The Early Modern Town

The Early Modern Town

A Reader

Edited with an Introduction
by Peter Clark

Published by Longman
in association with
The Open University Press

Longman Group Limited London

*Associated companies, branches and representatives
throughout the world*

*Published in the United States of America
by Longman Inc., New York*

Selection and editorial matter
© The Open University 1976

First published 1976

Library of Congress Cataloging in Publication Data
Main entry under title:
The Early modern town.

Includes index.
1. Cities and towns, Medieval—Great Britain—Addresses, essays, lectures. I.
Clark, Peter.
HT133.E2   301.36'3'0942   76-7041
ISBN 0 582 48404 9 (cased)
ISBN 0 582 48405 7 (paper)

Set in IBM Baskerville 9 on 10pt
Printed in Great Britain by   /
Whitstable Litho Ltd., Whitstable, Kent

Contents

List of Figures

Preface

The articles and extracts printed in this book have been selected because of the important light they shed on the early modern town, particularly in England. As well as illuminating major urban themes like civic ceremony, the economic structure and the life-style of the ruling elite, they explore the main types of urban community at the time, from the market towns to the great metropolis of London and the new industrial centres. In addition, there are introductory chapters on the literature and methodology of urban history in the West since the war, on the concept of the pre-industrial city and on the European city in general.

The majority of items have previously appeared in books or periodicals which are not readily accessible to the student or general reader. By collecting them together it is hoped that this volume will help to promote and facilitate the growing interest both in urban history and in social history as a whole. At the same time it must be stressed that the Reader forms part of an integrated teaching system for Open University students taking the Arts Faculty course, English Urban History 1500-1780. It is thus related to other material available to students. Opinions expressed in the volume are not necessarily those of the Open University.

I am indebted to Peter Burke, Clive Baldwin, Charles Phythian-Adams and Jenny Clark for their help in the preparation of this collection.

30 January 1976   P.A.C.

Acknowledgements

We are grateful to the following for permission to reproduce Copyright material —
The Athlone Press, University of London, for the article entitled: 'The elizabethan merchants of Exeter' by W. G. Hoskins taken from *Elizabethan Government and Society* edited by S. T. Bindoff, J. Hurstfield and C. H. Williams, 1961; The Cambridge University Press for the article entitled: 'The market towns' by Alan Everitt taken from *The Agrarian History of England and Wales* Vol. 4 edited by Joan Thirsk, 1967; Cassell and Collier Macmillan, New York for the article entitled: 'A backward glance: A forward look' retitled for this edition as 'The nature of the pre-industrial city' by G. Sjoberg taken from *The Pre-industrial City*, 1960; The Economic History Review for the article entitled: 'Places of origin of a group of immigrants into Sheffield 1624-1799' by E. J. Buckatzsch taken from the *Economic History Review*, 2nd series, II, 1949-50; Hodder and Stoughton Ltd, London, for the article entitled: 'Socio-economic status and occupations in the city of London at the end of the seventeenth century', by D. V. Glass taken from *Studies in London History* edited by A. E. J. Hollaender and W. Kellaway, 1969; Macmillan London and Basingstoke for the article entitled: 'English provincial towns in the early sixteenth century' taken from *Provincial England* by W. G. Hoskins, 1963; Martinus Nijhoff's Boekhandel for the article entitled: 'London as an "Engine of economic growth".' by F. J. Fisher taken from *Britain and the Netherlands:* 1V The Hague, 1971, edited by J. S. Bromley and E. H. Kossman; Professor W. E. Minchinton for the article entitled: 'Bristol-metropolis of the west in the eighteenth century', taken from *Transactions of the Royal Historical Society*, 5th series, 1V, 1954; Mr. J. F. Pound for the article entitled: 'The social and trade structure of Norwich 1525-1575' taken from *Past and Present* No 34, 1966; Routledge and Kegan Paul, London, and the University of Toronto Press for two articles entitled: 'Ceremony and the citizen: the communal year at Coventry 1450-1550' by C. Pythian-Adams, and 'A provincial capital in the late seventeenth century: the case of Norwich' by Penelope Corfield taken from *Crisis and Order in English Towns 1500-1700*, edited by P. Clark and P. Slack, 1972; Professor W. G. Rimmer for the article entitled: 'The evolution of Leeds' *Thoresby Society Transactions* Vol 50, 1967; Weidenfeld and Nicholson, London, for the article entitled: 'Pre-modern towns. taken from *Capitalism and Material Life* 1400-1800, by F. Braudel, 1973.
The publishers wish to thank Brenda Hall (Society of Indexers) for compilation of the index.

1 Introduction: the early modern town in the west
Research since 1945 [1]

Peter Clark

Urban history is at last finding its feet [1]. 'History goes to town', cried the heading of a recent review article on British urban studies. Interest has grown rapidly since the last war not only in Britain but throughout the West, and a number of journals and the like have sprung up to cater specifically for urban historians. Interest has also started to spill over into university teaching. In 1975 as many as fifty-eight British universities and colleges were offering courses in urban history or with an urban history component [2]. From 1977 the Open University will be presenting its own course on English urban history 1500-1780 with about 600 students a year [3].

At the same time, there is no room for complacency. In Britain much of the published work has been concerned with industrial urbanisation. By comparison with the mass production of the modern urbanists, research on the early town has tended to develop along cottage industry lines. Nonetheless, progress is now being made in most Western countries in the study of early modern urban society. This is hardly surprising. Not only are historians increasingly aware of how much the Victorian city owed to developments of the pre-industrial period, but towns provide some of the most exciting sources for the study of demographic, social, economic and other structures in early modern society.

The purpose of this introduction is modest. It is an attempt to take stock of some of the more important literature on the early modern town in Western Europe and the United States, in order both to gain an idea of the kinds of problems which are exercising historians in different countries and to learn from the variety of approaches being employed. In addition, the survey will endeavour to put in perspective the extracts and essays which form the main body of the reader.

Western Europe and North America

One of the major problems which has retarded research on the early modern town in the West has been the absence of any acceptable framework for analysis. A valiant effort to overcome this problem is G. Sjoberg's *The Preindustrial City* (New York, 1960), an extract from which appears as chapter 2. Sjoberg tries to outline a model of the town whose features are applicable to all non-modern societies. Many of his ideas are interesting and stimulating, but the total picture, with its data drawn from a wild miscellany of periods and cultures, fails to convince. Sjoberg's model is only of limited value for the analysis of the Western European or North American town [4]. More specific studies of the Western city in the early modern period also have drawbacks. F. Rörig has some general comments on the town at the end of the Middle Ages, but his perspective is dominated by German urbanisation. F. Braudel's survey of the early modern town (chapter 3 below) is a splendid *tour de force*, scurrying from one brilliant insight to the next. His concept of the West as having three basic types of town — open towns, closely related to their hinterlands, closed towns, 'closed in on themselves in every sense', and state towns, subject to the prince — is especially interesting. Having said this, however, the piece is too impressionistic to give any systematic idea of the total structure of urban society, while there is an over-emphasis on the great primate cities to the relative neglect of the innumerable smaller centres.

Other general work on the Western city is thematic. R. Mols has collected a vast array of data on urban populations and from this one can discern the main trends in urban development: the great demographic upswing of the sixteenth century, followed by a fairly widespread contraction during the seventeenth, and selective recovery in the next century. Unfortunately, Mols's data is patchy in quality and once again there is a preoccupation with the larger cities [5]. The multivolume history of European urbanisation by E. A. Gutkind is primarily concerned with planning and architecture [6]. On a more detailed level the most interesting piece of comparative work on the early modern city is P. Burke's attempt to compare Venice and Amsterdam at the height of their prosperity by an analysis of their ruling elites. If this is not completely successful, it is a result not of the approach, which works well, but of the scale and complexity of the two communities [7].

Compared with the dearth of material on the general nature of urban society in the West during our period, there is ample work on the towns of individual countries, particularly in northern Europe. Thus we already know a good deal about Dutch and Belgian towns. The Low Countries formed one of the most urbanised areas of Europe during the pre-modern period. In the early sixteenth century the greatest density of communities lay in the south, in Flanders and Brabant; there were the great commercial and industrial centres of Antwerp, Bruges, Brussels and Ghent, all probably with populations of over 30,000. During the next hundred years or so the main focus of urban growth moved to the north, to the provinces of Holland and Utrecht, which after the revolt against Spain in the late sixteeenth century formed part of the new Dutch Republic. Here, within a radius of twenty-one miles was a constellation of eight major cities: Amsterdam, Leyden, Haarlem, Utrecht, Gouda, Delft, Rotterdam and The Hague. The population of this urban network soared from under 100,000 in 1514 to nearly half a million in the mid-seventeenth century.

Belgian historians have been mainly interested in medieval towns and we have no overall picture of later urban developments in the south. The Golden Age of the Dutch city is better displayed. Useful light is shed on the general economic and social structure of Dutch towns by J. De Vries who shows the close relationship between urban growth and rural change and argues that the urban expansion of the sixteenth and seventeenth centuries was fuelled by a vigorous inflow of rural immigrants underpinned by a major *per capita* advance in Dutch agricultural productivity [8]. A more bread-and-butter survey of Dutch towns in the seventeenth century, by H. Klompmaker, constructs a somewhat artificial urban typology categorising towns according to their economic function — as ports, transhipment centres and so on. More interesting are his comments on major changes during the period: on the way that Amsterdam exploited the economic problems of some of the older industrial centres in order to enlarge its own power and influence; on the growth of civic oligarchy even in towns like Utrecht and Dordrecht where craft workers had previously retained some say in municipal politics [9].

As for the different sectors of the urban hierarchy, the leading cities have received greatest attention. In the case of Antwerp most work concentrates on the city's rapid rise from the late fifteenth century: by the 1520s it had a population of about 50,000. Fundamental to the city's success were the location there of one of the great medieval fairs; its role as the main entrepôt for English cloth, Portuguese spices and German minerals; and its novel development as a financial centre where the new absolutist rulers of Western Europe could raise loans. All this is discussed in the wide-ranging analysis of Antwerp's rise by H. van der Wee. At the same time, W. Brulez has stressed the need to be aware of the basic traditionalism of many aspects of Antwerp's economy, arguing that 'there was no sharp contrast between the trade of Bruges [its old rival] and that of Antwerp, neither in the products, nor in the leading groups of merchants, nor, finally, in the international character of the trade'. This traditionalism is also evident in the careers of individual merchants [10]. On a general note, E. Sabbé presents a well-rounded picture of the city at its peak with a valuable analysis of its physical growth, of magisterial encouragement of alien merchants through civic liberalism, and of the cultural patronage of its great merchants reaching a climax in the splendidly Italianate townhall 1561-66 [11].

By the 1560s Antwerp had passed its peak, adversely affected by the changing currents of international trade, by repudiations of government debts, and by growing political and religious instability which exploded in the Dutch revolt. Badly affected by the war and recaptured by Spain in 1585, the city soon lost half its population, many citizens fleeing to the north. The severity of the crisis is well illustrated by E. Scholliers who indicates that the dearth year 1587 caused a virtual collapse of real wages and living standards. However, with the restoration of peace after 1609 Antwerp partially recovered: immigration increased to boost the population; merchants found new outlets to the sea and luxury industries expanded. This modest revival continued until the last decades of the century when general European war inaugurated a period of prolonged depression for Antwerp and other towns in the southern Netherlands [12].

Our knowledge of developments in other cities is less complete. Thus there are no major depth studies of Amsterdam. Only Burke has sought to relate together the economic, political and cultural order of the city, and this is mainly from the patrician point of view. Other studies focus primarily on the complex structure of Amsterdam's commerce, though J. G. van Dillen explains how the city's economic power gave it considerable political leverage in the Dutch Republic. Amsterdam was by far and away the largest and wealthiest Dutch city in the seventeenth century, with a population rising from just over 100,000 in 1622 to about 200,000 by 1680 [13]. For much of the period its two nearest rivals were Haarlem and Leyden with about 40,000 inhabitants each. While little has been done on Haarlem, F. Daelemans has combined listings of population and city rents for the 1580s to examine Leyden's socio-economic structure. Daelemans shows that the city's rapid growth in the late sixteenth century was due to the flight there of many workers from the south. As elsewhere, there was a close correlation of poverty, low household size and cheap housing. Also interesting is the position of agriculture as the second main occupation in the city [14]. By the late seventeenth century Haarlem and Leyden were being overtaken by Rotterdam as the leading city after Amsterdam; the background to this development is explored in several short studies [15]. As for the south, seventeenth century Antwerp was closely pursued by a number of cities — Ghent, Brussels and Liège — all with populations of more than 40,000. J. Craeybeckx has argued that Ghent's buoyancy owed much to the prosperity of its linen industry [16].

The high level of urbanisation in the Low Countries is demonstrated by the fact that many of the medium-sized towns were on a par with the largest English provincial towns. One fairly typical middling centre was Nijmegen, which had 11,000 people. In the late sixteenth century Nijmegen suffered serious economic difficulty as a result of war, trade disruption and agricultural disorder: the position was especially bad in the 1590s. The southern town of Louvain likewise faced major economic crisis at this time, with a large increase in the number of its poor as the textile industry decayed [17]. In the case of the smaller towns we know most about their economic and social role. Thus there is evidence of the continuing importance of the market town for its rural hinterland in eighteenth-century Gelderland, while Faber's study of Friesland has indicated the emergence in some towns of a prosperous middle and shop-keeping class [18].

So far as specific urban themes or problems are concerned, Dutch and Belgian historians have made a considerable advance in the study of demographic and socio-economic structures. One of the best population studies is Hélin's *La Démographie de Liège*. Overcoming the many problems caused by the multiplicity of parishes, Hélin examines the age structure, birth rates and mortality levels of the citizenry. Particularly interesting is her data on the wide discrepancies in age weighting, household size, number of servants and level of celibacy between the wealthy central parishes and the much poorer suburbs. The former had fewer children, larger households, more unmarried people and many more servants than the latter. She also indicates the importance of immigration (particularly of female servants) which helped maintain the city's population in the eighteenth century. Throughout there are valuable comparisons with other European towns [19]. More limited research has also been done on Bruges and the small Flemish town of Eeklo [20].

International commerce is well covered, particularly that centred on Antwerp and Amsterdam. We also know something about the structure of merchant wealth, with investment in real property serving not as a first step towards abandoning the merchant class, but as a means of ensuring a regular and stable income, as a form of security for loans and, on occasion, as an opportunity for speculation. By contrast, less work has been done on internal trade despite its obvious importance for the provisioning of the increased urban population and for the spread of conspicuous consumption among the upper and middling ranks of Dutch society. One of the few important pieces on the food trade is van Uytven's account of the development of the brewing industry at Louvain [21].

Much of the debate on social structure and change centres on the hoary question of whether the Dutch revolt involved widespread social revolution. According to Scholliers, poverty and social tension were rife in mid-sixteenth century Antwerp. Polarisation was acute between the citizenry and those numerous workers not admitted to civic freedom, as well as within the established crafts — between privileged masters and poor journeymen. Here, it is argued, outbursts of religious violence and radicalism coincided with periods of food shortage and unemployment. The Hungarian Marxist historian T. Wittman has gone further and suggested that the lower orders and the deprived played a major role in the capture of Flemish towns in the 1570s by forces opposed to Spanish rule. Certainly there can be little question that social distress was widespread in many towns, both north and south, during the late sixteenth century [22]. In fact the socio-economic order remained extremely fragile into the eighteenth century. At Louvain, for instance, the bad harvest year 1739-40 caused a subsistence crisis with famine followed by epidemic disease, riots and an upsurge of crime [23].

Interest in the urban politics of the Low Countries has been mainly confined to the larger centres, with studies on town finance and the patrician class of sixteenth-century Louvain, and on the Amsterdam burghers and their power. However, D. J. Roorda's study of party and faction in the late seventeenth century looks at the political upheavals in both large and small Holland and Zeeland towns. At this time the major Dutch cities 'cultivated the grand style of independent city republics. Thus they liked to call their burgomasters "consuls", and eagerly aspired after the mastery of the surrounding countryside'. In numerous towns 1672 witnessed anti-oligarchic movements. Members of the upper class, excluded from power by oligarchic cliques, joined forces with the middling and lower orders in towns, and with the Orangist party in central government to overthrow the established municipal oligarchies. As a result, there was some change in the personnel of the ruling groups but their social composition and power remained much as before, and the growth of oligarchy continued unabated. At Nijmegen we can see the narrow patrician class of the eighteenth century leading a very comfortable existence: even the burdensome business of poor relief had been delegated to the parish authorities [24].

On the cultural front, urban religion is mainly discussed in the context of the Dutch revolt. At Deventer A. C. F. Koch argues that a small Calvinist minority drawn from the substantial members of local society exploited the occupation of the city by anti-Spanish forces in 1579 to outflank and frighten the Catholics, who had most support among the wealthiest and poorest citizens. Similar work on Ghent has indicated that the Calvinist following there came mostly from the upper and middle classes [25]. Other aspects of urban culture have been tackled by several British historians: A. C. Carter on the English Reformed Church at Amsterdam, one of many foreign churches; P. Burke on the artistic patronage of the Amsterdam burghers and K. Fremantle on the splendour of that city's Palladian town hall, erected in the 1650s to celebrate Amsterdam's political and economic supremacy [26]. G. L. Burke's general survey of *The Making of Dutch Towns* is a useful guide to the topographical and architectural development of Amsterdam, Haarlem and some of the smaller cities, whose magistrates preferred modest, functional buildings to the baroque grandeur increasingly in vogue elsewhere [27].

By contrast with the Low Countries work on the early Scandinavian towns can be dealt with briefly. B. Lager's research on Stockholm has suggested that the late sixteenth-century city may have experienced considerable population expansion with an increase in the size of the non-citizen class and the development of suburbs: in the 1580s the population was probably in excess of 5,000 [28]. For the later period one of the most interesting studies is P. Thestrup's account of living standards in eighteenth-century Copenhagen. At this time Copenhagen's population was roughly equivalent to that of all the other Danish towns put together: it doubled between 1728 and 1800, to over 100,000. As in other major European cities immigration was high and there was a substantial surplus of women over men. Thestrup uses special consumption tax records in conjunction with wage rates and mortality figures in an attempt to assess living standards. In the final analysis the data is inconclusive, but the rigorous approach to the sources is stimulating. Thestrup is particularly good on the problems of constructing a price index for an age when sharp price rises almost certainly led to marked shifts in consumption patterns. The other side of the coin to Copenhagen's prosperity was the decay of the smaller market centres, many of them, as in Zealand, with less than a thousand inhabitants. These suffered not only from the trading competition of Copenhagen merchants but also from the rivalry of rural craftsmen (encouraged by landowners) and from the general stagnation in farming [29].

In Germany students of the pre-modern town have put most emphasis on the medieval period, the great age of the German city. The sixteenth to the eighteenth centuries, years of urban decline at the hands of the Princes, have been somewhat neglected, with the exception of the Reformation era. In consequence we have no good working framework for the study of the early modern city [30].

Of the few brief forays into the general analysis of German urban development, mainly for the close of the Middle Ages and start of the sixteenth century, one of the best is P. Dollinger's study of social groupings. This argues that there was increasing social conflict and polarisation in many fifteenth-century towns between patricians and ordinary burghers. From the start of the next century conflict came out onto the streets, triggered off by heavy taxation. In 1513 there were risings in a dozen cities, in both north and south Germany. Subsequently various small cities in south-west and central Germany supported the Peasants' Revolt (1525), while elsewhere Protestant activists exploited social divisions to further their cause. More directly related to the Reformation is B. Moeller's work on the Imperial cities and Protestant ideology. Moeller argues that there was a disintegration of communal cohesion before the Reformation and that the Protestant tenets of Zwingli and Bucer in particular appealed to many townsfolk because they seemed to support the concept of a resuscitated civic community. Moeller, however, tends to see the cities as essentially passive recipients of Protestant teaching. This view has been criticised by B. Hall who argues for the importance of non-religious factors in the Reformation: economic and social unrest; divisions between city oligarchs and craft gilds, and growing population pressure which increased the number of inhabitants excluded from civic affairs [31].

Two other comparative studies of German towns should also be mentioned. Dollinger examines the great confederation of Baltic coast ports called the Hanseatic League. This is done primarily from a political and diplomatic viewpoint and most of the discussion relates to the years of medieval success. Nonetheless, there is a useful account of the Hanseatic decline in the sixteenth century as a result of the collapse of their main market at Bruges, growing south German commercial competition, and internal dissension caused by the Reformation. A more important work is Mauersberg's study of Basle, Hamburg, Frankfurt am Main, Hanover and Munich from the fifteenth century to the nineteenth. The first three cities enjoyed considerable autonomy for much of the period, while the others were capitals of princely states (Braudel's 'state towns'). Mauersberg examines the economic and social structures of the traditional community and some of the pressures for change. Among the main obstacles to economic rationalisation and more capitalist organisation were the gilds. At the same time, he shows that despite gild opposition there was some marked liberalisation of social structure, growing capital accumulation and the rise of financiers. Also significant was the development of a legal climate favourable to trade expansion. Where the study is weakest is on the demographic front: the population estimates are surprisingly crude [32].

The comparative approach is, as we have seen, one of the strong points of German urban history. On the other hand, most of the comparative work is limited to the larger cities. At the start of the sixteenth century there was a cluster of about ten first rank centres with populations between 20,000 and 30,000: among these were Cologne (the largest), Magdeburg, Danzig, Nuremburg, Augsburg, Strassburg and Vienna. Below them was a substantial second tier of cities, a number of which, like Hamburg, Bremen, Erfurt, Frankfurt and Ulm, had populations in excess of 10,000. Many of these larger centres were imperial cities, possessing regalian rights which made them virtually independent (there were about sixty-five imperial cities in the 1520s). However, the following two centuries saw the growing importance of state capitals like Vienna, Berlin and Munich. At the bottom of the German urban hierarchy were the two or three thousand small towns, some with populations as low as a few hundred [33].

Individual studies, like the comparative analyses mentioned above, show the same bias towards the major cities. Thus there are a number of works on Nuremburg, described by Bodin as 'the greatest, most famous, and best ordered of all the imperial cities'. G. Strauss has contributed a well-rounded portrait of the early sixteenth-century city. Much of the discussion centres on the success of the closed ruling elite in overcoming the threat posed by the Reformation to the city's internal cohesion and political autonomy. Unfortunately, there are important gaps on population structure and social change. Other work on the city includes analysis of the patrician class and detailed accounts of the progress of Reform with particular stress on the important part played by the legal profession [34]. For Strassburg there are two important studies spanning much of the early modern period. The first, by M. U. Chrisman, argues that the impact of the Reformation on the political and economic order of the city was limited; even the old ecclesiastical organisation survived in a truncated form. The most crucial areas of change in Strassburg were education, where a coordinated system of learning was established from primary classes to the city university, and social welfare, where Reform facilitated the development of more systematic poor relief. The second study, by F. L. Ford, looks at the city in the seventeenth and eighteenth centuries. By then the imperial city was in decline: its oligarchy increasingly ossified, its population stagnant after a series of plagues, and its political and cultural influence on the wane. The city's annexation by France in 1681 completed its political and cultural eclipse: French officials pulled most of the administrative strings and civic culture was infiltrated by French salon manners. Nevertheless, all this was made tolerable by the revival of trade during the eighteenth century and renewed population growth [35]. In the case of Vienna its metropolitan development came late. In the seventeenth century it was still a rather cramped fortress city threatened by the Turk (as in the siege of 1681). During the eighteenth century, however, with peace secured and the growth of the Habsburgs' centralised bureaucracy, Vienna acquired a large array of government institutions and public buildings, and a population of about 206,000 (1782). Finally, a recent study of Frankfurt provides a detailed description of the social and economic background to the political conflict which erupted in the city in the early eighteenth century [36].

What of the second-rank and smaller German towns? The rich archival sources available in many middle-sized German cities make possible such studies as R. W. Scribner's account of the highly unstable social and economic background to the Reformation at Erfurt and the divisive role of Lutheranism. Also valuable is C. Friedrichs' quantitative study of Nördlingen (population 7,500 in 1597). This argues that the seventeenth-century city saw growing class consciousness among the craftsmen, as they found their traditional opportunities for social mobility threatened by the decline of the gilds, their main protectors, and by the growth of the putting-out system in industry [37]. For the smaller, less thoroughly documented towns we have to rely heavily on the important study by M. Walker. Looking mainly at centres in the south, he argues for the continuing importance of community cohesiveness, traditional gilds and narrow localism in these towns right into the eighteenth century, though by then a growing number faced pressure from their merchants to relax their economic controls in order to benefit from general trade expansion. Walker is especially valuable on the politics and mentality of the small town [38].

As for the specific functions of German towns, most work has been oriented towards constitutional, political and religious history in a traditional vein. Although there is a growing interest in social history among German historians, much of the work in this field, especially for the smaller towns, is highly localised in approach [39]. The precise demographic consequences of the Thirty Years War are still somewhat obscure, though the impact of the war was probably large-scale. One of the best studies of urban population is E. Woehlkens' analysis of the impact of disease on the small town of Uelzen in Lower Saxony. As well as plotting the topography of epidemics (such as the major outbreaks of 1597 and 1599) with the use of detailed street maps, he also discusses the effect of disease on the local economy [40].

By contrast with German urbanists, French historians have been particularly concerned with the early modern period. An important source of inspiration has been the *Annales* school which under the leadership of Marc Bloch and Lucien Febvre has pioneered interest in the town and especially in its economic and social features. Since the war there have been a number of major French monographs on towns during the period [41].

As elsewhere syntheses are still in short supply. The best short introductions to the French town are offered by P. Goubert. From these one can see the continuing importance of the great provincial cities in early modern France: 'Paris did not reach the half-million mark until the eighteenth century, and could not muster more than two per cent of the [national] population; there were six towns of sixty to a hundred thousand people; about ten with thirty to forty thousand; fewer than fifty with ten to fifteen thousand plus a few dozen big market towns and small administrative centres: barely . . . fifteen per cent of the population'. Of the leading centres outside Paris, Rouen and Lyon were regional capitals, Amiens and Troyes great merchant cities and Dijon, Aix, Toulouse and Rennes seats of provincial Parlements [42].

As with most of the super-cities of early modern Europe, our knowledge of Paris is fragmentary with French studies limited to specific problems. American scholars have offered one or two rounded pictures but these have been more descriptive than analytical [43]. The major provincial cities have fared better. Lyon and the great ports of Marseille and Bordeaux are particularly well covered. For Lyon the sixteenth century started off with a tremendous burst of prosperity and growth. Its early importance as an international fair centre spilled over into the development of important industries, particularly textiles, and its population of about 120,000 was surpassed by Paris alone. However, the second half of the sixteenth century, with its religious wars and commercial instability brought economic decline with towns-people shifting their investments to the countryside. R. Gascon's work is mainly concerned with the urban economy and its problems, but extra light is shed by N. Z. Davis on social developments. In particular we can see how the city's early prosperity attracted large numbers of poor immigrants. Growing poverty and social disorder precipitated a shake-up in poor relief with the establishment of a central agency, the Aumône Générale, to supervise the different types of relief. Significantly, this plan won support from both Catholics and Protestants. Davis also sheds light on the growth of Protestantism in the city, especially among women and craftsmen [44]. For the later period J-P. Gutton's volume on poverty in Lyon and its region has detailed information on the mixture of repression, welfare and reform which characterised eighteenth-century relief. Eighteenth-century Lyon is also the subject of an important monograph by M. Garden. Garden surveys the whole panorama of Lyon society: the demographic structure and steady population increase caused both by immigration and by natural growth (a significant change from the past); the prosperity of the silk industry; the increasing polarisation of wealth and the social order; the dominant political position of the bourgeoisie; and the cultural developments in the city, notably the large-scale new building by the merchant and manufacturing interests [45].

Multivolume studies have appeared on the ports of Marseille and Bordeaux. After earlier difficulties both cities enjoyed tremendous economic growth and prosperity in the second half of the period: Marseille used its powerful commercial base in the Mediterranean to diversify into the Atlantic and Eastern trades; Bordeaux became the leading colonial port. At Bordeaux the upper classes enjoyed a lively intellectual life and there was extensive reconstruction of merchants' houses, while the city attracted an increasing number of poor migrants [46]. The northern ports of Rouen and Le Havre also flourished in the eighteenth century. Le Havre rose rapidly as a centre for the slave and colonial trades and the Rouen merchants invested in and profited from allied industrial developments (sugar-refining and cotton manufacture) [47].

The ports were undoubtedly the leading growth sector of French urban society in the second half of our period. By comparison, the inland centres had more erratic fortunes. Toulouse, for example, had reached the peak of its prosperity in the fifteenth and early sixteenth centuries as a busy industrial, administrative and university town. Because of the late sixteenth-century religious wars the urban economy suffered protracted depression and difficulty, and recovery was only slowly making itself felt by the end of our period [48]. Amiens, the great northern textile city, also experienced severe economic difficulty particularly in the late seventeenth and early eighteenth centuries. According to P. Deyon, the population reached its peak in the 1630s; thereafter there were recurrent crises as the cloth industry suffered from foreign and rural competition, with a *crise de subsistence* in 1692-94. Deyon also throws interesting light on the social structure, political organisation and religious life of the city (stressing the persistence of primitive concepts of belief). In another study, on Lille, also a major textile city, Deyon shows that the economic pattern was somewhat different, with the main population growth between 1677 and 1740 followed by stagnation as the city suffered from rural cloth production [49].

Work on the second-rank French cities is thinner on the ground. Only Beauvais (population 13,000) and Bayeux (about 7,000) have received full-dress treatment. For Beauvais and its region there is P. Goubert's magisterial study of demographic and socio-economic life. Up to the 1630s the picture is one of general urban growth with an increasing population and developing textile industry. The next century, however, was one of bleak decline with population decay punctuated by terrible crises (as in the 1690s) and the contraction of the textile industry. City fortunes were heavily influenced by the expansion and subsequent depression of local agriculture. Only after 1730 was there renewed economic and population growth and a decline in the incidence of food shortages. Bayeux followed a similar path during the seventeenth century. There were periods of major demographic difficulty 1600-40 and 1680-1720. After 1720 the population recovered sharply, but there was no parallel economic growth: agricultural production remained deficient; the clothing industry was under-capitalised and more and more vulnerable to English competition; the general economic base contracted as prosperous citizens withdrew. The result was a massive growth of poverty, over-powering the town. While M. El Kordi looks at the general economic and demographic background to the town's plight, O. Hufton relates it to political change and the outbreak of the French Revolution [50].

By comparison with Germany and England, France seems to have had a lower incidence of small towns. Some of the best work has been done by M. Lachiver on Meulan. Lachiver attempts to reconstitute a significant part of the town's population between the seventeenth and the nineteenth centuries. This reveals the late age of marriage and high infant mortality rates of the early period; during the eighteenth century there was some reduction in the level of infant mortality, but the main reason for the population upturn was extensive immigration from the country-side. Immigration also played an important part in the early eighteenth-century growth of Thonon discussed by R. Tinthoin. Here one can also see the rural aspect and localised economy of the town. For the sixteenth century there is P. Tucoo-Chala's account of urban growth at Pau in Navarre. Established in the late fifteenth century as an administrative centre, the town only slowly acquired marketing and other economic, political and cultural functions [51].

As we have already noted, the French forte is undoubtedly the urban monograph: the various functions and processes of urbanisation attract rather less interest. Such thematic studies as we have reveal a social and economic motif. As well as work on the overseas trade of sixteenth century ports like Nantes, there are forays into the growing sophistication of the Paris food market, which by 1700 was attracting supplies from as far afield as Picardy and Normandy, and into the growing land investments of the Parisian bourgeoisie south of the city [52]. We also know something about the contentious question of popular disorder: tax and food riots were endemic throughout the seventeenth and eighteenth centuries. For the later period there are valuable studies of the urban poor, their numbers swollen by rural migration. In Paris they were increasingly concentrated in the suburbs to the east and south of the city: in one parish it was said that 70 per cent of the inhabitants were 'so poor that they could not subsist either in illness or even in health without the help of charities' [53]. For the upper classes there is evidence of increasing social segregation and class consciousness. If we are to believe J-C. Perrot, the traditional status divisions in urban society were replaced by new divisions based on wealth and fiscal standing. Evidence of this can be found in the massive rebuilding of many French towns with select areas for the rich and new quarters for the poor, in the growth of worker solidarity, and in the decline of communal rituals and the advent of new ceremonies specifically for the lower or upper classes. A more static analysis of urban society from A. Daumard and F. Furet examines social structure and social mobility in Paris in the mid-eighteenth century, using the evidence of marriage contracts. Though some of the arguments are rather tendentious the piece makes a number of interesting points: on the high level of rural immigration into the poorer occupational groups; on the attractions of domestic service for the junior offspring of the upper classes who regarded it as the back door to aristocratic patronage and promotion; and on the tendency of the merchant class to recruit new members from the children of merchants, mainly Parisians [54].

Most of our information about urban politics in the sixteenth and seventeenth centuries is derived from the monographs mentioned above. In general it seems clear there was a progressive development of civic oligarchy. One reason for this was the sale of municipal offices to prosperous townsmen from the late seventeenth century; another the growing level of royal intervention in towns which turned local officials into part-time civil servants. In consequence there was mounting reluctance among wealthy citizens to serve and many incumbents were obliged to stay at their posts for long periods. Urban dependence on the government was accentuated by the heavy indebtedness of town treasuries in the seventeenth century caused by large-scale royal taxation. From the 1660s and 1670s town government was very much under the thumb of royal agents even in major cities like Paris and Bordeaux [55].

What about urban culture? Increasing stress is being put on the important role of civic ceremony, both as an integrative force in the town and as an outlet for communal tension, at least in the early part of the period. Thus N. Z. Davis argues that abbeys of Misrule, neighbourhood groups of young and old with their own officials and feasts, were common in sixteenth-century Lyon, Rouen and other centres. Even religious riots might assume ritual characteristics [56]. As yet we have no major research on the religious upheavals in sixteenth-century French towns as a result of the Reformation. The seventeenth century saw a major counter-offensive by the Catholic Church with the establishment of many new religious houses in towns. Educational change has been examined mainly from the viewpoint of book-ownership. For sixteenth-century Amiens we have a detailed study of the types of people owning books and what they read. By the second half of our period the French publishing industry was increasingly centralised in Paris under government control [57]. Paris also led the way in the great rebuilding of French towns which occurred in the seventeenth and eighteenth centuries. From the early seventeenth century Italian style architecture and planning were starting to change the physical image of the capital under royal auspices. Hence the splendid mansions which were constructed in the Place Royale and the Place Dauphine for the great aristocracy now increasingly attracted to Court [58].

Despite the apparent reluctance to adopt a more comparative approach French scholars are undoubtedly opening up important new avenues in urban history. Nor is their interest confined to French towns. The study of Swiss, Italian and Spanish towns has benefited considerably from their work. Thus one of the more interesting pieces on the early modern Swiss town is L. Henry's analysis of the demographic history of the Genevan patriciate from the sixteenth century to the twentieth. Rigorous quantitative work on a collection of family pedigrees allows Henry to conclude that the main impetus for demographic growth in the city in the sixteenth and early seventeenth centuries came from the low marriage age and associated high fertility level: the mortality rate was high. The second half of our period, however, saw a declining population as the deteriorating city economy forced many young men to emigrate. In consequence the marriage rate fell, the age at marriage for women increased and some form of contraception was used. One reason for Geneva's early prosperity was its role as an international trade centre [59]; another was its importance as the leading citadel of sixteenth-century reform, attracting large numbers of foreign Protestants. Kingdon has described the involvement of Genevan missionaries in the French religious wars, while Monter's general study of the city is largely concerned with the religious and political manoeuvring in the early sixteenth century, though he does point up the considerable tension between the international outlook of the religious refugees and the intensely local interests of the city fathers. Elsewhere Monter emphasises the increasing tendency towards oligarchy in late sixteenth-century Geneva, encouraged by growing civic indebtedness. The only other Swiss town for which we have significant work is Basle. According to P. G. Bietenholz, Basle, like Geneva, exercised considerable cultural influence in France mainly through the city's printing presses which were well known for their humanist and liberal output [60].

Compared with the north European city, the Mediterranean city in this period has been seriously neglected. Apart from the flashes of insight offered by F. Braudel in his tableaux of Mediterranean society, both the Italian and Iberian city remain in the shadow. This is especially paradoxical since Italy was the most urbanised region of Western Europe for much of the pre-modern era. In the sixteenth century Rome, Venice and Milan each had between 100,000 and 200,000 inhabitants and Naples over 250,000. There were also a large number of second-rank centres like Florence, Palermo, Genoa and Bologna, with between 50,000 and 100,000 people [61]. The most striking case of neglect is Naples, the largest city in the West until the rise of London. We have so far only a sketchy idea of the background to its growth: the important luxury and textile industries; its role as the political and social capital of Spanish Italy; and the vast influx of peasantry fleeing from signeurial oppression in the countryside [62]. Of the other main centres only Venice and Rome have received detailed treatment. Indeed, research on Venice has reached near saturation point. The upsurge of poverty in the sixteenth century and the efforts of the patrician class to cope with the problem through new forms of relief; the difficulties of Venetian trade and shipping due to Turkish incursions in the east and Dutch and English piracy in the west; the growing interest of the patrician class in estates on the mainland rather than trade; the flowering of Venice as a cosmopolitan centre in the fields of art and publishing; the timing of the city's decay in the late sixteenth century. All these problems have been investigated in increasingly repetitious detail [63]. For the later period, we know of the city's relegation to a regional role, the decay of its trade and industry, the growing exploitation of its mainland colonies to prop up its ailing patrician power [64].

Rome has to be content with a single major study. This is J. Delumeau's remarkable if rather disorganised account of the sixteenth-century city, which describes how the Counter-Reformation Popes redesigned the Roman townscape with wide streets, great squares and public fountains to make the city the unquestioned capital of a newly reorganised Catholic Church. It was an heroic task made possible in part by the arrival of bullion from the Spanish Indies (St Peter's alone gobbled up 44 tons of fine silver for its fittings). The new papal metropolis was also kitted out with a large bureaucracy and a luxury economy. To support all this the countryside was sucked dry and great numbers of poor peasants poured into the city, begging from rich visitors. Vagrancy had to be alleviated by the reorganisation of poor relief with the provision of new hospitals and the like. By 1600 the population had doubled to over 100,000 and the figure continued to rise in the seventeenth century [65].

So far as one can judge, most Italian towns suffered considerable upheaval in our period: the population expansion of the sixteenth century caused widespread poverty and food shortage, while the next century brought general economic and demographic decay. E. Cochrane looks at the decline of Florence after the return of the Medici Princes in the 1520s mainly from the angle of personality and political intrigue. Rather better is M. Berengo's analysis of Lucca in the sixteenth century which indicates the growth of oligarchy, economic difficulty and the revival of Catholicism due to the Counter-Reformation [66]. On Pavia there is Zanetti's important study of urban provisioning. This demonstrates the inability of local agriculture to keep pace with the city's population expansion. To try and deal with the problem and prevent famine the city introduced an elaborate system of food controls, along with public storehouses and food imports. Nonetheless, the position was particularly difficult in the periods 1520-40 and 1580-99. By the late seventeenth century the situation had begun to ease as population pressure decreased. Finally, P. Earle has shown how the Adriatic port of Ancona developed in the early sixteenth century from a regional centre to an international entrepot outbidding Venice in trade with the Levant [67].

In the early part of our period Iberian towns were doing rather well: Seville and Lisbon both tripled their populations to well over 100,000 by the start of the seventeenth century; Granada, Valencia and Madrid had 60-75,000 and second rank towns like Toledo, Valladolid and Barcelona had over 20,000. The following century or so was, however, probably a time of growing difficulty for all but the largest centres. Unfortunately, our information is too incomplete to be dogmatic. There are no general surveys of urban development during this period and only a handful of specific studies. The most impressive analysis of a Spanish town is that by the Frenchman, B. Bennassar, on Valladolid in the sixteenth century. In the early decades of the century the city was at its peak of prosperity, the largest centre of old Castile and the capital of the newly united kingdom of Spain. The period 1540-60 was one of great brilliance with the conspicuous consumption of the aristocracy who flocked to the city supporting substantial population growth. But from the 1560s the lights went out: the seat of government moved from the city; Valladolid stagnated and then declined after the demographic crisis of the 1590s caused by plague [68]. Another French scholar, P. Chaunu, has studied Seville, looking mainly at its great Atlantic trade. From this one can see that the port's two principal spurts of expansion were 1504-50 and 1562-92; after a plateau of prosperity 1592-1622, war and other difficulties caused severe depression in the city's colonial trade. More light is shed on Seville by R. Pike, whose work indicates the permanent damage done to the city by the demographic difficulties at the end of the sixteenth century [69].

For Toledo we have several short studies. J. P. Molenat considers the city's active role in the revolt of the Communeros against the Crown in the 1520s, and argues that this was a response to increasing royal and seigneurial interference in the preceding period which had deprived the city of much of its ancient jurisdiction and property. M. Weisser and D. Ringrose have examined the reasons why the city, which grew rapidly between 1530 and the 1570s and was at the height of its prosperity as a textile and marketing centre in the second half of the sixteenth century, suffered a dramatic collapse in the early seventeenth century, losing half its population. Weisser stresses the severe down-turn from the 1590s in the population of the city's hinterland, which undermined the rural textile industry (whose products Toledo marketed) and reduced regional demand for the city's goods and services. Further blows came from the growth of foreign competition in textiles and from the slump in trade with the Levant in the 1620s. Ringrose emphasises the close connection between the fall of Toledo and the rise of Madrid, the latter's population trebling between 1597 and 1630 to about 180,000. Madrid not only encroached on Toledo's hinterland, but attracted away many of the city's businessmen, who obviously hoped to do better catering for the Court and attendant aristocracy now established in Madrid [70].

As for smaller towns, Bennassar has outlined the decline of Medina del Campo in the sixteenth century as its international fair decayed and it was forced back onto its agricultural markets and cloth and leather industries. The picture was brighter at Leon which enjoyed a moderate prosperity from its textile industry and important service sector, though by the eighteenth century Leon too was in decline as cloth manufacture contracted [71].

The other literature on the early modern town in Spain is mainly concerned with population and town planning. Bennassar looks in detail at the traumatic impact on towns of the epidemics of the 1590s, with the old ruling elites losing power briefly in some centres; J. Fayard and C. Larquié suggest that Madrid's growing population in the seventeenth century included a large army of rural poor, many of them from the depressed areas of the north and west [72]. While poverty reared its unpleasant head, the Crown and aristocracy pressed ahead with the rebuilding of

Spanish cities. The country's mixed heritage of Christian and Muslim townscapes was transformed in this period by Italian concepts of the planned town with great squares and monumental official buildings. The city was thus redesigned to demonstrate its subordination to the state [73].

To conclude this discussion of work on towns outside the British Isles it may be useful to say a few words on American urban history. Progress here has been less spectacular than for the nineteenth and twentieth centuries and most of the discussion has been linked, directly or indirectly, to questions about the nature of the American Revolution. As a consequence, American studies often exhibit a strong political and ideological bias [74].

So far we have no convincing general outline of urban development in colonial America to use as a framework for analysis. C. Bridenbaugh has looked at the leading cities during the colonial period, but he is mainly concerned with their social and institutional development and his approach is rather old-fashioned. J. P. Greene has contributed a valuable comparative essay on the main American port towns — Boston, New York, Philadelphia, Baltimore, Charleston and one or two others — during the eighteenth century. This stresses the close connection between the towns' port activity and their general trading function, with particular regard to their hinterlands. Unhappily, all too little is said about the inland towns [75]. Part of the problem in establishing a general picture of the American town is that the different groups of colonies varied considerably in their urban experience. Whereas the New England colonies were the most urbanised and tended, superficially at least, to follow the English pattern, the southern colonies had few significant towns, while the middle colonies of New Jersey, New York and Pennsylvania stood somewhere in between. Most American historians tend to argue that there were two or more discrete urban systems during the colonial period.

Not surprisingly, the New England town has attracted greatest attention. According to E. M. Cook there were five main types of town in the New England urban hierarchy: first, the main cities like Boston and New Haven with their acute concentrations of wealth, complex economies based on commerce and local government, and elaborate political structures and leadership patterns; second, the numerous county towns with a less acute social order but an obvious ruling elite; third, the suburban towns, outside the cities, which had similar social and political structures to the county towns; fourth, the self-contained towns, basically agricultural with more open social and political orders; fifth, the frontier towns with fairly fluid structures. The last two types merged into rural society [76].

Detailed discussion of urban development has focused mainly on the smaller towns. Boston, which by the early eighteenth century had a population of 16,000 or so, needs far more analysis. Rutman's study of the early years of the city is mainly descriptive, primarily concerned with how the original concept of a godly civic commonwealth disintegrated as population and trade expanded. Shorter and better is Henretta's examination of Boston's growth in the late seventeenth century as the leading port in the Atlantic trade, and the consequent decline in farming activity and increase in social polarisation: by the 1760s 29 per cent of the male inhabitants were propertyless. As a leading port Boston was highly vulnerable to the infections introduced by visiting ships. J. B. Blake offers a rather pedestrian survey of the city's stumbling efforts to improve public health, mainly under the lead of English-inspired doctors [77].

As for the smaller communities slowly moving from rural to urban status, K. A. Lockridge has looked at Dedham, P. J. Greven at Andover and M. Zuckerman at a variety of centres. The Dedham study argues that the harmony and coherence of the early settlement gave way in the late seventeenth century to a more open and contentious society before its transformation into an increasingly divided and stratified community before the Revolution. Particularly interesting is the trend away from oligarchy in the late seventeenth century. While Lockridge is mainly concerned with social and political change, Greven uses demographic analysis, including family reconstitution, to provide the core data for his picture of Andover. There the trends were similar to those at Dedham. While the seventeenth-century settlement was characterised by stability and integration under firm patriarchal rule, the eighteenth century witnessed mounting population pressure (caused by low mortality, early marriage and high fertility), land scarcity, a move from the land into trade, and growing emigration to other areas: all this eroding the old stability. Zuckerman's argument, couched almost entirely in terms of political and social attitudes is rather different, suggesting the continuing importance of social cohesion, homogeneity and consensus in New England towns into the eighteenth century [78]. None of these studies, however, has gone unchallenged. J. P. Greene has argued that not only are developments in these smaller centres, at the bottom of the urban ladder, discussed without reference to the experience of the more important towns, but that both Dedham and Andover were exceptionally sluggish in their rate of economic growth; Zuckerman is accused of ignoring evidence of change [79].

What about the towns of the middle colonies? By the mid-eighteenth century Boston had lost its earlier commercial primacy and both New York (population 32,000 in 1790) and Philadelphia (population 42,000) were muscling in on the lucrative trade with Britain. New York may have been busier in the early part of the century but the late eighteenth century saw Philadelphia the leading city in colonial America. Though we still know relatively little about New York, Philadelphia is in reasonable focus. A. N. B. Garvan has described William Penn's vision of the city as a residential centre with parks and uniform streets, a vision that turned it into one of the most impressive colonial towns. We also know of the city's commercial activities, with the early grain trade with the West Indies giving way to large-scale and highly profitable exports to Britain: in return British goods poured through Philadelphia to its increasingly prosperous hinterland. As for politics, S. B. Warner has discussed the strong sense of community in political life, encouraged by the committee system of municipal government. Also interesting is J. T. Lemon's account of the great city's impact on smaller Pennsylvanian towns: the county seats within 30 miles of Philadelphia languished, while those further away did much better [80].

New York and Philadelphia had no real rivals in the middle colonies during this period. Annapolis, the capital of Maryland from the 1690s, was a much smaller centre. Originally an administrative town, the increasing prosperity of the colony's tobacco planters encouraged its development as a focus for conspicuous consumption and later as an export centre for tobacco. After the Revolution Annapolis lost out to the growing importance of Baltimore in foreign trade and returned to its earlier role as a small administrative and retail town. E. C. Papenfuse presents an excellent account of the way the town adjusted to its diminished role — an important subject too often overlooked by urbanists [81].

In the southern colonies the economy was dominated by the planters who traded direct with British merchants and their agents. Towns were few and far between. The most important was Charleston (population about 16,000 in 1790). This enjoyed an important trade with the West Indies and later with Great Britain (exporting rice and indigo), while it also served as a social centre for the planters. Williamsburg, the capital of Virginia, was considerably smaller and primarily a political and social centre, providing balls, races and other diversions for the landed classes. By the mid-eighteenth century it may have had a limited marketing function, both in the export of tobacco and grain and the import of luxury goods. At the same time recent attempts to show that the century saw a general growth of small market centres in the south have been heavily discounted: some of the putative market towns seem to have comprised only a couple of stores and a handful of people [82].

We have already noted the high political content in most case studies of colonial towns. The same bias is also evident in thematic studies. One of the best of these is B. C. Daniels's account of the ruling elite of three major Connecticut towns, where he shows the dominant role of civic oligarchy in the eighteenth century based on wealth, family connections with the founders of the original settlement, and superior education. Also interesting is R. E. Wall's discussion of the Massachusetts urban franchise in which he argues, contrary to Lockridge, that there was a progressive reduction in the franchise in most centres during the seventeenth century. For the eighteenth century G. B. Nash demonstrates the growth of political party and conflict in Boston, New York and Philadelphia with pamphleteering, clubs, mobs and violence developing rather as in eighteenth-century London. Another urban theme explored by American scholars has been town planning. J. W. Reps has demonstrated that virtually all American towns 'began as planned communities', their designs influenced by the Ulster planted towns of the seventeenth century and by the rebuilding of London after the Great Fire. The general adoption of a fairly simple gridiron plan was 'a conscious reaction against the irregularities of English cities' in this period [83].

What does this collage of recent work by continental and American urbanists tell us about the early modern town and its study? As far as the tempo of work is concerned, there can be no doubt that the most important advances are now taking place in northern Europe: we know all too little about the Mediterranean city. While the French with their excellent notarial and parish records are busily excavating the social and economic structures of individual cities, the Germans have more comparative, thematic interests, particularly concerned with urban politics and class, and the Dutch and Belgians are essentially pragmatic, looking at almost all aspects of urban society.

In spite of the obvious differences of national approach, there are, however, a number of general conclusions we can draw from this recent work on the early modern town. The evidence cited above would suggest that it was a time of acute difficulty for many continental centres. Town populations rose dramatically in the sixteenth century (mainly as a result of immigration) and generally stagnated in the seventeenth, only to expand again in the following century. Urban economies failed to meet the demographic challenge: industrial activity, already unstable in the sixteenth century, had declined in the majority of towns by the late seventeenth century: the subsequent revival was selective and many old industrial towns continued to contract. Eighteenth-century prosperity was heavily biased towards the major administrative or political cities and the great ports with their lucrative colonial trades. The divergence between demographic and economic trends meant the growth of large-scale poverty, with vast numbers of vagrants and beggars tramping into towns and exacerbating the plight of the growing number of native poor. The reorganisation of poor relief in many sixteenth-century towns, both Catholic and Protestant, was no more than a palliative, and the pressure of increasing poverty induced a major long-term restructuring of urban society. The social order became more polarised and stratified; rich and poor were steadily segregated. On the political front, urban oligarchy was increasingly the norm, buttressed by central governments which now to a growing extent interfered in the running of civic administration and eroded civic liberties. Urban politics, particularly in the smaller towns, also slipped under the influence of local landowners. Outside pressures likewise reshaped the cultural role and image of towns. Most spectacularly, many towns were rebuilt in the Italian style to demonstrate their loyalty and subordination to the Prince. Printing, so vital to the transmission of urban values, was centralised, usually under the lock and key of royal censors. Urban religion and ritual, formerly manifestations of civic cohesion, tended to fragment and develop on class lines.

Needless to say, not all of these critical developments affected every country at the same time or with the same degree of intensity. The Italian and Spanish towns may have been the earliest and worst affected; the Dutch towns probably suffered least. In North America significant urban development only occurred towards the end of our period and so most towns escaped the worst effects of the urban crisis found in Western Europe. Even here, however, there are clear signs of community disintegration, social polarisation and political oligarchy before the Revolution.

The British Isles

How does the study of the British town in the early modern period fit into the general picture just painted for the Continent and North

America? Like the Dutch and Belgians, British urbanists have been fairly pragmatic in their approach. To some extent this reflects the variegated background to urban studies, especially in England [84]. When interest in the town first developed in the last century most work took the form of urban biographies which sought to recapture the life of one community over an extended period, looking in particular at its institutional progress. This biographical approach has continued to influence postwar urbanists and has led to several notable studies, including those by Sir Francis Hill on Lincoln [85]. Another important influence has come from local history with its strong interest in topography and social change. Initially the pursuit of Victorian 'antiquarian societies with their charabancs of clergy and gentlefolk', local history gained professional recognition with the advent in the 1890s of the *Victoria County Histories*. While some of the early publications had a preoccupation with the Middle Ages, recent volumes have shed valuable light on a considerable number of early modern towns [86]. There can be little question that local history has gained immeasurably in recent years from the academic inspiration of H. P. R. Finberg and W. G. Hoskins. The latter's studies of the early modern town are major pioneering pieces. Thus the two essays printed below (chapters 4, 7) show a keen eye for economic structure, social change and the physical face of the town; they exemplify the local history approach at its best. Last but not least, British urban history has also been influenced by the fact that a number of urbanists have been economic historians by training. This may help to explain that we know much more about the ports (with their quantifiable customs records) than we do about the much larger number of inland towns.

Despite their rather complex parentage there have been some important advances since the war in the study of the early modern town. Progress has been greatest for England and Scotland. Considerably less is known about Welsh and Irish towns. Nonetheless, as we shall see, the general picture of the British town is starting to come into focus.

As yet we have no general study of urban society in the British Isles as a whole, but a number of broad surveys have appeared for the different component countries: in the case of England, P. Clark and P. Slack have examined the sixteenth and seventeenth centuries and C. W. Chalklin the eighteenth century [87]; for Scotland we have incisive accounts by T. C. Smout; and for Wales an interesting sketch by G. D. Owen [88]. From these one can see that for much of the period the structure of British urban society was rather different from that elsewhere in Western Europe. Whereas France, Germany and the Netherlands had a number of first-rank cities, in Britain only London stood in the same class during the sixteenth and seventeenth centuries; the other metropolitan centres of Dublin and Edinburgh trailed well behind. Even leading provincial centres like Norwich, Bristol and York were barely second-rank cities by continental standards. British urban society had, in fact, a strong bias towards the smaller country towns with populations of up to about 5,000 or 6,000 in England, 3,000 in Scotland and barely 2,000 in Wales or Ireland. At the same time, the last part of the period witnessed important changes and by the late eighteenth century Britain had acquired a substantial number of major industrial towns and international ports.

Looking at studies of individual communities, it is obvious that the larger established cities have come off best. London's spectacular rise in the sixteenth and early seventeenth centuries, during which it quadrupled its population to over 250,000, has attracted considerable attention. The best general analysis, stimulating and short, is F. J. Fisher's 'London as an "Engine of Economic Growth" ', which appears as chapter 9. This investigates the complex question of the interaction of London and the provinces, focusing on the city's growing importance as the economic and social centre of the kingdom. A multitude of specific studies have also appeared: on London's development as the hub of overseas and internal trade and as a focus of conspicuous consumption by the ruling classes [89]; on the craft gilds and apprentices [90]; on the plight of the lower orders [91]; on civic government and the city's somewhat erratic involvement in the English Revolution [92]; on London's role as an educational and cultural centre [93]. For the later half of the period E. A. Wrigley has written a lengthy account of the modernising function of the metropolis in pre-industrial England, with particular stress on demographic and economic developments. Though part of a multivolume general series on the capital, G. Rudé's study of Hanoverian London is primarily concerned with the distended underbelly of metropolitan society — the poor, the criminal and the malcontent. For a convincing picture of the eighteenth-century metropolis as a whole one must still return to M. D. George's pre-war masterpiece [94]. Among more detailed studies, D. V. Glass's paper on 'Socio-economic status and occupations in the City of London at the end of the seventeenth century' is of particular interest and is printed here as chapter 10. We also have useful pieces on the business community and foreign trade [95]; on metropolitan politics [96]; and on suburban building in both the East and West Ends [97]. By the late eighteenth century London's cultural splendour was already starting to look tarnished and inviting attack, as we can see from George's exhibition of graphic art from Hogarth to Cruikshank [98].

Over the Scottish border the leading city for most of the period was Edinburgh which ranked as the third largest city in the British Isles (after London and Dublin) with a population reaching about 57,000 in 1755. As with London, Edinburgh's importance rested on a wide range of commercial, industrial, political and cultural functions. The early city is somewhat neglected. However, W. S. Reid has analysed the rapid success of the Reformation there from the 1560s under the leadership of the merchants, who not only had strong trading ties with England and other Protestant states, but who were alienated from the Catholic Crown by the latter's fiscal exactions and support for the city craft gilds (hostile to the merchant interest). Most work on the city is, predictably, concerned with the golden age of the eighteenth century. N. T. Phillipson has explained the way that Edinburgh, though deprived of its status as a national capital after the Union (1707), continued to develop as a social and intellectual centre encouraged by the reform of Edinburgh University and the formation of literary clubs and improvement societies. By the 1750s the city was patronised by a large number of wealthy landowners profiting from the growth of Scottish trade and agriculture after the Union. To house this fashionable elite the city fathers organised the planning and building of a classical 'new town'; a development which is delineated in splendid detail by A. J. Youngson [99].

Dublin also did well in the second half of our period. As the headquarters of the English colonisation of Ireland the city had grown steadily in the years up to 1640. During the Irish Rebellion of the 1640s Dublin was the only major centre to escape capture by the Catholics, though it inevitably suffered some of the side effects of the troubles. From the 1650s it recovered rapidly and by the close of the century its population of about 60,000 was second only to that of London. Not only was it an important political centre after the Restoration, but it attracted the residence and lavish expenditure of the landed classes. The city was also the country's leading port and presided over a network of internal trade; by the early eighteenth century it had a flourishing textile industry. As in London and Edinburgh, urban prosperity went hand in glove with upper-class housing; some of the new suburban developments which appeared from the late seventeenth century, like that of the Earl of Longford to the south of the city, were probably modelled on the aristocratic encampments in the West End of London. Decay only set in at the end of the period [100].

So much for the metropolitan centres. What about the main regional cities? In England work has appeared on most of the provincial capitals. Two important articles on Norwich are printed below: the first, by J. F. Pound (chapter 6), looks at the trade structure of the Tudor city and points to the growing importance of its distributive and service sectors; the second, by P. Corfield (chapter 11), shows that despite the city's increasing regional importance as a social centre in the late seventeenth century, the local textile industry continued to play a vital part in the city economy; when exactly the industry declined remains in dispute [101]. Interesting work has also been done on the city's social problems and political leadership [102]. Exeter has also been the subject of a number of important studies, including W. H. MacCaffrey's general survey of the city 1540-1640, Hoskins' work on the Elizabethan merchants (chapter 7) and on the city's growing economy after 1688, and W. B. Stephens' examination of the seventeenth-century port [103]. At York we know of the serious economic and demographic difficulties of the early sixteenth-century city (with the decline of industry), and of the city's subsequent revival as the leading distributive and social centre in the north [104].

Information on Bristol is less complete. All too little is available on the city's economic contraction in the Tudor period, though Bristol's revival in the seventeenth century is reasonably well-established. For the Georgian period W. E. Minchinton's article (chapter 14) paints a rosy picture of the city's economic, social and cultural importance in western England, its prosperity fuelled by the lucrative colonial trades [105]. Newcastle is probably the least well served of the English provincial capitals. Apart from R. Howell's analysis of the city during the English Revolution, the picture is fragmentary with little on the city's dual function as the leading coal port in the kingdom and as the main regional centre in the north-east [106]. Outside England the picture is also hazy, though towns like Cork (population about 25,000 in the late seventeenth century) and Aberdeen (about 12,000) almost certainly had considerable regional significance.

How much do we know about the country towns? In England most attention has been directed at the hundred or so larger centres, the boroughs. Thus we have useful surveys of Leicester, Lincoln, Stamford and Coventry, which suggest that these like many other similar towns suffered considerable social and economic difficulty in the sixteenth and seventeenth centuries, though their fortunes were beginning to stabilise by the eighteenth [107]. As for detailed studies, the most provocative is A. Dyer's book on Tudor Worcester. This presents an array of quantified data from probate and civic records and argues that Worcester deviated from the general rule and actually enjoyed industrial growth in the sixteenth century. Confidence in the argument is somewhat undermined, however, by the absence of any careful discussion of the problems posed by the sources used [108]. For the later period there is a useful crop of work. K. A. Adey blames the decline of Stafford in the late seventeenth century on its isolation from new industrial development; H. Thorpe shows how eighteenth-century Lichfield came to terms with a similar problem and learnt to thrive [109]; and J. D. Chambers, J. Prest and J. D. Marshall discuss the role played by textile manufacturers in the eighteenth-century growth of Nottingham, Coventry and Kendal respectively [110].

The Tudor and early Stuart period saw the smaller country towns, the market towns, doing better for themselves than the larger centres. All this is ably described and explained by A. Everitt's analysis of the market centres (chapter 8), which shows how their prosperity relied heavily on the growth of internal trade. More static examination of the economic structure of these small towns is also to be found in articles by J. Patten and J. Cornwall [111]. In addition, we have one or two surveys of market town networks. What happened in the late seventeenth and eighteenth centuries? How far was the earlier period of prosperity followed by decay and eclipse for the smaller centres as agriculture stagnated and as the direction of internal trade tended to move in favour of the larger country towns with their better communications? And was there some kind of limited revival in the course of the eighteenth century with the renewal of agricultural expansion, as the Georgian rebuilding of numerous market towns would suggest? At present these vital questions remain unresolved, though important research is under way in the field [112].

Scottish and Welsh country towns seem to have followed the same pattern as their English cousins. In Scotland the ordinary royal burghs were the rough equivalent of the English boroughs, though their populations were usually substantially smaller. In the sixteenth and seventeenth centuries they suffered increasing economic competition, firstly from the aggressive merchants of Edinburgh and secondly from the growing activity of the smaller baronial burghs which with the support of local landowners sought to curtail the trading privileges of the larger towns. The royal burghs also suffered from the wars of the period and from internal dissension between the established merchant elite and the newly formed craft companies. But by the eighteenth century, at least some of the royal burghs had recovered their vitality, helped by the expansion of trade with England and the colonies and by the phasing out of their more restrictive commercial practices. As for the baronial burghs, the market towns of Scotland, G. S. Pryde has shown how these small centres, closely integrated with the local agrarian economy, grew in number and importance from the late fifteenth century, enjoying their heyday in the generation before the Union. However, with the growth of longer-distance trade in the eighteenth century the smallest centres declined [113].

In Wales the old fortified boroughs established during the English colonisation of the Middle Ages lost their military and political *raison d'être* with the Act of Union in 1536. A number of the walled towns decayed and urban growth moved away to more open towns, 'New Towns', as at Denbigh, which grew up outside the walls of the semi-ruinous old town, or market centres like Dolgellau or Presteigne which had close ties with the adjoining countryside. As in England the market towns, particularly in the south, enjoyed a remarkable vitality in the sixteenth and seventeenth centuries. By the early eighteenth century, however, the main growth points were larger towns and ports such as Swansea and Cardiff, which were benefiting from the expansion of trade with England, particularly the coal trade. Small towns such as Neath fell under the increasing domination of local landowners [114].

In Ireland we know most about the country towns planted in Ulster during the seventeenth century. Prior to this the only towns of any significance in the region were Carrickfergus and Newry. The Plantation led to the development of larger centres like Belfast and Londonderry (controlled by the London craft companies) and a variety of smaller market towns. Expansion was at first retarded by politcal instability and the Irish rebellion of the 1640s. Belfast still had only about 4,000 inhabitants by the end of the century. But the growth of trade with England, the development of Irish agriculture and the spread of the linen industry led to a marked upswing in urban fortunes during the eighteenth century with both ports and inland towns, county centres and market towns enjoying considerable growth and prosperity as evinced by the rebuilding of numerous town centres. By then Belfast was the second city in Ireland [115].

While the sixteenth and seventeenth centuries thus proved a time of expansion for the small market towns of the British Isles, and a time of difficulty for many of the larger urban centres, the eighteenth century saw the pendulum swing once more in favour of the latter. London and the leading regional cities all flourished; so did many of the main country towns. Most striking was the prosperity of the major ports, benefiting as on the continent largely from the growth of the colonial trades. As we know, some, like Exeter and Bristol, were also provincial capitals; others, such as Hull, Liverpool and Glasgow, rose on the back of trade alone. For Hull, G. Jackson paints an interesting picture of the port's overseas trade with the Baltic and its important coastal and hinterland trade (the port serving as the principal outlet for the swiftly growing Yorkshire textile industry). Unfortunately the study provides only a hazy outline of the general urban context of Hull's commercial growth [116]. In the case of Glasgow we also know most about the city's rapid economic expansion from the late seventeenth century as its merchants gained a leading share of the tobacco trade with the American colonies; by the late eighteenth century this commercial expansion was spilling over into large-scale industrial development [117]. Liverpool has had considerable attention. Already increasingly important in the late seventeenth century as a leading port in Irish commerce and the salt trade, the town made rapid strides in the next century, assuming a dominant position in the slave trade and acting as the principal outport for the new industrial centres of the north-west: by the 1760s it had a population (including the suburbs) of about 70,000. As for Liverpool's political progress, the late seventeenth century saw the rising merchant elite fight hard to emancipate itself from the tutelage of local landowners. By 1700 the battle was mostly won, and as F. Vigier has demonstrated in an interesting comparison of Liverpool and Manchester during the Industrial Revolution, the city oligarchs were able to devote their whole attention to improving the facilities of the port and to increasing the profits of the mercantile interest. Almost all other problems of the rapidly growing town were ignored [118].

Urban growth in the eighteenth century was also marked by the rise of a variety of new towns: industrial towns, dockyard centres and spas. Good recent work on the early industrial towns is still in short supply. For Manchester we have to rely mainly on Vigier, who argues that while the town's lack of corporate institutions may have encouraged economic expansion, it also led to uncontrolled urban growth and widespread social misery [119]. Information on Birmingham, the other leading centre, is fragmentary [120]. We do have more on Leeds: W. Rimmer's able account of the town's development into the eighteenth century is printed below (chapter 12). For the last part of our period R. G. Wilson points to the essential conservatism of the Leeds merchant class exemplified by their unwillingness to move from marketing to manufacturing cloth; factory production in and around the city was inaugurated by country clothiers [121]. The Yorkshire metalware town of Sheffield increased its population eightfold between 1700 and 1788, to over 26,000. Much of this growth came from long-distance immigration, the scope of which can be judged from E. J. Buckatzsch's paper on Sheffield migrants which appears as chapter 13. Other work on Sheffield and the smaller towns of Oldham and Halifax has been sketchy [122].

The dockyard towns and spas are also under-represented in recent literature. Work on the former is limited to a few brief forays, despite the fact that Chatham, Portsmouth and Plymouth Dock were among the most rapidly growing urban centres of the late seventeenth and early eighteenth centuries: by the 1740s Plymouth had 14,000 and Portsmouth over 10,000 inhabitants [123]. As for the spas, those new leisure centres catering for the increasingly prosperous landed and commercial elites, most work has been done by urban geographers. Even Bath, accounted in 1728 'the capital and most public and gay place in Europe', has been described primarily in terms of its architecture. We need to know much more about its clientele, its social institutions, its medical practitioners, its close ties with the capital and the provisioning of the 30,000 or so people who lived there by the end of our period. By comparison with Bath, most of the other spas, such as Scarborough and Tunbridge Wells, were relatively small-scale, but their social and cultural significance far transcended their size and deserves analysis [124]. From the mid-eighteenth century the spa began to lose out to the seaside resort in fashionable popularity. An early resort was Margate in Thanet, patronised from the 1730s by Londoners who travelled there by Thames hoy or coach. Nonetheless, as J. Whyman has argued, the resort's major growth only came after the end of the century with the development of the packet-boat and then the railway, bringing hordes of middle-class Londoners to the sea [125].

Overall, then, British urban historians have tended to concentrate most on the larger, traditional towns and have shown less concern with the smaller market centres or the new towns, for which the sources are more intractable. Even so, there is an interesting array of material on the various types of community in the early modern period. In thematic studies the output has been more disappointing. Not only have certain aspects of the town, like its cultural role, received scant discussion, but too many studies are marred by the absence of a comparative approach and a surprising lack of rigour in the use of sources. British historians lag well behind their continental colleagues in the study of urban population. Most research has been limited to the simple calculation of annual baptisms and burials. Only one or two scholars have struck out into the more exciting field of family reconstitution with all the light that this can shed on age at marriage, family size and the age structure of the population. Even here there is a disconcerting reluctance to follow the French example and discuss the limitations of the documents being exploited, including the extent of under-registration in parish records and the distorting effects on the data of physical mobility [126]. It is now widely recognised that there was a high level of mobility in England in the sixteenth and early seventeenth centuries, with migration rather than natural population increase the cause of most urban growth. More information is needed on the phenomenon in the rest of the British Isles and on the changing pattern of migration after the Restoration. How far, for instance, was there a reduction in the level of mobility, followed by a revival in the mid-eighteenth century [127]?

In the case of the urban economy substantial work has been done on the ports [128] and industrial activity [129], but the economic structures of the old inland towns have received less systematic analysis. There have been several analyses of the occupational structure, using the evidence of freemen's registers, and we know something of the disintegration of the old gild order. We have already noted Everitt's account of the growth of internal trade centred on the market towns and more detailed studies also exist for some of the more important towns [130]. On the other hand, numerous problems remain unsolved, including the state of the urban property market, the development of credit, the growth of the urban professions (lawyers, doctors and the like), and the impact on business of the repeated agrarian crises of the sixteenth and seventeenth centuries. Again we know a reasonable amount about textile manufacture, but house-building and brewing, two growth industries of the sixteenth and seventeenth century economy, await attention, though we do have excellent accounts for the following period [131]. Most surprising is the failure to follow the agrarian historians and tap the vast collections of probate records, both wills and inventories, which survive for much of the early modern period. These are particularly illuminating for the changing pattern of urban wealth and economic activity.

Research on the social order has been strongly oriented towards poorer townsfolk. Various studies have described the growth of poverty before 1640, with the usual small groups of elderly and impotent poor overshadowed by the massed ranks of unemployed labourers and artisans, many of them newly arrived from the countryside. There is also detailed work on the wide range of private, municipal, and statutory relief mobilised to alleviate the problem [132]. Even here, gaps in our knowledge exist. How far did the new relief prevent starvation? How much popular discontent was there, and what forms did it take? Is it right to regard the numerous alehouses which sprang up in many sixteenth century towns as victualling and lodging houses for the new influx of poor? The situation after 1660 is also rather unclear, though it may be that widespread poverty only occurred in the larger cities; elsewhere the problem was probably contained and only threatened to get out of hand again with the demographic upturn of the late eighteenth century [133].

Unlike the German urbanists British historians have shown only minor interest in town rulers. If they are considered at all it is mainly in their role as businessmen. Hoskins' study of the Exeter merchants (chapter 7) sketches in their background, political function and standard of living, but much more systematic work is needed on these topics, looking not only at the merchant group but also at the professional men who played an increasingly important part in seventeenth-century towns. For the later Stuart period Everitt has argued that merchants and professional men joined up with a number of minor landowners to form a pseudo-gentry class aping the manners and attitudes of the country gentry. One of the central institutions of fashionable society in this later period was the great urban inn, which served as a political, commercial and social meeting place for the upper classes of both town and countryside [134].

Until recently most of the discussion of urban politics has revolved around the parliamentary career of the main boroughs. The growth of outside interference in elections and the expansion of the urban franchise have tended to be considered in isolation from general developments in municipal politics, including the rise of civic oligarchy, the deterioration in civic finances, and the increase in political dissension within towns. Work on the latter has been scanty and we also need to know more about the system of rewards and patronage which compensated town magnates for civic service, and about the development of a permanent bureaucratic machinery which provided towns with sufficient administrative continuity to weather the recurrent storms in local politics during the period [135].

For urban culture we do at least have C. Phythian-Adams' perceptive account of the fabric of ceremonial life in Coventry before the Reformation: this appears as chapter 5. Nevertheless, more insight is needed into the growth of magisterial pomp and circumstance in the later period, and into the survival of popular ritual, now increasingly focused on the alehouse. Ceremony and ritual did not disappear after the Reformation so much as develop new, stratified, class dimensions [136]. The urban context of reform also needs clarification. Why did urban elites in most sixteenth-century towns (outside Ireland) assume a leading role in the propagation of Puritanism, and from where did the later religious sects get their support? The survival of urban dissent into the eighteenth century and the role of the old Puritan strongholds as early Methodist centres is another pressing question [137]. Urban education has been examined primarily from the angle of endowed schools — grammar and charity schools. Diocesan court records, however, are packed full of references to the unendowed grammar and petty schools which proliferated in most English towns during the Tudor period. The decisive role played by the growing supply and ownership of books in informal learning also deserves comment. By the early eighteenth century most English towns had their own booksellers [138].

Fortunately, the last few years have seen a spate of work on the British townscape. For England, Hoskins and others have described how the early modern period saw two important phases of private building: the first in the late sixteenth and early seventeenth centuries when town merchants rebuilt, extended and refurbished their houses, mostly employing traditional building materials; the second period, from the end of the seventeenth century, characterised by the use of new materials (brick and stone) and the adoption of the classical architectural style. Here the model was the new building which sprang up in London with the reconstruction after the Great Fire and the development of the aristocratic West End. The provincial customers included both merchants and pseudo-gentry. By the end of the eighteenth century we also see the appearance of distinctive back-to-back housing in the new industrial towns [139]. In Scotland there seems to have been some improvement in housing in the sixteenth and seventeenth centuries, but the main burst of activity coincided with the increased prosperity created by the Union. Not only was there a good deal of new Palladian building in the major cities (notably Edinburgh and Glasgow), but even smaller country towns like Inverary were planned and rebuilt in the Italian style. Similar developments occurred in Ireland: Dublin, Belfast and many of the Ulster country towns acquired a new classical townscape in the eighteenth century [140].

The increasing dominance of London in the cultural life of the British Isles for much of our period is now generally accepted. On the other hand, there is also considerable evidence of a revival of urban culture in the provinces in the eighteenth century. We noted earlier the intellectual renaissance of Edinburgh in the mid-eighteenth century, and Dublin may have enjoyed a more limited flowering somewhat earlier. By the end of our period a number of English provincial centres had their own philosophical and scientific societies, particularly the industrial towns like Birmingham, Derby and Manchester. The powerful cultural influence of the great provincial cities of the nineteenth century was already starting to make itself felt [141].

What then can we conclude about the study of the early modern town in the British Isles? In general one can say that the approach has been pragmatic, more wide-ranging but less rigorous than the French, less comparative than the German. The closest parallel is probably with work in the Low Countries. At the same time, British urban historians are now in the process of establishing a framework for analysis and debate: the urban hierarchy and some of the major functions of towns have been identified and we have some insight into the broad pattern of urban development. This is an important advance.

As for the town and its problems, we can see that British urban society, like its continental counterpart, suffered widespread economic, social, political and cultural dislocation. On the other hand, it also seems likely that the urban crisis was less severe and less prolonged than it was in other parts of Western Europe. By the late eighteenth century Britain had taken the lead in Western urbanisation.

Notes

Abbreviations *Econ H R: Economic History Review; J Econ Hist: Journal of Economic History; VCH: Victoria County History; WMQ: William and Mary Quarterly.*

1   I am grateful to T. Barnard, P. Burke, H. Diederiks, J. Elliot, F. Fernandez-Armesto, C. Friedrichs, A. Kreider and P. Morgan for their advice in the preparation of this survey.

2   *The Times Literary Supplement,* 27 December 1974; *Urban History Yearbook: 1976* (Leicester, 1976), p. 35 *et seq.*

3   For information contact the Student Enquiry Service, The Open University, Milton Keynes, Bucks.

4   For critical reviews see those by S. Thrupp in *Comparative Studies in Society and History* iv (1961-2), 60 *et seq.*; L. Mumford in *American Sociological Review* xxvi (1961), 656-7; and P. Burke in *Urban History Yearbook: 1975* (Leicester, 1975), p. 13 *et seq.*

5   F. Rörig, *The Medieval Town* (London, 1967); R. Mols, *Introduction à la démographie historique des villes d'Europe* (3 vols, Louvain, 1954-56); F. Dainville, 'Grandeur et populations des villes au XVIIIe siècle', *Population* xiii (1958), 459-80 combines Mols's data on population size with evidence on physical size to produce a ranking order of the main urban centres.

6   E. A. Gutkind, *Urban Development in Southern Europe* (London, 1969); *Urban Development in Western Europe* (London, 1971).

7   P. Burke, *Venice and Amsterdam* (London, 1974).

8   For a survey of recent Belgian work: *Cahiers Bruxellois* xv-xvi (1970-71), part 3, 251-77. J. De Vries, *The Dutch Rural Economy in the Golden Age* (London, 1974), esp. p. 84 *et seq.*

9   H. Klompmaker, 'Les villes Neerlandaises au XVIIe siècle', *Recueils de la Societé Jean Bodin* vii (1955), 578 *et seq.*

10   H. van der Wee, *The Growth of the Antwerp Market and the European Economy* (3 vols, Louvain, 1963), esp. ii, 113 *et seq.*; W. Brulez, 'Bruges and Antwerp in the 15th and 16th centuries: an Antithesis?', *Acta Historiae Neerlandicae* vi (1973), 1-26; also J. A. van Houtte, 'Anvers aux XVe et XVIe siècles', *Annales E-S-C* xvi (1961), 248-78; R. Doehaerd, *Études Anversoises* (3 vols, Paris, 1962-63); W. Brulez, *De Firma della Faille . . .* (Brussels, 1959).

11   E. Sabbé, *Anvers: metropole de l'occident* (Brussels, 1952); see also the account of Antwerp in G. D. Ramsay, *The City of London in International Politics at the Accession of Elizabeth Tudor* (Manchester, 1975), ch. 1.

12   E. Scholliers, 'De levensstandaard der arbeiders op het einde der XVIe eeuw te Antwerpen', *Tijdschrift voor Geschiedenis* lxviii (1955), 80-103; J. A. van Houtte, 'Declin et survivance d'Anvers . . .', *Studi in Onore di A. Fanfani,* v (Milan, 1962), 705-726.

13   P. Burke, *Venice and Amsterdam*; V. Barbour, *Capitalism in Amsterdam in the 17th Century* (Baltimore, 1950); W. J. van Hoboken, 'The Dutch West India Company . . .', in J. S. Bromley and E. H. Kossmann, eds, *Britain and the Netherlands: I* London, 1960), ch. 3; M. Bogucka, 'Amsterdam and the Baltic in the first half of the seventeenth century', *Econ H R,* 2nd ser., xxvi (1973), 433-47; J. G. van Dillen, 'Amsterdam's rôle in 17th-century Dutch politics . . .', in J. S. Bromley and E. H. Kossmann, eds, *Britain and the Netherlands: II* (Groningen, 1964), ch. 7; see also J. J. Murray, *Amsterdam in the Age of Rembrandt* (Newton Abbot, 1972).

14   F. Daelemans, 'Leiden 1581 . . .', *A. A. G. Bijdragen* xix (1975), 139-215.

15   A. M. van de Woude and G. V. Mentink, 'La population de Rotterdam . . .', *Population* xxi (1966), 1165-90; S. C. van Kampen, *De Rotterdamse Particuliere Scheepsbouw . . .* (Born-Assen, 1953).

16   J. Craeybeckx, 'Les industries d'exportation dans les villes Flamandes . . .', *Studi in Onore di A. Fanfani: IV* (Milan, 1962), 413-68.

17   P. H. M. G. Offermans, *Arbeid en levensstandaard in Nijmegen 1550-1600* (Zutphen, 1972); R. van Uytven, 'De Sociale Krisis der XVIe eeuw te Leuven', *Revue Belge de Philologie et d'Histoire,* xxxvi (1958), 356-87.

18   H. K. Roessingh, 'Beroepen bedriif op de Veluwe . . .', *A. A. G. Bijdragen* xiii (1965), 181 *et seq.*; J. A. Faber, 'Drie Eeuwen Friesland . . .', *ibid.*, xvii (1) (1972).

19   E. Hélin, *La démographie de Liège aux XVIIe et XVIII siècles* (Brussels, 1963).

20   A. Wyffels, 'De omvang en de evolutie van het Brugse bevolkingscifer', *Revue Belge de Philologie et d'Histoire* xxxvi (1958), 1243-74; A. de Vos, 'De Omvang en de Evolutie van het Eeklose Bevolkingscifer . . .', *Cinq études de démographie locale* (Brussels, 1963), 123-50.

21   H. Soly, 'The "betrayal" of the sixteenth-century bourgeoisie: a myth?' *Acta Historiae Neerlandicae* viii (1975), 31-49; R. van Uytven, 'De Leuvense bier industrie . . .', *Bijdragen voor de Geschiedenis der Nederlanden* xvi (1961), 193-227.

22   E. Scholliers, 'Vrije en onvrije arbeiders voornamelijk te Antwerpen . . .', *Bijdragen voor de Geschiedenis* xi (1956), 285-322; T. Wittman, *Les Gueux dans les 'bonnes villes' de Flandres* (Budapest, 1969).

23   G. van Houtte, *Leuven in 1740 een krisisjaar* (Brussels, 1964).

24   R. van Uytven, *Stadsfinanciën en Stadsekonomie te Leuven* (Brussels, 1961), French summary p. 653 *et seq.*; P. Burke, *Venice and Amsterdam*, p. 40 *et seq.*; D. J. Roorda, 'Party and faction . . .', *Acta Historiae Neerlandica* ii (1967), 188-221; see also *idem*, 'The ruling classes in Holland in the 17th century', in Bromley and Kossmann, *Britain and the Netherlands* ii, ch. 6; F. H. M. C. Adriaens, *De Magistrat van Nijmegen . . . 1750-1800* (Nijmegen, 1956).

25   A. C. F. Koch, 'The Reformation at Deventer in 1579-1580 . . .', *Acta Historiae Neerlandicae* vi (1973), 29 *et seq.*; M. Delmotte, 'Het Calvinisme in de verschillende bevolkingslagen te Gent 1566-1567', *Tijdschrift voor Geschiedenis* lxxvi (1963), 145-76.

26   A. C. Carter, *The English Reformed Church in Amsterdam in the 17th Century* (Amsterdam, 1964); P. Burke, *op. cit.* (n. 4); K. Fremantle, *The Baroque Town Hall of Amsterdam* (Utrecht, 1959).

27   G. L. Burke, *The Making of Dutch Towns* (London, 1956), chs 6-9; see also A. M. Lambert, *The Making of the Dutch Landscape* (London, 1971), chs 4-5.

28   B. Lager, *Stockholms Befolkning Pa Johan III: s tid* (Stockholm, 1962).

29   P. Thestrup, *The Standard of Living in Copenhagen 1730-1800* (Copenhagen, 1971); J. Jorgensen, 'The economic condition of Zealand provincial towns in the 18th century', *Scandinavian Economic History Review* xix (1971), 1-11.

30   For a survey of recent German work: *Cahiers Bruxellois, op. cit.* (n. 8), p. 240 *et seq.*; see also E. Keyser, *Bibliographie zur Städtgeschichte Deutschlands* (Cologne, 1969).

31   P. Dollinger, 'Les villes Allemandes . . .', *Recueils . . . Jean Bodin* vii (1955), 390 *et seq.*; B. Moeller, *Reichsstadt und Reformation* (Gütersloh, 1962): an expanded English edition by H. C. E. Midelfort and M. U. Edwards, *Imperial Cities and the Reformation* (Philadelphia, 1972); B. Hall, 'The Reformation city', *Bulletin of the John Rylands Library* liv (1971-72), 103 *et seq.* For a Marxist line on the social and economic context of reform see J. Schildhauer, *Soziale, politische und religiöse Auseinandersetzungen in der Hansestädten . . .* (Weimar, 1959).

32   P. Dollinger, *The German Hansa* (trans, D. S. Ault and S. H. Steinberg, London, 1970), part 3; H. Mauersberg, *Wirtschafts und Sozialgeschichte zentraleuropäischer Städte . . .* (Gottingen, 1960).

33   Mols, *op. cit.* (n. 5), ii, 509-11.

34   G. Strauss, *Nuremberg in the Sixteenth Century* (London, 1966); G. Hirschmann, essay in H. Rössler, ed., *Deutsches Patriziat 1430-1740* (Limburg, 1968); essays by G. Seebass, P. N. Bebb, J. Spielvogel in L. P. Buck and J. W. Zophy, eds, *The Social History of the Reformation* (Columbus, Ohio, 1972), pp. 17-40, 52-90.

35   M. U. Chrisman, *Strasbourg and the Reform* (London, 1967); F. L. Ford, *Strasbourg in Transition* (Cambridge, Mass., 1958); for the French angle see G. Livet, *L'Intendance d'Alsace sous Louis XIV* (Paris, 1956), p. 331 *et seq.*

36   G. Klingenstein, 'Vienna nel Settecento; alcuni aspetti di una trasformazione', in A. Caracciolo, ed., *Dalla città preindustriale alla*

città de capitalismo (Bologna, 1975), 55-65 (I am indebted for this reference to Prof. H. J. Dyos). See also briefly: J. Stoye, *The Siege of Vienna* (London, 1964), 64 *et seq.*; O. Brunner, 'Hamburg und Wien... 1200-1800', in O. Brunner *et al.*, eds, *Festschrift Hermann Aubin Zum 80 Geburtstag* (Wiesbaden, 1965), ii, 479-94; G. L. Soliday, *A Community in Conflict: Frankfurt society in the 17th and 18th centuries* (Dartmouth, 1974).

37   R. W. Scribner, 'Civic unity and the Reformation in Erfurt', *Past and Present*, no. 66 (1975), 29-60; C. R. Friedrichs, 'Capitalism, mobility and class formation in the early modern German city', *Past and Present*, no. 69 (1975), 24-49.

38   M. Walker, *German Home Towns 1648-1871* (London, 1971).

39   There are a few welcome exceptions to this tendency: for example, the collection of essays on the patrician classes in Rössler, *op. cit.* (n. 34). See also the varied mixture of social history items in E. Maschke and J. Sydow, eds, *Gesellschaftliche Unterschichten in den Südwest-deutschen Städten* (Stuttgart, 1967), and *Städtische Mittelschichten* (Stuttgart, 1972).

40   G. Franz, *Der Dreissigjährige Krieg und das deutsche Volk* (3rd edn, Stuttgart, 1961); E. Woehlkens, *Pest und Ruhr im 16. und 17. Jahrhundert* (Hanover, 1954).

41   F. Bedarida, 'The growth of urban history in France', in H. J. Dyos, ed., *The Study of Urban History* (London, 1968), 48 *et seq.*; for the best bibliography see P. Dollinger and P. Wolff, *Bibliographie d'histoire des villes de France* (Paris, 1967).

42   P. Goubert, *The Ancien Régime* (trans. S. Cox, London, 1973), esp. ch. 9; 'Economie et urbanisme en France dans la première moitié du XVIIe siècle', in P. Francastel, ed., *L'Urbanisme de Paris et l'Europe 1600-1680* (Paris, 1969), 39 *et seq.*

43   L. Bernard, *The Emerging City: Paris in the age of Louis XIV* (Durham, N. Carolina, 1970); O. Ranum, *Paris in the age of Absolutism* (London, 1968).

44   R. Gascon, *Grande commerce et vie urbaine...* (2 vols, Paris, 1971); N. Z. Davis, *Society and Culture in Early Modern France* (London, 1975), chs 1-3.

45   J. P. Gutton, *La Société et les pauvres... la généralité de Lyon 1534-1789* (Paris, 1972); M. Garden, *Lyon et les Lyonnais au XVIIIe siècle* (Paris, 1971).

46   G. Rambert *et al.*, *Histoire de Marseille* (Paris, 1949-   ), esp. vols iii-vi; R. Boutruche, *Bordeaux de 1453 à 1715* (Bordeaux, 1966); F. G. Pariset, *Bordeaux au XVIIIe siècle* (Bordeaux, 1968); J. P. Poussou, 'L'émigration bazardaise à Bordeaux...', *Les Cahiers du Bazardais* vi (1964), 28-38.

47   P. Dardel, *Commerce, industrie et navigation à Rouen et au Havre au XVIIIe siècle* (Rouen, 1966); *Navires et marchandises dans les ports de Rouen et du Havre au XVIIIe siècle* (Paris, 1963).

48   P. Wolff, *Histoire de Toulouse* (2nd edn, Toulouse, 1974); J. Estèbe, 'La bourgeoisie marchande... au XVIe siècle', *Annales du Midi* lxxvi (1964), 457-67; J. Godechot, 'L'histoire sociale et économique de Toulouse au XVIIIe siècle', *ibid.*, lxxviii (1966), 363-74.

49 P. Deyon, *Amiens capitale provinciale* (Paris, 1967); 'Dénombrements et structures urbaines', *Revue du Nord* liii (1971), 495-503.

50 P. Goubert, *Beauvais et le Beauvaisis de 1600 à 1730* (2 vols, Paris, 1960); M. El Kordi, *Bayeux aux XVIIe et XVIIIe siècles* (Paris, 1970); O. H. Hufton, *Bayeux in the Late Eighteenth Century* (Oxford, 1967).

51 M. Lachiver, *La Population de Meulan . . . 1600-1870* (Paris, 1969); also *Histoire de Meulan et sa Region* (Meulan, 1965); R. Tinthoin, 'Essai de Géographie urbaine historique . . . Thonon dans la première moitié du XVIIIe siècle', *Revue de Géographie Alpine* lx (2) (1972), 341-58; P. Tucoo-Chala, 'Un exemple d'essor urbain: Pau au XVIe siècle', *Annales du Midi* lxxviii (1966), 345-61.

52 J. Tanguy, *Le Commerce du port de Nantes au milieu du XVIe siècle* (Paris, 1956); J. Meuvret, *Études d'histoire économique* (Paris, 1971), 199-230; M. Venard, *Bourgeois et Paysans au XVIIIe siècle* (Paris, 1957).

53 B. Porchney, *Les Soulèvements populaires en France de 1623 à 1648* (Paris, 1963), 132-260; R. Mousnier, *Peasant Uprisings* (trans. B. Pearce, London, 1971), 38 *et seq.*; G. Rudé, *The Crowd in History* (London, 1964), *passim*; L. A. Tilly, 'The food riot as a form of political conflict in France', *Journal of Interdisciplinary History* ii (1971-2), 23-57; J. Kaplow, *The Names of Kings: the Parisian laboring poor in the 18th century* (New York, 1972); O. Hufton, *The poor of Eighteenth-century France 1750-1789* (Oxford, 1974), *passim*.

54 J. C. Perrot, 'Rapports sociaux et villes au XVIIIe siècle', *Annales E-S-C*, xxiii (1968), 241-67; A. Daumard and F. Furet, *Structures et Relations Sociales à Paris* (Paris, 1961).

55 N. Temple, 'Municipal elections and municipal oligarchies in 18th-century France', in J. F. Bosher, ed., *French Government and Society 1500-1850* (London, 1973), 70-91.

56 Davis, *op. cit.* (n. 44), ch. 6; but see the criticism of this view of religious riot by J. Estèbe, 'Debate', *Past and Present*, no. 67 (1975), 127 *et seq.*

57 A. Labarre, *Le Livre dans la Vie Amiénoise du Seizième siècle* (Paris, 1971); H. J. Martin, *Livre pouvoirs et société à Paris au XVIIe siècle* (2 vols, Geneva, 1969).

58 P. Francastel, 'Paris et la création urbaine en Europe au XVIIIe siècle', in Francastel, *op. cit.* (n. 42), 15 *et seq.*; J. P. Babelon, *Demeures Parisiennes sous Henri IV et Louis XIII* (Paris, 1965).

59 L. Henry, *Anciennes familles Genèvoises* (Paris, 1956); J. F. Bergier, *Genève et l'économie Européenne de la Renaissance* (Paris, 1963).

60 R. M. Kingdon, *Geneva and the Consolidation of the French Protestant Movement 1564-1572* (Geneva, 1967); E. W. Monter, *Calvin's Geneva* (London, 1967); *Studies in Genevan Government 1536-1605* (Geneva, 1964); see also R. M. Kingdon, 'Social welfare in Calvin's Geneva', *American Historical Review*, lxxvi (1971), 50-69; P. G. Bietenholz, *Basle and France in the 16th Century* (Toronto, 1971); see also J. Rosen, 'Prices and public finance in Basle 1360-1535', *Econ H R*, 2nd ser., xxv (1972), 1-17.

61   F. Braudel, *The Mediterranean and the Mediterranean World in the Age of Philip II* (trans. S. Reynolds, 2 vols, London, 1972), esp. i, 312-54; Mols. *op. cit.* (n. 5), ii, 505-9.

62   Braudel, *op. cit.*, i, 345-7; C. Petraccone, 'Note per la storia della popolazione di Napoli fra XVI e XIX secolo', Caracciolo, *op. cit.* (n. 36), 95-101.

63   J. Hale, ed., *Renaissance Venice* (London, 1973); P. Burke, *Venice and Amsterdam;* B. Pullan, *Rich and Poor in Renaissance Venice* (Oxford, 1971); B. Pullan, ed., *Crisis and Change in the Venetian Economy* (London, 1968); a good general survey is F. C. Lane, *Venice: a maritime republic* (Baltimore, 1973), ch. 17 *et seq.*

64   M. Berengo, *La società veneta alla fine del settecento* (Florence, 1956).

65   J. Delumeau, *Vie économique et sociale de Rome dans la seconde moitié du XVIe siècle* (2 vols, Paris, 1957-9).

66   E. Cochrane, *Florence in the Forgotten Centuries* (London, 1973); M. Berengo, *Nobili e mercanti nella Lucca del Cinquecento* (Turin, 1965).

67   D. Zanetti, *Problemi Alimentari Di Una Economia Preindustriale* (Turin, 1964); see also G. Aleati, *La Popolazione di Pavia durante il dominio spagnolo* (Milan, 1957); P. Earle, 'The commercial development of Ancona, 1479-1551', *Econ H R*, 2nd ser., xxii (1969), 28-44.

68   Mols, *op. cit.* (n. 5), ii, 518-19; B. Bennassar, *Valladolid au siècle d'or* (Paris, 1967).

69   P. and H. Chaunu, *Séville et l'Atlantique,* vol. viii (Paris, 1959); R. Pike, *Aristocrats and Traders: Sevillian society in the 16th century* (London, 1972).

70   Essay by J. P. Molénat in *Mélanges de la Casa de Velazquez,* viii (1972), 327-77; M. Weisser, 'The decline of Castile revisited: the case of Toledo', *Journal of European Economic History* ii (1973), 614-40; D. Ringrose, 'The impact of a new capital city: Madrid, Toledo and New Castile, 1560-1660', *J Econ Hist* xxxiii (1973), 761-91.

71   B. Bennassar, 'Medina del Campo . . .', *Revue d'Histoire Économique et Sociale* xxxix (1961), 474 *et seq.*; V. F. Vargas, *La Poblacion de Leon en el siglo XVI* (Madrid, 1968); J. L. Martin Galindo, *La Civdad de Leon en el siglo XVIII* (Leon, 1959).

72   B. Bennassar, *Recherches sur les grandes épidémies dans le Nord de l'Espagne* (Paris, 1969); J. Fayard and C. Larquié, 'Hôtels Madrilènes et démographie urbaine au XVIIe siècle', *Mélanges* iv (1968), 229-58.

73   L. Torres Balbas *et al.*, *Resumen Historico del Urbanismo en España* (Madrid, 1954); J. Gallego, 'L'urbanisme de Madrid au XVIIe siècle', Francastel, *op. cit.* (n. 42), 251 *et seq.*

74   For a survey of American work: E. E. Lampard, 'American historians and the study of urbanization', *American Historical Review* lxvii (1961-2), 49-61.

75   C. Bridenbaugh, *Cities in the Wilderness . . . 1625-1742* (New York, 1960); *Cities in Revolt . . . 1743-1776* (New York, 1955); J. P.

Greene, 'Economic function and the growth of American port towns in the eighteenth century', *Perspectives in American History* viii (1974), 123-86.

76 E. M. Cook, 'Local leadership and the typology of New England towns, 1700-85', *Political Science Quarterly* lxxxvi (1971), 586-608.

77 D. B. Rutman, *Winthrop's Boston* (Chapel Hill, 1965); J. A. Henretta, 'Economic development and social structure in colonial Boston', *WMQ*, 3rd ser., xxii (1965), 75-92; J. B. Blake, *Public Health in the Town of Boston 1630-1822* (Cambridge, Mass., 1959).

78 K. A. Lockridge, *A New England Town: the first hundred years* (New York, 1970); P. J. Greven, *Four Generations: population, land and family in colonial Andover, Massachusetts* (Ithaca, 1970); M. Zuckerman, *Peaceable Kingdoms; New England towns in the eighteenth century* (New York, 1970); see also P. Smith, *As a City upon a Hill* (London, 1966).

79 J. P. Greene, 'Autonomy and stability: New England and the British colonial experience ...', *Journal of Social History* vii (1974), 171 *et seq.*

80 J. P. Greene, 'Economic function', *op. cit.* (n. 75); A. N. B. Garvan, 'Proprietary Philadelphia as artifact', in J. Burchard and O. Handlin, eds, *The Historian and the City* (Cambridge, Mass., 1963), 177-201; J. J. McCusker, 'Sources of investment capital in the colonial Philadelphia shipping industry', *J Econ Hist* xxxii (1972), 146-57; S. B. Warner, *The Private City: Philadelphia in three periods of its growth* (Philadelphia, 1968), 3-45; J. T. Lemon, 'Urbanization and the development of 18th-century south eastern Pennsylvania . . .', *WMQ*, 3rd ser., xxiv (1967), 501-33.

81 E. C. Papenfuse, *In Pursuit of Profit: the Annapolis merchants in the era of the American Revolution* (Baltimore, 1975).

82 J. P. Greene, 'Economic Function', *op. cit.* (n. 75); J. H. Soltow, *The Economic Role of Williamsburg* (Charlottesville, 1965); J. A. Ernst and H. R. Merrens, 'Camden's turrets pierce the skies . . .', *WMQ*, 3rd ser., xxx (1973), 549-74; H. Wellenreuther, 'Urbanization in the colonial South: a critique', *ibid.*, xxxi (1974), 653-71.

83 B. C. Daniels, 'Family dynasties in Connecticut's largest towns 1700-1760', *Canadian Journal of History* viii (1973), 99-110; R. E. Wall, 'The Decline of the Massachusetts franchise 1647-1666', *Journal of American History* lix (1972-73), 303-10; G. B. Nash, 'The transformation of urban politics 1700-1765', *Journal of American History* lx (1973-4), 605-32; J. W. Reps, *The Making of Urban America* (New York, 1965); J. W. Reps, *Tidewater Towns: city planning in colonial Virginia and Maryland* (Williamsburg, 1972).

84 For a wide-ranging account of the development of British urban studies see H. J. Dyos, 'Agenda for urban historians', in Dyos, *op. cit.* (n. 41), 16 *et seq.*; see also the perceptive article by A. Sutcliffe, 'The condition of urban history in England', *The Local Historian* xi (1974), 287 *et seq.*; and P. Clark and P. Slack, eds, *Crisis and Order in English Towns 1500-1700* (London, 1972), pp. 1-2.

85 J. W. F. Hill, *Tudor and Stuart Lincoln* (Cambridge, 1956); *Georgian Lincoln* (Cambridge, 1966); see also J. Simmons, *Leicester: Past and Present*, vol. i (London, 1974).

86   For example, *VCH, Warwickshire* vol viii (Warwick and Coventry) and *Yorkshire; The City of York,* and *East Riding* vol 1 (Hull).

87   Clark and Slack, *op. cit.* (n. 84), ch. 1; P. Clark and P. Slack, *English Towns in Transition 1500-1700* (London, 1976); C. W. Chalkin, *The Provincial Towns of Georgian England* (London, 1974), ch. 1-2.

88   T. C. Smout, *A History of the Scottish People 1560-1830* (London, 1969), chs 7, 15; also *idem, Scottish Trade on the Eve of Union 1660-1707* (Edinburgh, 1963), ch. 7 *et seq.*; G. D. Owen, *Elizabethan Wales* (Cardiff, 1964), ch. 2.

89   See also: the introductory account of the Tudor city in G. D. Ramsay, *The City of London in International Politics,* ch. 2; F. J. Fisher 'The development of London as a centre of conspicuous consumption in the 16th and 17th centuries', *Trans. Royal Historical Society,* 4th ser., xxx (1948), 37-50; R. G. Lang, 'London's aldermen in business: 1600-1625', *Guildhall Miscellany* iii (1969-71), 242-64; 'Social origins and social aspirations of Jacobean London merchants', *Econ H R,* 2nd ser., xxvii (1974), 28-47; R. Brenner, 'The social basis of English commercial expansion 1550-1650', *J Econ Hist* xxxii (1972), 361-84.

90   B. W. E. Alford and T. C. Barker, *A History of the Carpenters' Company* (London, 1968); J. S. Watson, *A History of the Salters' Company* (Oxford, 1963); J. R. Kellet, 'The breakdown of gild and corporation control over the handicraft and retail trade in London', *Econ H R,* 2nd ser., x (1957-58), 381-94; S. R. Smith, 'The social and geographical origins of the London apprentices 1630-60', *Guildhall Miscellany* iv (1971-73), 195-206.

91   D. Cressey, 'Occupation, migration and literacy in East London', *Local Population Studies,* no. 5 (1970), 53-60; A. B. Appleby, 'Nutrition and disease: the case of London 1550-1750', *Journal of Interdisciplinary History* vi (1975-76), 1-22.

92   F. F. Foster, 'Merchants and Bureaucrats in Elizabethan London', *Guildhall Miscellany* iv, 149-60; V. Pearl, *London and the Outbreak of the Puritan Revolution* (London, 1961); 'London Puritans and Scotch fifth columnists . . .', in A. E. J. Hollaender and W. Kellaway, eds, *Studies in London History* (London, 1969), 317-31; J. E. Farnell, 'The usurpation of honest London householders: Barebones' Parliament', *English Historical Review* lxxxii (1967), 24-46; R. Brenner, 'The Civil War politics of London's merchant community', *Past and Present* no. 58 (1973), 53-107.

93   W. K. Jordan, *The Charities of London 1480-1660* (London, 1960); e.g. B. Gibbons, *Jacobean City Comedy* (London, 1968).

94   E. A Wrigley, 'A simple model of London's importance in changing English society and economy 1650-1750', *Past and Present,* no. 37 (1967), 44-70; G. Rudé, *Hanoverian London 1714-1808* (London, 1971); see also his *Paris and London in the Eighteenth Century* (London, 1970); M. D. George, *London Life in the Eighteenth Century* (London, 1st edn, 1925; 2nd edn, 1965).

95   R. Grassby, 'The personal wealth of the business community in seventeenth-century England', *Econ H R,* 2nd ser., xxiii (1970), 220-34; 'English merchant capitalism in the late 17th century', *Past*

and Present, no. 46 (1970), 87-107; D. W. Jones, 'London merchants and the crisis of the 1690s', in Clark and Slack, *op. cit.* (n. 84), ch. 9.

96   D. Allen, 'The role of the London trained bands in the exclusion crisis 1678-1681', *English Historical Review*, lxxxvii (1972), 287-303; L. S. Sutherland, *The City and the Opposition to Government 1768-1774* (London, 1959); 'The city of London in eighteenth-century politics', in R. Pares and A. J. P. Taylor, eds, *Essays Presented to Sir Lewis Namier* (London, 1956), 49-74; N. Rogers, 'Aristocratic clientage, trade and independency: popular politics in pre-radical Westminster', *Past and Present*, no. 61 (1973), 70-106; G. Rudé, *Wilkes and Liberty* (Oxford, 1962).

97   T. F. Reddaway, *The Rebuilding of London after the Great Fire* (London, 1951); M. J. Power, 'East London housing in the seventeenth century', in Clark and Slack, *op. cit.* (n. 84), ch. 7; J. Summerson, *Georgian London* (London, 1945); see also F. M. L. Thompson, *Hampstead Building a Borough 1650-1964* (London, 1974), ch. 1.

98   M. D. George, *Hogarth to Cruikshank: social change in graphic satire* (London, 1967); A. J. Weitzman, 'Eighteenth-century London: urban paradise or fallen city?', *Journal of the History of Ideas* xxxvi (1975), 469-80.

99   W. S. Reid, 'The coming of the Reformation to Edinburgh', *Church History*, xlii (1973), 27-44; N. T. Phillipson, 'Culture and society in the eighteenth-century province: the case of Edinburgh and the Scottish Enlightenment', in L. Stone, eds., *The University in Society* (London, 1975), ii, 407-48; see also A. Law, *Education in Edinburgh in the 18th Century* (London, 1965); A. J. Youngson, *The Making of Classical Edinburgh* (Edinburgh, 1966).

100   T. C. Barnard, *Cromwellian Ireland* (Oxford, 1975), 77-89; R. A. Butlin, 'The population of Dublin in the late 17th century', *Irish Geography*, v (2) (1965), 51-66; N. T. Burke, 'An early modern Dublin suburb . . .', *ibid.*, vi (1972), 365-85; J. G. Simms, 'Dublin in 1685', *Irish Historical Studies*, xiv (1964-65), 212-26; D. T. Flood, 'The decay of Georgian Dublin', *Dublin Historical Record* xxvii (1974), 78-100.

101   M. F. L. Pritchard, 'The decline of Norwich', *Econ H R*, 2nd ser., iii (1950-51), 371-7 argues for industrial decline by the mid-eighteenth century; J. K. Edwards, 'The decline of the Norwich textiles industry', *Yorkshire Bulletin of Economic and Social Research* xvi (1964), 31-41 suggests a later decline.

102   J. F. Pound, ed., *The Norwich Census of the Poor: 1570* (Norfolk Record Soc., xl, 1971); J. T. Evans, 'The decline of oligarchy in 17th-century Norwich', *Journal of British Studies* xiv (1974), 46-76.

103   W. T. MacCaffrey, *Exeter 1540-1640* (2nd edn, Cambridge, Mass., 1976); W. G. Hoskins, *Industry, Trade and People in Exeter 1688-1800* (2nd edn, Exeter, 1968); W. B. Stephens, *Seventeenth-Century Exeter* (Exeter, 1958); see also E. M. Carus-Wilson, *The Expansion of Exeter at the Close of the Middle Ages* (Exeter, 1963).

104   *VCH, York*; D. Palliser, 'York under the Tudors: the trading life of the northern capital', in A. Everitt, *Perspectives in English Urban*

History (London, 1973), ch. 2; 'Epidemics in Tudor York', *Northern History* viii (1973), 46 *et seq.*

105 J. Vanes, ed., *The Ledger of John Smythe 1538-1550* (London, 1974), introd.; *Bristol Record Society* xvii (1951), xix (1955), xxiv (1966), xxv (1968), xxvii (1974); see also P. McGrath, ed., *Bristol in the Eighteenth Century* (Newton Abbot, 1972).

106 R. Howell, *Newcastle-upon-Tyne and the Puritan Revolution* (Oxford, 1967); for the early eighteenth century see the discussion of Tyneside merchants in E. Hughes, *North Country Life in the Eighteenth Century*, vol. i (Oxford, 1952), ch. 2.

107 Simmons, *op. cit.* (n. 85); *VCH, Leicestershire* vol. iv; W. G. Hoskins, *Provincial England* (London, 1963), ch. 5; Hill, *op. cit.* (n. 85); A. Rogers, ed., *The Making of Stamford* (Leicester, 1965), 58 *et seq.*; *VCH, Coventry.*

108 A. D. Dyer, *The City of Worcester in the 16th Century* (Leicester, 1973).

109 K. A. Adey, 'Seventeenth-century Stafford: a county town in decline', *Midland History* ii (1973-74), 152-67; H. Thorpe, 'Lichfield: a study of its growth and function', *Staffordshire Historical Collections* (1950-51), 171-97. At Colchester there was a variation on the same theme: the eighteenth-century town declined as a textile producer but developed quickly as a fashionable social centre with 'pleasant houses, elegant shops and smarter inns': A. F. J. Brown, 'Colchester in the 18th century', in L. M. Munby, ed., *East Anglian Studies* (Cambridge, 1968), 146-73.

110 J. D. Chambers, 'Population change in a provincial town: Nottingham 1700-1800', D. V. Glass and D. E. C. Eversley, eds, *Population in History* (London, 1965), 334-53; J. Prest, *The Industrial Revolution in Coventry* (Oxford, 1960); J. D. Marshall, 'Kendall in the late 17th and 18th Centuries', *Transactions of the Cumberland and Westmorland Antiquarian and Archaeological Society*, new ser. lxxv (1975), 188-257.

111 J. Patten, 'Village and town: an occupational study', *Agricultural History Review* xx (1) (1972), 1-16; J. Cornwall, 'English country towns in the fifteen-twenties', *Econ H R*, 2nd ser., xv (1962-63), 54-59.

112 H. B. Rodgers, 'The market area of Preston in the 16th and 17th centuries', *Geographical Studies* iii (1956), 46-55; R. Millward, 'The Cumbrian town between 1600 and 1800', in C. W. Chalklin and M. A. Havinden, eds, *Rural Change and Urban Growth 1500-1800* (London, 1974), ch. 8; see also C. W. Chalklin, 'A seventeenth-century market town: Tonbridge', *Archaeologia Cantiana* lxxvi (1961), 152-62; G. H. Kenyon, 'Petworth town and trades 1610-1760', *Sussex Archaeological Collections* xcvi (1958), 35-107. We look forward in particular to the work of Dr J. Chartres of Leeds University.

113 W. M. MacKenzie, *The Scottish Burghs* (Edinburgh, 1949); G. S. Pryde, ed., *The Court Book of the Burgh of Kirkintilloch 1658-1694* (Scottish Hist. Soc., 3rd ser., lxiii, 1963), pp. lviii-lxxxix; also C. McWilliam, *Scottish Townscape* (London, 1975), ch. 3-4.

114 H. Carter, 'Phases of town growth in Wales', in Dyos, *op. cit.* (n. 41), esp. p. 237 *et seq.*; J. Thirsk, ed., *Agrarian History of England and Wales,* iv (Cambridge, 1967), 121 *et seq.*, 142 *et seq.*, 589 *et seq.*; W. S. K. Thomas, 'Tudor and Jacobean Swansea', *Morgannwg* v (1961), 23-48; M. I. Williams, 'Cardiff — its people and its trade 1660-1720', *ibid.* vii (1963), 74-97; R. D. Till, 'Proprietary politics in Glamorgan . . . Neath 1696-1794', *ibid.* xvi (1972), 37-52.

115 G. Camblin, *The Town in Ulster* (Belfast, 1951), chs 2, 4, 6, 8-9; J. C. Beckett, R. E. Glasscock, eds, *Belfast: the origin and growth of an industrial city* (London, 1967), chs 3-4.

116 G. Jackson, *Hull in the 18th Century* (London, 1972); for the earlier period: R. Davis, *The Trade and Shipping of Hull, 1500-1700* (York, 1964).

117 T. C. Smout, 'The development and enterprise of Glasgow 1556-1707', *Scottish Journal of Political Economy* vii (1960-61), 194-212; T. M. Devine, 'Glasgow merchants and the collapse of the tobacco trade 1775-1783', *Scottish Historical Review* lii (1973), 50-74.

118 F. E. Hyde, *Liverpool and the Mersey: an economic history of a port 1700-1970* (Newton Abbot, 1971), chs 1-3; T. C. Barker, 'Lancashire coal, Cheshire salt, and the rise of Liverpool', *Trans. Historical Soc. Lancs. and Cheshire* ciii (1952), 83-101; M. Mullett, 'The politics of Liverpool 1660-88', *ibid.*, cxxxiv (1973), 31-56; F. Vigier, *Change and Apathy: Liverpool and Manchester during the Industrial Revolution* (London, 1970), chs 3-4. Another north-western port which prospered due to the colonial and coal trades was Whitehaven: J. E. Williams, 'Whitehaven in the eighteenth century', *Econ H R*, 2nd ser., viii (1955-56), 393-402.

119 Vigier, *op. cit.*, chs 5-6; W. H. Chaloner, 'Manchester in the latter half of the eighteenth century', *Bulletin of the John Rylands Library* xlii (1959-60), 40-60.

120 C. Gill and A. Briggs, *History of Birmingham* (Oxford, 1952), i; R. A. Pelham, 'The migration of the iron industry towards Birmingham', *Birmingham Arch. Soc. Transactions* lxvi (1950), 142-9; M. J. Wise, 'Birmingham and its trade relations in the early eighteenth century', *University of Birmingham Historical Journal* ii (1949-50), 53-79; B. M. D. Smith, 'The Galtons of Birmingham . . .', *Business History* ix (1967), 132-50.

121 R. G. Wilson, *Gentlemen Merchants: the merchant community in Leeds 1700-1830* (Manchester, 1971); M. W. Beresford and G. R. J. Jones, eds, *Leeds and its Region* (Leeds, 1967), chs 11-12; W. G. Rimmer, 'The industrial profile of Leeds 1740-1840', *Thoresby Society Publications* l (1965-68), 130-57; F. Beckwith, 'The population of Leeds during the Industrial Revolution', *ibid.*, xli (1946-53), 118-96.

122 D. Hey, *The Rural Metalworkers of the Sheffield Region* (Leicester, 1972); also D. L. Linton, ed., *Sheffield and its Region* (Sheffield, 1956), p. 155 *et seq.*; J. Foster, *Class Struggle and the Industrial Revolution* (London, 1974), p. 22 *et seq.* (Oldham); M. E. François, 'The social and economic development of Halifax', *Proceedings of*

the Leeds Philosophical and Literary Society (Lit. and Hist. Section) xi (1964-66), 217-80.

123   D. C. Coleman, 'Naval dockyards under the later Stuarts', *Econ H R*, 2nd ser., vi (1953-54), 134-55; C. Chalklin, 'The making of some new towns, c. 1600-1720', in Chalklin and Havinden, *op. cit.* (n. 112), ch. 9 (Portsea).

124   For a general survey see J. A. Patmore, 'The spa towns of Britain', in R. P. Beckinsale and J. M. Houston, eds, *Urbanization and its Problems* (Oxford, 1968), 47-69; R. Neale, 'Society, belief and the building of Bath 1700-1793', in Chalklin and Havinden, *op. cit.* (n. 112), ch. 10; Chalklin, 'The making of some new towns', in *ibid*, ch. 9.

125   J. Whyman, 'A Hanoverian watering-place, Margate before the railways', Everitt, *Perspectives*, ch. 5; see also W. J. Smith, 'Blackpool . . . 1740-1851', *Trans. Lancs. and Cheshire Antiquarian Soc.* lxix (1959), 70-103.

126   M. Drake, 'An elementary exercise in parish register demography', *Econ H R*, 2nd ser., xiv (1961-62), 427-45; Chambers, *op. cit.* (n. 110); Beckwith, *op. cit.* (n. 121); E. A. Wrigley: 'Mortality in pre-industrial England: the example of Colyton, Devon, over three centuries', *Daedalus*, lxlvii (2) (1968), 546-80; 'Family limitation in pre-industrial England', *Econ H R*, 2nd ser., xix (1966), 82-109; M. F. and T. H. Hollingsworth, 'Plague mortality rates by age and sex in the parish of St Botolph's . . . London 1603', *Population Studies* xxv (1971), 131-46.

127   A. F. Butcher, 'The origins of Romney Freemen, 1433-1523', *Econ H R*, 2nd ser., xxvii (1974), 16-27; P. Clark, 'The migrant in Kentish towns 1580-1640', in Clark and Slack, *Crisis and Order* (n. 84), ch. 4; J. Patten, *Rural-Urban Migration in Pre-Industrial England* (Oxford School of Geography cyclostyled paper, 1973).

128   For example, D. M. Woodward, *The Trade of Elizabethan Chester* (Hull, 1970); W. B. Stephens, 'The cloth exports of the provincial ports, 1600-1640', *Econ H R*, 2nd ser., xxii (1969), 228-48; A. A. Ruddock, 'London capitalists and the decline of Southampton in the early Tudor period', *ibid.* ii (1949-50), 137-51; J. Webb, *Great Tooley of Ipswich* (Ipswich, 1962).

129   See above; also N. B. Harte and K. G. Ponting, eds, *Textile History and Economic History* (Manchester, 1973), esp. chs 3-6, 9.

130   Hoskins, *Provincial England*, p. 94 *et seq.*; D. M. Palliser, 'The trade gilds of Tudor York', in Clark and Slack, *Crisis and Order* (n. 84), ch. 3; L. Fox, 'The Coventry guilds and trading companies', in *Essays in Honour of P. B. Chatwin* (Oxford, 1962), 18 *et seq.*; J. Youings, *Tuckers Hall, Exeter* (Exeter, 1968); T. C. Mendenhall, *The Shrewsbury Drapers and the Welsh Wool Trade in the 16th and 17th Centuries* (Oxford, 1953).

131   Chalklin, *Provincial Towns*, ch. 3 *et seq.*; P. Mathias, *The Brewing Industry in England 1700-1820* (Cambridge, 1959); for an illuminating case study of provincial medicine: F. M. Valadez and C. D. O'Malley, 'James Keill of Northampton . . .', *Medical History* xv (1971), 317-35.

132   P. Slack, 'Poverty and politics in Salisbury 1597-1666', Clark and
      Slack, *Crisis and Order* (n. 84), ch. 5; 'Vagrants and vagrancy in
      England 1598-1664', *Econ H R*, 2nd ser., xxviii (1974), 360-79; J.
      Webb, ed., *Poor Relief in Elizabethan Ipswich* (Suffolk Record Soc.,
      ix, 1966); J. F. Pound, 'An Elizabethan census of the poor',
      University of Birmingham Historical Journal viii (1962), 135-51.

133   For eighteenth-century relief: R. V. H. Burne, 'The treatment of the
      poor in the eighteenth century in Chester', *Journal of the Chester
      Archaeol. Soc.* lii (1965), 33 *et seq.*; P. H. Goodman, 'Eighteenth-
      century poor law administration in the parish of Oswestry', *Trans.
      Shropshire Archaeol. Soc.*, 3rd ser., lvi (1957-60), 328 *et seq.*

134   A. Everitt, *Change in the Provinces: the seventeenth century*
      (Leicester, 1972), 43 *et seq.*; 'The English urban inn, 1560-1760', in
      Everitt, *Perspectives*, ch. 4.

135   But see D. Hirst, *The Representative of the People?* (Cambridge,
      1975), chs. 3, 5; R. L. Bushman, 'English franchise reform in the
      17th century', *Journal of British Studies* iii (1963), 36-53; P.
      Williams, 'Government and politics in Ludlow, 1590-1642', *Trans.
      Shropshire Archaeol. Soc.*, lvi (1957-60), 282-94. For towns and the
      English Revolution: D. Underdown, *Pride's Purge* (Oxford, 1971),
      40 *et passim*; A. M. Johnson, 'Politics in Chester . . . 1640-62', Clark
      and Slack, *Crisis and Order*, ch. 6. For the later period: A.
      Temple Patterson, *A History of Southampton: 1700-1835* vol. i
      (Southampton, 1966), esp. chs 2-3; Evans, *op. cit.* (n. 102); R. C.
      Latham, ed., *Bristol Charters 1509-1899* (Bristol Record Soc., xii,
      1947); also W. J. Shelton, 'The role of local authorities in the
      provincial hunger riots of 1766', *Albion*, v (1973-74), 50-66.

136   D. M. Bergeron, *English Civic Pageantry* (London, 1971).

137   But see D. M. Palliser, *The Reformation in York* (Borthwick Papers
      no. 40, York, 1971); P. S. Seaver, *The Puritan Lecture-
      ships . . . 1560-1662* (Stanford, Calif., 1970); A. Brockett, *Noncon-
      formity in Exeter 1650-1875* (Manchester, 1962).

138   J. Lawson, *A Town Grammar School through Six Centuries* (Oxford,
      1963) (Hull); *The Endowed Grammar Schools of East Yorkshire*
      (York, 1962); B. Simon, ed., *Education in Leicestershire 1540-1940*
      (Leicester, 1968), chs 1-3; P. Clark, 'The ownership of books in
      England 1560-1640: the example of some Kentish townsfolk', in L.
      Stone, ed., *Schooling and Society* (Baltimore, 1976), ch. 4; J.
      Fawcett, 'Eighteenth century Norfolk booksellers . . .', *Trans. Cam-
      bridge Bibliographical Soc.* vi (1972), 1 *et seq.*

139   For plans of early towns see M. D. Lobel, ed., *Historic Towns*
      (1969-   ); G. Burke, *Towns in the Making* (London, 1971), chs 5-6;
      M. Laithwaite, 'The buildings of Burford', in Everitt, *Perspectives*,
      ch. 3; D. Portman, *Exeter Houses 1400-1700* (Exeter, 1966); S. D.
      Chapman, ed., *The History of Working Class Housing* (Newton
      Abbot, 1971), chs 3-4; M. Beresford, 'The making of a townscape:
      Richard Paley in the east end of Leeds, 1771-1803', Chalklin and
      Havinden, *op. cit.* (n. 112), ch. 11.

140   McWilliam, *op. cit.* (n. 113), chs 3-4; I. G. Lindsay and M. Cosh,
      Inverary and the Dukes of Argyll (Edinburgh, 1973); Camblin, *op*

cit. (n. 115) chs 8-9; M. Craig, *Dublin 1660-1860* (London, 1952).

141 For the provincial press: G. A. Cranfield, *The Development of the Provincial Newspaper* (Oxford, 1962); A. E. Musson and E. Robinson, 'Science and industry in the late eighteenth century', *Econ H R*, 2nd ser., xiii (1960-61), 222-44; *Science and Technology in the Industrial Revolution* (Manchester, 1969), ch. 4; R. E. Schofield, *The Lunar Society of Birmingham* (Oxford, 1963).

2 The nature of the pre-industrial city

Gideon Sjoberg

Throughout this work the burden of our argument is that pre-industrial cities and the feudal societies that support them, whether past or present, or in divergent cultural settings, share an imposing number of structural characteristics. Similar in many facets of their ecology, as well as in their class, familial, economic, political, religious and educational structures, they differ dramatically from industrial cities and societies. Although we are cognisant of the variations among pre-industrial cities through time and across cultural boundaries, our task has been the search for similarities in these communities, particularly in those features that set them apart from industrial cities.

No claim is made that every pre-industrial city displays each one of the traits delineated in the preceding chapters. Nevertheless, non-industrial, or feudal, cities evince a startling degree of communality. Remember, we have introduced into our 'constructed type' only those traits for which empirical evidence is at hand for cities in at least several divergent cultural systems.

Although empirical illustrations are offered throughout to buttress our generalisations, these are merely suggestive of the wide range of supporting data available! Complete documentation of each proposition would have resulted in a set of volumes of unmanageable proportions, our theses smothered in a welter of technical details.

Granted that the materials on pre-industrial cities are of uneven quality, and that hiatuses exist, they are nonetheless more extensive than most readers might assume. Those who desire further particulars, as well as a fuller picture of specific cities, should examine the cited works; these serve as an introduction to a voluminous body of literature.

We undertook this research in the belief that systematisation of existing data, and their interpretation into some meaningful whole, is a desideratum in American social science, geared as it is to absorption with particulars. The fundamental premise of this work is that social science in general, and sociology in particular, to fulfil the requirements of a science, must seek to isolate the common elements in societies and cultures. It is only by abstracting out the universal, or near-universal, traits in pre-industrial cities that one really discovers and explicates what is unique. The more materials on cities around the world that I examine, the more I

G. Sjoberg, 'A backward glance: a forward look', from *The Preindustrial City*, New York, Collier-Macmillan, 1960, Chapter 11, pp 321-35.

am convinced that too many social scientists assume uniqueness where such does not exist.

Our primary intention has been to analyse feudal cities and their societies and thereby to provide a perspective for a clearer understanding of modern industrial orders. But we are jumping slightly ahead of ourselves. We need first to synopsise the structure of the non-industrial city, and then restate the theory underlying our work. After this we consider the possible utility of our typology for future research, most perceptibly in underdeveloped countries. Lastly we pose the query: What is transpiring in contemporary pre-industrial cities and what will be the possible end result as these are swept up in the tidal wave of industrialisation?

The pre-industrial city in capsule form

Cities of this type have been with us, present evidence indicates, since the fourth millennium BC, when they first began their development in the Mesopotamian riverine area. Before long, in response to the growing technology and a variety of political forces, city life proliferated over a broader area. To an astonishing degree, pre-industrial cities throughout history have prospered or floundered, as the case may be, in accordance with the shifting tides of social power.

In terms of their population these cities are the industrial city's poor relations, few ranging over 100,000 and many containing less than 10,000 or even 5,000 inhabitants. Their rate of population growth, moreover, has been slow and variable as well, in accordance with the waxing and waning of the supportive political structure. Yet throughout the shifting fortunes of empire, and the concomitant oscillation in population growth and decline, certain persistent structural characteristics signalise pre-industrial cities everywhere.

As to spatial arrangements, the city's centre is the hub of governmental and religious activity more than of commercial ventures. It is, besides, the prime focus of elite residence, while the lower class and outcaste groups are scattered centrifugally toward the city's periphery. Added to the strong ecological differentiation in terms of social class, occupational and ethnic distinctions are solemnly proclaimed in the land use patterns. It is usual for each occupational group to live and work in a particular street or quarter, one that generally bears the name of the trade in question. Ethnic groups are almost always isolated from the rest of the city, forming, so to speak, little worlds unto themselves. Yet, apart from the considerable ecological differentiation according to socio-economic critieria, a minimum of specialisation exists in land use. Frequently a site serves multiple purposes — e.g., it may be devoted concurrently to religious, educational and business activities; and residential and occupational facilities are apt to be contiguous.

As to class, one is born into a particular stratum and usually must live out his life in accordance with the rights and duties of his position. Few aspects of daily activity escape the pervasive influence of class. A small urbanised, privileged group commands the local community and the society and is nourished by the lower class and an outcaste group; this last, by performing functions considered defiling and beyond the bounds of respectability, is ostracised by both the lower and upper strata. Social mobility in the city, at least as viewed over several generations, seems, relative to the industrial norms, inconsequential. The small upper class, immediately identifiable by its dress, speech and personal mannerisms, controls the key organisational units of government, religion and education in the city and society. Distinctive familial arrangements and clear avoidance of economic activity mark the elite as well. Of course, as earlier emphasised, there are contrary forces at work that disturb these neat arrangements.

The pre-industrial urbanite functions within a family system and subordinates himself to it. One consequence is that, typically, marriages are arranged by families, not by individuals. The large extended family, with numerous relatives residing in a single 'household' — i.e., one that is a functioning social unit — is the ideal toward which all urbanites strive, though a sizeable, closely knit family is generally attainable only by the upper class. Economic circumstances prevent the urban poor and the peasantry alike from maintaining large households; for them the *famille souche* is more normal.

The men in the family lord it over the women; but though the latter are relegated to a humbler position, they are protected to a degree by the rigid sexual division of labour. Upper-class women, moreover, are isolated from most aspects of community life. Those in the urban lower class, like the rural women, play a rather more salient role in family affairs and are accorded wider freedom and responsibility in the community than are the elite womenfolk, though by no means to the degree permitted the males, nor to the extent enjoyed by the industrial city's women. Added to the profound status differentiation by sex in the feudal city is the sharp age-grading; the older family members dominate the younger, both as between generations and between siblings.

The family is the key socialisation agency in the community and serves, for the women and children, and men to a lesser degree, as the focus of leisure-time activity. But more than this, given the low level of social mobility, a man's family is the chief determinant of his future career, be this in the topmost levels of the governmental, educational, or religious bureaucracies or, in the case of the commoners, in the lower-status jobs. Personnel are recruited according to kinship or personalistic criteria far more than on objective, universalistic grounds.

Economic activity is poorly developed in the pre-industrial city, for manual labour, or indeed any that requires one to mingle with the humbler folk, is depreciated and eschewed by the elite. Except for a few large-scale merchants, who may succeed in buying their way into the elite, persons engaged in economic activity are either of the lower class (artisans, labourers and some shopkeepers) or outcastes (some businessmen, and those who carry out the especially degrading and arduous tasks in the city).

Within the economic realm the key unit is the guild, typically community-bound. Through the guilds, handicraftsmen, merchants and groups offering a variety of services attempt to minimise competition and determine standards and prices in their particular spheres of activity. Customarily also, each guild controls the recruitment, based mainly on kinship or other particularistic ties, and the training of personnel for its specific occupation and seeks to prevent outsiders from invading its hallowed domain.

The production of goods and services — by means of a simple technology wherein humans and animals are almost the only source of power, and tools to multiply the effects of this energy are sparse — is accomplished through a division of labour which is complex compared to that in the typical folk order but, seen from the industrial city's vantage point, is surprisingly simple. Very commonly the craftsman fashions an article from beginning to end and often markets it himself. Although little specialisation exists in process, specialisation according to product is widespread. Thus each guild is concerned with the manufacture and/or sale of a specific product or, at most, a narrow class of products.

Little standardisation is found in prices, currency, weights and measures, or the type or quality of commodities marketed. In the main, the price of an item is fixed through haggling between buyer and seller. Different types and values of currency may be used concurrently within or among communities; so too with weights and measures, which often vary as well among the crafts. The marketing procedure is further complicated by the extensive adulteration of produce, forcing the buyer to be wary in every transaction; the quality of commodities is rarely, if ever, guaranteed.

The expansion of the economy is limited not only by the ruling group's negation of economic activity, the lack of standardisation, and so on, but very largely also by the meagre facilities for credit and capital formation.

Turning from the economy to the political structure, we find members of the upper class in command of the key governmental positions. The political apparatus, moreover, is highly centralised, the provincial and local administrators being accountable to the leaders in the societal capital. The sovereign exercises autocratic power, although this is mitigated by certain contrary forces that act to limit the degree of absolutism in the political realm.

The sovereign, and the societal leaders in general, along with the bureaucracies they control, base their authority upon appeals to tradition and to absolutes. The political bureaucracy, and the educational and religious systems as well, are characterised by rigid hierarchical arrangements; notwithstanding, the lines of authority in decision-making are most imprecise. The result is that decisions are arrived at not according to impersonal rules but rather with reference to the 'persons' involved. Bureaucratic personnel are selected mainly on individualistic grounds — i.e., according to whether they have the correct community, kinship and friendship ties. Clientele are served on a similar basis, which means that the elite determine policy to their own advantage. These patterns, combined with the lack of a fixed salary system, are conducive to graft and, from the point of view of industrial-urban systems, marked inefficiency. Nevertheless, as we have sought to show, this bureaucracy can, from the perspective of the pre-industrial system, be considered quite rational in its operation.

Like the political structure, that pertaining to religion is a potent force making for order in the pre-industrial city. The religious personnel, as well as religious beliefs and practices in general, are rent by the same upper-lower-outcaste divisions that prevail in other areas of activity. Upper-class persons occupy the topmost positions in the hierarchy; furthermore, the elite's religious norms conform most closely to those enunciated in the sacred writings, understandable only to this literate group, whereas the values and norms of the lower strata, most notably those of the outcastes, are apt to deviate considerably from the ideal.

The religious norms, deriving from the religious values and in turn reinforcing them, are highly prescriptive. One's day-by-day behaviour is largely governed by religious injunctions, and few areas of activity — be these family life, politics, economics, education, or whatever — escape their pervasive influence. Moreover, the periodic religious ceremonies, in which a large segment of the community may participate, are one of the few mechanisms the city possesses for integrating disparate groups in an otherwise segmented community.

Strong reliance is placed upon protective, restorative and predictive magic for assisting the individual in adjusting to the natural-divine order, something taken as an absolute, a given. The elite itself, lacking as much as the common man the means to manipulate and revise the social and physical world, employs magical practices freely. And a good part of the magic is integrated into the religious body of knowledge.

Relative to the industrial-urban community, communication in the feudal city is achieved primarily by word-of-mouth, specialised functionaries serving to disseminate news orally at key gathering points in the city. Members of the literate elite, however, communicate with one another to a degree through writing. And the formal educational system depends upon the written word, the means by which the ideal norms are standardised over time and space.

Only the elite, however, have access to formal education. And the educational and religious organisations, with few exceptions, are inter-digitated. The curriculum in the schools, whether elementary or advanced, is overwhelmingly devoted to predication of the society's traditional religious-philosophical concepts. The schools are geared not to remaking the system but to perpetuating the old. Modern science, wherein abstract thought is coherent with practical knowledge and through which man seeks to manipulate the natural order, is practically non-existent in the non-industrial city. The emphasis is upon ethical and religious matters as one is concerned with adjusting to, not overcoming, the order of things. In contrast, industrial man is bent upon revising nature for his own purposes.

Theoretical orientation

Inasmuch as pre-industrial cities in numerous divergent cultural milieu display basic similarities in form, some variable other than cultural values, in the broad sense, must be operative; regularities of this sort are not the result of mere chance.

Here technology — viz., the available *energy*, *tools* and *know-how* connected with these — seems the most satisfactory explanatory variable [1]. This mode of reasoning should not commit us in any way to credence in technological determinism or unilinear evolution; indeed we firmly reject these stands. In point of fact, we make frequent reference to social power in accounting for the fluctuating fortunes of cities and the fate of technology and give due recognition to its role in producing organisation in the society. Nor do we ignore values. These, we have remarked in a number of contexts, account for certain divergencies from our constructed type; too, some values tend to be correlated with a specific level of technology; as a notable instance, the scientific method has built-in values that must be diffused, along with the energy sources, tools and requisite know-how, to underdeveloped areas if these are to industrialise. Further, we see the city *per se* as a variable to be reckoned with; rural and urban communities are in many ways intrinsically different. Although we lend priority to technology, we cannot dispense with the other variables enumerated.

With these qualifications (and we hope the reader will keep them ever in mind), it seems clear that the transition from the preliterate to the feudal level, i.e., to the pre-industrial civilised order, or from the latter to the industrial-urban society is associated with certain crucial advances in the technological sphere. The very emergence of cities is functionally related to the society's ability to produce a sizeable surplus; and the orientation, quite late in history, to an industrial base made possible a kind of city never before imagined. To minimise technology, as to ignore the value system, would be poor procedure.

As has been asseverated time and again, we have been searching for similarities among cities in feudal societies, rather than areas of cultural divergency. Our primary vantage point has been the industrial city — though we have maintained awareness of the relations between folk and feudal orders as well. Our hypothesis that pre-industrial and industrial cities are fundamentally distinctive entities is unmistakably borne out by the existing data.

Having taken technology as the dominant variable for explicating the divergencies between pre-industrial and industrial cities, and their respective societies, we then proceeded to set this analysis within the context of contemporary structural-functionalism — with one outstanding modification: we introduced the concept of contradictory functional requirements, or what are termed 'imperatives', 'prerequisites', 'necessary conditions' and other sociologisms [2]. Eschewing an excessive preoccupation with staticism and neatly integrated wholes, the proclivity of so much structural-functional analysis, we perceive the operation of contradictory structures, each 'essential' to the system, yet at odds with one another. This is obviously the source of some of the strains that pervade even the relatively static non-industrial civilised society. Phrased differently, it is not just societies in some stage of transition from one fundamental form to another that undergo strain and tension; so-called 'non-transitional' orders, either feudal or industrial, are plagued with self-inconsistencies.

As an illustration of our recourse to structural-functional analysis, may we briefly review certain aspects of the class system in the pre-industrial city. Some segment of the populace must be freed from food production or other physical labour so that it can devote its time to governing others. The labour force must be controlled and integrated, goods must be syphoned off from the hinterland to feed the city, political stability must be maintained, and so on. A leisure class can be considered a 'requirement' if the city is to operate with a limited technology. And at the same time, this privileged element is created by the technology (advanced as it is over that in the folk order), though the size of this group is firmly restricted, for in the absence of machines the populace must labour long and hard to support even a few in leisured status.

We can go a step farther and state that if this stratum is to persist it must bar ingress into its ranks from below; the result is an overwhelming tendency towards autocratic rule and a rigid class system wherein one's status is generally ascribed by birth. The political, religious and educational hierarchies all intensify this by staffing the key posts on particularistic, primarily kinship, grounds. More, the elite legitimises its dominance by appeal to absolutes and to tradition. Just as the existence of this class is made possible by the prevailing technology, so too, its autocratic rule and obstruction of social mobility for others are fostered by the technology which permits, and requires, few experts, no mass education, and so forth.

Nevertheless, in the matter of exclusiveness, though a considerable amount of it is permitted the elite, such cannot be fully achieved, for contradictory forces are at work. On the one hand the elite scorn, and attempt to ostracise, businessmen on a number of counts — most notably the fact that the latter's field lends itself to the amassing of wealth, and therefore possible upward mobility, by commoners who possess special talents for manipulation. This is an obvious threat to the elite's position, based as it is on kinship and reinforced by appeals to absolutes and to tradition. Yet because the city, to be a city, must allow for commercial activity, and because the upper class itself requires wealth if it is to maintain eminence, successful businessmen, if not from outcaste ethnic groups, can occasionally utilise their monetary gains to purchase upper-class status. Because the elite require the services of merchants, they nurture them, paving the way for a partial undermining of their own position. Although the pre-industrial city's, and the society's, internal structures reinforce one another to a high degree — a 'circularity' that actually makes exposition difficult — the component parts are at times at odds with one another, generating stresses within the system.

When comparing the pre-industrial and industrial city types, bear in mind that while each generates its own dominant patterns — e.g., the pre-industrial city emphasises class rigidity and particularism, the industrial city class fluidity and universalism — countervailing forces operate within both cities. Neither absolute rigidity nor extreme fluidity is achievable. Most writers ignore this, choosing to analyse systems in terms of fictional types; we have selected a more empirical orientation despite a resulting degree of muzziness; indeed the latter is characteristic of reality itself.

An ideological issue looms before us. Most treatments of feudal orders are essentially moralisations as to the merits or demerits of these societies' world outlook. 'Conservatives' look back in praise on what they consider to be a glorious past and lament the expansion of industrialisation [3]. The 'liberals' look back in shame and anger. We have attempted to tread a narrow line between these extremes. Although continually contrasting the feudal city with the industrial type, we do acknowledge the former's contributions to man's heritage. But we shun the interpretations of writers of Mumford's persuasion, who glamorise the medieval European city, or of some social scientists who, incredibly, are unaware of the stark poverty of the lower classes in ancient cities [4]. It is preferable to accept the pre-industrial city for what it is, realising its positive contributions but noting its deficiencies as well. We shall not cheer, neither shall we weep, as it fades from the scene.

One final comment on our theoretical approach. Throughout, recognition has been given to the theoretical distinctions between a city and a society. But empirically these fuse — our efforts to analyse one force us to treat the other. In practice, the city is our starting point, but we have branched outward from it to encompass the total feudal order. This work is, in the end, a survey of the pre-industrial civilised society with special emphasis upon the city, the hub of all major activity therein.

Utility of this typology for research and analysis

The ultimate test of our constructed type, of course, is its long-run utility for interpreting empirical phenomena. It does seem to enlarge one's purview of pre-industrial cities and feudal societies. For this reason the typology should prove useful to historians, anthropologists and archaeologists attempting to reconstruct the social arrangements in cities long since dead. Certain aspects of their life ways lie forever beyond our grasp. The only reasonable alternative is extrapolation to the past from data on more recent feudal cities, utilising in the process, recent advances in the social scientist's knowledge of social systems. Knowing 'what to expect' in earlier cities imparts fuller meaning to written records and permits more satisfactory reconstructions where gaps exist in the data. A salient weakness in much historical research is the tendency to assume uniqueness for much of the social phenomena encountered; all manner of false interpretations ensue. Such is 'historicism', ultimately a denial of objective generalisation as the goal of social science. A considerable proportion of sociologists, bound as they are to the American social scene, are unwitting proponents of this myopic approach.

This study will perhaps encourage some scholars to focus attention upon the pre-industrial cities that survive today; in turn, the data amassed on these can be used to refine our constructed type. Such need not be an end in itself. Acute awareness of the social structure of pre-industrial civilised societies and their cities is essential for anyone who hopes to understand current processes in societies now changing over from feudal to industrial modes of organisation. In this connection, it is instructive that some writers see regularity in form across industrial systems yet implicitly deny uniformities of structure for pre-industrial civilised societies. But that such regularities abound should be apparent to any observer of these societies who attains a broad space-time overview. It is these uniformities that provide a 'yardstick' for measuring and interpreting across cultural boundaries the significant social changes that are occurring. So much of the analysis of social change in India, China, the Middle East and other underdeveloped areas thus far has been accomplished with no real effort to isolate the underlying structural themes that run through these varying cultures. Surprising, yes, but nonetheless true. Only through the use of some kind of 'standard', like the one offered herein, against which to measure change, can we determine whether one society (with its cities) is relinquishing its traditional forms more rapidly than others. For as statistics on industrialising societies becomes quantitatively and qualitatively more adequate, firmer generalisations concerning these fundamental processes should become possible.

It is high time sociologists in general, not just the few, began to deal with the industrial urbanisation process in underdeveloped countries. The repercussions of this revolution throughout the world are devastating. And the impact of these changes on social science theory, sociological theory in particular, bids fair to be revolutionary as well.

Scanning the history of sociology, we see that sociologists today who are attempting to understand the nature of change in 'underdeveloped' countries (by no means a satisfactory term) are more closely akin theoretically to the German social thinkers than to the typical French, English, or American social scientists [5]. The explanation seems to be that Germany in the latter part of the nineteenth century experienced a rather sudden transition from (to employ the terminology of those who wrote about it) 'feudalism' to 'capitalism'. Most German social scientists, including Max Weber, Sombart, Tönnies, and a host of others, were concerned with the breakup of the old and its replacement by the new. But lamentably, their analyses in general were Europe-bound. Yet how could it have been otherwise? They were writing in an era before industrialisation had taken firm hold in Japan, before the Communists' will to industrialise Russia and China, before the upsurge of movements intent upon adopting the new technology in societies the world over. The future of social science theory — the ethnocentrism of urban sociology notwithstanding — lies in its long-run ability to explain the current processes on the world scene. Our effort is a step in this direction.

The pre-industrial city in transition

The heyday of the pre-industrial city is past. A few cities of this type persist in almost pure form, but in the face of industrialisation they are fast relinquishing their special characteristics. The dissolution before our very eyes of a city-type that has existed for fifty-five centuries or more is deserving of some attention. Contrarily, the traditional social structure does not evanesce as rapidly as might be imagined. Unlike the folk society, it possesses remarkable capacities for stemming, at least for a time, the tides of change; its complex institutional apparatus — above all its literate elite — are potentially powerful forces of resistance.

Pre-industrial urban forms continue to dominate the cityscape in India, the Middle East, in sections of Latin America and elsewhere. Even where industrialisation is well advanced, as in Japan, survivals of traditional forms crop up on every hand, and efforts by the old elite to maintain the past in the face of a veritable avalanche of industrialising influences continue strong.

Notes

1   For other sociologists who have given attention to the technological variable see: Francis R. Allen *et al.*, *Technology and Social Change*, New York: Appleton-Century-Croft, 1957. Unfortunately, some sociologists tend to drift into a materialistic interpretation of technology, something we have tried to avoid.

2   The terminology of structural-functionalism is by no means satisfactory. We perhaps favour the term, 'requirements', but we have utilised it more or less synonymously with those listed in the text as well as introducing the concept of 'correlates'. We can, obviously, be called to task for this 'looseness', but we believe the context will aid the reader in defining the terms. This approach seems preferable to repeating the terms, 'requirements' or 'necessary conditions' *ad infinitum* — when these concepts themselves are subject to mis-interpretation.

      Concerning the label, 'contradictory functional requirements', we emphasise that this must not be confused with the concept, 'dysfunction'. The latter, as employed by sociologists, still stresses the internal harmony of social systems, quite at variance with our approach.

3   For example, Friedrich Georg Juenger, *The Failure of Technology*, Chicago: Henry Regnery, 1956.

4   For example, Lewis Mumford, *The Culture of Cities*, New York: Harcourt, Brace, 1938. Pulgram, for one, leaves the impression that Italy under the Romans was more prosperous than it is today — disregarding completely two millennia of technological progress. Ernst Pulgram, *The Tongues of Italy*, Harvard University Press, 1958, pp. 34-6.

5   The dominant concern in present-day American sociology is comparing the real with the ideal norms (the informal with the formal), not contrasting the past with the present. Undoubtedly a reflection of the growing maturity of the urban industrial society, such an orientation is of little value in studying underdeveloped countries.

      Because of these differing emphases among sociologists, there is a good deal of unnecessary polemic. Writers concerned with the real *versus* the ideal often attack the past-*versus*-present, or the developmental, theorists on spurious grounds. Many recent criticisms of Weber's ideal type formulation of bureaucracy, for example, stem from sociologists' failure to realise that Weber was not studying deviations from the ideal, but rather contrasting traditional society with his so-called 'capitalist' one. To play the record over again: keep clearly in mind what is being compared!

3 Pre-modern towns

Fernand Braudel

The towns are so many electric transformers. They increase tension, accelerate the rhythm of exchange and ceaselessly stir up men's lives. They developed out of the oldest and most revolutionary division of labour: the fields on the one hand and the activities described as urban on the other. 'The contrast between town and country begins with the transition from barbarism to civilisation, from the tribal régime to the state, from the individual locality to the nation, and recurs in all history of the world until our own days'. Karl Marx wrote these lines in his youth.

Towns are also oppressive, parasitical formations. 'Herodotus was already speaking of the millet-eaters north of the Black Sea who grew corn for the Greek cities.' This town - country confrontation is the first and longest class struggle history has known. We should not pass censure or take sides: these parasitic towns also embodied the intelligence, risk, progress and modernity towards which the world was slowly moving. They had the finest foods, the luxury industries, brisk currencies and soon calculating, clear-sighted capitalism. To the rather unwieldy body of the state they lent their irreplaceable vitality. They were the accelerators of all historical time. Which does not mean that they did not make men suffer throughout the centuries, including the men who lived in them.

The town: a definition

The ideal would be to define the town in itself, outside the economy or civilisation containing it. There are two conditions for this: that all towns have certain common characteristics, and that such characteristics more or less persist from one period to another. But who would seriously deny it? As historians, we have put the original and creative power of Western towns too much in the limelight and unintentionally underestimated and neglected the others. Nonetheless, a town is a town wherever it is. 'Only primitive or undeveloped societies have not experienced the urban phenomenon', and this urban phenomenon necessarily presupposes certain recurring features. Even Black Africa had its towns. Even the

F. Braudel, 'Towns', from *Capitalism and Material Life 1400-1800* (trans. M. Kochan), Weidenfeld and Nicolson, 1973, Chapter 8, pp. 373-440.

pre-Columbian civilisations had their successes: Tenochtitlan (Mexico), Cuzco.

We ought therefore to rediscover one basic language for all the cities of the world within their very depths and beyond their varied and original images — the uninterrupted confrontation with the countryside, a prime necessity of daily life; the supply of manpower, as indispensable as water to the mill-wheel; the aloofness of the towns, that is to say their desire to be marked off from others; their situation necessarily at the centre of a network of communications; their relation to suburbs, secondary cities often their servants and even their slaves.

Minimum size

The town, an unusual concentration of men and houses, close together, often joined wall to wall, is a demographic anomaly. Not that it is always 'full of people' or, as Ibn Batouta said, admiring Cairo, a 'restless sea' of men. There are towns that have barely begun being towns and also some extensive villages that exceed them in numbers of inhabitants. Examples of this are the enormous villages in Russia, now and in the past, the country towns of the Italian *Mezzogiorno* or the Andalusian south, or the loosely woven clusters of hamlets in Java, which has remained an 'island of villages up to the present time'. But these inflated villages, even when they were contiguous, were not necessarily destined to become towns.

Numbers are not the only consideration involved. The town only exists as a town in relation to a form of life lower than its own. There are no exceptions to this rule. No privilege serves as a substitute. There is no town, no townlet without its villages, its scrap of rural life attached; no town that does not supply its hinterland with the amenities of its market, the use of its shops, its weights and measures, its moneylenders, its lawyers, even its distractions. It has to dominate an empire, however tiny, in order to exist.

Varzy, now in the Nièvre, barely numbered 2,000 inhabitants at the beginning of the eighteenth century. But it was well and truly a town, with its own bourgeoisie. There were so many lawyers there that one wonders what they could really have done, even in the midst of an illiterate peasant population who obviously had to resort to the pens of others. But these lawyers were also landowners. Other members of the bourgeoisie were masters of ironworks or tanneries, or wood merchants profiting from the traffic in 'lost logs' along the rivers, sometimes involved in the colossal provisioning of Paris, and owning forests as far as the distant Barrois. This is really a typical case of a small Western town. There are thousands of similar examples.

Numbers certainly determine the character of the town. All the same, they have to be specified with a certain accuracy. Present-day statistics use an arbitrary figure — 2,000 inhabitants for French censuses — to distinguish between towns and smaller rural communities. If we wanted to follow this procedure for the past — a risky method — the dividing line would need to be lowered considerably. Before 1500, 90 per cent to 95 per cent of the towns known in the West had fewer than 2,000 inhabitants. A fairly reliable calculation for the 3,000 places in Germany that had been granted the status of cities gives an average population of no more than 400 individuals. There were, therefore, some very small towns there, well below the size of Varzy, caught up in a rural life which submerged them but which they nonetheless transformed, preparing the way for certain developments for the benefit of more important towns which they supplied with manual labour, apprentices and even skilled workers.

This was the case in the West, where so many urban constellations revolved around one dominant town. But China had similar hierarchies (*Fou*, town of the first order, *Tcheou* of the second, *Hien* of the third), and in poor provinces there were rudimentary towns, because of the 'need to control half-savage peoples who were impatient of the yoke of authority'. A German doctor who passed through a small town on the road from Yedo (Tokyo) in Japan in 1690 counted 500 houses there, including the suburbs — a detail that alone would prove it really was a town. But, of course, these figures are only valid when seen in relation to the whole population.

In English America, around 1700, Boston numbered 7,000 inhabitants, Philadelphia 4,000, Newport 2,600, Charlestown 1,100 and New York 3,900. However, bricks had replaced wood in house-building after 1642 in New York (at that time Nieuwe Amsterdam), an obvious symptom of urbanisation. Moreover no one would not acknowledge the urban character of the centres — even when they were still small-scale. In 1690 the urban concentration made possible by a total population of some 200,000 people dispersed over a vast expanse represented 9 per cent of the population. There probably was more or less the same proportion between towns and villages in Germany in 1500 (10 per cent).

Nevertheless the urban population in Flanders and Brabant a century earlier is said to have already been 50 per cent of the total population, the proportion for western and central Europe towards the end of the eighteenth century being 20 to 25 per cent; for France, which had remained rural, only 16 per cent. On the other hand, half the population of England according to certain calculations was grouped in the towns in about 1700. But this remains questionable (it would be more accurate to say 30 per cent).

With a non-rural population in the vicinity of 50 per cent or even 40 per cent, an entire region automatically and under its own impetus moved into the category of a modern economy, freed from the rural hold and relieved of a heavy primary sector. And this shift was a considerable event in itself. The census of 1795 recorded a rural population of only 45·6 per cent of the total in the Netherlands province of Overijssel; it had crossed the line. In the East, in Muscovy where everything was behind, towns represented 2·5 per cent of the total population in 1630, 3 per cent in 1724, 4 per cent in 1796 and 13 per cent in 1897.

Division of labour

The essential problem at the beginning and throughout the life of towns in Europe and elsewhere remains the same: the division of labour between the countryside and the urban centres, a division which has never been perfectly defined and which calls for continual reassessment, because the positions of the partners change incessantly. The formula is always being recast in one or the other direction.

The urban problem consists of separating out certain activities in a partnership which was originally a joint one. Economists would describe it as detaching the specialised 'secondary' sectors from a primary sector incorporating the whole. In theory (and only in theory), the merchants, the functions of political, religious and economic control, and the craft activities, would move over to the town side. However, the complete span of professions can only spread out in a town of a certain size, for instance Frankfurt-am-Main or Strasbourg. Numbers alone allow this elementary rationalisation. It cannot occur in the small towns where manpower is too limited and which all continue to ensure the exploitation of their own land.

In fact town and countryside never separate like oil and water because the bond uniting them neither breaks nor pulls one way only. They separate and draw closer together at the same time, split up and then regroup. Even in Islamic lands the town does not ignore or exclude the countryside, despite the steep gulf separating them. It even develops efficient agriculture and market-gardening activities around it. Certain water-channels along urban streets are extended to the gardens of nearby oases. The same symbiosis occurs in China where the countryside is fertilised with refuse and rubbish from the town.

But there is little point in trying to demonstrate what is self-evident. Until very recently every town had to have its foodstuffs within easy reach. An economic historian familiar with the statistics estimates that from the eleventh century a centre holding 3,000 inhabitants had to have the lands of some ten villages at its disposal in order to live, or approximately 8·5 km^2, 'in view of the low yield of agriculture'. In fact the countryside has to support the town if the town is not to live in a constant state of anxiety with regard to its subsistence. It can be fed by large-scale trade only partially and in rare circumstances. And this applies only to privileged towns such as Florence, Bruges, Venice, Naples, Rome, Peking, Istanbul, Delhi and Mecca.

Moreover even the large towns continued to engage in rural activities up to the eighteenth century. In the West they therefore housed shepherds, gamekeepers, agricultural workers and vine-growers (even in Paris). Every town generally owned a surrounding area of gardens and orchards inside and outside its walls, and fields farther away, sometimes divided into three breaks, as in Frankfurt-am-Main, Worms, Basle and Munich. In the Middle Ages the noise of the flail could be heard right up to the *Rathaus* in Ulm, Augsburg or Nuremburg. Pigs were reared in freedom in the streets. And the streets were so dirty and muddy that they had to be crossed on stilts, unless wooden bridges were thrown across from one side to the other. The main streets of Frankfurt were hurriedly covered with straw or wood shavings on the eve of the fairs.

As for the innumerable small towns, they were barely outside the framework of country life. All the same, Weinsburg, Heilbronn, Stuttgart and Esslingen in vine-growing lower Swabia took it upon themselves to send the wine they produced to the Danube, and wine was an industry in itself. Jerez de la Frontera, near Seville, stated in answer to an inquiry in 1582 that 'the town has only its harvest of wine, corn, oil and meat', which were enough for its wellbeing and to keep its trade and its workers alive. Algerian pirates were able to take Gibraltar by surprise in 1540 because they knew the customs of the place and chose the time of the grape harvest. All the inhabitants were outside the walls, sleeping in their vineyards. True, towns everywhere guarded their vineyards jealously. Hundreds of municipal magistratures every year — in Rothenburg in Bavaria or in Bar-le-Duc, for example — proclaimed the opening of the grape-harvest when the 'vine leaves have taken on that yellow hue that proclaims their ripeness'. Florence itself received thousands of barrels every autumn and was transformed into an enormous market for new wine.

Townsmen in those days were often only semi-townsmen. At harvest-time artisans and others left their houses and trades behind them and went to work in the fields. This was true of busy, overpopulated Flanders in the sixteenth century. It was also true of England, even on the eve of its industrial revolution; and of Florence where the very considerable art of wool was primarily a winter activity in the sixteenth century. A diary kept by Jean Pussot, master-carpenter of Rheims, shows greater interest in vintages, harvests, the quality of the wine, and corn and bread prices, than in the events of political or craft life. At the time of the French Religious Wars the people of Rheims and the people of Epernay were not on the same side and both harvested their vines well escorted. But our carpenter notes, 'the thieves of Epernay took the herd of pigs away from the town [of Rheims] . . . they took them to the aforesaid Epernay on Tuesday the thirtieth day of March 1593'. It was not only a question of knowing who would win, the Leaguers or Henry IV, but of who would salt and eat the meat. Things had barely changed in 1722 when a treatise on economy deplores the fact that artisans instead of peasants took a hand in agriculture in small and even princely towns in Germany. It would be better if everyone 'kept in his own station'. Towns would be cleaner and healthier if they were cleared of livestock and their 'large stores of manure'. The solution would be 'to ban agriculture to towns and craftsmen and to put it in the hands of those suited to it'. Artisans would have the advantage of selling to the countrymen in proportion to what the countrymen would be assured of selling regularly to the town. Everyone would gain thereby.

If the town did not completely surrender the monopoly of crops of stock-raising to the countryside, conversely the countryside did not give up all its 'industrial' activities in favour of nearby towns. It had its share of them, although they were generally those activities the towns were glad enough to leave to them. For a start the villages had never been without craftsmen. Cartwheels were manufactured and repaired locally in the village itself by the wheelwright and ringed with iron by the blacksmith (the technique spread at the end of the sixteenth century). Every large village had its shoeing smith. Such activities could still be seen in France until the beginning of the twentieth century. Moreover, in Flanders and elsewhere, where the towns had established a sort of industrial monopoly in the eleventh and twelfth centuries, town industries surged back towards the rural outskirts on a vast scale in about the fifteenth and sixteenth centuries in search of cheaper manpower, outside the protection and meticulous supervision of the urban craft guilds. The town lost nothing thereby, controlling as it did the wretched rural workers outside its walls and managing them as it wanted. But the ungenerous division provoked quarrels. In any case in the seventeenth century, and even more in the following century, villages resumed a very large part of craft activities.

The same division was to be found elsewhere, but organised differently — in Russia, India and China for example. In Russia the greater part of the industrial tasks fell upon the villages, which were self-supporting. Urban agglomerations did not dominate or disturb them as in the towns in the West. There was as yet no real competition between townsmen and peasants. This is clearly explained by the slow rate of urban growth. There were probably a few large towns, despite the accidents they suffered. (Moscow, burned by the Tartars in 1571 and set alight by the Poles in 1611, would appear to have contained not fewer than 40,000 houses in 1636.) But in a poorly urbanised country, villages were necessarily forced to do everything by themselves. Apart from which the owners of large estates organised certain paying industries with their serfs. The long Russian winter therefore did not bear the sole responsibility for the lively activity of these country-dwellers.

The village in India was similarly self-sufficient. A lively community, capable on occasion of moving *en bloc* to escape some danger or too heavy oppression, it paid taxes to the town but only called on it for rare commodities (iron tools for example). In China the country craftsman supplemented his hard life by work in silk or cotton. His low standard of living made him a formidable competitor with the town craftsman. An English traveller (1793) registered surprise and delight at the unwonted sight of peasant women near Peking breeding silk worms and spinning cotton: 'which is in general use for both sexes of the people, but the women are almost the sole weavers throughout the Empire'.

The town and newcomers (the poor)

A town would probably cease to exist without its supply of new people. It attracts them. But they often come of their own accord towards its lights, its real or apparent freedom, and its higher wages. They come too because first the countryside and also other towns no longer want them and reject them. The standard stable partnership is between a poor region with regular emigration and an active town: Friuli in relation to Venice — the *Furlani* supplied it with its common labourers and servants; the Kabylias in relation to Algiers under the pirates — the mountain-dwellers went down to dig the gardens in the town and surrounding countryside; Marseilles and Corsica; the towns of Provence and the *gavots* of the Alps; London and the Irish. But every big town would have many different places of recruitment.

In Paris in 1788:

The people known as common labourers are almost all foreigners.
The Savoyards are decorators, floor polishers and sawyers: the
Auvergnats . . . almost all water-carriers; the natives of Limousin are
masons; the Lyonnais are generally porters and chair-carriers; the
Normans, stone cutters, pavers and pedlars, menders of crockery,
rabbit-skin merchants; the Gascons, wigmakers or *carabins* [barbers'
assistants] ; the Lorrainers, travelling shoemakers or cobblers. . . .
The Savoyards live in the suburbs; they are organised by rooms,
each run by a chief or an old Savoyard who is treasurer and tutor
to the young children until they reach an age to govern themselves.

A certain Auvergnat who hawked rabbit skins, buying them
individually and reselling them in quantity, travelled around 'so overloaded
that one looks [in vain] for his head and arms'. And of course, all these
poor people bought their clothes at the secondhand shops on the quai de
la Ferraille or the Mégisserie where everything was bartered. 'Someone
[goes into] the shop as black as a crow and leaves it green as a parrot.'
     But the towns did not only welcome poor wretches such as these.
They also recruited at the expense of the bourgeois in neighbouring or
distant towns: rich merchants, masters and craftsmen (whose services were
sometimes fought over), mercenaries, ships' pilots, professors and doctors,
engineers, architects, painters. Thus the points from which apprentices and
masters of its *Arte Della Lana* came to Florence in the sixteenth century
could be marked on the map of northern and central Italy. In the
preceding century they had come in a steady stream from the Netherlands.
The origins of new citizens in a lively town like Metz or Constance for
example (the latter from 1367 to 1517) could equally well be marked on a
map. In each case it would disclose a wide area associated with the life of
the town concerned. Perhaps this might after all be the same area that
would be marked out by the radius of its commercial relations, if we put
in the villages, towns and markets that accepted its systems of measures or
money, or both, or which, failing that, spoke its dialect.
     Such constant recruitment was a matter of necessity. Before the
eighteenth century the town had scarcely any excess of births over deaths.
It suffered from too high an incidence of mortality. If it was to grow, it
could not do so by itself. Socially as well, it left the lowly tasks to new
arrivals. Like our over-pressurised economies today, it needed North
Africans or Puerto Ricans in its service, a proletariat which it quickly used
up and had quickly to renew. The existence of this wretched and lowly
proletariat is a feature of any large town.
     An average of 20,000 people died in Paris every year, even after the
1780s. Some 4,000 ended their days in the poor-house, either at the
Hôtel-Dieu or the Bicêtre. The dead were 'sewn up in sacking' and buried
unceremoniously in the paupers' grave at Clamart, which was sprinkled
with quick lime. A hand-drawn cart carried the dead southwards from the
Hôtel-Dieu every night. 'A mud-bespattered priest, a bell, a cross' — such
was the true funeral procession of the poor. Everything about the
poor-house 'is hard and cruel'; 1,200 beds for 5,000 to 6,000 sick people.

'The newcomer is bedded down beside a dying man and a corpse . . .'

And life was no kinder in its beginnings. Paris had 7,000 to 8,000 abandoned children out of some 30,000 births around 1780. Depositing these children at the poor-house was an occupation in itself. The man carried them on his back

> in a padded box which can hold three. They stand in their swaddling clothes, breathing through the top . . . When [the carrier] opens his box, he often finds one of them dead; he completes his journey with the other two, impatient to be rid of the load. . . . He immediately sets off once more to start the same task, which is his livelihood, over again.

Many of these abandoned children came from the provinces. Strange immigrants indeed.

The aloofness of towns

Every town is and wants to be a world apart. It is a striking fact that all of them or nearly all between the fifteenth and eighteenth centuries had ramparts. They were held in a restrictive and distinctive geometry, hence cut off even from their own immediate surrounds.

Insecurity and ramparts   The first point is security. Protection was only superfluous in a few countries; in the British Isles, for example, there were practically no urban fortifications. They were thus spared a lot of useless investment, according to economists. The old city walls in London had only an administrative function, although temporary fear on the part of the Parliamentarians in 1643 caused fortifications to be hurriedly built around the town. Nor were there any fortifications in the Japanese archipelago, which was also protected by the sea, nor in Venice, an island in itself. There were no walls in self-confident countries like the vast Osmanli Empire which had ramparted towns only on its threatened frontiers — in Hungary facing Europe, in Armenia facing Persia. Both Erivan (where there was a small force of artillery) and Erzerum (crowded by its suburbs) were surrounded by double walls (though not earthworks) in 1694. Everywhere else the *pax turcica* brought about the ruin of the ancient ramparts. They deteriorated like the walls of abandoned estates, even the wonderful ramparts at Istanbul inherited from Byzantium. Opposite, in Galata, in 1694, 'the walls [are] half-ruined and the Turks do not seem to be thinking of rebuilding them'.

No such confidence was to be found anywhere else. Urban fortification became the general rule across continental Europe (Russian towns were ramparted to a greater or lesser degree and depended on a fortress as Moscow depended on the Kremlin), across colonial America, Persia, India and China. Furetière's *Dictionnaire* (1690) defined a town as the 'home of a large number of people which is normally enclosed by walls'. But the definition was not valid for the West alone.

[*Section on Chinese towns omitted.*]

The wall frequently enclosed a portion of fields and gardens together with the town. This was for obvious reasons of supplies in case of war. Such was the case with the ramparts rapidly constructed in Castile in the eleventh and twelfth centuries around a group of villages at some distance from each other, with enough space left between them to hold the flocks in case of emergency. The rule is valid wherever, in anticipation of a siege, ramparts enclosed meadows and gardens, as in Florence, or arable land, orchards and vineyards, as in Poitiers. In fact Poitiers' walls, even in the seventeenth century, were almost as extensive as those of Paris, but the town took a long time to grow into this outsize garment. Similarly, Prague took a long time to fill up the space left between the houses of the 'small town' and the new ramparts built in the middle of the fourteenth century. The same applied to Toulouse from 1400; and to Barcelona, which took two centuries (until about 1550) to reach the ramparts reconstructed around it in 1359 (on the site of the presentday Ramblas).

The scene was the same in China: one town on the Yang-tse-Kiang 'has a wall ten miles in circumference, which encloses hills, mountains and plains uninhabited because the town has few houses and its inhabitants prefer to live in the very extensive suburbs'. In the same year, 1696, the upper part of the capital of Kiang-Si sheltered 'many fields and gardens, but few inhabitants'.

The West had long ensured security at a low cost by a moat and a perpendicular wall. This did little to interfere with urban expansion — much less than is usually thought. When the town needed more space the walls were moved like theatre sets — in Ghent, Florence and Strasbourg for example — and as many times as was required. Walls were made-to-measure corsets. Towns grew and made themselves new ones.

But constructed and reconstructed walls did not cease to encircle towns and to define them. They were boundaries, frontiers, as well as protection. The towns pushed the maximum of their craft activity, and particularly their heavy industries, to the periphery, so much so that the wall was an economic and social dividing line as well. As the town grew it generally annexed some of its suburbs and transformed them, pushing activities foreign to strictly urban life a little farther away.

Plans in a chessboard design   Western towns developed gradually and in a haphazard way. That is why their plans are so complicated. Their winding streets and unexpected turnings are quite unlike the pattern of the Roman town, as it still survives, in fact, in a few cities descended from the classical period: Turin, Cologne, Coblenz, Ratisbon. But the Renaissance marked the first development of deliberate town planning, with the flowering of a series of supposedly 'ideal' geometric plans in chessboard pattern or concentric circles. This was the spirit in which the widespread urban development in the West remodelled squares and rebuilt districts acquired from the suburbs.

This new coherence and rationalisation were even better expressed in the new towns where builders had a free hand. Furthermore it is curious that the few examples of chessboard-pattern Western towns before the fifteenth century corresponded to deliberate constructions, built *ex nihilo*. Aigues-mortes, a small port that Saint Louis bought and reconstructed in order to have an outlet on the Mediterranean, was an example. So was the tiny town of Mompazier (in the Dordogne), built by order of the King of

England at the end of the thirteenth century. One of the squares of the chessboard design corresponded to the church, another to the market place, surrounded by arcades and equipped with wells. Other examples were to be found in the *terre nuove* of Tuscany in the fourteenth century, Scarperia, San Giovanni Valdarno, Terranuova Bracciolini and Castelfranco di Sopra. But the town planning honours lists get rapidly longer from the sixteenth century. One could give a long list of the towns built on a geometric plan, like the new Leghorn after 1575, Nancy, reconstructed from 1588, or Charleville from 1608. The most extraordinary case was still St Petersburg, to which we will return. Founded late, almost all the towns of the New World were similarly constructed on a prearranged plan. They formed the largest family of chessboard towns. Those in Spanish America were particularly characteristic, with their streets cutting the *cuadras* at right angles and the two main roads converging on the *Plaza Mayor* where stood the cathedral, the prison and the town hall — the *Cabildo*.

The chessboard plan poses a curious problem, taking the world as a whole. All the towns in China, Korea, Japan, peninsular India and colonial America (not forgetting those in Rome and certain Greek cities) were planned according to the chessboard pattern. Only two civilisations built confused and irregular towns on a large scale: Islam (including northern India) and the West in the Middle Ages. One could lose oneself in aesthetic or psychological explanations of these choices by civilisations. There is no doubt that the West was not harking back to the needs of the Roman camp in America in the sixteenth century. What it established in the New World was the reflection of modern Europe's interest in town planning, an urgent taste for order. It would be fascinating to go beyond the numerous manifestations of this taste and investigate its living roots.

Towns, artillery and carriages in the West

Western towns faced severe problems from the fifteenth century onwards. Their populations had increased and artillery made their ancient walls useless. They had to be replaced at all costs, by wide ramparts half sunk in the ground, extended by bastions, terrepleins, 'cavaliers', where loose soil reduced possible damage from bullets. These ramparts were wider horizontally and could no longer be moved without enormous expense. And an empty space in front of thse fortified lines was essential to defence operations; buildings, gardens and trees were therefore forbidden there. Occasionally the empty space in the requisite spot had to be recreated by pulling down trees and houses. This was done in Gdansk (Danzig) in 1520, during the Polish-Teutonic war and in 1576 during its conflict with King Stefan Batory.

The town's expansion was thus blocked and it was often, more often than previously, condemned to grow vertically. Houses were very early on being built in Genoa, Paris and Edinburgh with five, six, eight and even ten storeys. Prices of plots rose incessantly and high houses became the general rule everywhere. If London long preferred wood to brick it was also because it made possible lighter, less thick walls at the time when four- to six-storey houses were replacing the old buildings, which generally had two. In Paris 'it was necessary to restrain the excessive height of houses . . . because a few individuals had actually built one house on top of another. Height was restricted [just before the Revolution] to seventy feet not including the roof.'

Having the advantage of being without walls, Venice could expand in comfort. A few wooden piles sunk in, stones brought in by boat, and a new district rose up on the lagoon. Heavy industry was very soon pushed back to the periphery, knackers and curriers to the island of Giudecca, the arsenal to the far end of the new district of Castello, glassworks to the island of Murano as early as 1255. It was a kind of modern 'zoning'. Meanwhile Venice spread out its public and private splendour on the Grand Canal, an old and abnormally deep river valley. Only one bridge, the Rialto bridge, made of wood and with a drawbridge (until the construction of the present stone bridge in 1587), linked the Fondaco dei Tedeschi (the present central post office) side of the canal to the Rialto square. This marked out the lively axis of the town — from St Mark's Square to the bridge via the busy street of the Merceria. It was thus a town with plenty of room, a comfortable town. But in the ghetto — a narrow, walled and artificial town — space was cramped and houses shot upward five or six storeys high.

When the carriage made its massive entry into Europe in the sixteenth century it posed urgent problems and made severe measures necessary. Bramante, who destroyed the old district around St Peter's in Rome (1506-14), was one of Baron Haussmann's first predecessors in history. Towns inevitably regained a little order, more air, better circulation, at least for a time. Pietro di Toledo (1536) chose the same type of reorganisation when he opened a few wide streets across Naples where, as King Ferdinand of Naples had said earlier, 'the narrow streets were a danger to the state'. The completion of the short but sumptuous rectilinear Strada Nuova in Genoa in 1547 represented a similar process, as did the three axes dug across Rome from the Piazza del Popolo at Pope Sixtus V's wishes. It was not by chance that one of them, the Corso, became the commercial street *par excellence* of Rome. Carriages and soon coaches entered the towns at top speed. John Stow, who was present during the first changes in London, prophesied (1528): 'The world runs on wheels.' Thomas Dekker said the same thing in the following century: 'In every street [in London] carts and Coaches make such a thundering as if the world ran upon wheels.'

Urban geography

We have no need to be apprehensive about calling on geography for its contributions. It probably has too much to say, but what it says is clear; it deals in known facts. There is no difficulty in summarising them.

The sites   Every town grows in a given place, is wedded to it and does not leave it, except for very rare exceptions. The site is favourable, to a greater or lesser degree; its original advantages and drawbacks stay with it for ever. A traveller who landed at Bahia (Salvador), then capital of Brazil

(1684), mentioned its splendour, the number of slaves 'treated', he added, 'with the utmost barbarity'. He also remarked on the defects of its site: 'The roads slope so steeply that horses harnessed to carriages would not be able to cope with them.' There were therefore no carriages, but beasts of burden and saddle horses. A more serious disadvantage was the sharp drop which cut off the city proper from the lower commercial town by the sea, so that it was necessary to 'use a sort of crane to bring merchandise up and down from the port to the town'. Today lifts accelerate the process, but it still has to be done.

In the same way Constantinople on the Golden Horn, the Sea of Marmara and the Bosporus, divided by large expanses of sea water, had to maintain a tribe of boatmen and ferrymen to make incessant crossings — not always without danger.

But these drawbacks were compensated by important advantages — if not, they would have been neither accepted nor tolerated. The advantages were generally those inherent in the location of the town in relation to neighbouring regions. The Golden Horn was the only sheltered port in an immense stretch of squally sea. The vast All Saints' bay facing Bahia (Salvador) was a miniature Mediterranean, well sheltered behind its islands and one of the easiest points on the Brazilian coast for a sailing ship from Europe to reach. The capital was only moved south to Rio de Janeiro in 1763 because of the development of the Minas Gerais and Goyaz gold mines.

Of course all these advantages could eventually be nullified. Malacca had century after century of monopoly; 'it controlled all the ships which passed its straits'. Then Singapore emerged from nowhere one fine day in 1819. A much better example still is the replacement of Seville (which had monopolised trade with the 'Indies of Castile' since the beginning of the sixteenth century) by Cadiz in 1685. This occurred because ships with too great a draught could no longer pass the bar of San Lucar de Barrameda, at the entrance to Guadalquivir. A technical reason was thus the pretext for a ruthless, though perhaps reasonable change, which nonetheless gave watchful international smuggling its chance in the vast Bay of Cadiz.

In any case, whether these advantages of location were liable or not to be superseded, they were indispensable to the prosperity of the towns. Cologne was situated at the meeting point of two separate shipping routes on the Rhine — one towards the sea, the other upstream — which met up along its quays. Ratisbon on the Danube was a reloading point for ships with too great a draught coming from Ulm, Augsburg, Austria, Hungary and even Wallachia.

Perhaps no site anywhere in the world was more privileged for short- and long-distance trade than Canton. The town was 'thirty leagues from the sea' but still felt the throb of the tide on its numerous stretches of water. Sea vessels, junks, or three-masters from Europe could therefore link up there with the small craft, the sampans, which reached all (or nearly all) interior China using the canals. 'I have quite often contemplated the beautiful views of the Rhine and the Meuse in Europe,' wrote J-F. Michel of Brabant (1753), 'but these two perspectives cannot provide a quarter [of what] that river of Canton alone offers for admiration.' Nevertheless Canton only owed its big chance in the eighteenth century to the Manchu empire's desire to keep European trade as far to the south as possible. Left to themselves, European merchants would have preferred to reach Ning Po and the Yang-tse-Kiang. They had a presentiment of Shanghai and the advantage of reaching the middle of China.

Geography in conjunction with the speed — or rather the slowness — of transport at the time also accounts for the very many small towns. The 3,000 towns of all kinds which Germany counted in the fifteenth century were so many relay points — four or five hours' journey away from each other in southern and western regions of the country, seven or eight hours in northern and eastern. And these breaks were not only situated at ports, between *venuta terrae* and *venuta maris,* as they said in Genoa, but sometimes between carts and river craft, the 'pack saddle used on mountain paths and the cart in the plain'. So true was it that every town welcomed movement, recreated it, scattered people and goods in order to gather new goods and new people, and so on.

It was this movement in and out of its walls that indicated the true town. 'We had a great deal of trouble that day,' complained Careri, arriving at Peking in 1697, 'because of the multitude of carts, camels and mares which go to Peking and return from it, and which is so large that one has difficulty in moving.'

Town markets   Town markets everywhere made this movement tangible. A traveller could say that Smyrna in 1693 'is only a bazaar and a fair'. But every town, wherever it may be, is first and foremost a market. If there is no market, a town is inconceivable. But a market can be situated near a village, even at a point in the open road or at an ordinary crossroads, without giving rise to a town. Every town, in fact, needs to be rooted in and nourished by the people and land surrounding it.

Daily life within a small radius was provided for by weekly or daily markets in the town; we use the word in the plural, remembering the various markets in Venice, for example, listed in Marin Sanudo's *Cronachetta.* There was the great market in the Rialto square, and near it the specially constructed *loggia* where the merchants assembled every morning. The market sagged under the weight of fruit, meat and game. Fish was sold a little farther on. There was another market in St Mark's Square. But every district had its own, in its main square. Supplies came from peasants from surrounding areas, gardeners from Padua, and boatmen, who even brought ewes' cheese from Lombardy.

[*Parisian examples are omitted.*]

The space nearest the town, from where, as in Leipzig, came delicious apples and much-prized asparagus, was only the first of the numerous circles surrounding it. In fact no town was without large gatherings of people and various assets, each involving a particular area around it and often spread out over wide distances. In every instance town life was linked to diverse areas that only partly overlapped. Powerful towns would very quickly, certainly from the fifteenth century, bring innumerable spaces into play. They were the instruments of long-distance relationships forming a kind of overall civic economy which they brought to life and from which they profited.

All these extensions belonged to one family of interrelated issues. Depending on the period, the town affected spaces that varied according to its size. It was by turns inflated and emptied according to the rhythm of its existence. Vietnamese towns were 'little populated on ordinary days' in the seventeenth century. But twice a month on days when the great markets were held they were the scene of very great animation. At Hanoi, then Ke-cho, 'the merchants are grouped in different streets according to their specialities; roads for silk, leather, hats, hemp, iron'. It was impossible to move amidst such a mob. Some of these market streets were shared by people from several villages who 'had sole privilege to set up shop there'. A historian has rightly said that these towns were markets rather than towns. We would prefer to call them fairs rather than towns, but town or market or fair, the result was the same — movements towards concentration, then dispersion, without which a somewhat accelerated economic life could not have been created, either in Vietnam or in the West.

The suburbs   All the towns in the world, beginning with those in the West, had their suburbs. Just as a strong tree is never without shoots at its foot, so towns are never without suburbs. They are the manifestations of its strength, even if they are wretched fringes, shanty towns. Shoddy suburbs are better than none at all.

Suburbs were made up of the poor, the craftsmen, the watermen, the noisy malodorous industries, cheap inns, posting houses, stables for post horses, porters' lodgings. Bremen turned over a new leaf in the seventeenth century: its houses were constructed in brick, roofed with tiles, its streets paved, a few wide avenues built. In the suburbs around it the houses still had straw roofs. To reach the suburbs was always to take a step downwards, in Bremen, London and elsewhere.

Triana, a suburb or rather an extension of Seville often mentioned by Cervantes, became the rendezvous for low-lifers, rogues, prostitutes and dishonest agents of the law. The suburb began on the right bank of the Guadalquivir, level with the bridge of boats which crossed the river towards the upper waters as London Bridge — on a different scale — crossed the Thames. Sea shipping arriving on the tide at Seville from San Lucar de Barrameda, Puerto Santa Maria or Cadiz was unable to go beyond this point. Triana would certainly not have had its violent character nor its pleasure gardens beneath their vine arbours if it had not had Seville by its side — Seville with its foreigners, 'Flemish' or otherwise, and its *nouveaux riches*, the *peruleros* who returned there from the New World to enjoy the fortunes they had made. A census in 1561 counted 1,664 houses and 2,666 families in Triana with four people per family — which meant really overcrowded accommodation and over 10,000 inhabitants, the substance of a town.

As dishonest work did not suffice, to support itself Triana had its artisans who produced varnished faience tiles — the blue, green and white *azulejos*, with their Islamic geometric patterns (these *azulejos* were exported all over Spain and to the New World). It also had craft industries producing soap — soft soap, hard soap and lye. Careri, who passed through it in 1697, noted that the town of Triana 'has nothing notable except a

Carthusian monastery, the Palace and the prisons of the Inquisition'. It is true that by then Seville had been dethroned by Cadiz and was no longer the same.

The relay town   Small towns inevitably grew up at a certain distance from large centres. The speed of transport, which moulded space, laid out a succession of regular stopping points. Stendhal was surprised at the relative tolerance large Italian towns showed towards the average and second-rate towns. They were opposed to these rivals — Florence seized half-dead Pisa in 1406; Genoa filled in the port of Savona in 1525 — but they did not suppress them, and for the excellent reason that they could not; they needed them. A large town necessarily meant a ring of secondary towns, one to weave and dye fabrics, another to organise haulage, a third as a sea port, like Leghorn in relation to Florence for example (Florence preferred Leghorn to Pisa, which was too far inland and hostile); like Alexandria or Suez to Cairo; Tripoli and Alexandretta to Aleppo; Jeddah to Mecca.

In Europe the phenomenon was particularly marked, and small towns were numerous. Richard Häpke was the first to use the expression an 'archipelago of towns' in relation to Flanders, showing its cities linked to each other and more still to Bruges in the fifteenth century, later to Antwerp. 'The Netherlands,' Henri Pirenne repeated, 'are the suburb of Antwerp', a suburb full of active towns. The same was true, on a small scale, of the markets around Geneva in the fifteenth century; of the local fairs around Milan at the same period; the series of ports linked to Marseilles on the Provence coast in the sixteenth, from Martigues on the pool of Berre up to Fréjus; or the large urban complex that connected San Lucar de Barrameda, Puerto de Santa Maria and Cadiz to Seville; or Venice's urban ring; or Burgos's links with its outer harbours (notably Bilbao) over which it long exercised control, even in its decline; or London and the Thames and Channel ports; or finally the classic example of the Hansa towns. At the lowest limit one could point to Compiègne in 1500 with its single satellite, Pierrefonds; or Senlis, which only had Crépy. This detail in itself passes judgment on the stature of Compiègne and Senlis. A series of these functional connections and dependencies could thus be drawn up: regular circles, lines and intersections of lines, single points.

But these patterns had only a limited duration. If traffic moved faster without changing its favourite routes, relay points were bypassed and went out of use.

Sébastien Mercier could even see this in Paris (1782):

Second- and third-class towns are imperceptibly becoming depopulated and the immense pit of the capital is not only devouring the gold of the parents but even the honesty and native virtue of their sons who pay dearly for the imprudent curiosity.

But it was a slow process.

François Mauriac tells of an English visitor he welcomed in south-west France:

He slept at the Lion d'Or hotel in Langon and walked about the small sleeping town in the night. He told me that nothing like it exists in England any more. Our provincial life is really a survival, what continues to exist of a world in the process of disappearing and which has already disappeared elsewhere. I took my Englishman to Bazas. What a contrast between this somnolent straggling village and its vast cathedral, evidence of a time when the capital of the Bazadais was a flourishing bishopric. We no longer think about that period when every province formed a world which spoke its own language and built its monuments, a refined and hierarchical society which was not aware of Paris and its fashions. Monstrous Paris which fed on this wonderful material and exhausted it.

In the event Paris was obviously no more to blame than London. The general movement of economic life alone was responsible. It deprived the secondary points of the urban network to the advantage of the main ones. But these major points, in their turn, formed a network amongst themselves on the enlarged scale of the world. And the process began again. Even the capital of Thomas More's island of Utopia, Amaurote, was surrounded by fifty-three cities. What a fine urban network! Each city was less than twenty-four miles from its neighbours, or less than a day's travelling. The whole order would have changed if transport had accelerated, however slightly.

Towns and civilisations: the case of Islam

Another feature common to all the towns, and one which was furthermore at the origin of their profound differences in appearance, was that they were all products of their civilisations. There was a prototype for each of them. Father du Halde writes in 1735: 'I have already said elsewhere that there is almost no difference between the majority of towns in China, so that it is almost enough to have seen one to get an idea of all the others.' We might well apply this rapid but by no means impetuous judgment to the towns of Muscovy, colonial America, Islam (Turkey or Persia), and even — but with much greater hesitation — Europe.

There is no doubt that there was a specific type of Islamic town to be found all over Islam from Gibraltar to the Sunda Isles, and this one case is a sufficient example of the obvious relationship between towns and civilisations.

Islamic towns were generally enormous and far away from each other. Their low houses were clustered together like pomegranate seeds. Islam prohibited high houses, deeming them a mark of odious pride (there were certain exceptions: in Mecca, Jedda, its port, and Cairo). As they could not grow upwards, they invaded public road systems, poorly protected by Muslim law. The streets were lanes which became blocked if two asses with their pack-saddles happened to meet.

[In Istanbul] the streets are narrow, as in our old towns [said a French traveller (1766)]; they are generally dirty and would be very inconvenient in bad weather without the pavements running along either side. When two people meet they have to step off the pavement or get out of the way into a doorway. You are sheltered from the rain there. The majority of houses have only one storey which projects over the ground floor; they are almost all painted in oil. This decoration makes the walls less dark and sombre. . . . All these houses, including even those belonging to the richest nobles and Turks, are built of wood and bricks and whitewashed, which is why fire can do so much damage there in so short a time.

[*Other examples are omitted.*]

The originality of Western towns

The West was, as it were, the luxury of the world. The towns there had been brought to a standard hardly found anywhere else. They had made Europe's greatness. But although this fact is very well known, the phenomenon is not simple. Specifying that something is superior means referring either to something inferior or to an average in relation to which that thing is superior. It means moving on sooner or later to an uncomfortable and deceptive comparison with the rest of the world. It is impossible, following Max Weber, to discuss costumes, money, towns and capitalism and avoid comparisons, because Europe has never stopped explaining itself 'in relation to other continents'.

What were Europe's differences and original features? Its towns were marked by an unparalleled freedom. They had developed as autonomous worlds and according to their own propensities. They had outwitted the territorial state, which was established slowly and then only grew with their interested cooperation — and was moreover only an enlarged and often insipid copy of their developments. They ruled their fields autocratically, regarding them as positive colonial worlds before there were such things and treating them as such (the states did just the same later on). They pursued an economic policy of their own via their satellites and the nervous system of urban relay points; they were capable of breaking down obstacles and creating or recreating protective privileges. Imagine the fine goings-on there would be if modern states were suppressed so that the Chamber of Commerce of the large towns were free to act as they wanted!

These old realities leap to the eye without the help of doubtful comparisons. They leap up to a key problem which can be formulated in two or three different ways: What stopped the rest of the towns in the world enjoying the same relative freedom? Or again — another aspect of the same problem — why was change a striking feature of the destiny of Western towns (even their physical existence was transformed) while the other cities have no history by comparison and seem to have been shut in long periods of immobility? Why were they like steam-engines while the others were like clocks, to parody Lévi-Strauss? In short, comparative history compels us to look for the reason for these differences and to attempt to establish a dynamic 'pattern' of turbulent urban evolution in the West, while the pattern of life in cities in the rest of the world runs in a long, straight and unbroken line across time.

Free worlds

Urban freedom in Europe is a classic and fairly well documented subject; let us start with it.

In a simplified form we can say:

1. The West well and truly lost its urban framework with the end of the Roman Empire. Moreover the towns in the Empire had been gradually declining from before the arrival of the barbarians. The very relative animation of the Merovingian period was followed, slightly earlier in some places, slightly later in others, by a complete halt.

2. The urban renaissance from the eleventh century was precipitated by and superimposed on a rise in rural vigour, a growth of fields, vineyards and orchards. Towns grew in harmony with villages and clearly outlined urban law often emerged from the communal privileges of village groups. The town was the country revived and remodelled. The names of a number of streets on the map of Frankfurt (which remained very rural until the sixteenth century) recall the woods, clumps of trees and marshland amidst which the town grew up.

   This rural rearrangement naturally brought to the nascent city the representatives of political and social authority: nobles, lay princes and ecclesiastics.

3. None of this would have been possible without a general return to health and a growing monetary economy. Money was the active and decisive element, come perhaps from afar (from Islam, according to Maurice Lombard). Two centuries before Saint Thomas Aquinas, Alain de Lille said: 'Not Caesar but money is everything now.' Money is the same as saying towns.

Thousands of towns were founded at that time, but few of them went on to brilliant futures. Only certain regions therefore were urbanised in depth, immediately distinguishable from the rest, and played an obvious central role: these were between the Loire and the Rhine, in upper and middle Italy, and at vital points on the Mediterranean coasts. Merchants, craft guilds, industries, long-distance trade and banks were quick to appear there, as well as a bourgeoisie and even some sort of capitalism. The formula so often used to describe this strong and privileged urban body can be repeated without misgivings: 'The town is a world in itself.' But to complete the process it had to break away from other human groups, from rural societies, and from old political connections. It even had to stand apart from its own countryside. The break was achieved either violently or amicably, but it was always a sign of strength, plentiful money and real power. Moreover towns only flowered at vital trade junctions.

Soon there were no more states around these privileged towns. This was the case in Italy and Germany, with the political collapses of the thirteenth century. The hare beat the tortoise for once. Elsewhere — in France, England, Castile, even in Aragon — the earlier rebirth of the territorial state restricted the development of the towns, which in addition were not situated in particularly lively economic areas. They grew less rapidly than elsewhere.

But the main, the unpredictable, thing was that certain towns made themselves into autonomous worlds, city-states, buttressed with privileges (acquired or extorted) like so many juridical ramparts. Perhaps in the past historians have insisted too much on the legal factors involved, for if such considerations were indeed sometimes more important than, or of equal importance to, geographical, sociological and economic factors, this latter category did count to a large extent. What is privilege without material substance?

In fact the miracle in the West was not so much that everything sprang up again from the eleventh century after having first been almost annihilated with the disaster of the fifth. History is full of those slow secular up and down movements, urban expansion, birth and rebirth: Greece from the fifth to the second century BC; Rome too; Islam from the ninth century; China under the Songs. But these revivals always featured two runners, the state and the town. The state usually won and the town then remained subject and under a heavy yoke. The miracle of the first great urban centuries in Europe was that the town won entirely, at least in Italy, Flanders and Germany. It was able to try the experiment of leading a completely separate life for quite a long time. This was a colossal event. Its genesis cannot be pinpointed with certainty, but its enormous consequences are visible.

Modern features of towns

The large cities, and the other towns they touched and to which they served as examples, built an original civilisation on the basis of this freedom and spread techniques which were new, or revived or rediscovered after centuries. They were able to follow fairly rare political, social and economic experiments right through to the end.

In the field of finance the towns organised taxation, finances, public credit and customs and excise. They invented public loans: the first issues of the Monte Vecchio in Venice could be said to go back to 1167, the first formulation of the Casa di San Giorgio to 1407. One after another they reinvented gold money, following Florence which minted the florin in 1252. They organised industry and the crafts; they reinvented long-distance trade, bills of exchange, the first forms of trading companies and accountancy.

They also quickly set in motion their class struggles. Because if the towns were 'communities' as has been said, they were also 'societies' in the modern sense of the word, with their pressures and civil wars: nobles against bourgeois, poor against rich ('thin people', *popolo magro*, against 'fat people', *popolo grasso*). The struggles in Florence were already more deeply akin to those of the French industrial early nineteenth century than conflicts of the Roman type (classical Rome of course). The drama of the *Ciompi* (1378) demonstrates it.

This society divided within itself also faced enemies from without — the worlds of the nobles, princes, peasants, everybody who was not a citizen. These towns were the West's first 'fatherlands'. And certainly their patriotism was for a long time to be more coherent and much more conscious than territorial patriotism, which was slow to appear in the first states. One can ponder this subject looking at an amusing picture representing the battle on 19 June 1502 between the Nuremburg burghers and the Margrave Casimir of Brandenburg-Ansbach who was attacking the town. Most of the townspeople are depicted on foot, in their ordinary clothes and without armour. Their leader, on horseback and dressed in a black suit, is chatting to the humanist Wilibald Pirckheimer, who is wearing one of the enormous hats of the period with ostrich feathers, and who (the fact is also significant) is leading a band of men to assist the rightful cause of the attacked town. The Brandenburg assailants are heavily equipped, armed horsemen, their faces hidden by the visors of their helmets. One group of three men in the picture could be taken as a symbol of the freedom of the towns against the authority of princes and nobles: two burghers with unshielded faces proudly frame an armoured horseman they are taking away — a prisoner and ashamed of the fact.

'Burghers', little 'bourgeois' fatherlands: these are convenient terms but highly imprecise. Werner Sombart has placed a good deal of emphasis on this birth of a society, and more still of a new state of mind. 'It is in Florence towards the end of the fourteenth century, if I am not mistaken,' he wrote, 'that we meet the perfect bourgeois citizen for the first time.' Perhaps. In fact the assumption of power (1293) by the *Arti Maggiori* — those of wool and of the *Arte di Calimala* — was the victory of the *nouveaux riches* and the spirit of enterprise in Florence. Sombart, as usual, preferred to place the problem on the level of states of mind and the development of rational spirit, rather than on the plane of societies, or even of the economy, where he was afraid of following in Marx's footsteps.

A new state of mind was established, broadly that of an early, still faltering, Western capitalism — a collection of rules, possibilities, calculations, the art both of getting rich and of living. And also gambling and risk: the key words of commercial language, *fortuna, ventura, ragione, prudenza, sicurta,* define the risks to be guarded against. It was certainly no longer a question of living from day to day, like the nobles, by somehow or other raising returns to the level of expenditure and letting the future take care of itself. The merchant was economical with his money, calculated his expenditure according to his returns, his investments according to their yield. The hourglass had turned back the right way. He would also be economical with his time: a merchant could already say that *chi tempo ha e tempo aspetta tempo perde,* which means much the same thing as 'time is money'.

Capitalism and towns were basically the same thing in the West. Lewis Mumford humorously claimed that capitalism was the cuckoo's egg laid in the confined nest of the medieval towns. By this he meant to convey that the bird was destined to grow inordinately and burst its tight framework (which was true), and then link up with the state, the conqueror of towns but heir to their institutions and way of thinking and completely incapable of dispensing with them. The important thing was that even when it has declined as a city the town continued to rule the roost all the time it was passing into the actual or apparent service of the prince. The wealth of the state would still be the wealth of the town: Portugal converged on Lisbon, the Netherlands on Amsterdam, and English primacy was London's primacy (the capital modelled England in its own image after the peaceful revolution of 1688). The latent defect in the Spanish imperial economy was that it was based on Seville — a controlled town rotten with dishonest officials and long dominated by foreign capitalists — and not on a powerful free town capable of producing and carrying through a really individual economic policy. Likewise, if Louis XIV did not succeed in founding a 'royal bank', despite various projects (1703, 1706, 1709), it was because the merchants 'were afraid . . . that the king would lay hands on the deposits in the bank'. Paris did not offer the protection of a town free to do what is wanted and accountable to no one.

Urban patterns

Let us imagine we are looking at a comprehensive history of the towns of Europe covering the complete series of their forms from the Greek town to the eighteenth-century town — everything Europe was able to build at home and overseas, in the Muscovite East and across the Atlantic. The abundant material could be classified in many ways according to political, economic or social characteristics. Politically a differentiation would be made between capitals, fortresses and administrative towns in the full meaning of 'administrative'. Economically, one would distinguish between ports, caravan towns, market towns, industrial towns and money markets. Socially, a list could be drawn up of *rentier* towns, and Church, Court or craftsmen's towns. This is to adopt a series of fairly obvious categories, divisible into subcategories and capable of absorbing all sorts of local varieties. Such a classification has its advantages, not so much for the overall problem of the town itself as for the study of particular economies limited in time and space.

On the other hand some more general distinctions arising out of the very process of town development offer a more useful classification for our purpose. The West has had three basic types of town in the course of its evolution (we are, of course, oversimplifying): open towns, that is to say not differentiated from their hinterland, even blending into it (A); towns closed in on themselves in every sense, their walls marking the boundaries of an individual way of life more than a territory (B); finally towns held in the whole known gamut of subjection by prince and state (C).

Roughly, A preceded B, and B preceded C. But there is no suggestion of strict succession about this order. It is rather a question of directions and dimensions shaping the complicated careers of the Western towns. They did not all develop at the same time or in the same way. Later we will see if this 'grid' is valid, as I think it is, for classifying all the towns of the world; if one of our categories (either simple or composite) can be invoked at the right moment to take in no matter what specific case no matter where.

Open towns: Ancient Greece and Rome   The ancient Greek or Roman town was open to its countryside and on terms of equality with it. Athens accepted within its walls as rightful citizens the Eupatride horse-breeders as well as the small vine-growing peasants so dear to Aristophanes. As soon

as the smoke rose above the Pnyx, the peasant responded to the signal and
attended the Assembly of the People where he sat beside his equals. At the
beginning of the Peloponnesian war the whole Attic countryside automatically converged on Athens, where it was swallowed up and settled,
while the Spartans ravaged fields, olive groves and houses. When the
Spartans fell back at the approach of winter, the small country folk retrod
the road to their homes. The Greek city was in fact the sum of the town
and its wide countryside. If this were so, it was because the town had only
just been born, only recently become a distinct entity in a given rural area
(a century or two is very little on this scale). Moreover the division of
industrial activities, source of discord in the future, did not enter into the
matter. Athens did have the Ceramic suburb where its potters lived, but
they had only small shops. It also had a port, Piraeus, swarming with
foreigners, freed men and slaves, where craft activity — we cannot call it
industry or pre-industry — was becoming firmly established. But this
activity came up against the prejudices of an agricultural society that
mistrusted it; it was therefore left to foreigners or slaves. Above all
Athens's prosperity did not last long enough for social and political
conflicts to come to a head there and push 'Florentine-type' conflicts to
the fore. We can just discern a few symptoms. Moreover the villages had
their craftsmen and forges where it was pleasant to go and get warm when
winter came. In short, industry was rudimentary, foreign and unobtrusive.
Likewise, roaming the ruins of old Roman towns, you leave the gates and
immediately find yourself in open country: there are no suburbs, which is
as good as saying no industry or active well-organised crafts in their proper
place.

Towns closed in on themselves: the medieval cities   The medieval city
was the classic type of the closed town, a self-sufficient unit, an exclusive
Lilliputian native land. Crossing its ramparts was like crossing one of the
still serious frontiers in the world today. You were free to thumb your
nose at your neighbour from the other side of the barrier. He could not
touch you. The peasant who uprooted himself from his land and arrived in
the town was immediately another man. He was free — or rather he had
abandoned a known and hated servitude for another, not always guessing
the extent of it beforehand. But this mattered little. If the town had
adopted him, he could snap his fingers when his lord called for him. And
though obsolete elsewhere, such calls were still frequently to be heard in
Silesia in the eighteenth century and in Muscovy up to the nineteenth.

Though the towns opened their gates easily it was not enough to
walk through them to be immediately and really part of them. Full
citizens were a jealous minority, a small town inside the town itself. A
citadel of the rich was built up in Venice in 1297 thanks to the *serrata*, the
closing of the Great Council to new members. The *nobili* of Venice
became a closed class for centuries. Very rarely did anyone force its gates.
The category of ordinary *cittadini* — at a lower level — was probably more
hospitable. But the Seigniory very soon created two types of citizen, one
de intus, the other *de intus et extra*, the latter full, the former partial.
Fifteen years' residence were still required to be allowed to apply for the
first, twenty-five years for the second. A decree by the Senate in 1386

even forbade new citizens (including those who were full citizens) from trading directly in Venice with German merchants at the Fondego dei Todeschi or outside it. The small folk in the town were no less mistrustful or hostile to newcomers. According to Marin Sanudo, in June 1520 when too many wretched peasants came looking for jobs or just a little bread, the street people attacked them. *'Poltroni,'* they shouted, *'ande arar'* ('Poltroons, go away and till the land').

Of course Venice was an extreme example. Moreover it owed the preservation of its own constitution until 1797 to an aristocratic and extremely reactionary régime, as well as to the conquest of Terra Firma at the beginning of the fifteenth century, which extended its authority as far as the Alps and Brescia. It was the last *polis* in the West. But citizenship was also parsimoniously granted in Marseilles in the sixteenth century; it was necessary to have 'ten years of domicile, to possess property, to have married a local girl'. Otherwise the man remained amongst the masses of non-citizens of the town. This limited conception of citizenship was the general rule everywhere. The town was nonetheless a whole, with its own statutes and its privileges in relation to state and nearby countryside. Even in a still poorly urbanised country like France these distinctions only disappeared with the abolition of privileges on the memorable night of 4 August 1789.

The main source of contention can be glimpsed throughout this vast process: to whom did industry and craft, their privileges and profits, belong? In fact they belonged to the town, to its authorities and to its merchant entrepreneurs. They decided if it were necessary to deprive, or to try to deprive, the rural area of the city of the right to spin, weave and dye, or if on the contrary it would be advantageous to grant it these rights. Everything was possible in these interchanges, as the history of each individual town shows.

As far as work inside the walls was concerned (we can hardly call it industry without qualification), everything was arranged for the benefit of the craft guilds. They enjoyed exclusive contiguous monopolies, fiercely defended along the imprecise frontiers that so easily led to absurd conflicts. The urban authorities did not always have the situation under control. Sooner or later, with the help of money, they were to allow obvious, acknowledged, honorary superiorities, consecrated by money or power, to become apparent. The 'Six Corps' (drapers, grocers, haber-dashers, furriers, hosiers, goldsmiths) were the commercial aristocracy of Paris from 1625. In Florence it was the *Arte de la lana* and the *Arte di Calimala* (engaged in dyeing fabric imported from the north, unbleached). But town museums in Germany supply the best evidence of these old situations. In Ulm, for example, each guild owned a picture hinged in triptych form. The side panels represented characteristic scenes of the craft. The centre, like a treasured family album, showed innumerable small portraits recalling the successive generations of masters of the guild over the centuries.

An even more telling example was the City of London and its annexes (running along its walls) in the eighteenth century, still the domain of fussy, obsolete and powerful guilds. If Westminster and the suburbs were growing continually, noted a well-informed economist (1754), it was for obvious reasons:

> These suburbs are free and present a clear field for every industrious citizen, while in its bosom London feeds ninety-two of all sorts of those exclusive companies [guilds], whose numerous members can be seen adorning the Lord Mayor's Show every year with immoderate pomp.

Let us come to a halt here before this colourful scene. And also for the moment let us pass over the free crafts around London and elsewhere which kept outside the guild-masterships and their frameworks, outside their constraint and protection. We will have occasion to mention them again.

Subject towns in the early modern period   Everywhere in Europe, as soon as the state was firmly established it disciplined the towns with instinctive relentlessness, whether or not it used violence. The Habsburgs did so just as much as the Popes, the German princes just as much as the Medicis or the kings of France. Except in the Netherlands and England obedience was imposed, sometimes with compensations and profitable agreements, as we have already said.

Take Florence as an example: the Medicis had slowly subjugated it, almost elegantly in Lorenzo's time. But after 1532 and the recapture of the town by Cosimo the process accelerated. Florence in the seventeenth century was no more than the Grand Duke's court. He had seized everything — money, the right to govern and to distribute honours. From the Pitti Palace, on the left bank of the Arno, a gallery — a secret passage in fact — allowed the prince to cross the river and reach the Uffizi. This elegant gallery, still in existence today on the Ponte Vecchio, was the thread from which the spider at the extremity of his web supervised the imprisoned town.

In Spain the *corregidor*, the urban administrator, subjected the 'free towns' to the will of the Crown. Of course the Crown left the small profits and the vanities of local administration to the small local nobility. It summoned the delegates of the town *regidores* (in which office could be bought) to meetings of the Cortes — formal assemblies eager to present their grievances but unanimously voting the king his taxes. In France the 'good towns' were just as much under orders. Though enjoying the privileges of their municipal corporations and their manifold fiscal exemptions, they did not prevent the royal government from doubling the *octrois* by its declaration of 21 December 1647 and allocating a good half of them to itself. Paris, equally under the royal thumb, helped — had to help — the royal treasury. Even Louis XIV did not give up the capital. Versailles was not really separate from nearby Paris, and the monarchy had always been accustomed to centre itself upon the powerful, redoubtable city. The monarch spent some time at Fontainebleau, Saint-Germain and Saint-Cloud. At the Louvre he was on the outskirts of Paris; at the Tuileries, almost outside Paris proper. In fact it was advisable to govern these overpopulated towns from a distance, at least from time to time. Philip II spent all his time at the Escorial, and Madrid was only at its beginnings. Later the Dukes of Bavaria were in Nymphenburg; Frederick II in Potsdam; the emperors next to Vienna in Schoenbrunn. Moreover to return to Louis XIV, despite everything he did not forget to assert his authority in Paris itself nor to maintain his prestige there. The two great royal squares, the Place des Victoires and the Place Vendôme, were built during his reign. The 'prodigious construction' of Les Invalides was undertaken at that time. Thanks to him, wide access roads where carriages flowed and military marches were organised opened Paris to its nearby countryside on the pattern of Baroque towns. Most important from our point of view was the creation in 1667 of a Lieutenant of Police with exorbitant powers. The second holder of this high office, the Marquis d'Argenson, nominated thirty years later (1697), 'assembled the machine — not the one that exists today', explained Sébastien Mercier, 'but he was the first to think of its main springs and mechanisms. One can even say that today this machine runs by itself.'

We know that later on the large towns blew up in the masters' hands: Paris in 1789, Vienna, Munich and Prague in 1848. We also know that the means of restoring them to order were quite slowly but effectively perfected: to abandon the town to the riots and then return there in full force. Windischgraetz set the example in Prague and Vienna. Versailles applied the method against the Commune in 1871.

[*Section on colonial, Russian and Eastern towns omitted.*]

Large towns

For a long time the only large towns had been in the East and Far East. Marco Polo's wonderment proclaimed the fact: the East was then the site of empires and enormous cities. With the sixteenth century, and more still during the following two centuries, large towns grew up in the West, assumed positions of prime importance and retained them brilliantly thereafter. Europe had thus made up for lost time and wiped out a deficiency (if deficiency there had been). In any case there it was, tasting the luxuries, the new pleasures and the bitterness of large, already over-large, towns. Was it necessary or advantageous to recreate Romes in the classical style? Or to imitate the very expensive luxury of the East?

The states

This late growth would have been inconceivable without the steady advancement of the states: they had caught up with the forward gallop of the towns. It was their capitals which were privileged, whether they deserved it or not. Thenceforth they vied with each other in modernity: which would have the first pavements, the first street lamps, the first steam pumps, the first effective system for supplying and distributing drinking water, the first numbered houses. All this was taking place in London and Paris during the period roughly preceding the French Revolution.

The town that did not grasp this opportunity was necessarily left behind. The more its old shell remained intact, the greater its chances of becoming empty. In the sixteenth century demographic growth had still favoured all the towns indiscriminately whatever their size — large or small. In the seventeenth political success was concentrated on a few towns to the exclusion of others. Despite the depressing economic situation they grew unceasingly, and continually attracted people and privileges.

London and Paris led the movement, but Naples was also in the running with its long-established privileges and with already as many as 300,000 inhabitants in the last years of the sixteenth century. Paris, which the French quarrels had reduced to perhaps 180,000 inhabitants in 1594, had probably doubled by Richelieu's time. And others fell into step behind these large towns: Madrid, Amsterdam, soon Vienna, Munich, Copenhagen and even more St Petersburg. America alone was slow to follow the movement, but its overall population was still very thin. The anachronistic success of Potosi (100,000 inhabitants around 1600) was the temporary success of a mining camp. However brilliant Mexico, Lima or Rio de Janeiro were, they were slow to collect sizeable populations. Rio had at the most 100,000 inhabitants around 1800. As for the hard-working and independent towns in the United States, they fell well below these princely achievements.

This growth of large agglomerations, coinciding with the first modern states, to some extent explains the older phenomenon of the large Eastern and Far Eastern cities — their size was not a function of the density of population, which would have had to be higher in the East than in Europe (we know this is not true), but due to their role as powerful political concentrations. Istanbul probably had 700,000 inhabitants as early as the sixteenth century, but an enormous empire stood behind the enormous town. Behind Peking, which numbered three million inhabitants in 1793, there stood a single and united China. Behind Delhi there stood an almost united India.

[*Indian and Japanese examples are omitted.*]

The function of capital towns

By the laws of a simple and inevitable political arithmetic, it seems that the vaster and more centralised the state, the greater the chance its capital had of being populous. The rule is valid for imperial China, Hanoverian England and the Paris of Louis XIV and Sébastien Mercier. It is even valid for the reasonably large town of Amsterdam, though abandoned by the Courts of the Stadtholder at the end of the seventeenth century.

These towns, as we will see, represented enormous expenditure. Their economy was only balanced by outside resources; others had to pay for their luxury. What use were they therefore, in the West, where they sprang up and asserted themselves so powerfully? The answer is that they produced the modern states, an enormous task requiring an enormous effort. They produced the national markets, without which the modern state would be a pure fiction. For, in fact, the British market was not born solely of the political union of England with Scotland (1707), or the Act of Union with Ireland (1801), or because of the abolition of so many tolls (advantageous in itself), or because of the speeding-up of transport, or the 'canal craze' or the surrounding sea (a natural encouragement to free trade). It was primarily the result of the ebb and flow of merchandise to and from London, an enormous demanding central nervous system which caused everything to move to its own rhythm, overturned everything and quelled everything. Added to this was the enormous cultural, intellectual and even revolutionary role of these hothouses. But the price demanded was very high.

Unbalanced worlds

The right balance had to be struck. Amsterdam was thus an admirable town. It had expanded fast: 30,000 inhabitants in 1530, 115,000 in 1630, 200,000 at the end of the eighteenth century. It aimed at comfort rather than luxury, intelligently supervising the enlargement of its districts. Its four semicircular canals, like the concentric rings of a tree, marked out the wide physical growth of the town between 1482 and 1658. Light and airy, with its rows of trees, quays and stretches of water, it kept its original character intact. Only one mistake, but a revealing one, was made: the Jordaan districts in the south-west were handed over to unscrupulous contracting companies. Foundations were badly made, canals were narrow; the whole district was situated below the level of the town. And naturally this was the chosen place for a mixed proletariat of Jewish immigrants, *marranos* from Portugal and Spain, Huguenot refugees fleeing France and the wretched of all nationalities.

There is a risk that the retrospective traveller may be disappointed in London, the largest town in Europe (860,000 inhabitants at the end of the eighteenth century). The life of the port was less active than he would suppose. Moreover the town had not taken full advantage of its misfortune (if one can put it that way) after the fire of 1666 to reconstruct itself in a rational manner, despite the plans put forward, in particular the very beautiful one submitted by Wren. It had grown up again haphazardly and only began to improve at the end of the seventeenth century when the large squares in the west were completed: Golden Square, Grosvenor Square, Berkeley Square, Red Lion Square, Kensington Square.

Trade was obviously one of the driving forces behind the monstrous agglomeration. But Werner Sombart has shown that 100,000 people at the most could have lived on the profits of trade in 1700. Taken all together, profits did not add up to the civil list allocation granted to William III, £700,000. London, in fact, lived primarily from the Crown, from the high, middle-grade and minor officials it maintained (high officials were paid in a lordly fashion, with salaries of £1,000, £1,500 even £2,000). It also lived from nobility and gentry who settled in the town, from representatives to the House of Commons who had been in the habit of staying in London with their wives and children since Queen Anne's reign (1702-14), and from the presence of bearers of government bonds whose numbers grew as the years went by. An idle tertiary sector proliferated, turned its stocks, salaries and surplus to good account and unbalanced the powerful life of

England to the advantage of London, making it into a unity and creating artificial needs.

The same thing happened in Paris. The expanding town outgrew its walls, adapted its streets to the traffic of carriages, planned its squares and collected an enormous mass of consumers. After 1760 it was full of building sites, where high lifting wheels, 'which raised enormous stones into the air' near Saint-Geneviève and in 'the parish of the Madeleine', were visible from afar. The elder Mirabeau, the 'Friend of Men', would have liked to drive 200,000 people out of the town, starting with royal officers and large landowners and ending up with litigants, who perhaps would have liked nothing better than to go back home. It was true that these wealthy classes and the unwilling spendthrifts supported 'a multitude of merchants, craftsmen, servants, unskilled labourers' and many ecclesiastics and 'tonsured clerics'! 'In several houses,' Sébastien Mercier reported, 'one finds a priest who is regarded as a friend and who is only an honest valet. . . . Then come family tutors who are also priests.' Not to mention bishops breaking residence requirements. Lavoisier drew up the balance sheet for the capital: under the heading of expenditure, 250 million livres for humans, 10 million for horses; on the credit side, 20 million in commercial profits, 140 in government bonds and salaries, 100 million from ground rents or from business activities outside Paris.

None of these facts escaped the observers and economists of the time. 'The wealth of the towns attracts the gay life,' said Cantillon. 'The great and the wealthy,' noted Dr Quesnay, 'have withdrawn to the capital.' Sébastien Mercier listed the endless 'unproductive elements' in the enormous town.

No [said an Italian text in 1797], Paris is not a real market place, it is too busy supplying itself; it only counts because of its books, the products of its art or fashion, the enormous quantity of money which circulates there, and the speculation on the exchanges, unequalled except by Amsterdam. All industry there is devoted exclusively to luxury: carpets from the Gobelins or the Savonnerie, rich covers from the rue Saint-Victor, hats exported to Spain and the East and West Indies, silk fabrics, taffetas, galloons and ribbons, ecclesiastical habits, mirrors (the wide silvering of which comes from Saint-Gobain), gold work, printing.

The same thing happened in Madrid, Berlin and Naples. Berlin counted 141,283 inhabitants in 1783, including a garrison of 33,088 people (soldiers and families), 13,000 bureaucrats (officials and families), and 10,074 servants; with the addition of Frederick II's court that made 56,000 state 'employees'. All in all, an unhealthy situation. Naples is worth looking at in greater detail.

Naples, from the Royal Palace to the Mercato

Both sordid and beautiful, abjectly poor and very rich, certainly gay and alive, Naples counted 400,000, probably 500,000 inhabitants on the eve of the French Revolution. It was the fourth town in Europe, coming equal with Madrid after London, Paris and Istanbul. A major breakthrough after 1695 extended it in the direction of Borgo di Chiaja, facing the second bay of Naples (the first being Marinella). Only the rich benefited, as authorisation to build outside the walls, granted in 1717, almost exclusively concerned them.

As for the poor, their district stretched out from the vast Largo del Castello, where the burlesque quarrels over the free distribution of victuals took place, to the Mercato, their fief, facing the Paludi plain that began outside the ramparts. They were so crowded that their life encroached and overflowed on to the streets. As today, washing was strung out to dry between the windows.

> The majority of beggars do not have houses; they find nocturnal
> asylum in a few caves, stables or ruined houses, or (not very
> different from the last) in houses run by one of their number, with a
> lantern and a little straw as their sole equipment, entry being
> obtained in exchange for a *grano* [a small Neapolitan coin] or
> slightly more, per night.

'They are to be seen there,' continued the Prince of Strongoli (1783), 'lying like filthy animals, with no distinction of age or sex; all the ugliness and all the offspring which result from this can be imagined.' These ragged poor numbered at the lowest estimate 100,000 people at the end of the century. 'They proliferate, without families, having no relationship with the state except through the gallows and living in such chaos that only God could get his bearing among them.' During the long famine of 1763-64 people died in the streets.

The fault lay in their excessive numbers. Naples drew them but could not feed them all. They barely survived. Next to them an undeveloped lower bourgeoisie of half-starved craftsmen also just managed to get by. The great Giovanni Battista Vico (1668-1741), one of the last universal minds of the West capable of speaking *de omni re scibili*, was paid forty ducats a year as professor at the University of Naples and only managed to live by private lessons, condemned 'to go up and down other people's staircases'.

Above this totally deprived mass let us imagine a super-society of courtiers, great landed nobility, high-ranking ecclesiastics, dishonest officials, judges, advocates and litigants.

One of the foulest areas of the town, the Castel Capuaro, was situated in the legal district. It contained the *Vicaria*, a sort of Parliament of Naples where justice was bought and sold and 'where pick-pockets lie in wait for pockets and purses'. How, asked a too rational Frenchman, how was it that the social structure remained intact when it was 'laden with an excessive population, numerous beggars, a prodigious body of servants, considerable secular and regular clergy, a military force of over 20,000 men, a multitude of nobles, and an army of 30,000 lawyers'?

But the system held as it had always held, as it held elsewhere and at small cost. In the first place these privileged people did not always receive rich livings. A man got a little money and moved up into the ranks of the nobles. 'The butcher we used to use has no longer practised except through his assistants since becoming a duke,' meaning since he bought a title to the nobility. But we are not forced to take *le Président de Brosses* literally. Above all, thanks to state, Church, nobility and goods, the town attracted all the surplus from the Kingdom of Naples, where there were many peasants, shepherds, sailors, miners, craftsmen and carriers inured to hardships. The town had always fed on this hardship outside its boundaries since Frederick II, the Angevins and the Spaniards. The Church — which the historian Giannone attacked in his vast pamphlet, *Istoria civile del Regno di Napoli* in 1723 — owned at the lowest estimate two-thirds of the landed property in the kingdom, the nobility two-ninths. This restored the balance of Naples. It is true that only one-ninth was left to the *gente piu bassa di campagna.*

When Ferdinand, King of Naples, and his wife Marie-Caroline visited Grand Duke Leopold and 'Enlightened' Tuscany in 1785, the unhappy King of Naples, more lazzarone than enlightened prince, grew irritated by the lessons set before him and the reforms held up for his admiration. 'Really,' he said one day to his brother-in-law, Grand Duke Leopold, 'I cannot understand what use all your science is to you; you read incessantly, your people do as you do, and your towns, your capital, your court, everything here is dismal and gloomy. As for me, I know nothing, and my people are still the gayest people of all.' But the old capital of Naples was the Kingdom of Naples, together with Sicily. In comparison little Tuscany could be held in the palm of a hand.

[*Sections on St Petersburg and Peking are omitted.*]

Ultimate journey: London

We could multiply our journeys and still change none of our conclusions. The luxury of the capitals had always to be borne on the shoulders of others. Not one of them could have existed from the work of its own hands. Sixtus V (1585-90), a pig-headed peasant, misunderstood contemporary Rome. He wanted to make it 'work' and plant industries there, a project which the facts rejected without the need for human persuasion. Sébastien Mercier and a few others dreamt of transforming Paris into a seaport in order to attract hitherto unknown activities there. Had it been possible to recreate Paris in the image of London, then the greatest port in the world, it would still have remained a parasitical town.

It was the same in all capitals, all the towns where the enlightenment and excess of civilisation, taste and leisure glittered: Madrid or Lisbon, Rome or Genoa, Venice, bent on surviving in its past greatness, or Vienna, at the peak of European elegance during the seventeenth and eighteenth centuries. And also Mexico and Lima. And Rio de Janeiro, capital of Brazil since 1763, which grew incessantly, becoming a handsome human creation within an already sumptuous natural setting, so that travellers would not recognise it from one year to the next. Or Delhi where the splendour of the Great Mogul survived, and Batavia where precocious Dutch colonialism put forth its most beautiful and already poisonous flowers.

London from Elizabeth I to George III

We come back from these far-off shores and return to Europe, where the example of London will enable us to conclude the chapter and, with it, the present volume. Everything about this prodigious urban development is known or knowable.

In Elizabeth's reign observers already regarded London as an exceptional world. For Thomas Dekker it was 'the Queene of Cities', made incomparably more beautiful by its winding river than Venice itself judged by the marvellous view of the Grand Canal (a very paltry sight compared with what London could offer). Samuel Johnson (20 September 1777) was even more lyrical: 'when a man is tired of London, he is tired of life; for there is in London all that life can afford.'

Growth vainly opposed   The royal government shared these illusions, but it was nonetheless in constant fear of the enormous capital. In its eyes London was a monster whose unhealthy growth had to be limited at all costs. What alarmed the influential and propertied classes was the invasion by the poor and the proliferation of hovels and vermin that meant a threat to the whole population, including the rich. 'And so a danger to the Queen's own life and the spreading of mortality of the whole nation,' wrote Stow, who feared for the health of Queen Elizabeth and the whole population of his town. The first prohibition on new building (with exceptions in favour of the rich) appeared in 1580. Others followed in 1593, 1607 and 1625. The result was to encourage the dividing-up of existing houses and secret construction work in poor brick in the courtyards of old houses, away from the street and even from minor alleys. What in fact ensued was a whole clandestine proliferation of hovels and shanties on lands of doubtful ownership. It was no great loss if one or other of these buildings fell victim to the law. Everybody therefore tried their luck, and the network, the labyrinth of lanes and alleys, and the houses with double, triple, even quadruple entrances and exits, grew up as a result. In 1732 London was said to have 5,099 streets, lanes and squares, and 95,968 houses. Consequently the rising tide of the London population was neither stemmed nor stopped. The town had 93,000 inhabitants in 1563; 123,000 in 1580; 152,000 in 1593-95; 317,000 in 1632; 700,000 in 1700; and 860,000 at the end of the eighteenth century (all these figures are more or less reliable). It was then the largest town in Europe. Only Paris could compare.

The Thames and the pool of London   London depended on its river. The town was shaped 'like a half moon' because of it. London Bridge, which joined the city to the suburb of Southwark and was the only bridge over the river (300 metres from the present bridge) was the outstanding feature of the landscape. The tide flowed up to this point. The pool, the basin, the port of London, was therefore situated downstream from the bridge, with its quays, its wharves and the often mentioned forest of masts (not without reason: 13,444 ships in 1798). Depending on the load to be discharged, these sailing ships made their way to St Catherine's quay, frequented by coal lighters from Newcastle, or to Billingsgate quay if they carried fresh fish or were involved in the regular service from Billingsgate to Gravesend. Feluccas, barges, tilt boats, ferry boats and barks supplied transport from one bank of the river to the other and from sea-going boats to the appropriate quays — an essential service when these quays were situated upstream from the port. Vintry wharf, which received casks from the Rhine, France, Spain, Portugal and the Canaries, was one such case. It was not far from the Steelyard (or Stilliard), which was the headquarters of the Hanseatic League until 1597 and 'reserved for tasting Rhine wines since the expulsion of foreign merchants'. A character in one of Thomas Dekker's plays says, 'I come to entreat you to meet him this afternoon at the Rhenish Wine house in the Stilliard. . . .'

The utilisation of the river tended to extend farther and farther downstream towards the sea, particularly as the docks — basins inside the bends of the river — were not yet dug, except one belonging to the East India Company (1656). A first impression of the commercial port can be gained either at Billingsgate or at the Tower of London wharf, or better still at the essential barrier, the Customs House, burnt down in 1666 but at once reconstructed by Charles II in 1668. In fact the scene extends as far as Ratcliff, 'infamous rendezvous of prostitutes and robbers', as far as Limehouse, with its lime kilns and tanneries, up to Blackwall, where the pleasure of looking at the anchored boats was balanced by 'the very strong smell of tar'. East London — naval, artisan and slightly dishonest — was not a pleasant sight, and its stench was only too real.

A poverty-stricken population saw the riches from the moored ships dangled before their eyes. In 1798: 'The immense depredations committed on every species of commercial Property in the River Thames, but particularly on West India produce, had long been felt as a grievance of the greatest magnitude. . . .' The 'river pirates' who operated in organised bands, stealing an anchor or a rope when the opportunity offered, were not yet the most dangerous of these thieves. The role was reserved for the night plunderers, the watermen and lightermen, the 'mudlarks', who excavated the river ostensibly searching for old ropes, old iron, or pieces of lost coal, and finally, at the end of the line, the receivers.

All these moralising indictments taken from a *Police Treatise* (1801) convey very precisely the atmosphere of the dubious world of the pool — a vast kingdom of water, wood, sail, tar and menial labour on the margin of the life of the capital but linked to it by routes. The Londoner generally only saw the point where these routes converged.

The north bank   London was primarily on the north bank of its river. The only bridge over it was a commercial street, lined with shops and difficult to cross, leading into a poor suburb, Southwark, the 'Bridge Without'. It contained a few taverns, five prisons of ominous renown, a few theatres and two or three circuses (the Bear Garden, the Paris Garden).

The real town was on the north bank, slightly higher than the opposite bank, with its two eminences, St Paul's Church and the Tower of London. It extended like a 'bridgehead northwards', for it was in a northerly direction that the succession of roads, lanes and alleys linking London to the counties and to the flourishing English countryside actually ran. The great axes, old Roman roads, were directed towards Manchester, Oxford, Dunstable (Watling Street) and Cambridge.

London was the concentrated area of houses, streets and squares along the river — all of them turning their backs on the town; but above all it was the city (160 hectares) as marked out by the old city walls. They stood on the site of the ancient Roman wall, but they had disappeared around the twelfth century on the river front, where quays, wharves and floating landing-stages had breached the useless protection very early on. On the other hand they survived in a broken line, very roughly forming an arc of a circle from Blackfriars Steps or Bridewell Dock up to the Tower of London. The line was cut by seven gates: Ludgate, Newgate, Aldersgate, Cripplegate, Moorgate, Bishopsgate and Aldgate. Facing each of these gates, far into the suburbs, there was a gate limiting the authority of London. The inner suburbs were 'liberties', districts (sometimes vast areas) outside the walls. Thus the gate in front of Bishopsgate was situated on the edge of Smithfield, west of Holborn. Likewise, going out of Ludgate, one had to walk right down Fleet Street in order to reach Temple Bar, level with the Temple of the ex-Templars at the entrance to the Strand. Temple Bar was an ordinary wooden gate for a long time. This was the way in which London, or rather the City, overflowed its restricted boundaries even before Elizabeth's reign, reaching places in the countryside near by and joining itself to them by a series of roads lined with houses.

In the time of Elizabeth I and Shakespeare the heart of the town beat inside the walls. Its centre was on the axis extending London Bridge northwards to Bishopsgate. The east/west axis was marked out by a series of streets from Newgate in the west to Aldgate in the east. Under Elizabeth the crossing point was situated about 300 yards from the Stock Market, at the west end of Lombard Street.

The Royal Exchange was a couple of steps away on Cornhill. It had been founded by Thomas Gresham in 1566 and at first was called the 'Bourse' (*Byrsa Londinensis, vulgo the Royal Exchange* ran the caption on a seventeenth-century engraving) in memory of the Antwerp Bourse. The name Royal Exchange had been granted to it by the authority of Elizabeth in 1570. According to witnesses it was a veritable Tower of Babel, especially around midday when the merchants arrived to settle their business. However the most elegant shops around its courtyards attracted a rich clientele. Both the Guildhall (more or less London's town hall) and the Bank of England's first home (it was housed in the Grocer's Hall, the grocers' warehouse, before occupying its sumptuous building in 1734) were not far from the Royal Exchange.

The intensity of London life also showed in its markets, West Smithfields for example, the vast area near the ramparts where horses and livestock were sold on Mondays and Fridays; or Billingsgate, the fresh fish market on the Thames; or the Leaden Hall towards the heart of the city, with its lead roof, an old corn warehouse where butchers' meat and leather were sold on a large scale. But it would be impossible to give a full account of those important centres, those taverns, restaurants and theatres which were generally on the periphery and therefore reserved for the populace, or later, in the seventeenth century, those coffee houses which were so well patronised that the government was already thinking about prohibiting them.

A second capital: Westminster　　But the City was never the only runner in the race on the banks of the Thames. In comparison Paris had a solitary fate. Westminster, upstream from London, was quite a different matter from Versailles (a late creation *ex nihilo*). It was really an old and living town. The Palace of Westminster, next to the Abbey, abandoned by Henry VIII, had become the seat of Parliament and the principal tribunals. It was the meeting place for lawyers and litigants. The monarchy had taken up its abode slightly farther away, in Whitehall, in the White Palace beside the Thames.

Westminster was therefore both Versailles and St Denis plus the Paris *Parlement* for good measure. We have used the comparison to indicate the powerful attraction this second pole exercised in London's development. For example Fleet Street, which belonged to the City, was the district of jurists, solicitors and attorneys and law students. It looked obstinately westwards. Furthermore the Strand, which was outside the City and which, some way away from the Thames, led to Westminster, became the district of the nobility. They established their houses there and soon another Exchange — a group of luxury shops — was opened there in 1609. Articles of fashion and wigs were the rage there from the reign of James I.

In the seventeenth and eighteenth centuries a broad movement pushed the town in all directions at once. Appalling districts grew up on the outskirts — shanty towns with filthy huts, unsightly industries (notably innumerable brickworks), pig raising, accumulations of refuse, and sordid streets. One such place was Whitechapel, where the wretched shoemakers worked. Elsewhere there were silk and wool weavers.

Fields disappeared from the immediate approaches to London except in the western districts where greenery crept in via the stretches of Hyde Park and St James's Park and the gardens of wealthy houses. In Shakespeare's and Thomas Dekker's day the town was still surrounded by green, open spaces, fields, trees and real villages where one could hunt duck and drop in at authentic country inns to drink beer and eat spice cakes or the *Islington White Pot*, a sort of custard which earned the village of Islington a reputation.

At that time 'the wind that blew in the outer districts of the capital', wrote Thomas Dekker's most recent historian 'was not always heavy and impure: in the theatres in the south, north and north-west there was all the gaiety of Merry England, and also its subtle and vibrant imagination which penetrated the suburbs . . . and the whole town'. Merry England, that is to say the England of the undisguisedly peasant centuries of the Middle Ages, was a romantic, not a false vision. But this happy relationship did not last.

The ever-expanding entity of London completed its split into two parts. The movement had begun a long time before. It accelerated after the Great Fire in 1666 which practically destroyed the heart, almost the whole of the City. Before this disaster (1662) William Petty had already explained that London, where the prevailing winds blew from the west, was growing westwards to escape

> the fumes, steams and stinks of the whole Eastery Pyle. . . . Now if it follows from hence that the Palaces of the greatest men will remove westward, it will also naturally follow that the dwellings of others who depend on them will creep after them. This we see in London where Noblemen's ancient houses are now become Halls for Companies, or turned into Tenements. . . .

A westwards slide of the London rich thus took place. If the centre of the town was still in the vicinity of Cornhill in the seventeenth century, today it is not very far from Charing Cross, at the west end of the Strand. It has shifted a long way.

The proletariat: Irish and Jews   Meanwhile the east and certain peripheral districts were becoming more and more proletarian. Poverty moved in and dug itself in wherever it found room in the London world. The darkest pages of the story concern two categories of outcasts: the Irish and the Jews from central Europe.

Irish immigration began early from the most famished districts of Ireland. The exiles were peasants condemned to a bare living at home by the land system and more still by the demographic growth that shook the island until the catastrophes of 1846. They were used to living with the animals, sharing their hovels with them, and feeding on potatoes and a little milk. Inured to hardship, not jibbing at any task, they regularly found work every haymaking time as agricultural workers in the countryside around London. From there a few pushed on up to London and hung on there. They crowded into sordid slums in the parish of St Giles, their fief, to the north of the City, lived ten or twelve to one windowless room and accepted wages well below the general rate, as dockers, milk carriers, labourers at the brickworks, even lodging-house keepers. Brawls broke out amongst them on Sundays during drinking sessions. And they engaged in pitched battles with the competing English proletariat.

The same tragedy was enacted with the Jews of central Europe, fleeing from persecution in Bohemia in 1744 and Poland in 1772. There were as many as 6,000 of them in England in 1734 and 20,000 in London alone in 1800. Against them was unleashed the most ugly and widespread hostility. Attempts by the synagogues to stop this dangerous immigration, which came via Holland, proved useless. What could these wretched people do once they arrived? The Jews already settled helped them but could neither drive them away from the island nor support them. London craftsmen rejected them. They were therefore of necessity dealers in old clothes and old iron — shouting through the streets, sometimes driving an old cart — as well as rogues, filchers, counterfeiters and receivers. Their late success as professional boxers, even as the inventors of a form of scientific boxing, did not restore their reputation, although Daniel Mendoza, a famous champion, founded a school.

The London drama — its festering criminality, its underworld, its difficult biological life — can truly be understood from this worm's eye view of the poor. It is to be noted, however, that the material situation on the whole improved, as it did in Paris, with street paving, water supplies, building controls and advances in lighting the town.

From London to Paris and back

What can we conclude? That London, alongside Paris, was a good example of what a capital of the *ancien régime* could be. A luxury that others had to pay for, a gathering of a few chosen souls, numerous servants and poor wretches, all linked however, by some collective destiny of the great agglomeration.

What did this common lot comprise? There was, for example, the dreadful filth and stench of the streets, as familiar to the lord as to the populace. It was probably the mass of the populace which created it, but it rebounded on everybody. Much of the countryside was probably relatively less dirty than the large towns until the middle of the eighteenth century, and the medieval city was a pleasanter and cleaner place to live in, as Lewis Mumford suggests. It did not sink under the weight of numbers, simultaneously bringing glory and poverty; it was wide open to the countryside and found its water locally inside its ramparts. In fact the enormous town could not cope with its ever-growing tasks or begin by assuring its elementary cleanliness. Security, the fight against fire and flood, supplies and public order took priority. And even if it had wanted to, it would have lacked the means. The worst material ignominies remained the general rule.

> The streets [a traveller tells us *à propos* Madrid (1697)] are always very dirty because it is the custom to throw all the rubbish out of the window. One suffers even more in winter because carts carry several barrels of water which are emptied into the streets in order to carry away the rubbish and let the filth run off; it often happens that one encounters torrents of this evil water which blocks one's way and poisons by its stench.

Paris was no better provided for. To walk in the streets was inevitably to get covered with mud because of the stream loaded with refuse running down the middle of the roadway. The 'height of the pavement' — which courtesy required be left for women and gentlefolk — along the houses offered better protection from this pestilential mud. But it was still necessary to hug the walls to avoid what was poured out of the windows. It was impossible to pay even a slightly ceremonial visit without taking shoes to change into — which was done in an antechamber — unless some means of transport was borrowed. At the beginning of the seventeenth century nobles and the fashionable world were still travelling around on horseback. Elegance required that this be done *en housse*, that is 'in silk stockings and [perched] on a velvet horse cloth'. Such was no longer the case by 1640 except for doctors and 'those who were not very well off'.

The vogue of the coach was launched. There were still no more than three or four in Paris in 1580, but now, if someone prided himself on elegance, 'one immediately asks: has he got a coach?'. Sedan chairs were then invented, economical because they were hired, as hackney carriages were hired later, and 'so useful in that having been shut up inside without dirtying oneself in the street, it can be said that one gets out as clean as out of a magician's box'.

All in all coaches and chairs were a guarantee of staying presentable when crossing the town as much as a means of transport. All the same everyone by this time was familiar with the smell of Paris — 'so detestable that it is impossible to remain there', said the Princess Palatine, desperate each time she had to leave Versailles for Paris. And visitors, even to the

Louvre or the Palais de Justice, still relieved themselves publicly, in broad daylight, at a bend in the corridor, without anyone bothering about it. The chambermaids at the Louvre, like everybody else, soiled the façades by throwing the contents of the night-commodes out of the windows.

And things only really changed with the nineteenth century. Viollet-le-Duc tells how in Louis XVIII's time — Versailles by then had made a few concessions to modernity — an old lady of the Court of Louis XV passed through a still foul corridor in the palace and regretfully exclaimed: 'That smell reminds me of a very beautiful time.'

Everything was due to numbers, excessive numbers of people. But the large town attracted them. Every person in his own way received a few crumbs from its parasitical life. And look at Paris: 'It attracts all the manufactured goods of the kingdom; but it has few factories because of the high cost of manpower . . . money rushes towards it in a great mass and all the more so in that it does not flow back to the provinces.' Paris 'sucks in all the goods and makes use of the whole kingdom. People there do not feel the calamities which sometimes afflict the countryside and the provinces.' But it was the same in Peking and Nanking, which were also snowed under with food and fruit from their countryside. London too continued to receive corn by boat from the Humber and coal by boat from Newcastle during the plague in 1665.

Their thieves themselves proved that there was always something to be gleaned from these privileged towns. Criminals inevitably gathered in the most luxurious of them.

In 1798 Colquhoun was deploring that: 'The situation . . . has changed materially since the dissolution of the ancient government of France. The horde of sharpers and villains, heretofore resorted to Paris from every part of Europe, will now consider London as their general and most productive theatre of action. . . .' Paris was ruined and the rats left the ship.

> The ignorance of the English language (a circumstance which formerly afforded us some protection) will no longer be a bar. . . . At no period was it ever so generally understood by foreigners; is the French language so universally spoken, by at least the younger part of the people of this country?

Town life and false prospects

There is no question of falling into step with such a sad conservative as Colquhoun. The enormous towns had their faults and their virtues. They created, let us repeat, the modern state, as much as they were created by it. National markets expanded under their impetus as did the nations themselves and modern civilisation which mingled its varied colours more in Europe every day. For the historian they are primarily a prodigious test of the evolution of Europe and the other continents. Interpreted properly, their study leads to a general and unusually comprehensive view of the whole history of material life.

On the whole what is at issue is growth in the economy of the *ancien régime*. The towns there were an example of deep-seated disequilibrium, asymmetrical growth, and irrational and unproductive investment on a nationwide scale. Was luxury — the appetite of these enormous parasites — responsible for it? This is what Jean-Jacques Rousseau says in *Emile*:

> It is the large towns that drain the state and create its weakness. The wealth they produce is an apparent and illusory wealth; it is a lot of money and little effect. It is said that the town of Paris is worth a province to the king of France; I believe that it costs him several of them; that Paris is fed by the provinces in more than one respect and that most of their incomes pour into that town and stay there, without ever returning to the people or the king. It is inconceivable that in this century of forward-looking people, there has been no one able to see that France would be much more powerful if Paris were annihilated.

This is of course an absurd comment, because the capitals of the *ancien régime* were not aberrant phenomena. They sprang naturally from the institutions of their times. We should rather say that the town was just not able to do better at that time, that it came up against obvious incapacities. It was, in Europe and elsewhere, what society, economy and politics allowed it to be. Suppose that a historian at the end of the eighteenth century, better informed than we are about the contemporary scene, had indulged in long-term forecasts. He would have asked himself whether these urban monsters in the West were not proof of a kind of seizing-up process analogous to what happened to the Roman empire with the deadweight of Rome, and China with the enormous inert mass of Peking in the far north; that is to say he would have asked if they were not ends of evolution instead of promises for the future, the forces they unleashed resulting in nothing more than themselves.

Such a judgment is obviously exaggerated. But it obsessed a historian of the calibre of Camille Julian, and 'the prose of the Roman Empire' which Hegel mentioned was after all the prose of its capital, Rome.

In any case it has been proved that these enormous urban formations are more linked to the past, to accomplished evolutions, faults and weaknesses of the societies and economies of the *ancien régime* than to preparations for the future. Werner Sombart saw the luxury of the large towns and states as an accelerator of capitalism. But what capitalism? Capitalism is protean, a hydra with a hundred heads. The obvious fact was that the capital cities would be present at the forthcoming industrial revolution in the role of spectators. Not London, but Manchester, Birmingham, Leeds, Glasgow and innumerable small proletarian towns launched the new era. It was not even the capital accumulated by eighteenth-century patricians that was to be invested in the new venture. London only turned the movement to its own advantage, by way of money, around 1830. Paris was temporarily touched by the new industry and then released as soon as the real foundations were laid, to the benefit of coal from the north, waterfalls on the Alsace waterways and iron from Lorraine. Sébastien Mercier's Paris was also the end of a material world. That which was born of the middle-class nineteenth century was worse perhaps for the working classes but it was no longer to have the same meaning.

4 English provincial towns in the early sixteenth century

W. G. Hoskins [1]

I

English historians have concentrated almost exclusively upon the constitutional and legal aspects of town development. They have concerned themselves with the borough rather than the town, with legal concepts rather than topography or social history, just as the agrarian historians have been preoccupied with the manor rather than the village. Local historians of towns and villages have, with two or three notable exceptions, followed suit in this ill-balanced emphasis. The result is that we know surprisingly little about the economy, social structure, and physical growth of English towns before the latter part of the eighteenth century.

Literary sources help us to form some idea about late medieval towns, but taken by themselves they can be misleading. Thus *The Italian Relation of England* [1], written about 1500, tells us that 'there are scarcely any towns of importance in the kingdom excepting these two: Bristol, a seaport to the West, and Boraco, otherwise York, which is on the borders of Scotland; besides London to the South'. English provincial towns may well have been small by Italian and Flemish standards but one cannot single out York for special mention without speaking equally of Norwich and Coventry, Exeter and Salisbury, Ipswich, Canterbury and Lynn, all of which were substantially wealthier than York at this date.

It is not until we come to Leland that we hear much of English towns in general, and even that is meagre and tantalising enough. Leland was an antiquary and was little interested in economic affairs. Many of his incidental descriptions of the countryside he traversed, and of the towns he visited, are of some value as contemporary evidence, but like most of his contemporaries he had eyes only for the cloth industry and for active markets, so far as economic matters were concerned. Repeatedly he tells us that a town 'standeth all by clothing' or is 'a good quick market', but beyond that he rarely ventures into the economic field; and where he does we may be led astray by his impressionistic picture.

Of Birmingham, for example, we are told that 'a great parte of the towne is mayntayned by smithes', who got their iron out of Staffordshire

W. G. Hoskins, 'English Provincial Towns in the Early Sixteenth Century', from *Provincial England*, Macmillan, 1963, Chapter 4, pp. 68-85.

and Warwickshire and their coal out of Staffordshire. We might be forgiven for envisaging Birmingham already as mainly a town of metal trades. The smiths, lorimers and nailers probably made more noise and show, but wills and tax assessments tell us that the wealthiest townsmen were still tanners and butchers, as in many other Midland towns. Leland in fact tells us very little about industrial and commercial England, valuable though he is as an occasional commentator; nor does he enable us to form the slightest idea of the comparative size and importance of towns.

If we wish to obtain an accurate picture of the English economy in the first half of the sixteenth century we must turn to the accounts and assessments of the lay subsidies of that period, above all to the comprehensive subsidies of 1523-27 and 1543-44; to the preliminary survey of 1522, in the few cases where it still survives; and, for some urban population figures, to the chantry certificates of 1545. These are the basic records that enable us to check and to amplify Leland's descriptions, and to place the towns in the order of their importance in the national economy.

This is no place to discuss the deficiences of the lay subsidy authorised in 1523 [2]. It is sufficient to say that it was by far the most comprehensive of any subsidy either before or after, that it was indeed the most all-embracing tax since the poll tax of 1377, and that, unlike that tax, it attempted a differential assessment of incomes from lands, of the capital value of personal estate, and of incomes from wages, all of which valuations bore some recognisable relationship to the true facts. It was a completely new valuation, abandoning altogether the assessments of the past which had become increasingly conventional and remote from reality [3]. The greater part of the subsidy was gathered in two instalments in the early months of 1524 and 1525 [4]. A third instalment in 1526 fell upon persons with lands to the value of £50 a year and over, and need not be considered in any account of the towns; and a fourth instalment, gathered in 1527, fell upon all who possessed personal estate to the value of £50 and more. I have used the totals of the first, second and fourth payments,

Table 4.1   Tax yield of London and 25 leading provincial towns in the subsidy of 1523-27 (to nearest pound)

London	£16,675	Lavenham	£402
Norwich	1,704	York	379
Bristol	1,072	Totnes	c. 317
Coventry	974	Worcester	312
Exeter	855	Gloucester	c. 307
Salisbury	852	Lincoln	298
Southwark	c. 790	Hereford	273
Ipswich	657	Yarmouth	260
Lynn	576	Hull	256
Canterbury	532	Boston	c. 240
Reading	c. 470	Southampton	224
Colchester	426	Hadleigh	c. 224
Bury St Edmunds	405	Shrewsbury	c. 220

so far as they are available, to draw up Table 4.1 showing the ranking, in order of taxable capacity, of the first twenty-five provincial towns, to which London has been added for the sake of comparison [5].

Neither Newcastle and Durham nor Chester and Carlisle were taxed in 1523. Of the economic importance of Chester, Carlisle and Durham we can form almost no idea; that they would have appeared somewhere in the above list is just possible. The omission of Newcastle is more serious, but can be rectified with some degree of confidence. In 1334 she stood third among the provincial towns in order of wealth, exceeded only by Bristol and York. Sixteenth-century musters, especially that for 1547, suggest that she was just about as populous as Bristol, and considerably more populous than York, Exeter, Salisbury and Coventry [6]. There can be little doubt that had Newcastle been taxed in 1523-27 she would have emerged as not lower than fourth among the provincial towns.

The preponderance of eastern England over the rest of the country was as marked in the early sixteenth century as it had been two hundred years earlier. If we define eastern England in its widest sense, to include what the geographers call the lowland zone, no fewer than sixteen of the leading twenty-five towns in 1334 lay in this half of the country, the remaining nine being divided equally between the Midlands, the west and the south. Two hundred years later the balance was much the same: fifteen of the leading twenty-five towns still lay on the eastern side, though there had been some internal changes of place; but there was also a noticeable tilting of the economic balance towards the west in the 1520s with the rise of Exeter, Totnes and Worcester. There had been other notable changes between the early fourteenth century and the early sixteenth. Most important of all was the greatly enhanced economic strength of London. Whereas in 1334 London had been just over three times as wealthy as the richest provincial town (Bristol), in the 1520s she was just about ten times as wealthy as Norwich, the leading provincial city, and more than fifteen times as rich as Bristol. Another remarkable change had been the emergence of Exeter and Coventry from comparative economic obscurity, and to a lesser degree of Canterbury and Reading, not to mention the two little cloth towns of Lavenham and Totnes.

In the main, the ranking of the towns according to their taxable capacity reflects also their ranking in terms of population, but there are some exceptions to this obvious rule where the presence of one or two exceptionally rich merchants inflated the wealth of the town dispro-portionately. We know little as yet about the population of the sixteenth-century towns, except at Coventry, where the mayor numbered the people in 1520 and made the total 6,601 [7]. London at this date had just about 60,000 people, possibly a little under [8]. Bristol pretty certainly had between 9,500 and 10,000 people, Exeter and Salisbury round about 8,000, Worcester about 6,000, Gloucester slightly over 4,000, Shrewsbury about 4,000. York, which had had nearly 11,000 people in the late fourteenth century, now had fewer than 8,000 in its four urban wards. For Norwich — the largest provincial city in both wealth and numbers — there is a lack of direct information, but the probability is that the city contained between 12,000 and 12,500 people in 1524 [9]. Thus only one provincial town in England contained more than 10,000 people, and not more than twelve or fourteen others exceeded 5,000.

A considerable number of towns, like Plymouth or Taunton, Northampton, Leeds or Wakefield, numbered from 3,000 to 4,000 people each, but the majority of active market-towns kept a consistent size with 200 to 300 households each, say from 1,000 to 1,500 people in all. In nearly every county one would have found half a dozen such towns. Even smaller were a number of towns that were nevertheless considered significant enough to be incorporated during the course of the century, towns such as Banbury, Bideford and Sutton Coldfield, with only six or seven hundred inhabitants each.

II

In certain towns one or two rich men dominated the place and gave it a standing which its numbers alone would not have justified. Coventry, Lavenham and Totnes are cases in point. Though only two-thirds the size of Bristol in population, Coventry ranked nearly as high in taxable capacity by reason of three rich men — Richard Marler, grocer, Julian Nethermill, draper, and Henry Pysford, merchant of the staple, all of whom were much wealthier than anyone in Bristol. Marler alone, one of the three or four richest merchants in provincial England, paid nearly one-ninth of Coventry's tax; and the three together paid a trifle more than a quarter of the total subsidy of the town. The little cloth town of Bradford-on-Avon in Wiltshire was completely overshadowed by Thomas Horton, one of the largest clothiers in the south of England. He paid no less than 70 per cent of the subsidy from the borough and was assessed at ten times the figure of the next wealthiest clothier. In the much larger town of Leicester, William Wyggeston the younger, merchant of the staple, was a similar magnate. He paid slightly over a quarter of the total subsidy. He and his cousin, William Wyggeston the elder, paid just under a third of the total subsidy between them. In the Suffolk cloth town of Lavenham, the eminent Thomas Spring III was equally dominant. He died shortly before the subsidy was levied, but the preliminary survey for it shows him to have been the richest man, other than some of the peerage outside London. At the time of his death he was lord of twenty-six manors in eastern England, and landowner in over a hundred others. His widow and daughter were assessed together on goods to the value of £1,333 6s 8d, still the highest assessment of any outside London and the peerage, and his son John at Bures, described as esquire, was assessed at the same time on £200 a year from lands [10]. At Lavenham the Springs paid 37 per cent of the total subsidy on goods in the town in 1524.

At Norwich, Robert Jannys, grocer, paid in subsidy practically as much as the entire city of Rochester and rather more than Richard Marler at Coventry; but in a larger and richer city he was not the same dominating figure as Marler. He paid one-fourteenth of the total subsidy, as against Marler's ninth. Similarly, at Exeter the merchant family of Crugge, represented by a widow and her son, paid one-tenth of the entire subsidy from the city in 1524.

In contrast to Norwich, Coventry and Exeter, neither Bristol nor Ipswich contained any over-mighty merchant family. At Ipswich the highest individual assessment was £300, at Bristol only £240. William Canynges, the most eminent provincial merchant of his age, had died fifty years earlier and his vast business had dissolved. Bristol had not collapsed or even gone into a decline as a result, because its economy was too broadly based; but in a lesser town the disappearance of a single dominating business or family, such as the removal of the Wyggestons from Leicester, might have a serious effect upon the whole community, above all in a time of economic and political changes when there were new opportunities waiting to be seized by energetic or visionary men.

The disappearance of the Canynges from Bristol illustrates, indeed, a general feature of the social and economic history of English towns, and that was the remarkable constancy with which successful urban families came and went in a matter of three generations at the most. No merchant patrician class ever formed in the English towns. Recruited largely from the younger sons of the free peasantry and the minor gentry of the adjacent countryside, the successful merchants returned to the land within a hundred years — usually much less — and their business dissolved into farms and fields, crops and stock. For a time, in the second and third generations, they might own a not inconsiderable amount of urban property, but there seems to have been no attempt to retain this at any time as a long-term investment.

It is sometimes said, and often implied, that the merchant class was recruited largely from landless men, often hardly better than vagabonds. Pirenne cites the remarkable case of Godric of Finchale, born of peasant stock in Lincolnshire towards the end of the eleventh century, who began his career as a beachcomber, made a lucky haul, started a pedlar's pack, and thereafter never looked back [11]. Such a start may have been commoner in the beginnings of mercantile society, but by the fifteenth and sixteenth centuries the successful merchant was far more likely to have started with a little property of his own, or at least with the financial and moral support of a franklin family behind him. Hooker's Commonplace Book at Exeter gives us potted biographies of all the sixteenth-century mayors, who were, with very few exceptions, merchants by calling. They had, again with few exceptions, come into the city from outside, some from far afield, from Wales, Cheshire, Suffolk and Worcestershire, others from the adjoining counties of Somerset and Dorset, and most from the Devonshire countryside. Of the Devonians who rose to be mayors of Exeter, the Periams, Hursts, Staplehills, Spurways and Peters, among others, were all members of franklin families with pedigrees and lands going back two or three hundred years; and those who came in from other counties were often similarly descended, like Richard Martyn (mayor in 1533), who was the second son of Sir Richard Martyn of Athelhampton in Dorset. It is significant that of all the mayors described by Hooker only one — Robert Tucker, mayor in 1543 — is described as 'of mean parentage' [12].

At Leicester, the substantial merchant family of Wyggeston had originated in the neighbouring village of Wigston whence they took their name, and where they had a pedigree and deeds going back well into the twelfth century. They had migrated to Leicester in the 1340s, but do not seem to have established themselves as considerable merchants until about a hundred years later. At Coventry, the immediate origin of the Marlers, who first appear in the town in the 1460s, is uncertain, but they are found as small landowners (perhaps of the peasant class) not many miles from Coventry in the early fourteenth century. London, too, recruited her merchant class to a marked degree from the younger sons of small landed families in the provinces — such as the Greshams of Norfolk, the Skevingtons of Leicestershire, the Cloptons of Warwickshire, and so on. They may have been landless in strict truth, but it was a considerable help to have behind one several hundred paternal acres and doubtless some liquid capital. In London and in the provincial towns the merchant class was constantly changing in composition, losing its successful members to the landed class and recruiting from the same class, though possibly from a lower level.

Once arrived in town, three generations usually sufficed to see the end of the commercial or industrial phase. There were three generations of Springs at Lavenham (*c.* 1400-1523), three merchant generations of Canynges at Bristol (*c.* 1369-1474), three of the Marlers at Coventry (1469-1540), three of the Wyggestons at Leicester (*c.* 1430-1536). It was rare for a successful merchant family to stay in town beyond the third generation: often they had left for a substantial country estate within two generations. This rapid extinction might be no matter for surprise in families that had achieved a comfortable fortune, but even among smaller and more humdrum businesses it seems to have been quite exceptional to go beyond the third generation. An examination of the Freemen's Register at Leicester [13], a great catalogue of the obscure, shows us that in the sixteenth and seventeenth centuries it was rare for any Leicester business to last a hundred years. The exceptions can certainly be counted on the fingers of one hand. Here it is not a matter of a large mercantile business being transmuted into lands, but of some more prosaic death from natural causes. The longevity of urban families and businesses would well repay further inquiry. Even below the ranks of the outstandingly successful, urban businesses were constantly changing in scope and personnel; and so consequently were town populations as a whole. The continual mobility of both urban and rural populations in the fifteenth and sixteenth centuries, and probably at an earlier period also, is very evident. Whether or not the labouring class was as mobile as the remainder of the population is another matter: the records of this class are particularly meagre. The poor have no annals, not even a tax assessment, that sad passport to immortality.

Urban property has been curiously little studied by economic and social historians in this country. In many continental cities, such as Arras, Barcelona and Lübeck, 'the upper layers of urban society in the Middle Ages sprang from the families which happened to own land in the towns in the early stages of their history, and got rich as the rents and land values of town property rose', but the history of this class is not everywhere so simple and uniform [14]. English towns have yet to be studied in this way, but even in the early sixteenth century it would be difficult to assert that urban incomes were derived to any noticeable extent from urban property, and equally hard to detect any sustained interest in urban property as an investment. If we may take the examples of the richest merchants in Bristol, Coventry and Exeter as a guide in this uncharted field, they do not suggest any marked, certainly not a prolonged, interest in such investment. It is true that William Canynges, at the time of his death in 1474, had accumulated fifty-five urban messuages among much other property, but there is no indication that his heirs kept this accumulation together. At Exeter, William Crugge, starting as a newcomer, had, at the time of his death in 1520, acquired nineteen houses in the city, which yielded £20 a year clear, but his son and heir had got rid of them all within a dozen years, while retaining most if not all the rural property. At Coventry, Richard Marler owned fifty houses in 1522, producing the respectable income of £41 3s 8d a year. A good deal of this was cottage property, let at rents of four to eight shillings a year, which suggests a deliberate investment policy, but again the accumulation was not kept together in the next generation [15].

The lack of any widespread or sustained interest in urban property investment is revealed again when the monastic property within the city of Exeter was thrown on to the market from 1539 onwards. Most of the leading citizens were but mildly interested in the acquisition of house property, and then only as potential warehouses rather than as residences. There is, however, some clear investment by a few in the middle years of the century, when five wealthy merchants bought ex-monastic house property to the tune of over a hundred pounds apiece. One merchant laid out no less than £309 16s 10d for property confined almost entirely to one parish and to tenements held at will [16].

Interest in urban property as an investment quickened noticeably later in the century, stimulated by the rapid growth of population, above all in the towns, in the last quarter of the century, and by the housing problems which this created. We must remember, too, that the comparative lack of interest in this field of investment in towns like Bristol, Exeter and Coventry in the late fifteenth century and the early sixteenth may well have arisen from the greater profitability of external and internal trading in particularly active towns. The house property market in such towns was extremely sluggish and uninviting, if we may judge by Norwich, where the act of 1534 for the re-edifying of void grounds within the city recites that a great number of houses had been destroyed in a fire twenty-six years earlier and had not yet been rebuilt. It would be interesting to discover in what kinds of towns, and among what kinds of people, urban property investment first becomes apparent to a noticeable degree. Stow has a number of references to building activity by Elizabethan merchants and shipwrights on the edge of London, particularly on the eastern side, and chiefly of cottage property for the swarming labouring population; and there are hints of building activity in the provinces about the same time [17].

III

When we turn to consider the occupations of English towns-people in the reign of Henry VIII, we are much in the dark, especially when we move away from the purely cloth towns. We know far more about the foreign trade of this country than we do of its internal economy, and more about the one great export industry at this time than about all the other industries put together. It is time we remedied this deficiency in our knowledge, and the following remarks are offered as a starting-point. They relate to a group of three Midland towns — Coventry, Northampton and Leicester — for which the necessary information is forthcoming, and they illustrate types of urban economy other than the purely 'cloth town'. At Coventry we are told the precise occupations of some 635 persons in the military survey of 1522; at Northampton the 1524 assessment for the subsidy gives us the occupations of 390 persons; and at Leicester the very full Freemen's Register serves the same purpose for several hundred persons round about these years [18].

We obtain a clear picture of the economy of these three towns if we list the twelve leading occupations in each:

Table 4.2   The leading occupations of three Midland towns in the early sixteenth century

	Coventry (1522)		Northampton (1524)		Leicester (1510-40)	
1.	Cappers	83*	Shoemakers	50	Butchers	27
2.	Weavers	41	Bakers	21	Shoemakers	24
3.	Shearmen	38	Tailors	20	Tailors	18
4.	Butchers	36	Weavers	20	Mercers	16
5.	Shoemakers	28	Tanners	15	Weavers	16
6.	Drapers	28	Mercers	15	Bakers	15
7.	Dyers	28	Butchers	14	Tanners	11
8.	Bakers	27	Glovers	13	Glovers	10
9.	Mercers	26	Fullers	12	Smiths	7
10.	Tailors	21	Drapers	9	Millers	7
11.	Tanners	15	Dyers	9	Barbers	7
12.	Smiths	14	Millers	9	Shearmen	7

* Includes 12 hatmakers.

It should be noticed that the Leicester figures cover a period of time (admissions to the freedom of the town) and that though the ranking of the occupations is comparable with that of the other towns, the individual totals are not.

Northampton and Leicester were towns of roughly equal size, with round about 3,000 people each in the 1520s. Coventry was rather more than twice as large, with 6,600 people. At Northampton, some sixty-three distinct trades are listed at this time; at Leicester about sixty, but here some may have escaped the Freemen's Registers; and at Coventry there were ninety separate trades. In Elizabethan Bristol there were over a hundred distinct trades for apprentices to choose from. If we group this diversity of occupations into certain well defined classes of trades, some profitable conclusions emerge. Coventry was primarily a textile town, though much less so than Lavenham in Suffolk, and of the three was the most markedly industrial in character. Northampton was less industrial in character, but showed a decided bent towards specialisation in the leather trades. Leicester had no marked industrial character, but a leaning towards the leather and allied trades was becoming evident by the first quarter of the sixteenth century.

When we consider the clothing trades, the food and drink trades, and the building trades, three groups which necessarily bulked large in any town economy, we observe an interesting similarity between the three towns which suggests a conclusion worthy of general application. The wholesale and retail clothing trades in each provided work for 14 to 15 per cent of the occupied population; the food and drink trades for 15 to 21 per cent; and the building trades for 4 to 7½ per cent [19]. These figures tend to suggest that in any English provincial town with the rudiments of an urban character, some 35 to 40 per cent of the population were employed in three fundamental groups of trades. Even in a more specialist textile town like Coventry, the proportion occupied in these trades is still as high as one-third. With results of this kind, we are beginning to get away from the stock picture of the cloth town and to appreciate something of the variety of urban economies.

Table 4.3   The trades of three Midland towns (classified as percentages of all occupations)

Trades	Coventry	Northampton	Leicester
Clothing	14	15	15
Food and drink	15½	15	21
Building	4½	7½	4
Leather (and allied)	11	23	19
Textile	33	13½	8½
Metal	8	3	3
Percentages of all occupations	86	77	70½

Minor, yet still significant, differences also reveal themselves in these towns, such as the marked leaning of Coventry towards the metal trades, which were roughly twice as important here as in the other two towns. Besides the universal smiths and pewterers, Coventry had girdlers, wiredrawers, nailers, cutlers, bladesmiths and locksmiths, spurriers and a spoonmaker. At Northampton, the building trades were appreciably more important than at Coventry and Leicester, the difference being due mainly to the greater number of masons and stone-slaters (helliers) in a town on the great belt of Jurassic building stone. It is curious to note, in passing, that timber building was replacing stone building in the town by the second quarter of the sixteenth century: Leland observes that all the old building is of stone, all the new of timber. Yet elsewhere it is stone building which replaces timber during the sixteenth century, as in the Cotswolds and in north Yorkshire for example. Is there some difference in the costs of town and country building at this date which would account for this apparent anomaly?

At Leicester the higher proportion of occupied persons in the food and drink trades is accounted for almost entirely by the particularly large number of butchers. Like the metal-workers of Coventry, the number of Leicester butchers suggests the development of a considerable market beyond the purely local. Unless the Leicester butchers were supplying meat to the London market, of which there is yet no evidence, they must have been more interested in providing hides for the local tanners than meat for the townspeople.

The size of local markets, and the magnitude of internal trade generally, is one of the more obscure aspects of English economic history. Unlike foreign trade, with its copious customs accounts and, later, port books, internal trade is documented only intermittently, as for example in lawsuits and occasionally in travellers' notebooks. But that it was vastly important even in the early sixteenth century is borne in upon one by a study of Leland's pages, in which he repeatedly singles out towns with markets above the ordinary level. In Northamptonshire, for example, Oundle was a particularly good market, and Wellingborough was 'a good, quik market toune', Berkhamsted is described as one of the best market towns in Hertfordshire; Kingston was the best market town in all Surrey. In the north, Manchester, with its two fair market-places, was the 'best buildid, quikkest, and most populus tounne of al Lancestreshire' — though in fact it had only about fifteen hundred people in the 1520s — and Leeds is described as having a more lively market than Bradford. Wakefield was better than either — so well served with meat and fish and all other victuals that an honest man could get a good meal for twopence.

Darlington and Wolverhampton were also specially commended by Leland as good market towns. Swaffham is described as 'one of the quikkest markettes of al Northfolk. . . . It stondith much by handy crafte men, and byers of grayne' — an unusually verbose entry for Leland which suggests that the occupational structure of Swaffham would be particularly interesting could we but unravel it [20]. Luton is noted as a specially good market for barley. The high importance of the weekly market in the life of most English towns is revealed, too, when the decay of a whole town, like Leominster, is attributed by Leland to the removal of the market; or when the unquestionable decay of Coventry by the middle of the sixteenth century is attributed by Dugdale to the dissolution of the religious houses of the town, which had attracted a great concourse of people to the town for the supply of their material needs [21].

The daily importance of shops and handicrafts is even more difficult to assess, but it is strongly suggested by the foregoing analysis of the three Midland towns, and indeed by a walk today around any small, non-industrial country town corresponding in size with its counterpart in Tudor England. We tend, I think, to overemphasise the exceptional features of economic life because the records are more voluminous in these fields. Economic historians at any rate should pay more attention to commonplace things — to the laundry bills, if you like, which H. A. L. Fisher so much despised — or at least to the humdrum tax assessments. The decline of the international fair in England is only one aspect of commercial history. Internal fairs may be less spectacular, but nonetheless important economically. Daily shops and weekly markets, consumer goods and services, servants and labourers, are no doubt all very dull to contemplate, but they are nearer to the truth of past urban economies than thoughtless clichés about cloth, wool and sheep.

We may put the comprehensive tax-assessment of 1524 to yet another use, and that is to ascertain the distribution of wealth in urban communities. It is possible, by comparing the preliminary survey — allegedly made for military purposes in 1522 — with the actual assessment of 1524, to discover what proportion of the town populations escaped the subsidy. At Coventry, for example, no fewer than half the population (699 out of 1,395 persons) were written off in 1522 as worth nothing in worldly goods. The subsequent tax assessment managed to rope in a few of them and to extract from each the minimum sum of fourpence; but even so some 48½ per cent of the population still escaped this sweeping subsidy. At Exeter, the only other sizeable town for which we have the relevant figures, the *nil* assessments amount to about 36½ per cent of the total population. The Exeter tax-collectors dug a little deeper into the pockets of the poor. At Leicester it has been calculated, from other records, that about one-third of the adult population escaped the net of the 1524 subsidy on the ground of poverty [22]. Thus in the larger towns of England at this date we may say that fully a third of the population — and considerably more in places — were so poor that they paid neither on the minimum level of wages nor the minimum level of goods. Poor widows were a large element in this propertyless class, as the Coventry survey shows: they were indeed the largest single class in that town.

Few wage-earners escaped the subsidy, and though the assessments vary from town to town in the carefulness of the definitions, we are able to ascertain the size of the urban wage-earning class with some degree of accuracy. When we discover that at Exeter those assessed on wages amount to 47 per cent of the taxable population, at Salisbury to 48 per cent, at Lavenham to 50 per cent, and at Dorchester to 43 per cent, we may feel some confidence in saying that in the larger English towns just about one-half of the taxable population belonged to the wage-earning class, most of them paying the minimum rate to the subsidy. If to these we add the lowest class of all, those without any recognisable means of subsistence, fully two-thirds of the urban population in the 1520s lived below or very near the poverty-line, constituting an ever-present menace to the community in years of high food prices or bad trade. The great mass of the wage-earning class clearly had no reserves at all with which to meet a bad spell.

These formed the broad base of the social pyramid in any given town. Roughly one-third of the population owned no property at all beyond the clothes they stood up in, the tools of their trade, and a few sticks of furniture: they lived at the level of Italian hill-peasants today. Another third of the population depended wholly or very largely on wages, and could exist with some degree of anxiety so long as work was regular and harvests about normal. Above this wide base, the pyramid rose through a middle class of prosperous artificers, merchants and professional men, to a needle-like point. Even in a semi-country town like Leicester, with no striking industrial development, we find that six families owned one-third of the taxable wealth of the town between them, and twenty-five persons, or 6 per cent of the taxable population, owned nearly three-fifths.

At Coventry and Exeter the facts are much the same. In the former, 2 per cent of the taxable population owned no less than 45 per cent of the taxable wealth, and 7 per cent owned just under two-thirds. At Exeter, too, about 7 per cent of the taxable population owned nearly two-thirds of the taxable wealth. At the other end of the social scale, two-thirds of the taxable population at Exeter paid the minimum rate to the subsidy [23]. Inequality in the distribution of worldly goods was already deeply rooted and strongly developed in English urban communities by the early sixteenth century, and marriage and inheritance had become powerful factors in the continuance and aggravation of this massive inequality. It is true that rich merchants died and no one might take their outstanding place in the town; that big businesses dissolved and passed away in the form of lands into non-urban hands; that the topmost point of the pyramid was periodically broken off. But this was only a temporary alleviation of the social tension. The oligarchy at the top of the social structure remained small and exclusive, and the wide and solid base of the pyramid did not grow any less.

The problem of poverty was one of the acutest of all domestic problems for the later Tudors, as the price-revolution took its course from the 1540s onwards. It was above all an urban problem, and it had little or nothing to do with the dissolution of the monasteries and the end of monastic alms-giving. The poor as a class had a far longer history, and there was already a tendency for them to be segregated within certain districts. Though there was still some mixture of social classes in the sixteenth-century towns, outside the one or two principal streets which had long been the preserve of the well-to-do, we find undoubted evidence also of the increasing separation of the poor in the extramural suburbs, and in back lanes and side-streets within the walled area. Certain parishes in old cities like York and Exeter were almost entirely populated by the labouring class in the 1520s, and other parishes were equally reserved for the plutocracy. Though still medieval in so many ways, the provincial towns of the early sixteenth century had some markedly modern characteristics, not least in the lineaments of their social structure.

Notes

Abbreviation: *PRO: Public Record Office*

1   *A relation, or rather a true account, of the isle of England, about 1500*, translated from the Italian by C. A. Sneyd (Camden Society, old series, xxxvii, 1847).

2   An account of the origin and incidence of the subsidy is given in the Introduction to *Suffolk in 1524: Subsidy Return* (Suffolk Green Books, no. x, Woodbridge, 1910). For the text of the Act of 1523, see *Statutes of the Realm*, vol. iii, pp. 230-41. The act did not extend to Queen Catherine, nor to the inhabitants of Ireland, Wales, Calais, Guernsey and Jersey. In England it excluded the English inhabitants of the Cinque Ports and the members thereof, the counties of Northumberland, Cumberland, Westmorland and Cheshire, the bishopric of Durham, the towns of Brighton and Westbourne, the wardens of Rochester Bridge, and the town of Ludlow.

3   There is no need to multiply examples; the treatment of Salisbury was typical enough of the new approach. In the tenth granted in 3 Henry VIII, Salisbury was called upon to pay £65 6s 10d. The lay subsidy in the same year yielded £143 16s 8d, while the subsidy of 1523-27 yielded £852 5s 7d.

4   All those assessed at £40 and over in lands or goods were required to pay the first instalment of the subsidy by way of an Anticipation in the autumn of 1523, but the tax so paid is included in the accounts and assessments of 1524.

5   The figures are extracted mainly from the totals returned to the Exchequer and may be found in PRO, Exchequer LTR, Enrolled Accounts (Subsidies), E 359/41. They have been supplemented where necessary by an examination of the particular assessments (E 179). Very occasionally both these sources fail to produce a complete answer, which accounts for the approximate figures attached to some towns in Table 4.1.

6   The quotas fixed in 1334 for the tenth, whenever it should be demanded, give as accurate a picture of the economic standing of the towns as we could hope for. They are conveniently gathered together in PRO, Exchequer KR Misc. Books, E 164/7. The details of the Newcastle musters in 1539 and 1547 are given in R. Welford, *History of Newcastle and Gateshead: sixteenth century* (1887), pp. 173-4, 244. There were 1,714 able-bodied men in the latter year. A conservative multiplier for arriving at the total population would be six, so that the town had rather more than 10,000 people in that year. Newcastle maintained her place as fourth among provincial towns during the seventeenth century. The number of hearths at Newcastle in 1662 was exceeded only by that at Norwich, York and Bristol (C. A. F. Meekings, *Dorset Hearth Tax Assessments, 1662-1664*, Appendix III (Dorchester, 1951)).

7   *The Coventry Leet Book*, ed. Mary Dormer Harris (1907-13), iii, 674-5.

8   J. C. Russell, *British Medieval Population* (1948), p. 298, suggests a population of 67,744 on the basis of the chantry certificates of 1545.

9   My estimates for Bristol, Exeter, Salisbury and York are based upon the taxable population in the 1524 assessments, as compared with the known Coventry totals. The estimates for Gloucester and Worcester are based upon the chantry certificates. For Norwich,

neither the chantry certificates nor the complete 1524-25 assessments survive, but I calculate (by comparison with the Exeter figures for 1524) that the complete Norwich assessment in 1524 would have contained about 1,320 names, giving a total population of just about 12,000. W. Hudson and J. C. Tingey, *Selected Records of the City of Norwich* (1906-10) vol. ii, p. cxxiv, say that 1,400 persons contributed to the subsidy of 1524 but give no authority for this statement. If it is correct, the maximum population for the city would be about 12,600.

10   Barbara McClenaghan, *The Springs of Lavenham and the Suffolk Cloth Trade in the 15th and 16th centuries* (1924), *passim*, for the possessions of Thomas Spring III. The Spring tax assessments of 1524 will be found in *Suffolk in 1524*, pp. 19, 24, 405. A transcript of the 1522 survey for Babergh hundred in Suffolk, which includes Lavenham, is to be found in the Ipswich public library.

11   H. Pirenne, *Economic and Social History of Modern Europe* (1936), pp. 47, 49, 163, 164. At Swaffham in western Norfolk there is a somewhat similar story about one John Chapman, a fifteenth-century merchant, who is supposed to have begun his successful career as a pedlar after finding (directed by a dream) a useful cache of goods. Such stories are not uncommon in other countries, and may have a considerable basis of truth, but they serve to show the rarity of the vagabond type becoming successful merchants rather than the opposite.

12   Exeter city records, Book 51, *passim*.

13   *Register of the Freemen of Leicester, 1196-1930*, ed. Henry Hartopp (2 vols, Leicester, 1927-31).

14   M. Postan, 'The trade of medieval Europe: the North', *Cambridge Economic History of Europe*, ii (1952), 172-3.

15   For Canynges's property see *The Antiquities of Bristow in the Middle Centuries*, ed. James Dallaway (1834), p. 192. For the Crugge property there are the wills and inquisitions post mortem of William Crugge and John Crugge in Somerset House and the PRO respectively. For Marler there is the survey of 1522 among the Coventry archives (Accounts Various, 18).

16   Joyce Youings, 'The city of Exeter and the property of the dissolved monasteries', *Transactions of the Devonshire Association*, lxxxiv (1952), 131, 139-40.

17   *Stow's Survey of London*, ed. Henry Morley (1893), pp. 375, 384, and *passim*. At Plymouth one of the principal merchants built a street which in 1584 was called 'Sperkes newe streate' and survives as New Street today. It was a middle-class street, judging by the remaining houses. At least two other streets in Elizabethan Plymouth were named after rich merchants, and the assumption is that they financed their building.

18   These figures cover most of the occupied persons in these towns. I have excluded from them all such general categories as labourers, servants and yeomen, who would, in any event, have been fairly evenly distributed among the principal crafts and trades of the town.

The Coventry survey has already been noted; the Northampton assessment is in PRO, E 179, 155/124.

19   Any system of classification is open to detailed objections, but in distinguishing the textile trades from the wholesale and retail clothing trades I have put the cappers and hatters of Coventry under textiles rather than clothing, as the trade was clearly producing mainly for an external market; and I have classified the shoemakers under leather and allied trades rather than clothing for the same reason.

20   The assessments for the subsidy of Swaffham do not give occupations (it is rare for these assessments to do so), and we know nothing more than Leland tells us.

21   Dugdale, in his *Antiquities of Warwickshire* (1656), observes that the city authorities purchased all the monastic lands in and near Coventry, and also all the lands of the gilds and chantries, but all this enterprise did 'not balance the Loss this City sustained by the Ruine of that great and famous Monastery, and other the Religious Houses. . . . For to so low an Ebbe did their Trading soon after grow, for want of such Concourse of People that numerously resorted thither before that fatal Dissolution, that many thousands of the Inhabitants to seek better Livelyhoods, were constrain'd to forsake the City.' The simultaneous decay of the cap and cloth trades was another important factor in Coventry's decline in these years.

22   The Exeter survey of 1522 is in the city archives (Misc. Book, 156a). It does not give occupations as the Coventry survey does, and is not so informative in other respects. The Leicester estimate is given by D. Charman in 'Wealth and Trade in Leicester in the Early Sixteenth Century', *Transactions of the Leicestershire Archaeological Society*, xxv (1949), p. 84.

23   For Leicester, see Charman, *op. cit.*, pp. 80-1. The figures for Coventry and Exeter are calculated from the 1524 subsidy assessments in the PRO.

5 Ceremony and the citizen: the communal year at Coventry 1450 – 1550

Charles Phythian-Adams

For urban communities in particular, the middle and later years of the sixteenth century represented a more abrupt break with the past than any period since the era of the Black Death or before the age of industrialisation. Not only were specific customs and institutions brusquely changed or abolished, but a whole, vigorous and variegated popular culture, the matrix of everyday life, was eroded and began to perish. At the very heart of social activity, before these changes were effected, lay the repetitive annual pattern of ceremonies and cognate observances peculiar to each local community. An enquiry into the contemporary relevance of such practices as a whole for a particular urban society may, therefore, help to promote a wider acknowledgment of the magnitude of the subsequent shift in the social and cultural environment.

Accordingly, this exploratory analysis will seek first to demonstrate some simple congruities between Coventry's late medieval social structure (that relatively enduring but adaptable framework of institutionalised positions and connective relationships) and its ceremonial or ritualised expression in action, in time – with respect to the local calendar – and on the ground. It will then become possible, secondly, to establish the extent and nature (rather than the social effects) of the subsequent change by briefly charting the rapid disintegration of what had once evidently formed a coherent ceremonial pattern.

Methodologically, such an approach is only possible if the evidence for unquestionably perennial customs may be extracted from a wide period. Here, however, in that minority of cases where the documentation is not contemporary, the evidence of survivals has not been trusted after 1640, and earlier justification for its use has always been sought where possible. While this reconstruction seems broadly appropriate to the century from 1450 to 1550, known structural modifications therein have had to be sacrificed at the altar of brevity. The picture probably remains truest for the generation living between 1490 and 1520 when the surviving evidence is peculiarly rich, and before the tempo of social change had been accelerated by the final collapse of the city's medieval economy [1].

Charles Phythian-Adams, 'Ceremony and the citizen: The communal year at Coventry 1450-1550', from P. Clark and P. Slack, eds, *Crisis and Order in English Towns 1500-1700*, Routledge, 1972, pp. 57-85.

Since the citizens of Coventry themselves were convinced that ceremonial proceedings like the Corpus Christi procession and plays contributed to 'the welth & worship of the hole body', it is first necessary to establish the composition of this entity whose welfare and dignity were thus promoted. That it included only those persons who shared the expense of attaining these ends, the members of craft fellowships, is put beyond dispute by the same and similar contexts. At this period, only the crafts had the power to admit those who would later be called Freemen; the city could merely register new apprentices and swear them to the franchise. Hence 'to be discomyned oute of this Cite' involved *inter alia* estrangement from a man's craft. Exclusion from the fellowship of building workers or journeymen dyers automatically meant the stigma of inferior status as 'only comen laborers' or mere servants. When all masters and journeymen annually processed in their respective companies at Corpus Christi-tide and on the eves of Midsummer and St Peter, therefore, the community in its entirety was literally defining itself for all to see [2].

There can be little doubt that practically every ceremony hereinafter to be discussed related to this restricted communal membership. In a total population of between 8,000 and 9,000 in 1500, all unqualified adult males, possibly 20 per cent of all householders to judge from extrapolating craft records, were excluded. So too, in effect, were all single females under forty. For all such women, whether or not they had served an apprenticeship, were specifically debarred from keeping house by themselves; in-service evidently being felt to be preferable even to their possession of a chamber, let alone a shop. Surviving lists of journeymen, moreover, contain no women's names. Marriage thus remained the only realistic avenue of admission to the community for females. It was therefore no accident that the wedding ceremonies of masters or journeymen were compulsorily attended by the groom's particular fellowship. In the case of the tanners, indeed, the journeymen were accustomed to attend the marriages of masters. But communal recognition clearly did not mean immediate occupational privileges even for a newly married woman. These probably had to await her (first) husband's demise — a fact which, no doubt, added a further level of meaning to the craft's attendance at his funeral [3].

Ceremonial occasions repeatedly underlined this peripheral status of wives. Men or boys played the female parts in the Corpus Christi plays and there is some evidence, at least from 1565, that the women sat separately in St Michael's, the larger of the two parish churches. Certainly it was unusual for them to be present at either gild or craft banquets with their menfolk. Master Cappers' wives rarely attended craft meetings until they were widows. Even 'the Mairasse & hir Sisters', the other civic officers' wives, dined apart from their husbands when the Queen sent a present of venison in 1474. An early seventeenth-century description of the mayoral inauguration, which evidently fossilised traditional practice, moreover, makes it clear that these ladies did not even attend the civic oath-taking. Instead, 'Old Mistress Maioris', the other officers' wives and the town sergeant, separately escorted the new mayoress to the church where they awaited the arrival of their husbands after the ceremony was over [4].

To all those outside or on the edge of the community, therefore, ceremonies must have been a constant reminder of its discrete and predominantly masculine identity. For those inside it, on the other hand, they were the visible means of relating individuals to the social structure. The sequence of oath-taking ceremonies, in particular, regularly punctuated the life cycle of the successful citizen from the moment he pledged himself to his city, his craft or his gild, to that later period in life when similar *rites de passage* admitted him to the authority which was the reward of advanced years. Initiation to the annually held senior craft office, some thirteen or fourteen years after joining, in the case of the Cappers for example, had a special significance in this last respect. For by the mid-sixteenth century, ex-officers were being termed 'the Auncente' or 'the moost auncient persones' of a craft — designations that implied more than official seniority when 60 per cent of the members of even a prosperous craft like the Cappers do not seem to have survived twenty years of membership, and at a period in which 'the best age' was considered over at forty. The civic sequence of office, furthermore, usually seems to have succeeded that of the craft except in the cases of the richest companies like the Drapers whose head masters appear to have been at least ex-sheriffs. Even though potential civic office holders often reached the top of their fellowships more rapidly than normal, it still took a further seventeen years on average to reach the appropriately designated position of 'alderman' from junior civic office [5].

The relevance of age to the oath-taking ceremonies, which accompanied every step on this ladder, was emphasised by the apparent timing of the citizen's progress through the two religious and social gilds of Corpus Christi and Holy Trinity. Usually within four years or so of being sworn to their fellowships, potential office-holders from the middling to wealthy crafts were pledging themselves to the junior gild of Corpus Christi. The composition of this fraternity seems to have been strongly biased to the less aged office-holders, a characteristic which was underlined by the admission of dependent young offspring of the city's elite. Despite the destruction of the Trinity Gild's register, there are indications that in mid-career, the successful citizen transferred from the junior to the senior fraternity. Certainly regular attendance at the former seems to have ceased at about the time a man assumed the shrievalty. Out of fifteen Cappers, moreover, who had held craft office prior to 1520, only six were still attending Corpus Christi gild banquets in or after that year, though all were yet alive. Since both fraternities were ostensibly focused on eternity, it seems reasonable to suggest that in such cases the same need was being met by the only alternative organisation available, the Trinity Gild. There remains, therefore, the strong implication that the senior fraternity was dominated by the ageing elite of the city — certainly the aldermen and probably the more elderly ancients of at least the wealthiest crafts [6].

The importance of this broad but basic age categorisation was brought out in inaugural ceremonies. In many crafts, authority was clearly conferred on new officers by the most senior members on behalf of the whole, the choice being made as with the Smiths by 'xij of the Eldest & discretest of the feliship'. In a rather more complex manner, the mayor and junior civic officers were secretly elected and sounded in mid-January by the aldermen, whose choice was formally rubber-stamped on the 25th at a purely ceremonial meeting of twenty-four men. Here, however, in those cases where it can be checked, attendance was divided between a contingent of more junior civic officers, particularly ex-sheriffs, headed by the Master of the Corpus Christi Gild who would himself be about to undertake the mayoralty within a year or two; and the ex-mayors, preceded by the Master of the Trinity Gild, who, by the early sixteenth century, was assuming his office immediately after relinquishing the mayoralty. When the civic oath-taking itself took place a week later, the ceremony heavily underlined the accountability of the new mayor to his senior colleagues. The incoming officers processed into St Mary's Hall where the retiring officers and aldermen were already symbolically in possession. At the culmination of the ceremony the new mayor was obliged to doff his hat, in the presence of the people, as a public gesture of deference to the old mayor and aldermen, 'intreating their loves and assistances'. Of the sheriffs and the coroner, on the other hand, he simply entreated assistance, while the junior civic officers and the rest were more tersely 'required' to do their duties [7].

Oath-taking ceremonies were thus of wider significance than purely technical exercises which related only to the specific institutions concerned; by following an established sequence, they also helped each time to transfer the initiate to another broad social age category. In a number of further ways, too, they invested office with solemn and social attributes over and above the practical demands of annual executive position. A corporate act of worship by all the participants, for example, seems to have been the normal custom at both craft and civic levels. In the early fifteenth century, the Tilers were accustomed to offer at High Mass in the White Friars before their election. The Mercers, on the other hand, were 'after election, to bringe the new Maister to churche' in Elizabeth's reign. The mayoral oath-taking ceremony, by the seventeenth century, was actually sandwiched between the first lesson and the sermon during morning prayer at the adjacent parish church of St Michael [8].

Such observances were not irrelevant in view of the officers' obligations. Medieval head masters of the Weavers were sworn, indeed, not only to be good and true to their craft but also to its chapel of St James the apostle. The mayor and his retinue were expected to attend church daily before the Reformation. As in other societies, furthermore, office was hedged with taboos. If even the job of town gaoler could be put at risk because its holder succumbed to the temptations of fornication, senior civic officers were specifically debarred in 1492 from adultery and usury as well. Regular worship and theoretically high standards of morality thus helped to legitimate authority in ways which transcended the group concerned [9].

Another seemingly supernumerary facet of inauguration ceremonies was the Choice Dinner. Either before the election as in the case of the Drapers, or after, like the Weavers and the Dyers (who in fact held a breakfast), it was customary for the old and/or new masters to bear at least a substantial proportion of the cost of a dinner for their company. After his oath-taking on Candlemas day, the mayor likewise had to throw a huge banquet at his own very considerable expense. Whether it was largely furnished by the incoming or the outgoing office-holder such an occasion was either the first or last formal exercise of his position. Despite subsidisation, however, it was also clearly meant to be an act of 'hospitality' and as such was an expression more of social than of official obligation and status [10].

The culminating procedure of inaugural ceremonies ensured that the citizen's new official status was unquestionably established outside the confines of his specific group in his own home neighbourhood. Most crafts probably observed the same custom as the Mercers who processed with the new masters 'from churche to the head-maisteres' houses'. Certainly the same effect was achieved when the master Dyers obeyed the order to fetch their under-master before the marching of the watch on Midsummer and St Peter's eves 'at hys howse, And from thence to goe to the head master's howse'. Likewise after the mayor's inaugural banquet, the civic body was accustomed to attend on the new and old mayors; first to the former's home, where the civic insignia, the sword and the mace, were symbolically deposited, and thence for the last time to the house of the retiring mayor. By making an officer's home a focus for his group, a man's social status outside it was also inevitably enhanced [11].

And indeed it was by the spectacular advertisement of specific status in general contexts that ceremony made its most vital contribution to the viability of the city's late medieval social structure. For office was otherwise unremunerative. Unpaid or underpaid and greedy of time, it was unpopular and hence compulsory on pain of fine for those elected. Apart from the possibility of future promotion and the actuality of present influence, therefore, the exaggerated social precedence of ceremonial occasions was an office-holder's basic reward. 'In every procession and all other Congregacions for Worschipp of the Citte and Welth of the seyd Crafte', the Weavers ordained in 1452-53, 'every man shall goo & sytt in order as he hath byn put in Rule of the seyd crafte.' Significantly, the worst punishment that could befall a contumacious ex-mayor after fine and imprisonment, was to be 'utterly abiect from the Counsell of the Citee & the Company of theym in all theire comen processions, ffestes, and all other assembles & from weryng of his cloke or skerlet in theire companyes'. In magnifying and publicising the importance of annually held offices, ceremony completed the transformation of wealth ownership into class standing for the upper levels of society [12].

It is therefore notable that the order of march laid down in 1445 for the massive processions at Corpus Christi and Midsummer was based not on a system of precedence reflecting some *economic* class division of society (which might, for example, have allotted an inferior position to the handicraftsmen), but on occupational groupings whose order was determined apparently by the contribution of each to civic office-holding. Leaving aside two misfits in this scheme — the combined fellowship of Pinners, Tilers and Wrights, and the craft of Weavers, who may have been the occasion of the ordinance — the order of precedence was simple. It began, in the junior position, with the Victuallers, all of whom, despite their wealth, were theoretically banned by parliamentary statute (even after 1512 at Coventry) from holding civic offices unless they suspended their occupations. Next came the leather and metal trades (though the identity of the latter grouping was somewhat blurred by the amalgamation of miscellaneous crafts with the fellowship of Cardmakers), neither of which were overly conspicuous for their tenure of offices. Last were the wool and textile occupations on which the prosperity of the city depended, culminating in the places of honour with the Dyers, Drapers and Mercers in that order. Not only were these the wealthiest companies in the city; they also furnished a disproportionate quota of its officers [13].

Civic office consequently lent prestige even to the crafts whose representatives held it, and though the order of march did not apparently vary with the occupation of the mayor, his own fellowship would often find a means of advertising its temporary prominence. As from 1533 the parvenu craft of Cappers aped a custom of the London companies by bearing a carnival-type giant, with illuminated eyes, through the dusky streets at Midsummer and St Peter's, on the increasingly numerous years in which their fellowship could boast any civic officer or Master of the Trinity Gild. Not to be outdone, the established company of Drapers in later years provided this titan with a spouse, though 'when Master Norton was mere' in 1554, they blasted off 12 lb of gunpowder [14].

Thus although ceremony obviously helped to transform the formal constitution of the city into some sort of social reality, conversely it was also a valued instrument through which the basic divisions of humanity, by sex, age and wealth, could be related to the structure of the community. In addition, ceremonial occasions often provided at least the opportunities for bringing together in celebratory circumstances those who might otherwise be opposed or separated in their respective spheres.

In this connection, little needs to be added to the preceding discussion of those almost wholly ceremonious institutions, the two gilds, whose formal non-charitable activities were restricted to the observance of obits and religious festivals, public processions, civic or gild inaugurations and regular sumptuous banquets. For the office-holding class, their membership cut horizontally, as it were, across those major vertical subdivisions of the community, the individual crafts, since there was no restriction by occupation. Even the seeming division into broad social age categories was significantly blurred within the junior fraternity. Only a minority of officers from the humbler crafts could afford to join it — between 1515 and 1524, for example, there were only five carpenters as members — and fewer still could have found the £5 admission fine to the Trinity Gild. As a result, elderly ancients, like the carpenter Robert Hammond, were to be found rubbing shoulders with the adolescent sons of aldermen at the proceedings of the Corpus Christi Gild [15].

The gulf between the senior civic officers and the current craft officers, whether or not they were gild members, was bridged at least twice during the year. It would seem that prior to 1545, the mayor at Midsummer and the two sheriffs at St Peter's were respectively accustomed to entertain at least the officers of the crafts after the marchings of the watch. The composition of the guests at these established 'drynkynges' is suggested in the craft accounts by gifts from the mayor of money for wine and cakes 'that we shold have had at Medssomer nyght' as from about that date: 'my wyn' as the head master of the Weavers once described it. There is, however, the further interesting possibility that whole fellowships were the beneficiaries of this largesse. The quantity of drink — three gallons or its equivalent cost the usual for the Weavers — would seem somewhat excessive even when, as in this instance, there may have been two rent-gatherers as well as the two keepers to help consume it. In fifteenth-century Bristol, all those 'persones of Craftes' who had actually attended the watch were to 'send ther own servantes and ther own pottes for the seide wyn', which was issued in quantities varying from two to ten gallons. Since some face-to-face contact does seem to be implied at Coventry, however, it is possible that the craft officers attended in person on their civic hosts in order to supervise the transfer of the bulk of the liquor for their members to imbibe elsewhere [16].

Evidence for structurally integrative commensality lower down the social scale is inevitably harder to find. But it is not impossible that other crafts practised the same custom as the Weavers, whose masters partook of a communal meal and drinking with their journeymen once a year in the early fifteenth century. Both Dyers and Smiths at least provided ale or wine for their journeymen at Corpus Christi, Midsummer and St Peter's [17].

On certain fixed occasions, however, commensality did express those topographical arrangements of the population which cut across formal social groups or groupings. For while in 1522-24 there was no mistaking the geographical concentration of some occupations in certain quarters of the city, even in the most extreme cases, the Butchers and the Cappers, there was considerable overlapping into different areas. To judge from ranking the wards by mean household sizes, other neighbourhoods, especially near the heart of the city, were similarly biased towards the wealthier levels of society, though none was totally exclusive. Taken as a whole, the social topography of Coventry was remarkable chiefly for the evident intermixture of all types of person [18].

It was this which gave significance to the social activities of the two huge parishes into which the city was divided. As elsewhere, the Holy Cake, for example, was consumed together in church by the parishioners after the celebration of Mass even in times of famine. On other occasions, in accordance with the instructions laid down for him in 1462, the first deacon of Holy Trinity was to serve the parishioners with 'bred & alle, and other thengs', at Mylborne's, Meynley's and other *diriges* 'made of the churche cost'. This is to say nothing of Whitsun ales and wakes at the feasts of dedication for which local evidence has yet to come to light [19].

A rather different kind of observance was the informal gathering around each of the bonfires that are known to have blazed on the streets during Midsummer and St Peter's nights. These occasions were widely acknowledged celebrations of neighbourliness. 'At Baptis-day with Ale and cakes bout bon-fires neighbours stood' carolled William Warner in his *Albion's England*, while at nearby Warwick, money was specifically bequeathed to the 'neyhboures of the other thre bonfyres' within a ward 'to make merry withall'. Stow stated quite categorically that in London, 'These were called Bone-fires, as well of amity amongst neighbours, that being before at controversie, were there by the labour of others reconciled, and made of bitter enemies, loving friends'. Topographical groupings when expressed in such convivial ways must have helped at least to encourage cross-cutting ties within the social structure [20].

Just as customary commensality served to promote cohesion within the community, so tensions stemming from rigidities within the social structure seem to have been provided with institutionalised outlets. The most clearcut example of what amounted to periodic relaxations of the social order was the Coventry Hock Tuesday play. The structural implications of this are perhaps best revealed by comparison with the practices of May Day, since these two occasions involved distinctly contrasted social age categories. May Day everywhere was, of course, primarily a festival of unmarried young people, the 'Maides and their Makes', as Ben Jonson characterised the Coventry participants; while Hock Tuesday concerned the women or the wives. In view of the markedly inferior status with regard to the opposite sex which females incurred as a consequence of the oath-taking ceremony of marriage, it is hardly surprising that the contrast between these two traditional observances was complete [21].

On May Day the relationship was one of equality expressed in friendly dance. The preoccupation with courtship and love-making hardly needs emphasising, but it is worth drawing attention to an aspect of popular symbolism which lay at the core of that seasonal rite. This was the widespread custom whereby yearning maidens on May Day in particular, and at other relevant moments in their lives, sported articles of clothing conspicuously embroidered with blue thread, for blue was the universal symbol of constant love. This simple practice, to which Coventry's dyeing industry traditionally catered and lent the term 'Coventry blue' because of its appropriate permanence, underlines what was probably a basic feature of May Day: the deliberate pairing-off by couples for the holiday as opposed to the unselective promiscuity implied in the more fevered castigations of certain Puritans [22].

By contrast, the Hock Tuesday play used the anonymity of a *generalised* division of the sexes to reverse temporarily the *in*equalities existing between married men and women through the medium of conflict. This play-cum-mock-battle, in celebrating the putative historic overthrow of the Danish yoke by the citizens of Coventry in particular, culminated in a much diluted dramatisation (with no doubt a reduced number of participants) of the rural custom by which the wives of the parish were accustomed to bind and/or heave the menfolk before releasing them on payment of a ransom. At Coventry, after the men had fought out the battle, the play harped on 'how valiantly our English women for loove of their cuntree behaved themselvez', and how the Danish warriors having been beaten down 'many [were] led captive for triumph by our English weemen'. For once there is no doubt that women did take part; references to feminine costume hire amongst the expenses of special performances of this play before Queen Elizabeth are conspicuously absent [23].

If relationships between the sexes concerned everyone in the community at an informal level, the position of mayor was the keystone in the formal structure of office-holding. It is, therefore, notable that at Christmas-time the mayoral dignity probably fell victim to institutionalised ridicule. Coventry then seems to have emulated that annual custom of a Lord of Misrule which was also to be found at Court, in great households, university colleges and the Inns of Court [24].

Now it may be that this personage represented or came eventually to represent no other function than that of 'Master of Merry Disports' or superintendent of the revels, a purely prestigious adjunct to the seasonal festivities and hence to the standing of the host. Yet there are a number of pointers which suggest that there may have been more to it than this. The very title, for example, indicates that he was Lord not of *un*ruliness and licence, though this may have been and indeed possibly was a consequence of his activities, but of *mis*-rule or mis-government. Early commentators like Polydore Vergil and Selden, moreover, were emphatic that Christmas was a season when the master of the house abdicated his position in order to obey or wait upon his own servants, one of whom would act as the Christmas Lord during the festivities. In the restricted context of a great man's home, some connection between misrule at Christmas and the normal sway of the household head (whether in a public or private capacity) during the rest of the year could hardly have been avoided [25].

It is in these circumstances that the urban version of this custom must be judged. For it is evident that Lords of Misrule pertained only to civic governors and not to other rich merchants or tradesmen. At Coventry and Chester they were associated with the mayor; at London with both the mayor and the sheriffs. It may also be significant that at Coventry in 1517 the Lord himself was one of the civic sergeants. Since mayors' sergeants were to be found at this time in the Corpus Christi Gild they clearly belonged to the office-holding class, and so may have been considered suitably dependable candidates for the festive post. Alternatively, there may even have been some form of deliberate status elevation within the body of civic officers for the duration of the holiday. Either way, the indications are that within the confines of his household or even elsewhere, the civic ruler had to be seen or known to put temporarily aside his formal status, in order to become, instead, the subject of satirical government: hence perhaps in part, the open house kept by the mayor for the whole twelve days at Coventry, at least in 1517, and the public processions of the London sheriffs with their respective Lords of Misrule through the streets of the capital [26].

The only other time of the year at which the social barriers were lowered was the period of early summer. In this instance it was the classic antipathy between town and country which was expressed, the sanctity of private property that was annually violated and the privileged immunity of the local landowning class which was breached. For the festivities of Midsummer, St Peter's and probably May Day required the lavish decoration of houses, halls and streets with birch boughs and blossoms, quite apart from Maypoles, all of which were most conveniently procured without permission or payment from nearby estates. Thus, when in 1480 the Prior of Coventry complained that every summer his underwood was being taken, the mayor had to invoke a widespread custom in answering the charge, 'remembryng that the people of every gret Cite, as London & other Citeez, yerely in somur doon harme to divers lordes & gentyles havyng wodes & Groves nygh to such Citees be takyng of boughes & treez, and yit the lordes & gentils suffren sych dedes ofte tymes of theire goode will'. In like manner the citizens of Leicester hacked down timber for use on May Day in the woods of Sir Henry Hastings in 1603, while the gardens of the gentry in the neighbourhood of Nottingham were being ransacked for flowers at Midsummer up to the reign of Charles I. It seems that at such times everyday rules did not apply, while the privileged class, whose interests normally ensured their preservation, was expected to acquiesce passively in their flagrant transgression [27].

The significance of all these practices lay not in the ways in which social tensions were haphazardly released but in the methods by which they were controlled. In the first place, such observances appear to have been the means of canalising traditional periods of licence — a process which seems to have been completed at Coventry during the fifteenth century. The Hock Tuesday play, created in 1416, for example, was clearly a deliberate urban rationalisation of contemporary bawdy practice in the rural Midlands generally. Accordingly Hock Monday, when the men usually bound the women in the country, withered away completely in an urban environment to become merely the Monday before Hock Tuesday. Local evidence for Christmas licence does not survive, but it is worth noting in passing that if Lords of Misrule did not originate during the fifteenth century, they only seem to have become generally popular towards its end. Midsummer and St Peter's were, however, indubitably times of extreme disorder and even riot. It was as a necessary response to this that the Prior of Coventry and other worried ecclesiastical dignitaries had suggested the inception of a special watch in 1421 to control 'the grett multytude of peopull' and to avoid the 'grett debate and man-slaughter and othure perels and synnes that myght fall, and late have fallen'. There is no evidence before 1445, however, that their recommendations were accepted [28].

These customs, secondly, had built into them, as it were, certain safeguards for the preservation of the structure. In all cases those in subordinate roles encroached in some way only on certain *attributes* of socially superior positions. At Hocktide representatives of the women overcame the menfolk in their unaccustomed masculine role as warriors and not as husbands or householders. In summertime the towns-people did not specifically attack the gentry class; they merely appropriated its property. Even at Christmas, the Lord of Misrule seems to have been a bad ruler rather than a 'mock mayor' or 'mayor of misrule'. If such customs deliberately distorted certain aspects of the social order, there was no question of altering the whole: in disfiguring the structure temporarily, the participants were in fact accepting the *status quo* in the long run [29].

And it was perhaps this emphasis on preserving and enhancing the wholeness of the social order which most distinguished the ceremonies of this late medieval urban community. In a close-knit structure composed of overlapping groups or groupings, where a change of status in one sphere so often could affect standing in another, ceremony performed a crucial clarifying role. It was a societal mechanism ensuring continuity within the structure, promoting cohesion and controlling some of its inherent conflicts, which was not only valued as contributing to the 'worship' of the city, but also enjoyed by contemporaries. Even in times of crisis the plays were performed and the watches marched. If anything, before 1545 the tendency was not to cut back on over-costly trappings but to preserve and elaborate them. A reforming Mayor in the 1530s was quite unable to stop accustomed drinkings even when craftsmen were being ruined by the expense. Feelings in favour of the Hock Tuesday and Corpus Christi plays, or some substitute for them, survived their formal abolition, and some way of observing Midsummer and St Peter's evidently outlived the watches. But the real significance which contemporaries attached to such practices may be better gauged by turning now to the cultural, temporal and spatial contexts in which they took place [30].

The citizen's year was marked by rather different seasonal quarter-ings to those which, according to Homans, characterised the openfield husbandman's calendar. At Coventry, the beginning of the year seems to have been determined by the long-standing tradition by which the city's Lammas pastures reverted to private hands on 2 February, the date at which the mayoral inauguration had also come to take place and from which the mayoral year accordingly began. It is more than probable that, as elsewhere, May Day was accepted as the start of summer, and the reopening of the Lammas lands to common pasturing on 1 August as the beginning of autumn. Judging from lighting regulations, winter was thought to lie between 1 November and 2 February. It seems indeed to have been a function of the city waits to emphasise this seasonal and predominantly pastoral framework. With the exception of the first quarter when they played from the first week in Clean Lent through to Easter, the waits performed nightly during the first part of each of these quarters, up to Midsummer, Michaelmas and Christmas respectively [31].

Cutting clean through this seasonal sectionalisation of the calendar, however, was another division of the year. In this instance, subdivision was by halves: a bisection made possible by that evident unity of the six months between 24-25 December and 24 June inclusively (182½ days), which stemmed from an oft-noted coincidence of Christian and archaic native practice. In the case of the Church, the outcome was to cram all the major observances connected with the birth, life, death and resurrection of Christ into these six months, the unity of which is still roughly expressed when reference is made to Christmas, Easter and Whitsun in preference to a strictly calendrical ordering. Even the movable feasts were tied in a way to Christmas: Lent could begin as early as 4 February, only two days after the feast of the Purification, logically the last rite of Christmas. Similarly, at the latter end of the moiety when Easter fell at its latest, the feast of Corpus Christi, the culminating festival of the cycle, coincided with Midsummer Day. Whatever the date of Easter, it seems reasonable to suggest that the very movability of the greatest feasts of the Church, and the universal custom of relational dating thereto, helped to invest the whole of this period with an appreciable quality of its own [32].

Through their origins and practice, moreover, native popular observances served to emphasise this unity. The widespread acceptance of the end of December as pertaining more logically to the succeeding than to the current year, for example, had its origins in remote antiquity: according to Bede, the heathen year, which also broke down into two halves, had begun on 25 December. In later times, the twelve days, of course, remained inseparable from Christmas itself and so acted as the connecting link with the following year. Events on each of these days were commonly seen as predictive of the weather or fortunes of the succeeding twelve months [33].

Such popular attitudes served also to bridge the gap between Christian observances. At Norwich, Lent was ushered in by the King of Christmas on Shrove Tuesday 'in the last ende of Cristemesse', 'as hath ben accustomed in ony Cite or Burgh thrugh al this reame'. In like fashion did native customs span the interval, when there was one, between the end of the movable Church cycle and Midsummer. There are indications, for example, that May games were played in London up to 24 June (though a command performance was once held on the following day before Queen Elizabeth). It may be significant in this connection that at the Coventry Midsummer watch in the 1550s, the Dyers' contingent was attended by a herdsman blowing his horn and someone 'carrying the tree before the hartt' — probably a reference to a 'company' of morris dancers with a maypole and other props. A relevant confusion in popular thought was also criticised by one puritan preacher who claimed that 'What offences soever happened from that tyme [Rogation] to Midsommer, the fumes of the fiers dedicated to John, Peter, and [though uncelebrated at Coventry] Thomas Becket the traytor, consumed them'. Any attempt at analysing popular culture has to take into consideration the ways in which religious and vulgar symbolism thus complemented each other and often merged into one [34].

Particularly notable in this respect was the manner in which the contrasted symbols of fare and vegetation were accepted in Coventry, as elsewhere, by both Church and layman alike during this temporal moiety. If at Christmas time, Holy Trinity church was ablaze with extra candles, the Smiths' craft also specifically employed 'iij tapers at Crystmas & a candle ageynst xij day', while both church and craft sported the obvious evergreens, holly and ivy. There is no need to dwell on the relevance of Candlemas, the ritualised burning of 'palm' leaves on Ash Wednesday, the bearing of 'palms' on Palm Sunday, nor on the hallowing of fire in church at Easter. The use of fresh foliage to decorate the city at the summer feasts has already been indicated as have the Midsummer bonfires. It is worth emphasising, however, that half the point of the marching watch seems to have been literally to carry fire through the streets. Each craft had its own special cresset bearers for this purpose, probably an urban echo of that rural custom of rolling burning wheels down hills to mark the summer solstice [35].

Also to be found in these six months were the extremes of sacred and profane drama with their common themes of birth, death and rebirth, and their corollary sexual relationships. Though Christmas mummers are not evidenced, the parish churches dramatised Palm Sunday with the unveiling of the Rood and Easter Day with the resurrection from the Easter sepulchre, while the crafts performed their plays at Corpus Christi. The intersex dramas or ritualised games of Hocktide and May Day have already been discussed, but as at nearby Leicester and Stratford-upon-Avon, it is likely that the procession which marked St George's Day (23 April) was also enlivened by some representation of the traditional fight with the dragon. A courtly version of what would probably have been stock practice was the highlight of Prince Edward's visit to Coventry on 28 April 1474 to observe a late St George's feast. This showed a King and a Queen 'beholdyng seint George savyng theire doughter from the dragon', a very similar tableau being presented before Prince Arthur in 1498 [36].

This temporal unit was further characterised by pronounced polarities in everyday activities and behaviour. On the one hand were the long period of Lenten diet, the accompanying civic enforcement of personal morality — the aldermen were specifically ordered to punish 'bawdry' during Clean Lent — and, more often than not, the eight-day Corpus Christi fair, that annual apogee of the city's economic endeavour. On the other were the traditional periods of licence and the only major extended holidays in the year. An obviously pre-Reformation ruling in a later sixteenth-century recension of the Cardmakers' ordinances was probably representative in permitting neither

> Cutinge, prickyng, doublyng, Crooking, nor Settinge, within the xij dayes at Christmas neyther at any Satterday, at after noone, after one of the clock, neyther on any Vygill Even after the same houre, . . . neyther shall they woork at any of the poynts above specyfyed in Easter weeke, neither in Whitsune week. . . . [37].

The contrast with the six months between 25 June and about midday on the vigil of Christmas (182½ days) was absolute. In this period there was no religious or popular symbolic coherence, there were no institutionalised extremes of behaviour and there were no extended holidays. Essentially this was a time for uninterrupted, normal economic activities, some of which, even in a city the size of Coventry, were still dependent on rural rhythms. The Lammas pastures could only have been free for use on 1 August if, as elsewhere, the hay harvest began at Midsummer, while the grain harvest made the few Michaelmas lands similarly available. More germane were the completion of sheep-shearing by mid-June and the wool sales which followed: new supplies may have been reaching the army of wool and textile workers soon after Midsummer. Similarly, if somewhat later in the year there was no early winter slaughtering in the locality to bring supplies of meat into the city, there were, very probably, sales of surplus stock well before Christmas. The importance of this generally drier season for travel, finally, emphasises the conspicuous number of fairs which at least the merchants might have wanted to attend. Coventry seems to have belonged to a minority in holding its own fair before Midsummer in nearly all years [38].

It is thus difficult to doubt the existence of a marked pre-Reformation dichotomy of the year, the two halves of which it is surely no exaggeration to denominate for convenience as respectively 'ritualistic' and 'secular'. It must be stressed, however, that this is to suggest not that the former necessarily saw a general slowing down of economic activity, but rather that the same routines continued to be carried out against an abnormal background. When ceremonies occurred in this half, they did so in a heightened context which was wholly absent in the secular moiety. It is therefore relevant to enquire into what sorts of ceremonies were most usually associated with each, leaving aside those largely administrative occasions which recurred half-yearly or quarterly like the ordinary meeting of crafts or the court leet, and arbitrarily fixed events like obits.

With this obvious proviso it is an interesting comment on the value attached to the ideal of local community, that the ritualistic half embraced every major public ceremony (St Peter's eve excepted) which formally interrelated separate whole groups or groupings of the social structure. Even as late as the seventeenth century, all the festival days on which the aldermen were to wear their scarlet fell in this period with the only exceptions of two post-medieval additions, 1 November and 5 November [39].

This emphasis on the ritualistic half was further brought out by the frequency of processions and occasions which, in so far as separate ceremonies pertained to similar structural relationships, seem to have been concentrated into sometimes overlapping temporal blocs. The half began by expressing the relation of the civic body to the community. If the retiring mayor was burlesqued over Christmas, his successor and junior colleagues were chosen and then approved in January prior to their inauguration before the citizens at Candlemas in, appropriately, St Mary's Hall. On the morrow of Lenten mortification, it was the turn of those socially cohesive topographical groupings, the parishes, which, from as early as the Palm Sunday processions through the entire Easter celebrations, seem to have been the unrivalled foci of ceremonial activity. It is even conceivable that the two sides in the Hock Tuesday play (ten days after Easter) originally represented the two parishes which, in any case, came into their own again with the normal Rogationtide processions. Hock Tuesday, however, could fall on any day between 6 April and 3 May, only two days after that other celebration of intersex relationships, May Day itself [40].

At this juncture the gilds and probably the civic body began to dominate the scene. There is some evidence to suggest that both gilds processed with their cross-bearers on St George's Day (23 April), Ascension (which fell between 30 April and 3 June), and Whit Sunday (10 May to 13 June). It is more than probable that the mayor and his brethren were associated with the first and, certainly in company with the commonalty, the last, which was indeed still an official festival day for aldermen in 1640. Not that the parishes were excluded — Holy Trinity, at least, also fielded its cross, banner and streamers on all three days [41].

The ceremonial activities of this ritualistic half reached a spectacular climax with four processions: on Corpus Christi day (21 May to 24 June), the following day — Fair Friday, Midsummer eve, and (for the sake of analytical continuity, though it belonged strictly to the secular half) five days later on St Peter's eve. In all of these, of course, the civic body was accompanied by the craft fellowships or, in the case of Fair Friday alone, two or three accoutred representatives [42].

In a very real sense the community thus ceremonialised itself *vis-à-vis* all its major activities, with a changing emphasis on worship, work and particularly authority. The ritualistic half may have begun with a parody of government, but it ended with the mayor processing as the king's representative backed by a token armed force provided by each company.

In more general fashion the frequent ultraformalisation of group inter-relationships throughout this half was conspicuously balanced by the structurally distortive customs of Christmas, Hocktide and Midsummer, which fell broadly at the beginning, middle and end of the period in question. It is thus tempting to see such practices as representing in this instance, not the exact opposite of everyday life, as has been suggested on general grounds by Dr Leach, but rather of communal ceremonialisation. For *both* ceremony *and* structural distortion operated on an exaggerated plane which was quite distinct from normality: the former idealised and the latter inverted social norms. Conceptually they complemented each other [43].

Whereas during the ritualistic half the component groups of the community were ceremonially interrelated in public, throughout the secular period the parts, on the whole, ceremonialised themselves in private. Perhaps to avoid the interruption of the next ceremonial 'season', this half was primarily concerned with the election of those officers who, unlike the mayor, could not be regarded as symbols of the community as a whole. Both gilds, for example, then elected their masters; the Trinity Gild on 18 October and the Corpus Christi Gild on 8 December. Ten out of the fourteen fellowships for which information survives or can be inferred, furthermore, also elected their officers in the secular half. There even remains, in some cases, traces of an occupational pattern. The elections of the 'textile' crafts, for instance, seem to have been fairly closely bunched. The Cappers who began in 1496 with 26 July, later changed to 7 August in 1520, while both the Weavers and apparently the Fullers favoured 25 July. The accounts of the latter were usually rendered on 23 November, a popular date for this, and the same day as the Dyers, the date of whose elections may thus be broadly inferred. By contrast, the Cordwainers and Tanners elected on or near 9 October and 16 October respectively, while the new master of the Butchers held his inaugural dinner on the 18th of the same month [44].

All the four fellowships whose elections overlapped into the ritualistic half chose their officers between Christmas and New Year's Day. The Tilers, who elected on 26 December (although the St Stephen's Day in question could conceivably have been 2 August), represent the only serious aberration in an otherwise remarkable overall pattern. The leet ordinance on the hybrid character of the fellowship of Cardmakers, Saddlers, Masons and Painters probably explains their date (29 December) during the holiday period when either disputes might in theory, perhaps, have been more easily avoided, or a mutually convenient date on which to meet, most readily found. Clearly the Mercers and Drapers, on the other hand, whose dates fell on 27 December and 31 December, had to fall in line with the elections to civic office which were due to take place during the succeeding month [45].

Differences between the two halves of the year were not restricted to the varying ceremonialisation of social structure, however; there were also significant contrasts in the actual territory over which open-air ceremonies took place. This was partly due to the peculiar topography of Coventry. For, firstly, at its heart lay what was virtually a single vast churchyard containing not only the two parish churches, but also the

Cathedral priory. Flanking it were the bishop's palace, and halls for priests, as well as the major civic administrative buildings like St Mary's Hall and the gaol, and finally the huge covered cloth-market, the Drapery. Since the approach to the cathedral and the circuits around the parish churches were mostly if not all known as 'procession ways', it is clear that this whole consecrated area constituted a ritual centre for the city. It is therefore noteworthy that the ceremonies in the early part of the ritualistic period were mainly confined to it. The mayoral inauguration was focused on St Michael's Church and St Mary's Hall, while the parochial processions around the churchyard on Palm Sunday, the Easter celebrations and quite possibly rather more elaborate occasions, as at Whitsuntide, were likewise restricted [46].

The city, secondly, was triangulated by gild chapels: the chapel of St Nicholas which belonged to the Corpus Christi Gild lay just outside Bishop Gate to the north-west; that of the Trinity Gild, St John Bablake, was situated just inside the Spon Gate at the western end of the city; and the unique craft-cum-gild chapel of St George which pertained to the Shermen and Tailors was attached to Gosford Gate itself, on the eastern side. Most probably, each of these was the departure point or destination of a major procession in the latter part of the ritualistic half. That at Corpus Christi must have started from St Nicholas chapel, where the host would have been consecrated, before proceeding through the streets until it reached what seems to have been the first pageant station at Gosford Gate where the plays were to begin. Since the Feast of the Nativity of St John the Baptist was the dedication day of the Trinity Gild chapel, and since the mayor who presided over the procession was accustomed to visit Bablake 'overnight' for *dirige*, 'dyvers consideracions & other great busynes', it is very possible that the riding on Midsummer's eve began there. (It will be recalled that following the watch, which evidently did not start until after dark, he was engaged in entertaining at least the craft officers.) More probably still, the St George's Day procession, after leaving Bailey Lane which skirted the churchyard centre, would have included a visit to the only chapel dedicated to that saint in the city and to an area customarily connected, at secondhand, with the chivalrous slaughter of monsters. A bone of the fabulous boar slain by Guy of Warwick hung at Gosford Gate, while a few hundred yards up the hill outside was a chapel dedicated to yet another dragon dispatcher, whose fame was locally celebrated, St Margaret [47].

During the ritualistic half, therefore, there seems to have been a movement of formal ceremony from the centre outwards to the limits of the city but no further. Nearly every other observance during this moiety was similarly confined. Hocktide games took place 'in' the city and not on adjacent waste ground; maypoles stood over the streets; bonfires burnt on them; 'pageants' trundled through them. The one part-exception would have been the Rogationtide processions which traced the parish boundaries outside as well as within the city. Such practices are not only a reminder that medieval streets were as important for recreation and marketing as for communication; rites and processions, like the carriage through the streets of the Corpus Christi host or the Midsummer fire, periodically added a mystical dimension to this utilitarian valuation of the immediate topographical context. While doing so, they underlined further the physical inescapability of communal involvement [48].

Though somewhat mitigated by the fewness of the occasions, a contrast was provided, once again, by the secular half. Here the emphasis was on the surrounding countryside, the city's fields and the *County* of Coventry. Communal participation, moreover, was attenuated. Attendance on the Chamberlains' annual Lammas ride (1 August), to oversee the renewal of common access to pasture land, for example, was restricted as from 1474 to those appointed, and after 1495 to representatives from each ward. What theoretically became a triennial activity as from 1469, the riding of the metes and bounds of the County of Coventry, also seems to have taken place in the secular half. If the intention to ride before the Michaelmas leet was sometimes announced at its Easter predecessor, the only surviving exact dates indicate that the execution was left to the last possible moment: 4 October in 1509 and 26-27 September in 1581. On the latter occasion, the party included not only a number of aldermen, sheriffs, other civic officers, and 'yonge men appoynted', no doubt as guardians of the future, but also 'dyvers others of everie Townshipp sommune within the forrens'[49].

The correlation between town and country, which seems to have been associated with this moiety, was emphasised in another way. For to accommodate the demands of the Exchequer year, the sheriffs for the county were sworn and so designated at the Michaelmas Leet in the secular half. When the same men appeared at the following Easter Leet in the ritualistic half, however, they did so only in their *civic* capacities as 'bailiffs'. It may not be too farfetched to suggest, therefore, that the marching of the watch on St Peter's eve in the first week of the secular half may have had an extra-urban bias. It was conducted by the sheriffs and not by the mayor; fines for non-attendance by craftsmen were, at least in one instance, less severe than at Midsummer; the city Weavers do not even seem to have participated; and there appears to have been no formally defined order of march by crafts. It is thus just possible either that there may have been some progression from township to township or, more likely, that county representatives joined the civic procession. Such an explanation might help to account for the overlap of this ritualistic activity into the secular half of the year [50].

Taken as a whole, however, Coventry's calendar seems to betray a conspicuous correspondence between social structure and its ceremonial-isation in time and space. That observances occasionally overlapped their temporal contexts cannot be denied, but by and large the intricate regularity of the pattern is remarkably clear. Reconstructed, it bears mute witness both to the communal quality of a late medieval urban society, particularly the evident subordination of the parts to the working of the whole, and to the pervasive role of the pre-Reformation Church and its practices in that community. Such a reconstitution also highlights the extent of the subsequent change: the destructive impact of the events of the mid-sixteenth century and the consequent obliteration of the estab-lished rhythm of life itself.

The modernisation of this late medieval framework was characterised by the triumph of the secular half over its ritualistic counterpart as, one after another, the principal ceremonies vanished. The important processions of St George's Day, Ascension, Whitsun and Corpus Christi were either unrecognisably altered or later abolished by the amalgamation of the Corpus Christi Gild in 1535 with the Trinity Gild, and their subsequent dissolution in 1547. At the same time, St George's chapel was probably abandoned though the Shermen and Tailors survived as a craft fellowship. Like London and Bristol, Coventry then also secured some respite from the summer watches, officially relinquishing that on St Peter's in 1549, though the last riding at Midsummer does not seem to have taken place until some fourteen or fifteen years later. Meanwhile, in 1552, a new October fair had been granted, and during the very year that the Queen had foisted a Catholic mayor on the city (1556), the mayoral inauguration had been moved from Candlemas to 1 November, a date with fewer papistical overtones. A first attempt at abolishing the Hock Tuesday play seems to date from 1561, but the insistence of the citizenry ensured its spasmodic resurrection thereafter. Thirty years later it was finally moved out of context to St Peter's eve, when its performance was theoretically to be restricted by confinement to the stages of the Corpus Christi 'pageants'. The sacred plays, for which these theatrical waggons had originally been designed, were last acted in 1579. For a few years, however, they were replaced by a safe Protestant substitute which, in 1591 at least, seems to have been performed at Midsummer. With the removal, finally, of all maypoles from the city in the same year, the ritualistic half no longer existed as a recognizable unit for both church and society [51].

The changing venue of ceremony was itself indicative of the nature of this momentous alteration in the yearly round. The only open-air ceremonies to survive, for example, were now justifiable on technical grounds alone: to proclaim the fair or to perpetuate the boundaries, of parish, field or county. With the emasculation of popular practices at May Day, Hock Tuesday or Midsummer, profane rites and even a recreation, like football in 1595, were banished from the streets. The Queen's highway was left to its purely materialistic functions. If the opportunity for popular participation in public rituals was consequently largely removed, that especial meaning which sacred ceremonies and popular rites had periodically conferred on the citizens' tangible environment also fell victim to the new 'secular' order. Ceremony and religion together withdrew indoors from the vulgar gaze. The formalisation of social structure was now passively restricted accordingly to the hierarchical seating arrangements within the parish churches. As a result, that unknown proportion of the population which bothered to attend them was automatically divided [52].

For, most significantly, formal communal processions had totally disappeared. The nearest the later sixteenth century could come to former practices was the Fair Friday display with its minimal craft representation. Indeed, until the days of the later Godiva procession (which in origin bore all the hallmarks of an advertising stunt), formal communal involvement of any sort was restricted to the annual mayoral inauguration, a largely indoor affair. The civic body may have ceremonially observed certain church festivals, but there is no evidence that anyone else took part [53].

The leading representatives of that simultaneously adjusting social structure, who had helped to bring about all these changes, may have belonged to a wider cultural and economic environment than their predecessors, but at least in one respect their societal horizons were narrower. By the seventeenth century the claims of the community, at this level, were yielding first place to class loyalties. With this development, the annihilation of what had evolved into a ceremonial system in the late medieval period, was closely connected. It was no accident that the elaborate official inaugurations which had characterised the old secular moiety alone survived untarnished, in the post-Reformation world, to dominate the altered and abbreviated ceremonial calendar of the Coventry citizen.

Notes

Abbreviations   *APC: Acts of the Privy Council; Bodl.: Bodleian Library, Oxford; LB: The Coventry Leet Book; LP: Letters and Papers of Henry VIII; VCH: Victoria County History.*

1   I am particularly grateful to Professor W. G. Hoskins under whose sympathetic aegis this investigation was begun while the author was Research Fellow in English Local History at the University of Leicester between 1966 and 1968; to Messrs A. A. Dibben, D. J. H. Smith and colleagues for multifarious assistance far in excess of their statutory duties; and to the Company of Cappers and Feltmakers of Coventry for permission to study their earliest account book. A full-scale study of Coventry society between 1480 and 1660 on social anthropological lines, which will amplify matters only touched on here, is currently in preparation. Unless otherwise specified all MS references relate to the Coventry Record Office.

2   M. D. Harris, ed., *The Coventry Leet Book (LB)* (Early English Text Society, 1907-13), p. 556; *ibid.*, pp. 655, 560; *ibid.*, p. 294; *ibid.*, pp. 653, 694; *ibid.*, p. 417; T. Sharp, *A Dissertation on the Pageants or Dramatic Mysteries Anciently Performed at Coventry (Dissertation)* (Coventry, 1825), pp. 22, 79-80, 161, n.f. 182-3; accession 241, original fols 2v., 4; cf. p. 78, below.

3   See my forthcoming study of urban population change in late medieval England with particular reference to Coventry 1480-1540; accession 100: Weavers 11 (unfol.), quarterage payments and journeymen's groats 1523-1537; A5, fols 152r., 164r., 173r.; Cappers and Feltmakers' Company MSS, first account book (Cappers' accs), fols 67v., 68r., 70v., 71r.; *LB*, pp. 568, 545; *ibid.*, p. 249; Cappers' accs fols 68r., 71r.; A5, *loc. cit.*; Weavers 2a, fol. 2v.; Weavers 2c, journeymen's orders; A99, fol. 2r.; accession 241, original fols 2v.-3r.; Weavers 2a, fol. 4r.; A5, fol. 1r.; cf. L. Fox, 'The Coventry Guilds and Trading Companies with Special Reference to the Position of Women', in *Essays in Honour of Philip B. Chatwin* (Oxford, 1962), pp. 13-26.

4   Accession 100: Weavers 11, 1524; A166 (with acknowledgment to Professor R. W. Ingram), extracts from St. Michael's vestry book; cf. A98, 'For comyng to the Churche'; A6, *passim*; Cappers' accs *passim*; *LB*, pp. 405-6; A34, fol. 269r.

5   *LB*, p. 560; Bodl. MS. Top Warwick c. 7 (Reader), fol. 118r.; A5, fol. 2r.; G. Templeman, ed., *The Records of the Guild of the Holy Trinity, St. Mary, St. John the Baptist and St. Katherine of Coventry* (Dugdale Society, XIX, 1944), p. 31. Calculations from Cappers' accs have been made on the basis of 'New Brethren' up to 1513. Weavers 2a, fol. 6r.; A98, rules 6 and 3; A110, rules 11, 13, 28; *LB*, p. 792; Reader 92v.; Bodl. MS. Top Warwick d. 4, fol. 19v.; accession 154, *passim*; Capers' accs, *passim*; *LB*, calculated from all those serving as warden or chamberlain between 1490 and 1520. Coventry's gerontocracy will be fully discussed in the larger work mentioned in n. 1.

6   Calculated for all Cappers in A6 between 1515 and 1524; Cappers' accs *passim*; A6, fols 206r. *et seq.* A microscopic examination of gild membership has yet to be completed.

7   *LB*, p. 743; *LP*, xii, 108; *e.g. LB*, pp. 604-5; A6, fol. 148r.; A34, fol. 269r.

8   Reader, fol. 217r.; A99, fol. 16v.; A34, fol. 269r.; Reader, fol. 100r.

9   Weavers 2a, fol. 7v.; *LB*, p. 662; *ibid.*, pp. 279, 544; M. Fortes, 'Ritual and office in tribal society', in M. Gluckman, ed., *Essays on the Ritual of Social Relations* (Manchester, 1962), pp. 82-3.

10   Phrase used in 1615, A98 (unfol.); Reader, fol. 92r.; Weavers 2a, fols 5v., 6; Reader, fol. 117r.; *LP*, xiv (1), 77; cf. Reader, fol. 100.

11   A99, fol. 16v.; Sharp, *op. cit.*, p. 183; A34, fol. 269v.

12   *LB*, p. 107; Templeman, *op. cit.*, p. 173; *LB*, pp. 619-21, 676-7; Weavers 2a, fol. 2v.; *LB*, pp. 670, 743; Weavers 2a, fol. 3v.; *LB*, p. 648.

13   *LB*, p. 220; *Statutes of the Realm*, 3 Hen. VIII c. 8; *LB*, p. 533; Templeman, *op. cit.*, p. 6, n. 5, the Mercers' Craft included Grocers, Merchants and perhaps Vintners.

14   G. Unwin, *The Gilds and Companies of London* (fourth edition, 1963), p. 269; Cappers' accs fols 45v. *et seq.*; *LB*, *passim*, and A7(a), *passim* — in a minority of years the junior civic officers cannot be ascertained; Sharp, *op. cit.*, pp. 203-5; accession 154, p. 34; the Drapers' possession of a male giant cannot be proved.

15   Templeman, *op. cit.*, pp. 152-9, 179-84; A6 and A5, *passim*; Templeman, *op. cit.*, p. 178; A6, fols 226r., 225r.; A5, fols 38v., 60r., 106v.

16   *LB*, p. 779; accession 100: Weavers 11 (unfol.) 1544, 1550, 1557; A5, fol. 140r.; E. W. W. Veale, ed., *The Great Red Book of Bristol* (Bristol Record Society, 1933), i, 125-6.

17   *LB*, p. 94; Sharp, *op. cit.*, p. 181, n.p.

18   A96; *Public Record Office* E 179/192/125; 1523 census; Phythian-Adams, *op. cit.*

19   J. C. Cox, *Churchwardens' Accounts* (1913), p. 58; *LB*, p. 669; T. Sharp, *Illustrative Papers on the History and Antiquities of the City of Coventry (Antiquities)* (corrected by W. G. Fretton, Birmingham, 1871), p. 123.

20   *LB*, p. 233; G. C. Homans, *English Villagers of the Thirteenth Century* (New York, 1960), p. 375; Sharp, *Dissertation*, pp. 175-6.

21   B. C. H. H. Percy and E. Simpson, eds, *Ben Jonson* (Oxford, 1941), vii, 785; Cox, *op. cit.*, pp. 64-5, 261-3.

22   Percy and Simpson, *op. cit.*, p. 785; J. Brand, *Observations on the Popular Antiquities of Great Britain* (1841), ii, 69, 59, 75, 80; B. Poole, *Coventry — its History and Antiquities* (Coventry, 1870), p. 358; Brand, *op. cit.* (1859 edition), i, 213.

23   E. K. Chambers, *The Mediaeval Stage* (Oxford, 1903), i, 155; Poole, *op. cit.*, pp. 51-2; Sharp, *Dissertation*, p. 128.

24   Chambers, *op. cit.*, pp. 403, 407, 418.

25   *Ibid.*, p. 403; Thomas Langley, *An Abridgemente of the Notable Worke of Polidore Virgile* (?1570), fol. *Cr*.; Sir F. Pollock, ed., *Table Talk of John Selden* (1927), p. 28.

26   British Museum, Harleian MS 6388, fol. 28v.; Chambers, *op. cit.*, p. 418; A6, fols 216r., 217v., 218r., 221v., 223r.; J. G. Nichols, ed., *The Diary of Henry Machyn* (Camden Society, xlii, 1848), pp. 28, 274.

27   *LB*, p. 233; Sharp, *Dissertation*, pp. 179-80; *LB*, p. 455; W. Kelly, *Notices Illustrative of the Drama and other Popular Amusements chiefly in the Sixteenth and Seventeenth Centuries, . . . Extracted from . . . Manuscripts of the Borough of Leicester* (1865), pp. 102, 72, 99; C. Deering, *Nottinghamia Vetus et Nova* (Nottingham, 1751), p. 124.

28   F. Bliss Burbidge, *Old Coventry and Lady Godiva* (Birmingham, n.d.), p. 218; n. 23, above; Brand, *op. cit.*, pp. 184-91; Cappers' accs fol. 68v.; cf. J. Latimer, *Sixteenth Century Bristol* (Bristol, 1908), p. 10 and Brand, *op. cit.*, p. 377; most early references to Lords of Misrule are sixteenth century: Chambers, *op. cit.*, pp. 403-18, cf. p. 173; *LB*, pp. 35, 220.

29   M. Gluckman, *Order and Rebellion in Tribal Africa* (1963), chap. iii; E. Norbeck, 'African rituals of conflict', *American Anthropologist*, lxv (1963), 1254-75; P. Rigby, 'Some Gogo rituals of "purification" — an essay on social and moral categories', in E. R. Leach, ed., *Dialectic in Practical Religion* (Cambridge, 1968), pp. 153-78; V. W. Turner, *The Ritual Process* (1969), pp. 170-8, 183-5.

30   Phythian-Adams, *op. cit.*; Cappers' accs fols 24r., 26v., 29v.; accession 100: Weavers 11, 1523; cf. Cappers' accs fols 24r. and 94r.; *LP*, xiv, 1, 77; A14(a), p. 216.

31   Homans, *op. cit.*, p. 354; E. O. James, *Seasonal Feasts and Festivals* (1961), p. 309; *LB*, p. 777; Sharp, *Dissertation*, p. 211.

32   James, *op. cit.*, pp. 291, 230, 225-6, 207-25.

33   M. P. Nilsson, *Primitive Time-Reckoning* (Lund, 1920), pp. 294-5; Chambers, *op. cit.*, pp. 247 n. 3, 269; Brand, *op. cit.*, pp. 478-80.

34   W. Hudson and J. C. Tingey, eds, *The Records of the City of Norwich* (1906), i, p. 345, n. 2, and unconvincing assertions, p. xc; Nichols, *op. cit.*, pp. 20, 89, 137, 201; cf. J. Godber, *History of Bedfordshire* (Luton, 1969), p. 170; Sharp, *Dissertation*, pp. 200-1; Brand, *op. cit.*, p. 308.

35   Sharp, *Antiquities*, pp. 123-4; Reader, fol. 84r.; accession 154, p. 41;
      cf. Brand, *op. cit.*, p. 305; Sharp, *Dissertation*, p. 184; Homans, *op.
      cit.*, pp. 369-70.

36   James, *op. cit.*, p. 272; cf, *LB*, p. lii, n. 12; Sharp, *Antiquities*, pp.
      122, 124; Kelly, *op. cit.*, p. 47; E. I. Fripp, ed., *Minutes and
      Accounts of the Corporation of Stratford-upon-Avon* (Dugdale
      Society, i, 1921), p. xix; *LB*, pp. 393, 590-1.

37   *LP*, iv (3), Appendix I; J. C. Jeaffreson, *Coventry Charters and
      Manuscripts* (Coventry, 1896), B48; Reader, fol. 95v.

38   Homans, *op. cit.*, p. 370; P. J. Bowden, *The Wool Trade in Tudor
      and Stuart England* (1962), p. 22 and cf. pp. 86-7, 91; P. J. Bowden,
      'Agricultural prices, farm profits and rents', in J. Thirsk, ed., *The
      Agrarian History of England and Wales* (Cambridge, 1967), p. 621;
      Alan Everitt, 'The marketing of agricultutal produce', *ibid.*, p. 533;
      F. Emery, 'The farming regions of Wales', *ibid.*, p. 121; H. P. R.
      Finberg, 'The genesis of the Gloucestershire towns', in H. P. R.
      Finberg, ed., *Gloucestershire Studies* (Leicester, 1957), pp. 86-8.

39   A14(b), p. 6.

40   Above, pp. 60-1, 67-8; Sharp, *Antiquities*, pp. 120, 122-3; cf. James,
      op. cit., pp. 300-4.

41   Sharp, *Dissertation*, p. 161; Templeman, *op. cit.*, p. 158; Poole, *op.
      cit.*, p. 211; A6, fol. 322r.; *LB*, pp. 588-9, 299-300; A14(b), p. 6;
      Sharp, *Antiquities*, p. 120. The evidence seems to be against a
      number of separate processions on each day. At Whitsun, for
      example, the gilds would hardly have segregated themselves from the
      Mayor's procession which contained their two Masters.

42   Above, p. 63; Reader, fol. 33. The Corpus Christi Gild may have
      processed as a separate entity on its major feast day, but no
      provision was made for this in Craft ordinances (e.g. accession 241,
      original fol. 2v.). There is evidence for processional activity by the
      Gild on the vigil: A6, fol. 325r.

43   Sharp, *Dissertation*, pp. 182-3, 192-5; Turner, *op. cit.*, pp. 168-9,
      176-7; E. R. Leach, *Rethinking Anthropology* (1966), p. 135; E. R.
      Leach, *Political Systems of Highland Burma* (Boston, 1965), p. 286.
      The logical opposite of everyday behaviour in Dr Leach's schema
      should surely be disguise or masquerade — even holiday as opposed
      to work.

44   Cf. Templeman, *op. cit.*, p. 157; *ibid.*, pp. 159, 152; A6, fols 332v.,
      347v.; *LB*, pp. 573, 670; Weavers 2a, fol. 6 and cf. fol. 5v. and
      accession 100: Weavers 11 (unfol.) 1523 expenses; accession 30, pp.
      10, 17; Reader, fol. 117r.; A98, rule 3; accession 241, original fol.
      4r.; Reader, fol. 100r.; *LB*, p. 743; A110, rules 22 and 20; A5, fol.
      21r.

45   Reader, fol. 217r.; *LB*, p. 205; A99, fol. 2r.; Reader, fol. 92r.

46   *LP*, xiii (2), 674; *VCH Warwickshire*, viii, 329; J. Speed, *Theatre of
      the Empire of Great Britaine* (1611), fols 49v.-50; Poole, *op. cit.*, p.
      203; A24, pp. 33, 32, 29; *LB*, pp. 460-1, 264, 299, 588; Sharp,
      Antiquities, pp. 122, 120; Cox, *op. cit.*, pp. 253-8; *LB*, p. 299.

47   Hardin Craig, ed., *Two Coventry Corpus Christi Plays* (Early English
      Text Society, E.S. 87, 1957), pp. xiii-xiv, 84-5; *LB*, p. 558:

significantly, a number of 'pageant houses' were conveniently sited nearby, e.g. *ibid.*, p. xiii, n. 2, A24, p. 8; Poole, *op. cit.*, p. 211; above, p. 64; *LB*, p. 589; Speed, *op. cit.*, fol. 49r.; *LB*, pp. 738, 291-2.

48   Poole, *op. cit.*, p. 90; A14(a), p. 216; *LB*, p. 233.

49   *LB*, pp. 843, 565; *ibid.*, pp. 348, 571, 622, 628, 821 — a special survey.

50   *Ibid.*, pp. 271-2 *passim*; *ibid.*, p. 791; Sharp, *Dissertation*, p. 182; accession 100: Weavers 11, Expenses 1523, *passim*; *LB*, p. 220; cf. Brand, *op. cit.*, pp. 337-8.

51   *LB*, pp. 722-3; cf. A99, fol. 2 (pre-1551: *ibid.*, fol. 2v.); *VCH*, *op. cit.*, p. 332; *APC*, new series, i, pp. 447, 422, and cf. Cappers' accs fol. 72; *LB*, p. 791; Sharp, *Dissertation*, p. 201 and cf. accession 100: Weavers 11, fols 53 *et seq.*; A5, fols 185r., 187r.; *Calendar of Patent Rolls, Edward VI*, iv, 380; *APC*, new series, v, p. 218; Bodl. MS Top Warwick d. 4, fol. 20; Craig, *op. cit.*, pp. xxi-xxii; A14(a), p. 216; *VCH, Warwickshire*, viii, 218.

52   A3(b), p. 13; Bodl. MS Top Warwick d. 4, fol. 36; A98 (unfol.) 'For comynge to the Churche'; Poole, *op. cit.*, p. 157.

53   Cf. accession 100: Weavers 9 (unfol.), 1622; Bliss Burbidge, *op. cit.*, p. 256; Cappers' accs fol. 208v.; A14(b), p. 6.

6   The social and trade structure of Norwich 1525–1575*

J. F. Pound

Some ten years ago, Professor Hoskins discussed the sources for a study of the social and trade structure of English provincial towns in the early sixteenth century, pointing out the value of the subsidy rolls for 1523-27 in this respect. As examples, he dealt with the economy of three Midland towns — Coventry, Leicester and Northampton — from both aspects [1]. Subsequent studies have been made of Exeter, the country towns of Buckinghamshire, Rutland and Sussex and of small towns in Devon [2]. Valuable as these studies are, they have all, necessarily, been written more from the point of social than trade structure and we know very little more about the occupations of English townspeople.

This article hopes to redress the balance to some extent. The complete subsidy roll for 1525 survives for Norwich, after London the largest and wealthiest town in England; and the names and assessments of those who paid the Anticipation in 1523 and who were sufficiently wealthy to contribute in 1527 are also available. The information contained therein can be related to the city's register of freemen to obtain a clear picture of the social and trade structure of early sixteenth-century Norwich. Other sources, which are discussed below, enable us to attempt a comparison of this picture with that prevailing fifty years later [3].

I

In 1525 the number of people called upon to pay the second instalment of the subsidy totalled 1,414. Assuming that one-third of the population was too poor to pay even the minimum of fourpence (probably a conservative estimate) and using a multiplier of six on the resulting figure of 2,121 we obtain a total of 12,726. It is unlikely that the city's population was in excess of this at that time and certainly it would not have exceeded 13,000, but it still made Norwich the second largest city in the kingdom. Its nearest rivals were Bristol with, perhaps, 10,000

* I should like to thank Professor W. G. Hoskins for his valuable criticism of this article.

J. F. Pound, 'The Social and Trade Structure of Norwich 1525-1575', *Past and Present*, no. 34 (1966), pp. 49-69.

inhabitants, Exeter and Salisbury with 8,000 and Coventry with 6,601 [4].

The familiar pyramidal structure prevailed in Norwich as elsewhere. At its apex were the city's wealthiest citizens, the twenty-nine men (2·05 per cent of the whole) who were considered worth £100 or more and who between them owned over 40 per cent of the city's wealth. Immediately below them, and forming an upper middle class, were those assessed on amounts varying between £40 and £99. This group, numbering a further fifty-two, or 3·68 per cent of the contributors, and those above them formed the Anticipation class, the men deemed sufficiently wealthy to pay their first year's contribution in advance. A further 204 people (14·14 per cent), paying on sums between £10 and £39, may also be considered middle-class, while the 141 assessed on amounts varying between £5 and £9 were comfortably off. Below this we are approaching those who were near poverty at times. Nearly 30 per cent of the city's population paid on assessments varying between £2 and £4 and a further 40 per cent paid on assessments of less than £2. Broad as this base was, at least one-third of the inhabitants — probably more — would have been too poverty-stricken to contribute at all, making more than 60 per cent of the citizens poor or very poor. The situation was not unusual. Professor Hoskins has suggested that fully two-thirds of the urban population in the 1520s lived below or very near the poverty line and the Norwich figures merely serve to confirm this.

Inequality of wealth was common in Tudor times and nowhere was it more marked than in the towns. Virtually everywhere a minority of people owned much of the taxable wealth. In Norwich about 6 per cent of the population owned approximately 60 per cent of the lands and goods. In Coventry 2 per cent owned 45 per cent of the property, at Exeter some 7 per cent owned almost two-thirds [5]. At Lavenham the Anticipation class, numbering nearly 12 per cent of the taxpayers, was in possession of over 80 per cent of the property. Fewer than 4 per cent of the Long Melford taxpayers owned 64 per cent of the town's wealth. In complete contrast, the 570 Norwich wage-earners (just over 40 per cent of the taxpayers) owned less than 4 per cent of the city's wealth. At Lavenham, the wage-earners, numbering just over half of the taxable population, owned less than 3 per cent of the property. The proportions were similar elsewhere, ranging from the 3·26 per cent owned by the Thetford wage-earners to the 7·05 per cent at Bury St Edmunds.

Usually, much of a town's wealth was in the hands of a few exceptionally rich men. Richard Marler, a Coventry grocer, and Thomas Guybon of King's Lynn, for example, each paid about one-ninth of their town's subsidy contributions, while William Wigston of Leicester paid just over one-quarter. The rich clothiers of Suffolk were even more out-standing. The widow and daughter of Thomas Spring of Lavenham, assessed on £1,000 and £33 6s 8d respectively, paid rather more than 30 per cent of the town's subsidy; Thomas Smyth of Long Melford, assessed on £600, contributed over 46 per cent [6].

Norwich had several wealthy men. Robert Jannys, grocer and alderman of the city, was assessed on £1,100 in 1523, his assessment almost equalling that of the entire city of Rochester. Thomas Aldrych, a

Table 6.1   Distribution of wealth at Norwich, 1525

Tax group £	Number in group	Percentage of taxpayers	Actual wealth of group £ s d			Percentage of total wealth
Under 2	570	40·37	570	6	8	3·83
2-4	416	29·46	1,037	0	0	6·96
5-9	141	9·98	869	13	4	5·84
10-19	124	8·78	1,484	13	4	9·97
20-39	80	5·66	2,016	0	0	13·54
40-99	52	3·68	2,850	6	8	19·15
100-299	25	1·77	3,585	0	0	24·90
300-500	1	·07	400	0	0	2·68
Over 500	3	·21	2,066	13	4	13·88
Unknown	2	·14	0	0	0	—
Totals	1,414	100·12	14,879	13	4	100·75

draper, was considered to be worth £700, John Terry, a grocer, £550 and Edward Rede and Thomas Pyckarell, mercers, £500 and £300 respectively. In all, thirty-two men were assessed on personal estate to the value of £100 or more in 1523.

In Norwich, at least, it seems probable that more people were called upon to contribute to the subsidy in 1525 than in the previous year, but many tax-payers had their assessments radically reduced [7]. In the absence of a complete 1524 return, it is impossible to give many details of lesser men but the Anticipation class were treated ever more generously in each successive year. Of the ninety-six people worth £40 and above who were taxed in both 1524 and 1525, fifty-six had their assessments reduced, four had them increased and thirty-six remained the same. Twenty-four of these had their assessments reduced yet again in 1527. Some of these reductions were considerable. Robert Jannys paid on £1,100 in 1524, £950 in 1525 and on only £600 in 1527. Aldrych's assessment of £700 in 1524 was reduced to £566 13s 4d the following year. Edward Rede's wealth allegedly fell from £500 in 1524 to £266 13s 4d three years later, Pyckarell's from £300 to £160 in the same period — virtually halved in both cases. In contrast, although on a more modest scale, Thomas Grewe, butcher, who contributed to the Anticipation in 1523 when only considered worth £30, was assessed on £66 13s 4d in 1527 — the year of his mayoralty [8].

Between the Henrician and Elizabethan periods little information is available on which to base an analysis of the city's social structure and it is not until the second decade of Elizabeth's reign that we are again in a position to attempt such a study.

As is well known, Elizabethan subsidy rolls give no real impression of a person's wealth, nor are they as all-embracing as those of the Henrician period. Nevertheless, with the 1525 assessments as a guide, and used in conjunction with the census of the Norwich poor, taken in 1570, and the yearly lists of contributors to poor relief between 1570 and 1580, we can obtain a reasonably accurate picture of the social structure of Elizabethan Norwich from this source.

Ostensibly, the majority of the contributors to the subsidy of 1576 were worth between £3 and £30 in either lands or goods, the lowest assessments of a common councillor and alderman being on £4 and £13 respectively; in 1525 the corresponding sums were £5 and £40. This suggests that those worth £13 and above in 1576 correspond to the Anticipation class of fifty years earlier and that the £4 men were similar in status to those worth £5 in the earlier period. Assuming this to be correct, and that the proportions in the various categories had not altered radically in the period under discussion, it is not too difficult to break down the rest of the subsidy roll into suitable groupings.

This leaves those not contributing to the subsidy to be accounted for — the men corresponding to the wage-earners and those worth between £2 and £4 in 1525. In the former case, we have no positive information and must assume that they still constituted about 40 per cent of the people above the level of very poor. For the other group there is some statistical detail. Between 1570 and 1580 the Norwich scheme for the relief of its destitute was in operation. An analysis of the census of the poor and the details of the scheme have been published elsewhere [9]. Here it is sufficient to note that for much of that decade some 950 men regularly contributed to poor relief. Very few of those capable of payment escaped, but to allow for some evasion the figure may be extended to 975 — 321 more than those paying subsidy. This difference, added to the 227 taxed on £3 in 1576, would appear to represent the £2-£4 group of 1525. With these points as a guide, a thorough analysis of the English contributors to the subsidy provides the details given in Table 6.2.

Table 6.2   Distribution of wealth at Norwich, 1576

Tax group	No. in group	Percentage
Wage-earners	650*	40·00
£3 men and others	548	33·72
4-5	165	10·15
6-7	78	4·80
8-12	83	5·11
13-19	60	3·69
20-24	25	1·54
25-30	11	·68
Over 30	5	·31
Totals	1,625	100·00

* Estimated number

The various categories had clearly altered little in the fifty-year period. It seems possible (indeed likely, bearing in mind the depression among the textile workers) that the city's social structure was broadening at the base, but to overstress this would suggest an absolute accuracy for the figures that they are unlikely to possess.

The bulk of the city's wealth remained in the hands of a few men. At the apex were the 1·85 per cent corresponding to the £100 plus class of fifty years earlier. Immediately below them were another 3·69 per cent comprising the rest of the 'Anticipation' class. Among this group were all the city's aldermen and the richest third of the common councillors. Exactly how wealthy they were is difficult to ascertain. Thomas Wilson, writing at the end of the sixteenth century, said that he knew of twenty-four Norwich aldermen worth at least £20,000 apiece, some much more, and several lesser citizens (the common councillors?) worth half as much [10]. The greater part of this wealth — in some cases, virtually all — was held in lands and, to a lesser extent, plate and jewels. Even so, fairly large sums of money were disbursed, on occasion, in aldermanic wills. Thomas Sotherton, mayor in 1605, bequeathed over £8,000 at his death in 1608. Thomas Whall, mayor in 1567, disposed of some £1,382 and Clement Hyrne left over £950. This was unusual. Average aldermanic wills dispose of something between £300 and £500 in cash [11].

The men allegedly worth between £8 and £12 in 1576 (the £20-£39 men of 1525) came next in the city's hierarchy. Among them were a majority of the city's common councillors (25). Below this, and including the rest of the city's ruling classes, were those worth between £4 and £7. They ranged from the moderately affluent to the comfortably off.

Apart from the very poor, the only other group about which we have positive information is that containing the £3 men and the residue of those called upon to contribute to poor relief. The poorest of these would have to accept wages at some time to maintain a reasonable existence; some may have been entirely dependent on wages. Those at the upper end would have led a reasonable if, at times, precarious existence. All of them were thought to be able to contribute at least a halfpenny a week to their less fortunate fellows.

The number of wage-earners is conjectural and it only remains to consider those at the very base of the social pyramid — the people deemed sufficiently poor to need fairly regular financial support. In contrast to the Henrician period, we know the exact number of this group or, at least, the number of those contained in the census. A total of 504 men, 831 women and 1,007 children were enumerated. The bulk of the men were textile workers (sixty-one worsted weavers alone) and labourers. Many were old, but most claimed to be in employment at the time their names were recorded [12].

The figures above suggest that the city's social structure changed little in the period under consideration. It remains to consider the trade structure of Norwich and the changes that took place in that sphere.

II

When we turn to the trades of the subsidy contributors it is immediately apparent that the normal picture of Norwich as a textile town needs some qualification. Of the 1,414 people who were taxed in 1525 approximately half (705) are identifiable as freemen, occupying between them seventy-nine different trades. The twelve leading occupations, listed in Table 6.3, give a clear picture of the city's trading interests.

Table 6.3   Twelve leading trades in Norwich, 1525

1.	Worsted weavers	131
2.	Tailors	51
3.	Mercers	44
4.	Butchers	33
5.	Grocers	27
6.	Carpenters	23
7.	Cordwainers	23
8.	Shearmen	23
9.	Bakers	21
10.	Shoemakers	21
11.	Masons	18
12.	Coverlet weavers	17
	Rafmen	17

Grouped into specific categories, the industrial character of the city emerges. Textiles, clearly, employed more people than any other grouping, the worsted weavers alone being almost three times as numerous as their nearest rivals, the tailors. Nevertheless, almost 70 per cent of the Norwich freemen were employed in trades other than textiles and even if the clothing trades are considered to be closely allied more than six people in every ten were engaged in different spheres. Of these, the distributive trades were the wealthiest by far, over 50 per cent of the city's Anticipation payers, with known occupations, being found among them. The mercers were particularly pre-eminent. Twenty of them paid the first year's contribution in advance and of these over half paid on sums of £100 and above. The grocers and drapers between them had a further sixteen people in this category, including Robert Jannys and Thomas Aldrych, the city's richest men.

The food and drink trades, the third largest grouping, employed more than 12 per cent of the Norwich freemen, the most numerous being the bakers, butchers and fishmongers. These trades also included a number of wealthy men, the three leading groups supplying over 85 per cent of the city's Anticipation payers.

The majority of the remaining freemen were engaged in the leather, building, clothing and metal trades. The first two of these, employing between them one-fifth of the city's freemen, were among the poorer occupational groupings, two-thirds of the builders and over two-thirds of the leather workers being worth less than £5 in personal estate. The bulk of the glaziers, masons and reeders in the building trades and the curriers, saddlers and shoemakers in the leather trades fell into this category. Rather more than one-half of the cloth workers and one-third of the city's metal workers could be considered poor but the majority ranged from being moderately well-off to affluent [13]. Table 6.4 summarises the position.

Table 6.4   Trade groupings in 1525 given as a percentage of the whole

Textiles	30·35
Distributive trades	17·87
Food and drink	12·77
Leather and allied	11·60
Building and allied	9·65
Clothing	8·23
Metal	4·96
Totals	95·43

Any system of classification is open to objections. For the purpose of the table above, the grocers are included with the distributive trades rather than food and drink and the cobblers, cordwainers, glovers and shoemakers with the leather trades rather than clothing.

With these points in mind, the Norwich trade structure makes interesting comparison with that of the three Midland towns analysed by Professor Hoskins. In all of them, the wholesale and retail clothing trades provided employment for 14 to 15 per cent of the occupied population, the food and drink trades for 15 to 21 per cent and the building trades for 4 to 7·5 per cent. These facts led Professor Hoskins to suggest that in every sixteenth-century town with the semblance of an industrial character the same trades would provide employment for between 35 and 40 per cent of the working population [14]. The trade structure of Norwich tends to confirm this, the three groupings actually employing just over 30 per cent of the city's freemen in 1525.

The proportion of people employed in the different trade groupings naturally differs from town to town. Coventry, like Norwich, employed a majority of people in the textile trades and in both towns the food and drink and leather trades were of some importance. In Leicester and Northampton the leather trades were of primary importance, many of the Leicester mayors being drawn from their ranks in the Elizabethan period [15]. All three Midland towns had more people employed in the wholesale and retail clothing trades than Norwich while the East Anglian town, in contrast, exceeded the Midland towns in the number of its builders.

The major occupations apart, all four towns had important subsidiary trade groupings. In Coventry and Norwich, the metal, as well as the leather, trades were of some significance. The proportion of building workers in Northampton was almost as high as that in Norwich and was twice as high as the same grouping in Coventry and Leicester. Textiles employed substantial minorities in both Leicester and Northampton.

Turning again to Norwich, we find that radical changes took place in the city's economy between 1525 and 1575. Whereas in the former year much — although by no means all — of the city's prosperity depended on the activities of its textile workers, by the second decade of Elizabeth's reign it relied increasingly on the activities of its grocers and the demands of the surrounding gentry and countryfolk for its wealth.

The change was brought about by the lessening demands for the city's products. As early as 1536 complaints were made that worsted could not be sold, one weaver, at least, attributing his failure to pay subsidy to that cause, and the tax commissioners were obliged to collect reduced amounts in the city. Competition abroad, where a better class of worsted was produced, caused considerable distress in Norwich and the government showed itself aware of the problem by making specific provision for the city's merchants to buy and sell worsted elsewhere. The decline continued, however. Up to 1535 between 1,000 and 3,000 Norwich worsteds were exported annually from Great Yarmouth. Thereafter the numbers fell steadily until by the third year of Elizabeth's reign no more than thirty-eight left for foreign markets [16].

In an attempt to restore the city's fortunes, new industries were fostered, the hatters becoming a separate company in 1543, the russell weavers in 1554. Neither trade was particularly successful. The hatters suffered from the apparent total inability of the city fathers to control their activities, with the result that inferior products were put on to the market. Initially, there was no effective training, no specific period of apprenticeship, and a number of people from depressed occupations (worsted weavers, shearmen, etc.) tried their hands at the new trade. The matter was not finally settled until the 1560s, several hatters in the meantime having left the city to escape possible gild restrictions. The russell weavers, when they began, introduced foreign craftsmen and repeatedly made better products than their continental rivals but their output was small, numbering only a few hundred cloths each year [17].

The depression did not affect those engaged in the purely textile trades alone. For much of the first half of the sixteenth century the Norwich mercers shared in the prosperity resulting from the boom in the cloth trade. Their wealth is apparent in their contributions to the subsidy of 1523-27 and in the fact that they held the mayoralty no fewer than fourteen times in the first half of the century. The slump which followed the saturation of the market in 1550 and the subsequent steady decline of Antwerp affected the mercers as a class, however, and they never regained their pre-eminent position. There were still forty-eight of them in Norwich in 1569 but the number of mercers admitted to the freedom of the city steadily declined and by the last quarter of the century they are no longer to be found among the twelve leading trades [18].

The various crises in the cloth trade, depreciation of the coinage and the rise in prices affected Norwich as elsewhere and some tradesmen attempted to solve the problem by emigration. In May 1549 the Common Council complained that masons, carpenters, reeders and tilers had left to find work in the country, the void created being filled by 'foreigners' and beggars. Significantly, it was in the same year that many of the latter element caused trouble in the city during Ket's rebellion and that Norwich became the first provincial city to inaugurate compulsory contributions to the relief of the poor [19].

To add to the trade depression, the city suffered severely from plague in 1556. No precise figures are available but Blomefield records the death of ten aldermen and a number of common councillors from this cause, classes that usually survived similar outbreaks in the Elizabethan period, and the poor almost certainly suffered severely [20]. Plague mortality and emigration from the city arrested the physical growth of

Norwich and by the second decade of Elizabeth's reign the population was little higher than in 1525 [21].

Despite the relatively static population, the number of freemen increased steadily throughout the fifty-year period under discussion. Between 1500 and 1529 the average number of annual admissions was twenty-eight. By the 1570s it had increased to forty-nine and it is thus possible to identify 1,250 men as freemen as against the 705 some fifty years earlier.

Even more than in 1525, an analysis of the occupations reveals how inadequate it is to describe Norwich as a purely textile town, little more than one freeman in five being thus engaged. There were as many engaged in the distributive trades as in textiles, the clothing trades employed almost one-sixth of them and one in ten found employment in building, leather work and the various food and drink trades. As in 1525, too, about one in twenty was a metal worker.

Table 6.5   Twelve leading trades in Norwich, 1569

1.	Worsted weavers	166
2.	Grocers	150
3.	Tailors	146
4.	Cordwainers	59
5.	Mercers	48
6.	Dornix weavers	35
	Hatters	35
8.	Tanners	34
9.	Bakers	32
10.	Carpenters	31
11.	Butchers	29
12.	Masons	26

Table 6.6   Trade groupings in 1569 given as a percentage of the whole

Distributive trades	21·44
Textiles	21·28
Clothing	14·88
Leather and allied	11·84
Food and drink	9·68
Building and allied	9·12
Metal	5·12
Totals	93·36

Looking more closely at these groupings, it becomes apparent that the most striking changes in the fifty-year period were the decline of the textile and, to a lesser extent, the food and drink trades, and the steady rise in numbers of those employed in the clothing and distributive trades. Despite a known increase of over 500 freemen in a virtually static population, the numbers engaged in the former trades altered little. In contrast, those employed in the clothing and professional trades more than trebled in number, those concerned with the distributive trades more than doubled and the numbers of building, leather, metal and woodworkers almost doubled [22].

The increased number of freemen and, in particular, the spheres in which they increased reflect a major change in the economy of the city. Much has been written about the decline of Norwich as a textile town and its subsequent revival with the coming of the New Draperies, but to paint a picture of complete economic stagnation before the coming of the Dutch and Walloons would be misleading in the extreme. Far from being a depressed town there is every evidence, textiles apart, that the economy of Norwich was in a very healthy state in the first decades of Elizabeth's reign, due, at least in part, to the increasing demands of the surrounding gentry. The number of tailors alone suggests a considerable extramural demand for clothing. If we add to this the large numbers of the occupied population engaged in the provision of food and drink, household goods and building facilities it becomes apparent that the city served a number of customers beyond its immediate precincts. At least 80 per cent of the freemen were engaged, directly or indirectly, in providing goods for the consumer, and it is hardly possible to envisage four people producing goods for the other one.

It seems fairly clear, in fact, that Norwich was becoming increasingly a centre of conspicuous consumption — a lesser London. On a reduced scale, the city had much the same advantages as the metropolis. The Duke of Norfolk held court there in a very real sense; the Quarter Sessions attracted the country gentry — and others — at frequent intervals; the city's grammar school took at least a portion of the country people; it was a minor port, albeit an inland one; and the great fairs, held at regular intervals throughout the year, brought in a vast concourse of people.

In this respect Norwich resembled many of the other large towns that played the part of capital cities to their regions. Professor Hoskins has pointed out that many towns of this type — Exeter, Salisbury, Newcastle and Bristol as well as York and Norwich — were in the process of becoming social capitals 'in which a growing proportion of the larger gentry had a town house to which they migrated for the winter months', while Professor Dickens noted the steady increase in number of those engaged in the 'luxury' trades at York, a town which, like Norwich, increased little in population during the sixteenth century [23].

That much of the demand in Norwich was for luxury goods is evidenced both by the increasing quantity of groceries imported and by the phenomenal rise of the grocers themselves (150 in 1569 against the 27 in 1525). By the 1570s the East Anglian ports were importing ever increasing quantities of sugar, molasses and syrup, figs and prunes, raisins and currants. In 1581 a cargo of 20,000 oranges and 1,000 lemons reached Norwich in time for the St Bartholomew's Fair. The grocers were not the only ones to take advantage of the opportunities offered, however. The Norwich mercers, possibly extending their activities, imported large quantities of French and sweet wines about the same time. The number of beer brewers increased considerably and most of them appear to have been at least moderately affluent. The innkeepers were able to make large profits on occasion, particularly when the Quarter Sessions brought in the justices and other notables, and by 1575 one had achieved aldermanic status. The business of the tailors increased only less than that of the grocers, while the ever increasing river traffic enabled John Stingate, keleman, to quote but one example, to leave over £250 to his children at his death, as well as real estate within the city. The development of the leather trades increased the status of the cordwainers, ordinances passed in 1561 allowing them to become common councillors for the first time. Richard Durrant, the Norwich bonesetter, prospered sufficiently to leave over £280 at his death in addition to large sums owed him, almost certainly, by wealthy patrons. This list is not exhaustive.

The increasing wealth of at least a section of the community is reflected, too, in the considerable building activity in Norwich between 1576-90, activity only temporarily halted by the various outbreaks of plague. There is evidence of an increasing substitution of brick for timber and slate for thatch, large quantities of bricks and tiles being brought up-river, mostly from the Low Countries. By 1580 the volume of river traffic had grown to such an extent that the authorities found it necessary to construct a new common staithe [24].

There was, of course, a reverse side of the picture. The census of the poor, taken in 1570, confirms the decline of the textile trades, over 50 per cent of the city's destitute being either labourers, textile workers or people of no specified occupation. Worsted weavers apart, cobblers, tailors and cordwainers were the most numerous individual trades to be found among them. The presence of ten hatters suggests that many in that trade were already encountering difficulties. More surprising is the presence of two goldsmiths and a silversmith, the latter being particularly interesting as no freeman followed this trade as a separate occupation until 1710. Altogether, just over 500 men practised ninety-seven different trades [25].

After 1575 the activities of the Dutch and Walloons brought further prosperity to Norwich for a while, many of the poorer inhabitants of the city being employed by them. The Spanish invasion of the Netherlands closed their markets at least temporarily, however, and it seems probable that the city's prosperity depended to a large extent on its extramural trade until at least the end of the sixteenth century [26].

III

The social structure and population of Norwich thus altered little in the fifty years between 1525 and 1575. In contrast, the city's trade structure, which was much more complex than is usually suggested, underwent a radical, if possibly temporary, transformation during this period. The textile trades, which were at least numerically superior in 1525, gradually declined and by 1575 there was an increasing demand for luxury goods. The change must not be overstressed. Many of the city's products went to feed and clothe the ordinary townsfolk and their country neighbours, and that their demands grew greater is evidenced by the increased number of cordwainers and tailors, to take but two of the most obvious examples. Nevertheless, the considerable rise in number of those trades catering mainly for the monied classes — the drapers, grocers and haberdashers, the scriveners, bladesmiths, goldsmiths and joiners — is a sure indication that Norwich was becoming increasingly attractive to the country gentry, many of whom had town houses there. The same situation was beginning to apply in all the provincial capitals. Professor Hoskins has suggested that the local gentry preferred to migrate to those places in the winter months rather than to London, which generally attracted the peerage and the larger gentry of the Home Counties [27].

With the steady development of the New Draperies in the seventeenth century, the fortunes of Norwich were again linked closely to the textile trades, the number of worsted weavers increasing fourfold within a comparatively short time [28]. Between 60 and 70 per cent of the city's freemen continued to be employed in other spheres, however, and there is every indication that the city became increasingly attractive as the capital city of its region. Its history in the seventeenth century must await further investigation.

Appendix 6.1   Trades of the freemen of Norwich

A – 1525   B – 1569

In 1525 a total of 705 freemen followed 79 trades.
In 1569 the number of freemen had increased to 1,250, the trades followed by them to 102.

Building and allied	A	B
Bricklayers	–	4
Carpenters	23	31
Folsterers	–	2
Freemasons	1	2
Glasswrights	2	–
Glaziers	10	11
Joiners	1	14
Masons	18	26
Millwrights	2	–
Painters	–	2
Reeders	8	9
Roughmasons	–	7
Sawyers*	2	–
Stainers	–	3
Tilers	1	3
Totals	68	114
Percentages	9·65	9·12

Woodwork	A	B
Basket-makers	–	2
Bowyers	1	2
Coopers	6	16
Fletchers	5	4
Gravers	2	–
Latheryvers	–	1
Pedmakers	–	1
Ploughwrights	1	2
Turners	–	4
Wheelwrights*	–	3
Totals	15	35
Percentages	2·13	2·80

Food and drink	A	B
Bakers	21	32
Beer brewers	4	18
Brewers	7	6
Butchers	33	29
Cooks	7	1
Fishermen	1	3
Fishmongers	11	14
Freshwater fishers	4	4
Fingerbread makers	–	1
Innkeepers*	–	7
Millers	2	2
Victuallers	–	3
Vintners	–	1
Totals	90	121
Percentages	12·77	9·68

Distributive trades	A	B
Apothecaries	–	2
Barbers	15	13
Drapers	13	24
Grocers	27	150
Haberdashers	3	20
Linen drapers	–	1
Mercers	44	48
Mercers and notaries	2	–
Merchants	–	2
Parchmeners	2	2
Rafmen	17	4
Wax chandlers	3	1
Totals	126	268
Percentages	17·87	21·44

Textiles	A	B
Calendrers	10	7
Coverlet weavers	17	4
Coverlet and dornix weavers	–	1
Dornix weavers	–	35
Dyers	16	13
Embroiderers	–	1
Felmakers	–	2
Fullers	7	1
Hairmakers	–	3
Linen weavers	–	2
Linen and woollen weavers	–	3
Russell weavers	–	2
Shearmen	23	18
Slaymakers	1	–
Staymakers	–	4
Thick woollen weavers	3	–
Weavers	1	1
Woolmen	3	1
Wool chapmen	1	–
Worsted shearmen	1	2
Worsted weavers	131	166
Totals	214	266
Percentages	30·35	21·28

Miscellaneous	A	B
Bookbinders	–	1
Limeburners	–	2
Ropemakers	–	2
Stringers	–	1
Totals	–	6
Percentages	–	0·48

Appendix 6.1 – continued

Clothing trades	A	B
Cappers	4	1
Hatters	–	35
Hosiers	2	2
Pointmakers	1	2
Tailors	51	146
Totals	58	186
Percentages	8·23	14·88

Professional	A	B
Barber surgeons	–	1
Courtholders	1	–
Musicians	1	1
Mayor's sergeants	1	–
Scriveners	5	18
Surgeons	–	3
Totals	8	23
Percentages	1·14	1·84

Metalwork	A	B
Bellfounders	–	1
Blacksmiths	–	11
Bladesmiths	4	12
Braziers	2	–
Cutlers	–	5
Farriers	–	1
Furbishers	–	–
Goldbeaters	1	–
Goldsmiths	5	9
Hardwaremen	1	–
Locksmiths	1	7
Pewterers	3	4
Pinners	6	5
Plumbers	–	1
Sheargrinders	1	–
Sievemakers	–	1
Smiths	9	6
Spurriers	2	1
Totals	35	65
Percentages	4·96	5·20

Leather and allied	A	B
Cobblers	1	7
Collar-makers	1	1
Cordwainers	23	59
Curriers	7	6
Glovers	2	13
Pattern-makers	2	–
Saddlers	7	17
Shoemakers	21	4
Skinners	3	7
Tanners	11	34
Totals	78	148
Percentages	11·60	11·84

Transport	A	B
Carriers	3	10
Carters	2	1
Kelemen	1	5
Loaders	1	–
Watermen	6	2
Totals	13	18
Percentages	1·84	1·44

* There were obviously innkeepers and wheelwrights in the first half of the century and sawyers in the second. The inclusion of the first two in Elizabeth's reign probably indicates growing pressure on certain trades to become freemen.

Appendix 6.2 Admissions to the freedom in Norwich 1500-1603

A – 1500-1529   B – 1530-1558   C – 1558-1580   D – 1581-1603   E – Total

Between 1500 and 1558, the total number of admissions to the freedom was 1,814, the number of trades followed was 113. In the Elizabethan period the respective figures were 2,025 and 123.

Food and drink

	A	B	C	D	E
Bakers	12	27	23	27	89
Brewers	9	8	10	1	28
Brewers of ale	–	–	1	1	2
Brewers of beer	2	12	21	20	55
Butchers	21	31	31	25	108
Cooks	5	4	4	5	18
Fishermen	2	3	–	2	7
Fishmongers	12	11	16	12	51
Freshwater fishermen	4	5	4	–	13
Fingerbread makers	–	–	1	–	1
Innkeepers	–	7	11	16	34
Maltsters	–	1	–	2	3
Millers	1	1	3	1	6
Oatmeal makers	–	–	1	–	1
Sugarbakers	–	–	1	–	1
Victuallers	–	–	4	1	5
Victuallers and brewers	–	1	–	–	1
Vintners	1	2	1	5	9
Totals	69	113	132	118	432
Percentages	8·36	11·43	12·31	12·38	11·25

Miscellaneous

	A	B	C	D	E
Ashburners	–	1	–	1	2
Bookbinders	–	1	–	–	1
Horseleeches	–	–	1	–	1
Knackers	–	–	1	–	1
Labourers	–	–	1	–	1
Limeburners	–	1	2	2	5
Printers	–	–	1	–	1
Ropemakers	–	–	–	2	2
Stringers	1	–	–	–	1
Totals	1	3	6	5	15
Percentages	0·12	0·30	0·56	0·52	0·39

Textile industry

	A	B	C	D	E
Bay weavers	–	–	–	4	4
Calendrers	11	9	2	2	24
Clothiers	–	–	1	7	8
Clothmakers	–	2	–	–	2
Clothshearmen	–	–	–	1	1
Clothworkers	–	–	2	2	4
Combers	–	–	–	1	1
Coverlet weavers	12	12	–	–	24
Dornix weavers	–	6	33	31	70
Dyers	9	17	6	4	36
Embroiderers	–	1	–	3	4
Feltmakers	–	–	–	9	9
Fullers	5	5	–	–	10
Hairmakers	–	1	1	–	1
Lacemakers	–	–	–	1	1
Linen weavers	–	1	6	1	8
Linen and woollen weavers	–	–	5	1	6
Russell weavers	1	2	2	–	3
Shearmen	31	29	13	8	81
Silk rasers	–	–	–	1	1
Slay makers	3	3	–	2	8
Tache makers	–	1	–	–	1
Thick woollen weavers	3	–	–	–	3
Tuft mockado makers	–	–	1	–	1
Twisterers	–	–	1	–	1
Upholsterers	–	1	–	2	3
Weavers	3	2	1	2	8
Wool chapmen	1	–	–	2	3
Wool combers	–	–	–	1	1
Woolmen	1	2	–	–	3
Woollen weavers	–	1	–	–	1
Worsted shearmen	3	1	1	2	7
Worsted weavers	160	115	107	56	438
Totals	243	206	183	145	777
Percentages	29·58	20·83	17·07	15·22	20·24

Appendix 6.2 – *continued*

Metal trades

	A	B	C	D	E
Armourers	—	—	1	—	1
Bellfounders	—	2	—	—	3
Blacksmiths	—	—	15	16	31
Bladesmiths	4	4	7	7	22
Braziers	3	1	7	1	6
Cutlers	—	4	5	7	16
Farriers	—	—	1	—	1
Furbishers	1	—	1	—	1
Goldbeaters	—	—	—	—	1
Goldfinders	—	—	—	—	1
Goldsmiths	5	1	7	7	30
Hardwaremen	3	11	—	—	4
Ironmongers	—	—	6	9	19
Lockmiths	2	2	6	9	14
Pewterers	2	3	6	3	18
Pinners	8	3	5	2	3
Plumbers	—	—	1	2	2
Sievemakers	—	—	1	4	58
Smiths	18	32	4	1	4
Spurriers	2	1	—	1	1
Tinkers	—	1	1	—	2
Wiredrawers	1	3	1	3	2
Totals	49	66	63	61	239
Percentages	5·94	6·67	5·88	6·40	6·23

Woodwork

	A	B	C	D	E
Basketmakers	3	2	1	3	9
Bowyers	2	2	—	—	5
Coopers	3	12	15	10	40
Fletchers	6	5	2	—	13
Gravers	6	—	—	—	10
Latheryvers	1	—	1	—	1
Organmakers	—	—	1	—	1
Pedmakers	1	1	2	1	2
Ploughwrights	1	—	—	1	3
Turners	1	1	2	3	4
Wheelwrights	3	3	3	3	9
Totals	22	31	25	17	95
Percentages	2·67	3·13	2·52	1·78	2·53

Building and allied

	A	B	C	D	E
Bricklayers	30	—	4	—	4
Carpenters	—	17	15	30	92
Foisterers	2	4	1	—	7
Freemasons	1	2	2	—	5
Glasswrights	3	—	—	—	3
Glaziers	6	9	9	8	32
Joiners	—	7	15	20	42
Masons	23	19	27	22	91
Millwrights	1	—	—	—	1
Painters	—	1	6	1	9
Reeders	10	3	15	6	34
Roughmasons	—	—	7	10	17
Sawyers	2	—	1	1	4
Stainers	—	2	—	—	2
Stainers and glaziers	—	—	—	—	1
Tilers	1	2	7	3	13
Totals	80	67	109	101	357
Percentages	9·69	6·77	10·17	10·60	9·32

Distributive trades

	A	B	C	D	E
Apothecaries	—	—	2	7	9
Barbers	16	18	8	12	54
Drapers	15	14	19	23	71
Grocers	37	84	116	77	314
Haberdashers	1	12	19	16	48
Linen drapers	—	—	2	—	2
Mercers	71	83	32	18	204
Mercers and notaries	2	—	—	—	2
Merchants	—	—	—	15	17
Merchant tailors	—	—	2	1	1
Parchmeners	3	2	3	2	10
Rafmen	23	9	—	—	32
Stationers	—	—	—	4	4
Wax chandlers	9	—	1	—	9
Woollen drapers	—	—	—	3	3
Totals	177	222	203	178	780
Percentages	21·45	22·45	18·94	18·65	20·32

Appendix 6.2 – *continued*

Leather and allied

	A	B	C	D	E
Bagmakers	1	2	–	–	3
Cobblers	–	1	8	8	17
Collar-makers	–	1	–	–	1
Cordwainers	22	38	60	66	186
Curriers	6	3	5	6	20
Glovers	1	12	17	31	61
Leather carvers	1	–	–	–	1
Leather dressers	–	–	–	3	3
Pattern-makers	3	–	–	–	3
Saddlers	8	10	9	9	36
Shoemakers	20	13	10	3	35
Skinners	4	3	10	3	20
Tanners	14	32	20	14	80
Totals	79	116	131	140	466
Percentages	9·58	11·73	12·22	14·69	12·14

Transport

	A	B	C	D	E
Carriers	1	8	10	2	21
Carters	2	1	–	–	3
Kelemen	1	8	5	1	15
Loaders	1	–	–	–	1
Watermen	–	1	2	–	3
Totals	5	18	17	3	43
Percentages	0·61	1·82	1·59	0·32	1·12

Professional

	A	B	C	D	E
Barber surgeons	–	–	1	1	2
Courtholders	–	–	1	–	1
Juris periti	–	2	–	–	2
Legis periti	–	2	–	–	2
Minstrels	–	1	–	–	1
Musicians	2	1	3	2	8
Scriveners	14	12	14	12	52
Scriveners and mercers	1	–	–	–	1
Serjeants	–	1	2	–	3
Surgeons	3	1	1	1	6
Swordbearers	1	–	1	–	2
Totals	21	20	23	16	80
Percentages	2·55	2·20	2·14	1·68	2·08

Clothing trades

	A	B	C	D	E
Cappers	3	12	–	–	15
Hatters	–	19	29	10	58
Hosiers	–	3	1	8	12
Jerkin makers	–	–	1	–	1
Pointmakers	5	–	3	1	9
Tailors	71	93	144	150	458
Totals	79	127	178	169	553
Percentages	9·58	12·48	16·60	17·73	14·40

	A	B	C	D	E
Grand totals	825	989	1,072	953	3,839

Notes

1   W. G. Hoskins, 'English provincial towns in the early sixteenth century', in *Provincial England* (London, 1963). The events leading up to, and details of, the subsidy are given in the introduction to *Suffolk in 1524: Subsidy Return* (Suffolk Green Books, x, Woodbridge, 1910) and it is not considered necessary to refer to them again here.

2   W. T. MacCaffrey, *Exeter, 1540-1640* (Cambridge, Massachusetts, 1958, [1st edition]); J. Cornwall, 'English country towns in the 1520s', *Economic History Review*, 2nd ser., xv (1962-63); Laura M. Nicholls, 'The lay subsidy of 1523: the reliability of the subsidy rolls as illustrated by Totnes and Dartmouth', *University of Birmingham Historical Journal*, ix, 2 (1964). These are, of course, only some of the more accessible accounts.

3   PRO E179/150/208; E179/150/218; E179/150/254. The trade structure has been worked out by relating the names in the subsidy rolls to the register of Norwich freemen.

4   Hoskins, *op. cit.*, p. 72.

5   *Ibid.*, p. 84.

6   PRO E179/150/263 for Thetford; *Suffolk in 1524*; pp. 19 and 24 for the Springs, p. 30 for Smyth, pp. 348-58 for Bury St Edmunds; *Norfolk Antiquarian Miscellany*, ii (Norwich, 1883), p. 406 for Guybon.

7   The Norwich subsidy roll for 1524 (PRO E179/250/264) is much mutilated, the names of the contributors from only three wards remaining in their entirety. In every case, fewer people paid than in the following year, the respective figures for 1524 and 1525 being: St Giles 15 and 33; Coslany 140 and 161; Fibridge 117 and 154. Almost 50 per cent (36) of these additional payers were wage-earners. In the two years, the sums on which the various contributors were assessed fell by some £1,500. In 1525 those paying subsidy were allegedly worth £14,880 (to the nearest £), the Anticipation class accounting for £8,902. As mentioned above, complete figures for the previous year are wanting, but we know from the Anticipation payments that those assessed on £40 and above were worth £10,328. If we add to this the £5,978 on which the men worth less than £40 were assessed in 1525 we obtain a total of £16,306, an approximate, and almost certainly a conservative, figure. In the same year the Coventry taxpayers were assumed to be worth £10,112. (I owe this latter figure to Professor Hoskins.)

8   PRO references quoted in note 3 above and, for Grewe, B. Cozens-Hardy and E. A. Kent, *The Mayors of Norwich, 1403 to 1835* (Norwich, 1938), p. 50.

9   J. F. Pound, 'An Elizabethan census of the poor', *Univ. of Birmingham Hist. Jl.*, viii (1962).

10   T. Wilson, 'The state of England, AD 1600', ed. F. J. Fisher, *Camden Miscellany*, xvi (1936).

11   Prerogative Court of Canterbury; 49 Windebanck, 57 Pyckering and 83 Drake, quoted, with reference to other aldermanic wills, in J. F. Pound, 'The Elizabethan Corporation of Norwich, 1558-1603'

(Birmingham Univ. MA thesis, 1962), pp. 64-6 and 82-95.

12   Pound, *loc. cit.*, pp. 138-9.

13   This information has been derived by comparing the trades of the freemen with their alleged wealth. It has not been thought necessary to produce a further table with the full details.

14   Hoskins, *op. cit.*, p. 80.

15   W. G. Hoskins, 'An Elizabethan provincial town: Leicester', in *Provincial England*, p. 108.

16   K. J. Allison, 'The Norfolk worsted industry in the sixteenth and seventeenth centuries', *Yorkshire Bulletin of Economic and Social Research*, xii, 2 (Nov. 1960); N. Williams, 'The maritime trade of the East Anglian ports, 1550-90' (Oxford Univ. DPhil. thesis, 1952), pp. 38 and 74.

17   K. J. Allison, 'The Norwich Hatters', *East Anglian Magazine*, xvi, 3, p. 138.

18   See Appendix 6.2.

19   D. Knoop and G. P. Jones, *The Medieval Mason* (Manchester, 1933), p. 209; Pound, 'The Elizabethan Corporation of Norwich', p. 194.

20   F. Blomefield, *History of Norfolk* (London, 1806), iii, p. 276.

21   This refers to the English population, the immigrants being excluded. If the 504 men included in the census of the poor are added to the 1,625 referred to in Table 6.2 we obtain a total of 2,129. Extending this to 2,200 to allow for possible omissions, and again multiplying by six, a total of 13,200 is obtained. It is most unlikely that the population was any higher than this. These figures are confirmed, to some extent, by the very full muster roll of 1569 which records the names of 2,285 men. The names of the 1,250 freemen referred to in the text were derived from this source. 'Muster Rolls: Henry VIII to Charles II', Norfolk Record Office archives, Case 13, Shelf a.

22   The trades of the freemen, in this case, have been obtained from P. Millican, *The Freemen of Norwich, 1548-1713* (Norwich, 1934). Some caution must be observed when talking of a decline in the food and drink trades as, during most of the period under discussion, the numbers admitted to the freedom of the city in these occupations remained fairly constant. The grocers, too, although primarily wholesalers and dealing in a variety of products, included a number of retailers in their ranks and were responsible for the importation of a considerable amount of food and drink.

23   Hoskins, *Provincial England*, pp. 86-7; A. Dickens, 'Tudor York', in *The City of York* (*Victoria County History, Yorkshire*, London, 1961), pp. 127-8.

24   Williams thesis, pp. 77, 205; Pound thesis, pp. 12, 41, 118-20; Norwich Consistory Court, 273 Flack.

25   Silver articles were, of course, made by the Norwich goldsmiths.

26   The Norwich authorities, on more than one occasion, pointed out the advantages accruing to the city since the arrival of the Dutch and Walloons: Pound thesis, pp. 318-9.

27   Hoskins, *Provincial England*, p. 87.

28   Information derived from Millican, *op. cit.*

7 The Elizabethan merchants of Exeter

W. G. Hoskins [2]

The first meeting of the Chamber, the governing body of Exeter, after the accession of Queen Elizabeth I, took place as usual in the ancient Guildhall that still stands in the High Street of the city, though it lacked in the autumn of 1558 its now-familiar renaissance portico. Of this assembly of twenty-four men, including the mayor, all but one were merchants. The single exception was Robert Chafe, an ecclesiastical official connected with the cathedral, a skilful and learned lawyer, 'a man of very good condition being of great modesty and gravity, very friendly and loving to all men', who was twice to be chosen mayor of the city — in 1568 and again in 1576 [1].

John Buller, as mayor, presided over this first Elizabethan assembly, but the father of the house was old William Hurst, now in his seventy-sixth year. He had been mayor as far back as 1524 and three times since, and three times had represented Exeter in parliament. He had come to the thriving city, the son of a South Devon yeoman, as long ago as 1497 and so could look back over sixty years in its streets, and to more than forty years of service on its governing body. Around this venerable figure on the benches of the Guildhall sat not a few prosperous men who had been his apprentices in their youth. Even at that great age, his fifth mayoralty — in 1561 — had yet to come and he had another ten years of life ahead of him [2].

The city governed by this assembly was one of the largest and wealthiest in Elizabethan England. It was the social and cultural capital of a large province, a cathedral city, an industrial town, and a busy port. In wealth and population, among the provincial towns, it ranked after Norwich, Newcastle and Bristol, and was the most important city between London and Land's End [3]. Yet it was very small in extent. A man could walk comfortably around the entire circuit of its walls in twenty minutes or so, for it was less than a mile and a half around. The entire area enclosed by these walls was but 93 acres, though to that one must add, by the year 1558, small suburbs outside all four gates which carried houses along the road in a ribbon development for possibly a couple of hundred yards in each direction. The extramural suburbs consisted almost entirely of working-class houses, except for a few merchant houses outside the West

W. G. Hoskins, 'The Elizabethan Merchants of Exeter', from S. T. Bindoff, J. Hurstfield, C. H. Williams, eds, *Elizabethan Government and Society*, London, Athlone Press, 1961, Chapter 6, pp. 163-87.

Gate in the principal industrial and commercial quarter. But the great majority of the merchant class lived within the walls, in one of half a dozen small, rich, central parishes, and in one or other of only half a dozen streets.

The merchant class was similarly small, compact, and closely interrelated by marriage. We can get a rough idea of its total size in a given generation from the number of admissions to the freedom of the city, a necessary qualification for all who practised as merchants whether they had been apprenticed in boyhood to an Exeter freeman or had come to the city from elsewhere as grown men. In the last quarter of the sixteenth century the number of merchants and mercers admitted to the freedom amounted to 104 [4]. We may reasonably assume that the average business life of a merchant was not much above twenty-five to thirty years, so that at any given time there may have been about a hundred merchants in the city. Such a figure is clearly only approximate, but it will not be far wrong: at its worst it serves to give us an order of magnitude.

The total population of the city in this generation was between 9,000 and 10,000 — about 2,000 families at the most. Of these, then, one family in every twenty was a merchant family [5] and belonged potentially to the governing class. From these alone, with very few exceptions, were chosen the mayors, sheriffs, and members of parliament for the city. The choice, indeed, was even finer, for within this small class there were closely-knit dynasties of the wealthiest merchants related to each other, often more than once over, by marriage. The fifty Elizabethan mayors — there were two mayors in some years because of early deaths — were chosen from twenty-six different families. But in this narrower field, too, marriages had united Hursts, Martins, and Peters, or Periams and Blackallers. In this way we are reduced to perhaps a score of ruling families in the Elizabethan city and this oligarchic rule carried over well into the seventeenth century [6].

In the smaller town of Leicester, the Elizabethan mayors were also drawn from twenty-six different families: but Leicester had just about one-third the number of families as Exeter [7], so to that extent its choice of mayor was far less oligarchic. At Norwich, by far the largest and richest of provincial cities, the forty-seven Elizabethan mayors were drawn from twenty-nine different families. Here, with a total population of well over 3,000 families, the field of choice was even narrower than at Exeter. The larger the town, the more oligarchic was its government likely to be in the sixteenth century. Yet there was a wider choice at Norwich as between occupations. Whereas at Exeter only four of the fifty mayors were chosen from outside the ranks of the merchants, at Norwich the non-merchant groups provided thirteen out of forty-seven mayors, drawing upon worsted and dornix weavers, a butcher, a baker, a saddler, a scrivener, and a goldsmith [8].

At Bristol, the second richest provincial city, the choice of mayor was more widely made. Of the eighteen mayors between 1558 and 1576, eight were not merchants, tanners and brewers being conspicuous in the list. After 1576, however, the merchants predominated heavily. Out of the next twenty-eight mayors only three were not merchants, and Mr McGrath has shown that in the seventeenth century the key positions of mayor, sheriff, and chamberlain were all held by merchants [9]. Mayors were chosen also from a much wider range of families than at Norwich or Exeter. No fewer than thirty-eight different families are represented in the mayoral list from 1558 to 1603. Bristol was, for some local reason, the least oligarchical of the large provincial cities, though it was becoming more so in the last quarter of the century.

The merchant class at Exeter, as in all the larger provincial towns, was recruited to a considerable extent from outside — not only from the surrounding countryside but from such distant parts as Wales, Cheshire, Worcestershire, or Suffolk. Younger sons of ability for whom there were no bright prospects at home would naturally tend to move to a thriving commercial city like Exeter; but their biographies by John Hooker make it clear that their destinies often depended upon some human accident and not upon any inhuman calculation of economic prospects. 'The girl at the door of an inn' is as important in this respect as the account book, perhaps more so.

So it was that Thomas Prestwood the elder, who died in the autumn of 1558, had come to Exeter from his native city of Worcester exactly thirty years earlier. His father,

> conceiving a good hope of him by reason of his pregnant wit and forwardness sent him to London, where he bound him apprentice unto a rich and wealthy merchant under whom he prospered and did very well. And upon occasion, being a traveller for his master and in his affairs, he came to this city [Exeter] and in course of time he became acquainted with the widow of one John Bodley of this city. She . . . having found favour in his sight, he made his master acquainted therewith and with his good favour he followed his former suit to the widow and obtained and married her. And then, leaving his master, he remained and dwelled in this city, and followed the trade of merchandise wherein he had been brought up, and did prosper very well and increased unto good wealth and riches . . . [10].

Thomas Prestwood followed a familiar pattern in marrying a rich widow. So did Thomas Bodley, the grandson of John Bodley, when he married the widow of a wealthy Totnes merchant in the summer of 1586, within four months of her husband's death. Nicholas Ball of Totnes, then one of the richest little towns in England, had made a fortune in a short space of time 'specially by trading for pilchers', and much of this fortune passed by the marriage of his widow to Bodley. The Bodleian Library is founded in part at least upon the humble pilchard.

The marriages of Prestwood and Bodley illustrate a general thesis: the influence of rich widows upon economic progress. In an age when men generally died young, the supply of active and wealthy widows was a noticeable feature of society. Many an enterprising young man in the sixteenth century owed his ultimate success to this simple biological fact.

Thomas Richardson, a merchant dealing principally in wines, mayor in 1566-67, had come to Exeter from Cheshire, through some personal relationship which is not made clear by Hooker.

By means of one Michael Lymett of this city, apothecary, he was brought to this city and served under the said Lymett. When he came to ripe years and was married, he kept a wine tavern and was a merchant adventurer for wines, and following that trade in good order and diligently he attained to good wealth and nobility, and did not only serve this city by retail but also all the gentlemen in the shire of Devon by the tuns and hogsheads, with whom he was in great credit and favour. He was of very good conditions and qualities, given to all good exercises and a good companion for any gentleman or honest man, whether it were shooting, bowling, or any other pastime. And albeit he were very honest, friendly, and courteous to all men, so would he not receive wrong at any man's hands, neither would he give his beard for the washing. He had passed and borne all the offices of the city, in every of which he used and behaved himself very well . . . for which he was well respected both in town and country.

Simon Knight, mayor in 1570 and again in 1579, was Somerset born, of good parentage.

His father having many other children brought him to this city and bound him apprentice unto a merchant named John Morgan, after whose death he served under Mr William Hurst, who, having a good liking of the towardness of the young man did employ him both at his side and beyond the seas, and he did so well follow his business that he prospered very well and was of good wealth and hability, and was at length twice mayor of this city. [He] did very well in the first, but in the latter he was so encumbered in litigious and troublesome matters that in following of them he was the more remiss in public matters . . . [But] well thinking of himself and standing in his own conceit to be wiser than others, and also for his too much jesting of other men, he was much blamed and the less liked.

Though the Elizabethan merchant class was liberally recruited from outside, more often than not from the younger sons of good families, it contained also a solid core of second-generation mercantile families. Such were the Periams, the Midwinters, Blackalls (or Blackallers), Martins, and Spicers. Some successful merchants failed to find successors in trade: their eldest sons either moved out to a country estate or withdrew their money from trade to use it in other ways: we shall return to this point later. But a few merchant families continued into the second, and occasionally into the third generation. Of these, the Periams were perhaps the most notable. The first of them in the city, William Periam, was the son of a franklin in the nearby parish of Broadclyst. He had been admitted to the freedom of the city as a capper in the same year as William Hurst (1504-05) and had flourished exceedingly, making most of his early fortune at least in the tin trade and dying a rich man. He was followed in business by his second son, John Periam, who was chosen mayor in 1563 and again in 1572. He was a zealous Protestant and had assisted Lord Russell during the Catholic rebellion of 1549 in the West 'with money and other necessaries to his great comfort'. As a consequence of this, he was obliged to spend several years abroad during Mary's reign, by which he lost nothing for he became the chief governor of the company of English Merchants in Antwerp. He was apparently an unlikeable man, for Hooker, though a good Protestant and therefore well disposed to Periam on religious grounds, speaks of him with modified approval as 'a very worthy man in many respects, and had many good parts in him'. Nevertheless, he made a good mayor of the city.

> His government was upright. A great favourer of the poor man's cause, an upright judge in all causes of law depending before him, severe against the wicked and lewd persons who received at his hands according to their deserts, and friendly and loving to the good and honest, and them he defended against all enemies . . . As he lived, so he died virtuously, godly, and in years, whose memory deserves not to be forgotten.

The Periams were perhaps a quick-tempered lot. Hooker tells us of William Periam, mayor in 1532, that 'he was but a plain dealing man, but rough and soon offended if he was abused and with wrongs he would not lightly lay up . . .' He remained a peasant for all his business acumen and wealth. And the temper of his son is revealed to us in his will. He had left 'to Jasper Horsey to fynde at one of the Universities £30'. In a codicil a few months later he tightened his bequest: 'Jasper Horsey only to have his legacy if he stand bound to be at one of the Universities there to study Divinity and so to be of the ministry.' A few days later, there was a row. Young Jasper was evidently not amenable to the dictates of old Periam. To the will was added:

> This I write 22 May 1573. Forasmuch as Jasper Horsey went from the house on Whitsunday morning very ungratefully and uncourteously not saying farewell to me or any of all the household, whereas he had been sufficiently brought up as I take it v or vi years, I having in remembrance this his ungratefulness give him only 40 shillings with his apparel and his books and nothing else, so god bless him.

John Periam was a great believer in education. His own father, rough as he was, had caused him 'to be brought up in knowledge and learning', later putting him as apprentice to a merchant. His own eldest son, William, he sent to the High School in Exeter and thence on to Oxford, where he became a fellow of Exeter College, apparently at the age of seventeen, in 1551. William Periam turned to the law, in which (surprisingly) Devonians had always shown unnatural abilities, and eventually became a judge (1581) and sat on the commission for the trial of Mary Queen of Scots. Down in Devon he had his country seat at Fulford, a few miles outside Exeter, not far from his younger brother, John, who had ceased also to have any interests as a merchant and lived, for the latter part of his life, as a country gentleman.

Once admitted to the freedom of the city, by apprenticeship or by fine, the merchant set up in business for himself. No Exeter merchant was substantial enough to own a whole ship, or even half a ship. The great majority joined with half a dozen others to fill a ship with cargoes. Harry Maunder (died 1564) owned 'half a quarter of a barke called the *Dragon*, of Topsham', valued at £8. George Hunt (died 1565) owned half a ship called the *George*, valued at £30. And the ships of the late sixteenth century were generally very small. Of the 123 ships that entered the port of Exeter in the year 1597-98 no fewer than ninety-six were of less than 30 tons. The average ship belonging to the port of Exeter was one of 20 to 30 tons. The largest in that year were the *Dolphin* of Exmouth (100 tons), the *Endeavour* of Topsham (80 tons), and the *Rose* of Exmouth (70 tons). A typical sort of ship was the *Robert* of Topsham, of only 20 tons, which came in from St Malo in Brittany with a cargo shared among eleven Exeter merchants; or the *True Meaning* of Kenton, of 30 tons, which came in from Bordeaux with a cargo of 24 tuns of Gascon wine shared between two Exeter merchants and one from Tiverton.

Even at the end of the century, too, the range of the Exeter merchant's trading activities was not great. Of the ships entering the port in 1597-98, nearly one-half were engaged in the coasting trade, mainly from Wales with coal, from London with mixed cargoes, and from other Devon ports. Of the fifty ships coming in from foreign ports, Brittany sent the most (18), and the 'salt ports' of western France were second with 16. Other French ports (Rouen and Bordeaux) accounted for four more. So three ships out of every four in Exeter's foreign trade came from or went to France. Of the rest, five ships entered from Newfoundland (mainly with salt fish), four came in from Middelburg or Danzig, and three from Madeira or Portugal. The merchants of Exeter were certainly not as adventurous and wide-ranging as those of Plymouth. Their trade with France was a long-established one and they felt little desire, apart from Newfoundland, to open up new lines of country. What they could not get from France, and to a limited degree from a few other foreign ports, they relied upon getting through the re-export trade from London. There was, at the end of the sixteenth century, the beginning of wider interests. By about 1600 a small trade with Ireland and with the Baltic had been developed, and we can detect the beginnings of the trade with Holland which was to become the greatest of all the Exeter trades during the latter half of the seventeenth century. There was, indeed, a more considerable trade with Spain than might appear from casual references in the port books. This trade was stopped for years by war, but it is significant that in 1580, for example, the biggest 'adventure' that William Chappell was engaged in was in Spain, where he had £322 owing to him. From Spain, when political conditions permitted it, came Spanish wool and Bilbao iron.

The inventories of Exeter merchants' personal estates tell us a good deal more about their trading activities than we could gather from the port books or custom accounts. Nearly every merchant at this period carried on a retail business through a shop on his premises. The list of people who owed money to Harry Maunder at his death in 1564 is probably typical of most merchants' businesses. There were 112 debtors, of whom no fewer than seventy-five owed small sums ranging from one penny to twenty shillings. These, and probably others, are clearly retail customers. Other debtors owed several pounds and are identifiable as wholesale buyers. Such are Thomas Richardson, the vintner, who owed £18 9s 8d, and Philip Yard of Exeter, also a vintner, who owed £9 6s 8d for sack.

Harry Maunder had an extensive business in Spanish iron, supplying numerous smiths in the city and for a dozen miles around. But besides wine and iron, he dealt in an extraordinary miscellany of commodities: the 'shop book' speaks of canvas, calico, figs, coal, tin, linen cloth, hops, grindstones, mustard mills, vinegar, raisins, dowlas, saffron, alum, playing cards, shirts, and woollen cards, while in the shop and warehouse we find many other commodities, such as brass, brown paper, soap, wax, kerseys, yarn, thread, silk, nails, buttons, parchment, lead, pepper, ratsbane, and Heaven knows what else.

Much went to other shopkeepers and to country gentry. The Elizabethan merchant covered the whole range of trading, rather indiscriminately, from direct import from overseas or London and the coastal ports, down to pennyworths of things sold in the shop. There is some indication, however, that by the early seventeenth century the keeping of a shop was regarded as beneath the dignity of a big merchant, and he was beginning to leave that to others. When John Periam, in the third generation of the family (1616), left £1,000 to be lent to five Merchant Adventurers of the city, trading beyond the seas, he stipulated that they should not be shopkeepers by retail.

The only inventories of personal estate to survive are those in the court of orphans records among the city muniments [11]. This court was set up in 1563 to safeguard the interests of widows and orphaned children where a citizen died leaving children under age. Hence the value of many estates is less than it would have been had the head of the family lived to his full term of years. On the other hand, it may well be argued that death in the forties or fifties was a common feature of sixteenth-century life and to that extent these records are more truly representative of the economic facts of merchant life than those drawn from men who all died of old age. A table of twenty-seven merchants' estates for the period 1564 to 1618 is therefore as instructive as any (Table 7.1).

The average merchant estate was one of £1,913 gross (that of John Aplyn, 1594). This compares very closely, as we might expect, with the average personal estate of a Bristol merchant (over a somewhat wider period) which Professor Jordan puts at £1,921. In the same period, the average (median) personal estate of a London merchant was £7,780 [12], about four times that of Exeter or Bristol men. About one-third of the Exeter merchants left personal estate valued at £3,000 or more.

It will be observed from the table opposite that there is often a considerable gap between the gross personal estate and the net estate. This gap is accounted for in two ways: by the money owing at the time of death by the dead man, and by the debts due to him which the executors write off as 'doubtful', or more usually, 'desperate'. The proportion of 'desperate debts' to the whole debt owing to the merchant's estate is often remarkably high. In some instances they were greater than the 'good debts'. An outstanding example is that of the rich merchant William Martyn, who died in 1609. The good debts amounted to nearly £1,542, and the desperate debts to over £2,633. William Spicer (1604) was owed £300 in good debts, but a further £662 of debts were written off as 'desperate'. No uniformity is observable in this respect.

Sometimes the desperate debts are less than one-tenth of the whole; in other cases they are as much as two-thirds of the whole debt due to the

Table 7.1   Exeter merchants' estates, 1564-1618

Name	Date	Gross personal estate	Net personal estate
		£	£
Harry Maunder	1564	556	360
Edmond Whetcombe	1565	791	710
Edward Lymett	1571	509	382
John Bodley	1572	156	146
Thomas Prestwood	1576	905	662
William Chappell	1580	2,378	2,265
Thomas Chappell	1590	3,266	3,225
Richard Swete	1591	1,485	708
John Follett	1591	255	135
Richard Mawdytt	1592	356	277
Richard Reynolds	1592	2,086	1,473
John Aplyn	1594	1,913	1,592
John Spurway	1595	1,074	862
Walter Horsey	1597	2,670	2,464
Richard Beavis	1603	3,492	3,063
William Spicer	1604	3,825	2,916
David Bagwell	1604	675	−102*
John Trosse	1605	236	166
Thomas Cooke	1606	3,000	1,716
Alexander Germyn	1608	986	551
Robert Parr	1608	3,976	2,223
John Plea	1609	827	713
Thomas Snowe	1609	2,032	1,818
William Newcombe	1609	2,174	2,037
William Martyn	1609	6,381	4,401
Thomas Mogridge	1617	5,189	4,343
John Lant	1618	7,317	4,664

* David Bagwell died young at St Malo. His debts amounted to £777, exceeding his assets at that time.

dead man's estate. Much must have depended upon whether England was at war with the country where the debtors lay; but it is also clear from many inventories that a high proportion of 'desperate debts' were purely local.

The variation from one inventory to another is so great, and must so often arise from accidental circumstances at the time, that an average proportion of bad debts to good is probably rather meaningless. All we can note is that the Elizabethan merchant had to reckon with the serious possibility that a considerable proportion of the money owing to him at any given time was going to be difficult to collect, and that a considerable residue might have to be written off as beyond hope of realisation. The estimate of 'desperate debts' was probably a rather subjective one also, and might be considerably amended before the estate was finally wound up. We see this in the case of Richard Swete (1591), where the original estimate at the making of the inventory was of £295 3s 11d in desperate debts. In what seems to be the final reckoning, the figure had been reduced to £46 8s 5d. Executors probably tended to take an extremely conservative view of debts outstanding as a precaution against arousing optimistic hopes in the widow, but hoped for better things eventually.

Table 7.2   Good debts and desperate debts, 1565-1617

Name	Date	Good debts	Desperate debts	Total debts due
		£	£	£
Edmond Whetcombe	1565	230	81	311
William Chappell	1580	902	113	1,015
Thomas Chappell	1590	957	21	978
Richard Beavis	1603	256	193	449
William Spicer	1604	300	662	962
Alexander Germyn	1608	257	270	527
Robert Parr	1608	1,958	1,310	3,268
John Plea	1609	350	38	388
Thomas Snowe	1609	696	52	748
William Martyn	1609	1,542	2,634	4,176
William Tothill	1609	201	95	296
Thomas Mogridge	1617	1,186	410	1,596

We also notice the great variation in the sums of ready money kept in merchants' houses at any particular time. This is largely a reflection of the opportunities for investment and also perhaps of the enterprise, or lack of it, manifested by different men of wealth.

The second smallest sum of ready money was left by one of the wealthiest merchants in the city. This was Thomas Prestwood, the son of the Thomas Prestwood already referred to. The inventory of his personal estate does not reveal his true wealth, for he had put a great deal of money into real estate — both farms in the countryside and houses in the city. His total personal estate was therefore comparatively small — only £905, less than half the average. In such cases as this the inventories can be quite misleading about a man's true wealth.

Thomas Prestwood senior had built up a substantial merchanting business, but then, Hooker tells us,

in his later age by little and little he gave over his trade of merchandise and employed his wealth in purchasing of lands and in building of houses, especially within the city, which do yet remain as goodly ornaments to beautify the same. He died in good age and left

his lands and possessions to his only son Thomas Prestwood . . .
who, beginning where his father left, did not much follow the trade
of merchandise in which also he was trained up, but lived rather as a
gentleman by his lands . . . .

Table 7.3   Ready money in merchants' houses

Name	Date	(nearest £)
		£
Harry Maunder	1564	69
John Bodley	1572	20
Thomas Prestwood	1576	25
William Chappell	1580	192
Thomas Chappell	1590	1,303
Richard Swete	1591	566
Richard Beavis	1603	410
Thomas Mogridge	1617	914

This is why there was so little ready money in the house at his death in
1576, and why also his shop — for he still continued to live in a merchant's
house in the High Street — contained nothing but a few oddments worth
less than £4 in all. When Thomas Prestwood the elder died in 1558 he
possessed the manors of Butterford, Tynacre, and Venny Tedburn, and
farms in a dozen other parishes, besides a tin-blowing mill and a
fulling-mill, and eight large houses in the city of Exeter. His son Thomas
inherited this estate, was styled gentleman, and divided his time between a
large town house in the High Street of Exeter and his 'mansion house' of
Butterford, some thirty miles away in the South Hams.

William Chappell, who died in the early months of 1580, 'was
brought up in the trade of merchandise and by the same he grew to good
wealth, and giving himself to purchasing of lands he in a manner gave over
his trade'. Hooker here gives a slightly false impression, for there is a very
marked difference between the financial affairs of Thomas Prestwood
(1576) and William Chappell (1580). Prestwood's inventory shows very
little ready money, the shop abandoned to the storage of junk, and very
small debts due to the estate. William Chappell's inventory also shows a
shop containing nothing but oddments, but a larger sum of ready money
(nearly £200), and very considerable trading interests. More than 40 per
cent of his large personal estate took the form of trading debts due to him,
and another 20 per cent was wrapped up in 'adventures abroad', most of it
'in the Isles' and in Spain.

Merchants' wills and inventories tell us little or nothing about their
real estate, which in some instances was substantial. At least half a dozen
Elizabethan merchants at Exeter founded landed families, as for example
the Hursts, the Martins, the Periams, the Davys, and the Prestwoods. The
real estate of old William Hurst, who died in 1568, was exceptionally large.
It included six manors, farms in more than a score of parishes, and a
certain amount of house-property. John Periam had probably inherited

some lands from his father William, but of these we know nothing. By 1572, when he made his will, he was able to set up his elder son William (the future judge and baron of the exchequer) with the manor of Pancrasweek and lands in Pyworthy, Ottery St Mary, and Pinhoe, while to his younger son he left houses in Exeter and lands in half a dozen other parishes. This was not a large accumulation by comparison with the Hurst estate, but that was quite untypical. The successful Exeter merchant could probably hope for the lordship of one or two manors, and to possess farms in perhaps half a dozen parishes. Many big merchants achieved less than this.

The majority of merchants in the Elizabethan period had begun their careers as apprentices to Exeter merchants, though there was, as we have seen, always a small but important influx of men who had been apprenticed elsewhere and who had come to the city as mature men. These are usually distinguishable in the city records by the fact that they obtain the freedom of the city, without which they could not trade within its bounds, by fine and not by apprenticeship. Those born in Exeter received their education at the High School, the only grammar school in the city. From this they passed on to a seven-year apprenticeship and then set up in business on their own account, unless, as in a few cases, they remained in the family business, like John Periam, or Thomas Prestwood, or Thomas Chappell.

Marriage was the next important step, and it was most likely to be to the daughter of a fellow-merchant. The close relationships by marriage among the leading Exeter merchant families at least (perhaps there was a slightly wider choice of partner among the lesser men) have been worked out by Professor MacCaffrey, and could certainly be paralleled in other commercial cities. By his marriage, then, the Exeter merchant became related to a more or less numerous group of leading families, and his social standing was henceforth assured. Sometimes the merchant married into a small landed family. Thomas Prestwood the elder married the widow of another Exeter merchant who had been the daughter of a Kingswear gentleman; and his son married the daughter of William Strode of Newnham near Plymouth.

As time went by his family grew. Nothing could be farther from the truth than that sixteenth-century children died like flies, or that the average family of survivors was a small one. Certainly it is not true of the latter half of the sixteenth century and of the first generation of the seventeenth. At Exeter the court of orphans records give us a good picture of the typical family. Out of thirty-three merchant households in the Elizabethan period, in which the father had died before his time, about one in seven (15 per cent) had seven, eight, or nine children. At the other end of the scale, one-third had only one, two or three children. The average number of children for the thirty-three households was 4·7; but against this we must set the fact that many men in the sample had died relatively young and before they could produce a 'normal' family. The largest single group (40 per cent of the total) had five or six children, and this must be regarded as the 'normal' family in this social class. Of all the children in the sample, 55 per cent were male, 45 per cent female.

A very small sample of merchant wills from Totnes, the wills moreover of men who lived (as far as we can discover) their normal term of life, shows forty-one living children in five well-to-do families, an average of eight per family. A fuller sample, were it obtainable, would unquestionably lower this remarkable figure; but it serves to indicate that our 'normal' figure for Exeter of five or six children is a very credible one. To this typical family of seven or eight, including the parents, we have to add probably two apprentices at any given time and at least a couple of maid-servants, giving us a household of some dozen people.

With such a high figure in mind, we need not be surprised at the number of rooms in the Elizabethan merchant's house as we find it described in the Exeter inventories. A sample of twenty houses described between 1564 and 1609 shows that only six were smaller than ten rooms, eleven contained ten to fifteen rooms, and three more than fifteen rooms [13]. The largest houses were those of Henry James (22 rooms) in 1578, and Robert Parr (20 rooms) in 1608. Seven of the eighteen houses had fourteen or fifteen rooms and may be regarded as the typical dwelling of the wealthier merchant.

There is good evidence for saying that houses became larger and grander during the Elizabethan period, either by additions to an existing house or through a complete rebuilding. Thus the inventory of Richard Beavis in 1603 shows a fifteen-room house of which at least two rooms are described as 'new'. More often, however, a completely new house was built on the site at some date in the Elizabethan period or in the early seventeenth century. In particular there seems to have been some considerable rebuilding in the 1550s and 1560s. We have already seen that Thomas Prestwood the elder built some good houses before he died in 1558, and there are dated houses (1564, 1567) still surviving in the High Street, as well as others of exactly the same design which no longer exist but which can be recovered in old drawings and photographs.

The fact that larger and more ostentatious houses were being built in increasing numbers is suggested by a civic by-law, made in 1563.

> For avoidance of sundry inconveniences which daily do grow by the excessive buildings in sailing [sealinge] themselves further out than it appurtaineth or should be used: it is ordered that no manner of person or persons shall build nor attempt to build any house or houses within this city outwards towards any of the streets whereby the same shall have any sailing into the streets without the view and assent of the mayor, aldermen, and of the chamberlain be first had therein.

On the same day (21 August 1563), Robert Hunte was ordered to pull down forthwith a room and a projecting window in it which exceeded the limits of an earlier regulation. This regulation permitted a room to be built outwards to a depth of four feet beyond the principal of the house, and a window to project not more than sixteen inches farther, giving a maximum total projection of five feet four inches beyond the principal. The new regulation, made the same day, fixed no maximum measurements for oversailing, but required each building to be inspected and approved by the mayor and others.

We learn a great deal from the inventories about the houses of Elizabethan merchants, though we cannot always be sure of their exact plan in default of surviving buildings. Several such buildings survive, but most have been altered internally to meet later needs and do not therefore help us as much as we could hope over the original Elizabethan plan. Indeed it is unrealistic to assume that there was a single type of house inhabited by merchants at this period. For one thing, the merchant class covered a wide range of worldly wealth. Table 7.1 shows that even in the limited period between 1590 and 1603 the richest merchant was worth ten times more than the smallest merchant and their houses would have been correspondingly different. And further, in any given generation (especially before the early seventeenth century), some merchants would have been living in houses that were survivors (slightly modernised perhaps) of the Middle Ages, while others were living in pure Elizabethan 'mansions' — for so they are repeatedly called in the records of the time — which were the result of a complete rebuilding on the old site.

To illustrate the variety of merchants' houses therefore we may take two or three examples in detail from the inventories. The house of Edmond Whetcombe, who died in 1565 worth just under £800, was one of only six rooms, or seven if we count the 'spence' separately. Apart from the shop, it had a hall, a parlour, kitchen and spence, and three bedrooms, called respectively, 'the Forechamber', the 'high chamber', and 'an other chamber'. It is difficult to be certain about the plan of this house and the disposition of the various rooms, but it may well have been a medieval hall-house of which a few (somewhat battered) still remain in the street where Edmond Whetcombe lived. The simple plan of shop, hall, parlour, and kitchen, with some chambers over, suggests a medieval house with a large open-roofed hall.

Nor was the six-roomed house of Richard Mawdytt very different at his death in 1592. He, too, was a small merchant worth only £356 gross. His house is described as consisting of a shop, a hall, parlour, and kitchen, and of three chambers (bedrooms) above — one over the kitchen, another over the parlour, and 'the maidens chamber'. Here there was pretty certainly no chamber over the hall, for the maidservants' chamber would have been a small one tucked away somewhere. It was still the open-roofed medieval hall, dating in all probability from the fifteenth century, like so many surviving examples in the city.

As against these smaller and older houses, occupied by the lesser merchants, we have the new-built grander houses of what may be called the civic merchants, that is those belonging or related to the governing oligarchy of the city and likely to fill the office of mayor, sheriff, or receiver. The house of Thomas Prestwood the younger (1576) is a fine example of this type, possibly one of the beautiful houses built by his father before 1558. Such houses, with fifteen or more rooms, are best described by means of conventional plans of each floor, which, while not accurate in every detail, give the essential disposition of the rooms beyond much doubt (see Fig. 7.1).

The Prestwood house, like all the larger town houses of the time, occupied a long narrow site, fronting on to the main street and running back to a small street which acted as what we should call a service road. A side-passage, running the length of the house and generally known as 'the entry' or occasionally as 'tween doors', gave access to the groundfloor rooms and finally emerged at the back gate. The total depth of the house and all its appurtenances was considerable — in all probability about 140 feet. The frontage, on the other hand, was probably no more than 20 to 24 feet [14].

On the ground floor the almost invariable plan of the larger house from the middle of the sixteenth century onwards was that of two blocks of building separated by a small courtyard. The front block contained the shop with a parlour behind, and possibly a spence or small buttery. The back block contained the kitchen, larder, main buttery, and any other domestic offices such as the brewhouse. Access between front and back blocks in bad weather was provided by a covered way, formed by the first-floor gallery being carried on a short colonnade.

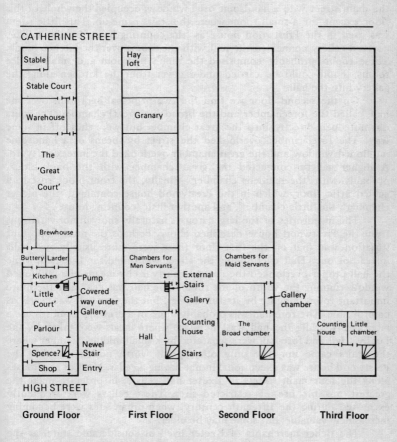

Fig. 7.1   Conjectural plan of the Prestwood house in 1576.
(Not drawn to scale)

Behind the kitchen block of the Prestwood house lay a much larger court, called the Great Court in the inventory, on the other side of which was the warehouse. Behind that again was a little court containing the stable with hayloft over, which abutted directly on to the back street and so completed the property. Above the warehouse in all probability was the granary. Stable and hayloft, warehouse and granary, could be serviced (in or out) by way of the back street. The problem of handling heavy or bulky loads on such a narrow urban site was easily solved. It is an arrangement we find all along the main streets of Exeter. Back streets run parallel to the High Street and Fore Street on both sides, and all the largest properties extended right through from the main street to the back street. Many do so to this day.

Access to the first floor of the front block was by means of a newel stair which carried on indeed up to the top of the house. In the Prestwood house, the hall, which was of course the principal living room, overlooking the main street with a handsome oriel window, occupied the whole of this floor except for a small room where the stairs came up. This little room was used in the Prestwood house as 'the counting house by the hall'. A covered gallery connected the hall with the rooms over the kitchen block. These rooms probably comprised the men's bedroom and small service rooms. Food could be carried under cover from the kitchen along the gallery into the hall.

On the second floor we find the two principal bedrooms over the hall, called the forechamber and the broad (i.e. great) chamber. The stairs did not open directly into the great chamber but were shut off in some way. The forechamber overlooked the street by means of a handsome mullioned window and the great chamber overlooked the inner courtyard. A higher gallery connected the great chamber with the back block, probably with 'the maidens chamber'. Finally, the front block rose to a gabled attic floor, which in the Prestwood house contained 'the higher chamber', the 'little chamber', and another little 'counting house'. . . .

The inventories of the larger houses naturally show minor variations from the Prestwood house described above. Perhaps the most important variation was that on the first floor there were more usually two halls instead of one. That overlooking the street was called the fore-hall, while the hall proper overlooked the central courtyard by means of a mullioned window running the width of the room. The hall was generally the more important room, judging by its furnishings, but the fore-hall was nearly as comfortable. The fore-hall was probably more of a drawing-room (to use a later term), while the hall was the place where meals were taken by the family. Hall and fore-hall were separated by a small middle chamber where the stairs came up. The only other point worth noticing is that the Prestwood house was exceptional in not having a cellar. Most of the houses along the four main streets of Exeter had cellars, in order to make the greatest possible use of restricted sites. These cellars were frequently excavated during the fifteenth century, when urban sites were becoming increasingly valuable; but some may be older.

The richer merchants of Exeter lived in considerable state, as the inventories show. Their plate, 'napery', and apparel, as listed in the inventories, are all very considerable, indeed ostentatious. It is not unusual to find plate worth £100 or more in a merchant's house. The mayor of Exeter was an important man and was expected to entertain well, and to live well when not entertaining. Although he received a large allowance from the Chamber, his expenses were usually higher than this [15]. Only a rich merchant could afford the honour, and John Woolcot was passed over for many years because he was not considered rich enough to sustain the dignity of the office.

Woolcot in fact finally achieved the mayoralty in 1565. Of him Hooker says:

> This mayor had passed all the offices towards the mayoralty for about 22 years past and by reason of his age and his small wealth it was not thought nor meant that ever the office of the mayoralty should have fallen unto his lot. Nevertheless, when the matter so fell out, and no means found how the same might be avoided, order was taken both that his house should be prepared and also he to be furnished with money for his diet with liberality. The Chamber did consider he was in times past a great merchant and adventured very much, whereby he had great wealth, but in the end his losses were so great that he was very poor and lived in very mean a state.

We know little that is personal of these merchants of Exeter beyond the brief glimpses Hooker gives us. John Woolcot was one of the old way of thinking.

> He was a zealous man in the Romish religion and too much addicted unto papistry, and in the commotion time [the local description for several generations afterwards of the rebellion of 1549] when the Commons of Devon and Cornwall were up in rebellion for the same, and he was in the city the time of the besieging of the same: yet his affection was such towards them that upon a day, when he was captain of the ward for the charge of the West Gate of this city, he went out at the West Gate to the rebels without any commission and had conference with them, which was not after forgiven but turned him to displeasure.

Hooker was an old Protestant and doubtless remembered where others charitably forgot. Many of the leading merchants in that year had been Catholics — the city seems to have been pretty evenly divided at the top — but the older generation were dying one by one, and the younger men seem to have changed over easily enough. Indeed, it was not always a case of conforming to the established order of the new Settlement. John Periam had assisted Russell to crush the Catholics in 1549 while old William Periam, his father, kept his Catholic sympathies to the end. One would give much to know what passed between father and son in that bad year; but we do not even have William Periam's will to guide us. He was still a Catholic a year or two before his death, when he refused to give up a chalice and a pair of vestments to the Commissioners for Church Goods. He had given these to his parish church of St Olave about 1547 and had taken them back again when the Commissioners appeared.

The Elizabethan merchants were probably Protestants to a man. Of Thomas Prestwood the younger we have a more certain glimpse. A man's character is revealed by what he reads (above all when he has to buy his own books) and Prestwood's books are very revealing. The inventory of 1576 speaks of 'two bibles, one of Geneva making, and Calvin's book [presumably the *Christian Institutes* published definitively in 1559], Turner's *Herbal*, two books of service, one book of *The Fall of Princes*, a bridgement of the Statutes, Hall's *Chronicles*, with divers other books of Latin, French and English'. Prestwood read at 'a desk for a book' in the hall, looking out onto the teeming High Street below, though it was quiet enough in the evenings. Everybody was indoors by nine o'clock, and most were asleep.

Most merchants, apart from their business, lived private lives. The opportunities for public service were very few. There were only twenty-four places on the Chamber and once admitted a man stayed on for life. Vacancies occurred only at long intervals on the death or disablement of a sitting member. The great majority even of the merchant class could not expect to reach the Chamber, least of all the mayoralty. Members of parliament for the city, sheriffs, and receivers, all were chosen from the Twenty-four. Beyond that, there were no opportunities for a man to make a public mark.

In the prime of his life, usually, the Exeter merchant made his will. By this he generally settled such real estate as he possessed — houses and other small properties in the city, farms, tithes, and even manors in the country if he were a successful man. He also distributed considerable sums of money among his wife and children. John Periam (*c.* 1510-73) disposed of nearly £3,000 in money by his will, chiefly to his two sons (William got £1,400, John £800, and an unmarried daughter £300). Some of the sons' money may have been reinvested in the family business. But it is evident that in many families, especially where a merchant died young and the court of orphans administered his estate, the distribution of his personal wealth must have involved the end of the business, rather like the savagery of death duties today. Of Alexander Germyn's net estate of £550 11s 5d (1608), his widow got about £367 (two-thirds of the whole) and the five children got about £36 14s 1d each. Robert Parr's nine children (1608) got £82 6s 10d each, the widow just over £740. Harry Maunder apparently left £360 net estate in 1564, with no surviving widow but nine children, each of whom got £40. So the Maunder business dissolved at once. Thomas Chappell left a widow and ten children in 1590, and even his large business (worth over £3,224 net) is heard of no more. Where the legacy was a large one, it may, as suggested above, have been reinvested in the business; or an elder son may have used his small inheritance to build up another business almost from scratch. But the general tendency was for a business to dissolve in every generation, mainly because its assets had to be realised and distributed among a considerable number of children. A large number of daughters was a particular misfortune from this point of view; the average merchant had to provide for the marriage of three or four daughters. Even here, a dowry might go to fertilise the son-in-law's own business. Only the really large businesses, however, could stand the effect of the merchant's death, and only these therefore survived into a second generation and, more rarely still, into a third.

In every generation, some merchants had left money for charities according to their means. Professor Jordan has recently traced the tremendous flow of charitable bequests in the sixteenth and seventeenth centuries, above all from the merchant class in the leading towns. How do the Exeter merchants stand up to this scrutiny?

A number of merchants took a special interest in the welfare of poor and friendless prisoners. Griffith Ameredith, who died in 1558, had been appalled in his lifetime by the way in which the bodies of those hanged were treated. They were brought back from the gallows, a mile or so outside the city, slung on a staff between two men, and having been brought to Exeter they were then flung into a grave in their clothes. Ameredith left a piece of property in east Devon, yielding 38 shillings a year, to provide a shroud and a coffin for each body. William Tryvett, mayor in 1573, bequeathed 'one great Brass Crock, to boil meat therein, for the Use of the Prisoners in the Southgate Prison'. The main flow of bequests was, however, for the relief of the poor, more especially those who were old, and for the encouragement by timely loans of young artificers. The largest single benefaction was that of William Hurst in 1567, when he founded an almshouse for twelve poor men and endowed it with lands to the value of £12 4s 0d per annum. Both Thomas Prestwood (1576) and John Davy (1599) left money also for the foundation of smaller almshouses.

In 1572 John Periam left £100, to be lent to two young merchants freely for four years in order to set them on their feet. And from 1599 onwards there was a steady flow of bequests designed to provide free loans for young artificers or tradesmen for a period of years. The main flow of benefactions at Exeter came, however, a generation or two later, well into the seventeenth century, and even then Exeter saw nothing to match the noble foundation of Peter Blundell, of a school at Tiverton (1599). But Blundell had accumulated a fortune as a cloth merchant at Tiverton, fourteen miles to the north, far beyond that of the richest merchant in Exeter at this time.

The rich merchant's funeral was usually a costly affair. For some of the lesser men a sum of £10 to £20 sufficed to cover all the charges; but Thomas Chappell's funeral in 1590 cost as much as £120, and Walter Horsey's £100 in 1597. The funeral charges of Thomas Prestwood in January 1577 amounted to a modest £12 7s 2d. This included the cost of ten yards of black cloth 'for the children's gowns and coats' £4, 'to a tailor for making the boys' coats, 3s', six shillings to a joiner 'for the chest', 'for a tombstone 13s 4d' and 'for engraving the Tombstone, 9s'. At William Newcombe's funeral in 1609 the mourning clothes cost £42, the actual burial in Cathedral £20, and finally — the closing scene in the life and death of the merchant — the funeral dinner, in the hall of his dwelling-house, costing £13 6s 8d. But it is, perhaps, more fitting to say farewell to the Exeter merchant as he is lowered into the grave, in the nave of his own little red-sandstone parish church to the mournful singing of the Vicars Choral and amid the darkening light of a cold January afternoon.

Notes

1   Exeter city records, Book 55 (known as John Hooker's Common-place Book), which contains a number of biographies of mayors written by Hooker from his personal knowledge. He was chamberlain of the city from 1556 until his death in 1601.

2   William Hurst is traditionally said to have died (in 1568) at the age of ninety-six, which would have made him eighty-nine at the time of his last mayoralty. The records show, however, that he was admitted to the freedom of the city by apprenticeship in 1504-05, probably at the age of twenty-one, so making his birthdate about 1483. This gives a more likely, though still remarkable, chronology for his public career.

3   For the ranking by wealth of English towns in the 1520s see W. G. Hoskins, 'Provincial towns in the early sixteenth century', *Transactions of the Royal Historical Society*, 5th ser., vi, 4-6. Since that time Coventry and Salisbury had both greatly declined, leaving Exeter in undisputed fourth place among the provincial towns.

4   The occupations of new freemen are not regularly stated in the records until 1575. The terms 'mercer' and 'merchant' were practically interchangeable at Exeter, as is abundantly clear from the records. I am indebted to Mr R. A. MacKinley, the keeper of the Exeter city records, for the use of his valuable lists of the freemen, as yet unpublished.

5   This estimate of an 'upper class' amounting to 5 per cent of the total population agrees substantially with the conclusions of Professor W. T. MacCaffrey, arrived at by an entirely different method, in *Exeter, 1540-1640* (1st edn., Cambridge, Mass., 1958) pp. 249, 250.

6   For more examples of merchant family alliances see MacCaffrey, *op. cit.* 254-6.

7   It had 591 families in 1563, say about 650 families during the later Elizabethan period.

8   For Norwich, see B. Cozens-Hardy and E. A. Kent, *The Mayors of Norwich, 1403 to 1835*.

9   P. McGrath, *Merchants and Merchandise in 17th-century Bristol* (Bristol Rec. Soc. xix), pp. xxv-xxvi. I am greatly indebted to Miss Elizabeth Ralph, the city archivist of Bristol, for preparing for me a list of the Elizabethan merchants of Bristol and their occupations. There is no complete printed list for this period.

10   Hooker, Commonplace Book, *loc. cit.* The city records show Thomas Prestwood admitted by fine to the freedom in 1528-29, and chosen for the Twenty-four on 27 September 1534. He was mayor in 1544-45 and in 1550-51, and sat in parliament as the member for Exeter from October 1549 until April 1552.

11   The entire contents of the Exeter probate registry were needlessly destroyed in an air-raid of May 1942, while the inventories preserved (if that is the correct word) at Somerset House are still inaccessible to students.

12   W. K. Jordan, *Philanthropy in England*, 376. The average personal estate for a provincial merchant at this period was £1,428: *ibid.* 336.

13   In counting rooms I have excluded the shop, cellar, warehouse, stables, and any 'domestic offices' such as a brewhouse.

14   The Prestwood house, which stood in St Stephen's parish, on the High Street and pretty certainly near St Stephen's church, has long ago been destroyed. Since the site is known, however, it is possible to give these measurements.

15   The mayor's allowance had been raised to £40 in 1551, to £66 13s 4d in 1564, to £80 in 1579, and to £120 before the end of the century.

8   The market towns

Alan Everitt

The market town

The number and origin of market towns

Despite the expansion of private bargaining in the sixteenth century, the market town was still, and was destined to remain, the normal place of sale and purchase for the great majority of country people. Scattered up and down the countryside, at intervals of every few miles, there were about 760 market towns in Tudor and Stuart England and fifty in Wales, each with its official weekly market day or days and its fairs held once or twice a year. Although the population of the country was less than one-tenth that of today, there were far more market towns than now. The intense localism of society and the absence of mechanical transport demanded their proliferation.

Some of these markets had been founded well before the Conquest, like Gloucester, Winchcombe and Bristol in Gloucestershire. Other early foundations, like Sevenoaks in Kent, originated spontaneously at casual or traditional meeting places, and never received an official charter [1]. But the great majority of markets came into existence in the period Professor Finberg has described as 'the golden age of borough-making in England', the two hundred years or so following the Norman Conquest. Of the thirty-four Tudor and Stuart market towns of Gloucestershire, all but five had been founded before the Black Death, and more than half before the reign of Edward I; they had existed for upwards of 250 years before our period began [2]. In Lancashire the peak of development came rather later, but there too more than half the thirty markets extant under the Tudors and early Stuarts had been flourishing for two centuries before 1500. Many new medieval towns were fresh creations on hitherto unoccupied sites; not infrequently, as at Newmarket, Northleach and Market Harborough, the new territory was carved out of the corner of an existing parish or group of parishes, whose boundaries often became a source of contention in the sixteenth century [3].

Despite this proliferation of markets, there were far fewer market towns and villages in the sixteenth century than three centuries earlier —

Alan Everitt, 'The Market Town', from J. Thirsk, ed., *The Agrarian History of England and Wales*, iv (Cambridge University Press) 1967, 467-506.

probably less than one-third as many. The population of the country may by that date have returned to or surpassed its former peak; but scores and hundreds of markets had perished in the generations following the Black Death, and were never revived. In Norfolk, where at one time there had been 130, there were now only thirty-one. In Gloucestershire, where there had formerly been at least fifty-three, there were now no more than thirty-four. In Lancashire, where charters were granted for no fewer than eighty-five markets and fairs, while a further fifty arose by prescription, there were in 1640 not more than thirty market towns in the county [4].

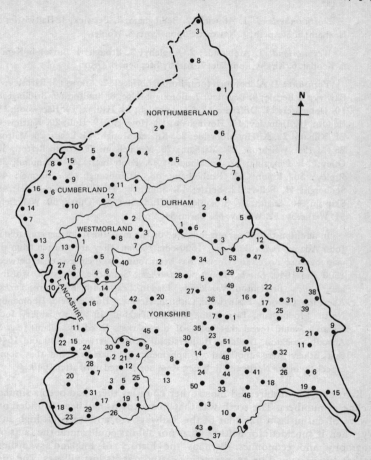

Fig. 8.1 Markets in northern England, *c.* 1500-1640.

Cumberland: 1. Alston; 2. Blennerhasset; 3. Bootle; 4. Brampton; 5. Carlisle; 6. Cockermouth; 7. Egremont; 8. Holme Cultram; 9. Ireby; 10. Keswick; 11. Kirkoswald; 12. Penrith; 13. Ravenglass; 14. Whitehaven; 15. Wigton; 16. Workington.

Durham: 1. Barnard Castle; 2. Bishop Auckland; 3. Darlington; 4. Durham; 5. Hartlepool; 6. Staindrop; 7. Sunderland.

Lancashire: 1. Ashton-under-Lyne; 2. Blackburn; 3. Bolton; 4. Burnley; 5. Bury; 6. Cartmel; 7. Chorley; 8. Clitheroe; 9. Colne; 10. Dalton-in-Furness; 11. Garstang; 12. Haslingden; 13. Hawkshead; 14. Hornby; 15. Kirkham; 16. Lancaster; 17. Leigh; 18. Liverpool; 19. Manchester; 20. Ormskirk; 21. Padiham; 22. Poulton-le-Fylde; 23. Prescot; 24. Preston; 25. Rochdale; 26. Salford; 27. Ulverston; 28. Walton-le-Dale; 29. Warrington; 30. Whalley; 31. Wigan.

Northumberland: 1. Alnwick; 2. Bellingham; 3. Berwick; 4. Haltwistle; 5. Hexham; 6. Morpeth; 7. Newcastle upon Tyne; 8. Wooler.

Westmorland: 1. Ambleside; 2. Appleby; 3. Brough; 4. Burton-in-Kendal; 5. Kendal; 6. Kirkby Lonsdale; 7. Kirkby Stephen; 8. Orton.

Yorkshire: 1. Aldborough (near Boroughbridge); 2. Askrigg; 3. Barnsley; 4. Bawtry; 5. Bedale; 6. Beverley; 7. Boroughbridge; 8. Bradford; 9. Bridlington; 10. Doncaster; 11. Driffield; 12. Guisborough; 13. Halifax; 14. Harewood; 15. Hedon; 16. Helmsley; 17. Hovingham; 18. Howden; 19. Hull; 20. Kettlewell; 21. Kilham; 22. Kirkby Moorside; 23. Knaresborough; 24. Leeds; 25. Malton; 26. Market Weighton; 27. Masham; 28. Middleham; 29. Northallerton; 30. Otley; 31. Pickering; 32. Pocklington; 33. Pontefract; 34. Richmond; 35. Ripley; 36. Ripon; 37. Rotherham; 38. Scarborough; 39. Seamer; 40. Sedbergh; 41. Selby; 42. Settle; 43. Sheffield; 44. Sherburn-in-Elmet; 45. Skipton; 46. Snaith; 47. Stokesley; 48. Tadcaster; 49. Thirsk; 50. Wakefield; 51. Wetherby; 52. Whitby; 53. Yarm; 54. York.

In addition to the markets indicated on the map, the following are listed in John Adams, *Index Villarum,* 1690 edn, *passim.* They are omitted from the map because no clear evidence has been found of their existence between 1500 and 1640. *Cumb.:* Longtown; *Durham:* Stanhope, Stockton, Wolsingham; *Lancs.:* Broughton; *Northumb.:* Elsdon, Learmouth, Rothbury; *Yorks.:* Aberford, Cawood, Easingwold, Gisburn, Hornsea, Huddersfield, Hunmanby, North Frodingham, Patrington, Thorne, Tickhill. In all probability local research would reveal that some of the markets listed by Adams (e.g. St Austell, Stockton, Dedham, Huddersfield) existed between 1500 and 1640; that others were unofficial or ephemeral in character; and that some, especially in the North and in Wales, were not created until after 1640.

In Kent and Devonshire and most other counties there had been a similar decline in numbers. The truth was that many towns had been founded on a wave of enthusiasm like that of the Railway Age, and were left high and dry when it subsided; for neither kings nor abbots could annul the facts of geography and economics. Perhaps the history of England's vanished market towns would be as interesting a study as its lost villages. The old market cross which today stands forlorn among the trees of Stapleford Park in Leicestershire, where the village too has now all but disappeared, bears silent testimony to the forgotten aspirations of scores of villages and their manorial lords in medieval England.

In the sixteenth and seventeenth centuries there were still many markets which hovered on the verge of extinction. That at Thornbury in

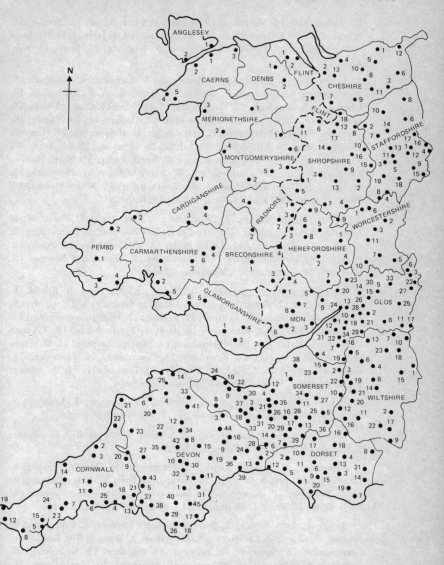

Fig. 8.2   Markets in western England and Wales, *c.* 1500-1640.

England

Cheshire: 1. Altrincham; 2. Chester; 3. Congleton; 4. Frodsham; 5. Knutsford; 6. Macclesfield; 7. Malpas; 8. Middlewich; 9. Nantwich; 10. Northwich; 11. Sandbach; 12. Stockport; 13. Tarvin.

Cornwall: 1. Bodmin; 2. Boscastle; 3. Camelford; 4. East Looe; 5. Falmouth; 6. Fowey; 7. Grampound; 8. Helston; 9. Launceston; 10. Liskeard;

11. Lostwithiel; 12. Marazion; 13. Millbrook; 14. Padstow; 15. Penryn; 16. Penzance; 17. St Columb Major; 18. St Germans; 19. St Ives; 20. St Stephen's by Launceston; 21. Saltash; 22. Stratton; 23. Tregoney; 24. Truro; 25. West Looe.

Devonshire: 1. Ashburton; 2. Axminster; 3. Bampton; 4. Barnstaple; 5. Bere Alston; 6. Bideford; 7. Bovey Tracey; 8. Bow; 9. Bradninch; 10. Chagford; 11. Chudleigh; 12. Chulmleigh; 13. Colyton; 14. Combe Martin; 15. Crediton; 16. Cullompton; 17. Dartmouth; 18. Dodbrooke; 19. Exeter; 20. Great Torrington; 21. Hartland; 22. Hatherleigh; 23. Holsworthy; 24. Honiton; 25. Ilfracombe; 26. Kingsbridge; 27. Lifton; 28. Membury; 29. Modbury; 30. Moretonhampstead; 31. Newton Abbot; 32. North Bovey; 33. North Molton; 34. North Tawton; 35. Okehampton; 36. Ottery St Mary; 37. Plymouth; 38. Plympton St Mary; 39. Sidmouth; 40. South Brent; 41. South Molton; 42. South Tawton; 43. Tavistock; 44. Tiverton; 45. Totnes.

Dorset: 1. Abbotsbury; 2. Beaminster; 3. Bere Regis; 4. Blandford; 5. Bridport; 6. Cerne Abbas; 7. Corfe Castle; 8. Cranborne; 9. Dorchester; 10. Evershot; 11. Frampton; 12. Lyme Regis; 13. Milton Abbas; 14. Poole; 15. Puddletown; 16. Shaftesbury; 17. Sherborne; 18. Sturminster Newton; 19. Wareham; 20. Weymouth; 21. Wimborne Minster.

Gloucestershire: 1. Berkeley; 2. Bisley; 3. Blockley; 4. Bristol; 5. Cheltenham; 6. Chipping Campden; 7. Chipping Sodbury; 8. Cirencester; 9. Coleford; 10. Dursley; 11. Fairford; 12. Falfield; 13. Frampton-on-Severn; 14. Gloucester; 15. Great Witcombe; 16. Horton; 17. Lechlade; 18. Leonard Stanley; 19. Marshfield; 20. Mitcheldean; 21. Minchinhampton; 22. Moreton-in-Marsh; 23. Newent; 24. Newnham; 25. Northleach; 26. Painswick; 27. Stow-on-the-Wold; 28. Stroud; 29. Tetbury; 30. Tewkesbury; 31. Thornbury; 32. Wickwar; 33. Winchcombe; 34. Wotton-under-Edge.

Herefordshire: 1. Bromyard; 2. Hereford; 3. Kington; 4. Ledbury; 5. Leominster; 6. Pembridge; 7. Ross-on-Wye; 8. Weobley; 9. Wigmore.

Monmouthshire: 1. Abergavenny; 2. Caerleon; 3. Chepstow; 4. Grosmont; 5. Monmouth; 6. Newport; 7. Raglan; 8. Usk.

Shropshire: 1. Bishop's Castle; 2. Bridgnorth; 3. Church Stretton; 4. Cleobury Mortimer; 5. Clun; 6. Ellesmere; 7. Ludlow; 8. Market Drayton; 9. Much Wenlock; 10. Newport; 11. Oswestry; 12. Prees; 13. Shipton; 14. Shrewsbury; 15. Tong; 16. Wellington; 17. Wem; 18. Whitchurch.

Somerset: 1. Axbridge; 2. Bath; 3. Bishop's Lydeard; 4. Bridgwater; 5. Bruton; 6. Chard; 7. Crewkerne; 8. Dulverton; 9. Dunster; 10. Frome; 11. Glastonbury; 12. Huntspill; 13. Ilchester; 14. Ilminster; 15. Keynsham; 16. Langport; 17. Martock; 18. Milverton; 19. Minehead; 20. North Curry; 21. North Petherton; 22. Norton St Philip; 23. Pensford; 24. Porlock; 25. Queen Camel; 26. St Michael Church; 27. Shepton Mallet; 28. Somerton; 29. South Petherton; 30. Stogumber; 31. Taunton; 32. Watchet; 33. Wellington; 34. Wells; 35. Weston Zoyland; 36. Wincanton; 37. Wiveliscombe; 38. Wrington; 39. Yeovil.

Staffordshire: 1. Abbots Bromley; 2. Betley; 3. Brewood; 4. Burton-upon-Trent; 5. Cannock; 6. Cheadle; 7. Eccleshall; 8. Leek; 9. Lichfield; 10.

Newcastle-under-Lyme; 11. Penkridge; 12. Rugeley; 13. Stafford; 14. Stone; 15. Tamworth; 16. Tutbury; 17. Uttoxeter; 18. Walsall; 19. Wolverhampton.

Wiltshire: 1. Aldbourne; 2. Amesbury; 3. Bradford-on-Avon; 4. Calne; 5. Castle Combe; 6. Chippenham; 7. Cricklade; 8. Devizes; 9. Downton; 10. Highworth; 11. Hindon; 12. Maiden Bradley; 13. Malmesbury; 14. Market Lavington; 15. Marlborough; 16. Mere; 17. Salisbury; 18. Swindon; 19. Trowbridge; 20. Warminster; 21. Westbury; 22. Wilton; 23. Wootton Bassett.

Worcestershire: 1. Bewdley; 2. Bromsgrove; 3. Droitwich; 4. Dudley; 5. Evesham; 6. Kidderminster; 7. Pershore; 8. Stourbridge; 9. Tenbury; 10. Upton-on-Severn; 11. Worcester.

Wales

Anglesey: 1. Beaumaris; 2. Newborough.

Breconshire: 1. Brecon; 2. Builth; 3. Crickhowell; 4. Hay.

Caernarvonshire: 1. Bangor; 2. Caernarvon; 3. Conway; 4. Nefyn; 5. Pwllheli.

Cardiganshire: 1. Aberystwyth; 2. Cardigan; 3. Lampeter; 4. Tregaron.

Carmarthenshire: 1. Carmarthen; 2. Kidwelly; 3. Llandilo; 4. Llandovery; 5. Llanelly; 6. Llangadog.

Denbighshire: 1. Denbigh; 2. Ruthin; 3. Wrexham.

Flintshire: 1. Caerwys; 2. Flint.

Glamorgan: 1. Bridgend; 2. Cardiff; 3. Cowbridge; 4. Llantrisant; 5. Neath; 6. Swansea.

Merioneth: 1. Bala; 2. Dolgelley; 3. Harlech.

Montgomeryshire: 1. Llanfyllin; 2. Llanidloes; 3. Montgomery; 4. Machynlleth; 5. Newtown; 6. Welshpool.

Pembrokeshire: 1. Haverfordwest; 2. Newport; 3. Pembroke; 4. Tenby.

Radnorshire: 1. Knighton; 2. New Radnor; 3. Presteigne; 4. Rhayader.

In addition to the markets indicated on the map, the following are listed in John Adams, *Index Villarum,* 1690 edn, *passim.* They are omitted from the map because no clear evidence has been found of their existence between 1500 and 1640. In **England** — *Cornwall:* Callington, Redruth, St Austell, Wadebridge; *Devon:* Sheepwash, Topsham; *Dorset:* Stalbridge; *Salop:* Hodnet, Shifnal; *Som.:* Castle Cary, Chewton Mendip, Stowey. In **Wales** — *Caerns.:* Criccieth; *Carms.:* Laugharne, Newcastle; *Denbs.:* Llangollen, Llanrwst; *Flint.:* St Asaph; *Glam.:* Caerphilly, Llantwitfarde, Penrice; *Mer.:* Dinas Mawddwy; *Pembs.:* Cilgerran, Fishguard, Narberth, Nevern, St David's, Wiston.

Gloucestershire maintained only the slenderest thread of life. The market at Waltham-on-the-Wolds in Leicestershire was described about 1670 as 'very inconsiderable and in a manner disused', while that of Billesdon was 'very mean'. That at Tutbury in Staffordshire was 'very inconsiderable, if one at all'; at Brewood 'almost discontinued'; at Great Eccleston in Lancashire 'so inconsiderable that it is not worth the taking notice of'; at

Fig. 8.3   Markets in eastern England, *c.* 1500-1640.

Bedfordshire: 1. Ampthill; 2. Bedford; 3. Biggleswade; 4. Dunstable; 5. Leighton Buzzard; 6. Luton; 7. Potton; 8. Shefford; 9. Toddington; 10. Woburn.

Berkshire: 1. Abingdon; 2. East Ilsley; 3. Faringdon; 4. Hungerford; 5. Lambourn; 6. Maidenhead; 7. Newbury; 8. Reading; 9. Wallingford; 10. Wantage; 11. Windsor; 12. Wokingham.

Buckinghamshire: 1. Amersham; 2. Aylesbury; 3. Beaconsfield; 4. Buckingham; 5. Colnbrook; 6. High Wycombe; 7. Ivinghoe; 8. Little Brickhill; 9. Marlow; 10. Newport Pagnell; 11. Olney; 12. Princes Risborough; 13. Stony Stratford; 14. Wendover; 15. Winslow.

Cambridgeshire: 1. Cambridge; 2. Caxton; 3. Ely; 4. Linton; 5. Littleport; 6. March; 7. Reach; 8. Wisbech.

Derbyshire: 1. Alfreton; 2. Ashbourne; 3. Bakewell; 4. Bolsover; 5. Chapel-en-le-Frith; 6. Chesterfield; 7. Derby; 8. Dronfield; 9. Tideswell; 10. Wirksworth.

Essex: 1. Aveley; 2. Barking; 3. Billericay; 4. Braintree; 5. Brentwood; 6. Burnham-on-Crouch; 7. Castle Hedingham; 8. Chelmsford; 9. Chipping Ongar; 10. Coggeshall; 11. Colchester; 12. Epping; 13. Great Dunmow; 14. Halstead; 15. Harlow; 16. Harwich; 17. Hatfield Broadoak; 18. Hornden-on-the-Hill; 19. Maldon; 20. Manningtree; 21. Newport; 22. Rayleigh; 23. Romford; 24. Saffron Walden; 25. Thaxted; 26. Waltham Abbey; 27. Witham.

Hampshire: 1. Alresford; 2. Alton; 3. Andover; 4. Basingstoke; 5. Christchurch; 6. Fareham; 7. Havant; 8. Kingsclere; 9. Lymington; 10. Newport; 11. Odiham; 12. Petersfield; 13. Portsmouth; 14. Ringwood; 15. Romsey; 16. Sandown; 17. Southampton; 18. Stockbridge; 19. Whitchurch; 20. Winchester; 21. Yarmouth.

Hertfordshire: 1. Baldock; 2. Barkway; 3. Berkhamsted; 4. Bishop's Stortford; 5. Buntingford; 6. Hatfield; 7. Hemel Hempstead; 8. Hertford; 9. High Barnet; 10. Hitchin; 11. Hoddesdon; 12. Rickmansworth; 13. Royston; 14. St Albans; 15. Sawbridgeworth; 16. Standon; 17. Stevenage; 18. Tring; 19. Ware; 20. Watford.

Huntingdonshire: 1. Earith; 2. Godmanchester; 3. Huntingdon; 4. Kimbolton; 5. Ramsey; 6. St Ives; 7. St Neots; 8. Yaxley.

Kent: 1. Appledore; 2. Ashford; 3. Bromley; 4. Canterbury; 5. Cranbrook; 6. Dartford; 7. Dover; 8. Elham; 9. Faversham; 10. Folkestone; 11. Goudhurst; 12. Gravesend; 13. Hythe; 14. Lenham; 15. Lydd; 16. Maidstone; 17. Milton Regis; 18. New Romney; 19. Northfleet; 20. Orpington; 21. Rochester; 22. St Mary Cray; 23. Sandwich; 24. Sevenoaks; 25. Sittingbourne; 26. Smarden; 27. Tenterden; 28. Tonbridge; 29. Westerham; 30. West Malling; 31. Woolwich; 32. Wrotham; 33. Wye.

Leicestershire: 1. Ashby-de-la-Zouch; 2. Billesdon; 3. Castle Donington; 4. Hallaton; 5. Hinckley; 6. Leicester; 7. Loughborough; 8. Lutterworth; 9. Market Bosworth; 10. Market Harborough; 11. Melton Mowbray; 12. Mountsorrel; 13. Waltham-on-the-Wolds.

Lincolnshire: 1. Alford; 2. Barton-upon-Humber; 3. Beckingham; 4. Binbrook; 5. Bolingbroke; 6. Boston; 7. Bourne; 8. Brigg; 9. Burgh-le-Marsh; 10. Burton-upon-Stather; 11. Caistor; 12. Crowland; 13. Dalderby; 14. Donington; 15. Folkingham; 16. Gainsborough; 17. Grantham; 18. Great Limber; 19. Grimsby; 20. Holbeach; 21. Horncastle; 22. Ketsby; 23. Kirton-in-Holland; 24. Kirton-in-Lindsey; 25. Lincoln; 26. Louth; 27. Market Deeping; 28. Market Rasen; 29. Market Stainton; 30. Saltfleet; 31. Sleaford;

32. Spalding; 33. Spilsby; 34. Stallingborough; 35. Stamford; 36. Tattershall; 37. Wainfleet.

Middlesex: 1. Brentford; 2. Edgware; 3. London; 4. Staines; 5. Uxbridge; 6. Westminster.

Norfolk: 1. Attleborough; 2. Aylsham; 3. Burnham Market; 4. Castleacre; 5. Cawston; 6. Cley; 7. Cromer; 8. Diss; 9. Downham Market; 10. East Dereham; 11. East Harling; 12. Fakenham; 13. Harleston; 14. Heacham; 15. Hickling; 16. Hingham; 17. Holt; 18. King's Lynn; 19. Loddon; 20. New Buckenham; 21. North Walsham; 22. Norwich; 23. Reepham; 24. Snettisham; 25. Swaffham; 26. Thetford; 27. Walsingham; 28. Watton; 29. Worstead; 30. Wymondham; 31. Yarmouth.

Northamptonshire: 1. Aynho; 2. Brackley; 3. Daventry; 4. Higham Ferrers; 5. Kettering; 6. King's Cliffe; 7. Northampton; 8. Oundle; 9. Peterborough; 10. Rockingham; 11. Rothwell; 12. Thrapston; 13. Towcester; 14. Weldon; 15. Wellingborough.

Nottinghamshire: 1. Bingham; 2. Blyth; 3. Mansfield; 4. Newark; 5. Nottingham; 6. Retford; 7. Southwell; 8. Tuxford; 9. Worksop.

Oxfordshire: 1. Bampton; 2. Banbury; 3. Bicester; 4. Burford; 5. Chipping Norton; 6. Deddington; 7. Henley-on-Thames; 8. Hook Norton; 9. Oxford; 10. Thame; 11. Watlington; 12. Witney; 13. Woodstock.

Rutland: 1. Oakham; 2. Uppingham.

Suffolk: 1. Aldeburgh; 2. Beccles; 3. Bildeston; 4. Blythburgh; 5. Botesdale; 6. Brandon; 7. Bungay; 8. Bury St Edmunds; 9. Clare; 10. Debenham; 11. Dunwich; 12. Eye; 13. Framlingham; 14. Hadleigh; 15. Halesworth; 16. Haverhill; 17. Ipswich; 18. Ixworth; 19. Lavenham; 20. Lowestoft; 21. Mendlesham; 22. Mildenhall; 23. Nayland; 24. Needham Market; 25. Newmarket; 26. Orford; 27. Saxmundham; 28. Southwold; 29. Stowmarket; 30. Sudbury; 31. Wickham Market; 32. Woodbridge; 33. Woolpit.

Surrey: 1. Chertsey; 2. Croydon; 3. Dorking; 4. Farnham; 5. Godalming; 6. Guildford; 7. Haslemere; 8. Kingston-upon-Thames; 9. Reigate; 10. Southwark.

Sussex: 1. Arundel; 2. Battle; 3. Brighton; 4. Chichester; 5. Cuckfield; 6. Ditchling; 7. Eastbourne; 8. East Grinstead; 9. Hailsham; 10. Hastings; 11. Horsham; 12. Lewes; 13. Midhurst; 14. Petworth; 15. Rye; 16. Shoreham; 17. Steyning; 18. Storrington; 19. West Tarring; 20. Winchelsea; 21. Worthing.

Warwickshire: 1. Alcester; 2. Atherstone; 3. Bidford-on-Avon; 4. Birmingham; 5. Coleshill; 6. Coventry; 7. Henley-in-Arden; 8. Kenilworth; 9. Kineton; 10. Nuneaton; 11. Rugby; 12. Shipston-on-Stour; 13. Solihull; 14. Southam; 15. Stratford-upon-Avon; 16. Sutton Coldfield; 17. Warwick.

In addition to the markets indicated on the map, the following are listed in John Adams, *Index Villarum,* 1690 edn, *passim.* They are omitted from the map because no clear evidence has been found of their existence between 1500 and 1640. *Bucks.:* Chesham; *Cambs.:* Soham; *Derbys.:* Winster; *Essex:* Dedham, Great Bardfield, Grays Thurrock, Rochford; *Hants.:* Bishop's Waltham, Brading, Fordingbridge, Overton; *Middx.:* Enfield; *Norfolk:* Castle Rising, Foulsham, Litcham, Methwold; *Surrey:* Ewell; *Warws.:* Polesworth.

Holme Cultram in Cumberland 'very mean'; at Ewell in Surrey 'so inconsiderable that it does not deserve the name'. The market at Heacham in Norfolk was extinguished by a great fire in Charles I's reign; that of St Mary Cray in Kent lingered on, though 'very inconsiderable', till the great storm of 1703, when its ancient market house was blown down, and its history came to an end [5].

On the whole, however, the process of elimination was not characteristic of the sixteenth century. Most markets were expanding again, many were obtaining new rights and franchises [6], and some were being refounded. Almost every county, moreover, could boast a few fresh creations: Ketsby in Lincolnshire in 1524, for instance; Sedbergh in Yorkshire and Little Brickhill in Buckinghamshire in 1526; Chertsey in Surrey in 1599; Aynho in Northamptonshire in 1622; Earith in Huntingdonshire about 1623; Stevenage in Hertfordshire in 1624; and Puddletown in Dorset in 1626 [7]. Generally speaking, these new grants were made to small places not destined to develop a truly urban status; but there were a number of important exceptions, particularly in the north of England. Several of the principal towns of modern Lancashire were emerging in this period and setting up markets of their own: Blackburn, Colne, Haslingden, Leigh, Padiham and Whalley among them [8].

Many of the new markets and extended franchises of the sixteenth century owed their origin to the spontaneous action of local people. Frequently they flourished for many years before any formal grant was sought by the lord of the manor or by the town tradesmen [9]. In all probability there were many unofficial markets of which we know nothing; for their life was often brief and fugitive, and it is only when disputes concerning their status arose that we hear of them. A case in point is that of the new wool market set up at Marshfield in Gloucestershire in Queen Elizabeth's reign. According to the citizens of. Bath, the inhabitants of Marshfield and the surrounding countryside had hitherto purchased their wool in *their* market; but early in Elizabeth's reign,

> perceiving your Majesty's said city of Bath to be infected and greatly
> visited with the plague, in such sort as the inhabitants of the country
> bordering upon . . . Bath did stay their repair to the said city upon
> the market days aforesaid for the buying or uttering yarn and other
> merchandises . . . the same inhabitants . . . of Marshfield very
> uncharitably, withal meaning in the same time of the said infection
> the utter subversion, ruin and decay of . . . Bath, did cause open
> proclamation to be made as well in . . . Somerset as also
> in . . . Gloucester[shire], that all your Majesty's subjects . . . might
> have their access to . . . Marshfield for the uttering and buying of
> yarn, woollen cloth, and other merchandise . . . And so by the
> uncharitable . . . devices of the said inhabitants of the town of
> Marshfield . . . the country people . . . do make their whole
> repair . . . to the town of Marshfield . . .

The little Gloucestershire town could claim ancient market rights, but not, it was objected, the further privilege of a wool market [10].

Another, and more auspicious, venture of local enterprise was the revival of the market at Westerham in Kent in James I's reign. Here the old market granted about 1337 to the then lord of the manor, the abbot of Westminster, had long since fallen into desuetude. So, too, had the markets granted to other villages in Holmesdale — Kemsing, Shoreham, Seal and Otford. Only Sevenoaks, at the junction of the roads traversing the valley had survived the vicissitudes of the late fourteenth and fifteenth centuries. The village of Westerham itself, however, still survived as a small trading centre, with its mercers', grocers' and bakers' shops, and its inns and alehouses. There was no other market, north and south, between East Grinstead and Bromley, a distance of thirty miles, nor, east and west, between Sevenoaks and Reigate, a distance of twenty miles. Towards the end of 1620, therefore, a group of local tradesmen joined together in an attempt to restore the market 'as it had been of ancient time'. Richard Dawling, a local grocer, 'went about to persuade divers other inhabitants of the said town of Westerham' to contribute to the expense of procuring a new grant, and Raphe Twigg, George Fuller, and nine others entered into a bond of £100 in support of his venture. After considerable delay a patent was obtained in the name of Sir Thomas Gresham, the new lord of the manor, who leased the market with its 'tollage, stallage and pickage', rent-free, to Dawling and Twigg. As Gresham himself was unwilling to incur expense in providing market facilities, he also leased to Dawling and Twigg a plot of land in front of the George and Dragon to erect shambles. The plot covered barely 300 square yards and the term of the lease was for twenty-one years only; the rent was only 12*d*, but the shambles were to revert to the lord at the end of the period. Well aware 'that the erecting of a market house and shambles would be a furtherance and increase of the [market], and would be very profitable for the general good', the two tradesmen erected thirteen shops or shambles on the site, and a stone 'market house with a lanthorne and a market bell'. The royal patent was publicly proclaimed, and the market formally declared open. Altogether Dawling and Twigg spent something like £300 in providing the new market — a very considerable sum for two village tradesmen of the reign of James I. Within fifty years Westerham developed into a centre of the Kentish cattle trade; and despite their complaints that other inhabitants refused to share the expenses and that they themselves were 'great losers' by it, both Dawlings and Fullers (as their monuments in the church indicate) played a conspicuous part in the prosperity of the town during the succeeding century [11]. The history of Westerham's refoundation can be taken as typical of that of many rising market villages in the later sixteenth and early seventeenth centuries.

The size and functions of market towns

Quite as various as the origins of market towns were their size and functions. Many markets were held in obscure villages unknown beyond their own borders, or inhabited, like Kirkby Moorside, only by poor people and cottagers [12]. Such places as Elham, buried in its downland valley, or Smarden in the Weald of Kent, or Billesdon in Leicestershire, or Bow and Bradninch in Devon, could scarcely be accounted urban even by Tudor standards. With a population of perhaps three or four hundred, their influence was confined to a few square miles of neighbouring countryside. Within that area each played a vital role in the lives of several thousand husbandmen and labourers.

More characteristic of Tudor England were the numerous market towns with a population of perhaps six hundred or one thousand, or occasionally two thousand, inhabitants. There were few counties without half-a-dozen such centres: Ashford, Cranbrook, Dartford, Faversham, Sevenoaks, Tonbridge, Tenterden and Sandwich in Kent, for example. Or Abingdon, Newbury, Wallingford, Windsor and Reading in Berkshire. Or Burton, Stafford, Lichfield, Newcastle, Tamworth and Wolverhampton in Staffordshire [13].

At the other end of the scale were the shire towns [14]. In each of the five large counties of the south-east of England there were two rival shire towns: Winchester and Southampton in Hampshire, Chichester and Lewes in Sussex, Canterbury and Maidstone in Kent, Colchester and Chelmsford in Essex and Bury St Edmunds and Ipswich in Suffolk. With a population usually of several thousand inhabitants, and with a long tradition of independence behind them, such towns influenced both the economy and the ways of thought of a wide tract of countryside. Bury St Edmunds, we are told, was accounted the place 'of most credit' in Suffolk, 'a fine neat town, and much inhabited by the gentry, who resort thither from all parts of the country'. Ipswich, with twice or thrice the population, was 'the most remarkable [town] towards the sea . . . a very fair and spacious town, well peopled and well traded too, adorned with fourteen churches for the service of God and many a fair and goodly edifice for private use'. Maidstone, already the social capital of west Kent, was described later by Daniel Defoe as 'a very agreeable place to live in, where a man of letters, and of manners, will always find suitable society . . . so that here is what is not often found, namely a town of very great business and trade and yet full of gentry, of mirth, and of good company' [15].

Towns like Maidstone, Ipswich and Bury were not only centres for the distribution and sale of agricultural produce, but also for its consumption. The feeding of the populace in towns like Canterbury and Bristol involved, in little, the same economic and administrative problems as that of London. In recalling the overwhelming preponderance of the metropolis in this period as a factor in agricultural marketing, the parallel growth of these provincial towns must not be overlooked. It was less meteoric, but it was nonetheless significant. The population of Norwich in Henry VIII's reign has been estimated at about 12,000 persons; of Bristol, about 10,000; of Salisbury, Exeter and York about 8,000 each; and of Coventry 6,600. Taken together, the inhabitants of these six places were equal in number to those of London [16]. By the time of the hearth tax London had far outstripped them; but, judged by the number of their hearths, there were then sixty provincial towns with an average of 6,000 or 7,000 inhabitants each, and a total population still exceeding that of London and Westminster [17].

The factors underlying the growth of towns from purely local markets to provincial centres were many and varied. The necessity of adequate roads and an extensive and varied hinterland are obvious. Quite as important was the presence of a sizeable river. Few major towns were situated away from navigable streams, and the growth of towns like Leicester was indubitably limited by their absence. Another important factor was the topographical suitability of the site. The expansion of Manchester, far excelling 'the towns lying round about it, both for the beautiful show it bears and the resort unto it of the neighbouring people', was evidently facilitated by the convenience of its market place, so 'remarkable . . . in those parts' for its size [18]. Many a market town like Brentford in Middlesex or Shaftesbury in Dorset was restricted by its 'narrowness and straytness' and 'by reason of the continual thorough-fare . . . of travellers through the same, whereby the said street became altogether unfit and inconvenient for the purpose'. At Brentford the townsmen eventually removed the market place to a new site in 'the orchard and backside of . . . the Crown' inn [19]. But generally the opposition of tradesmen with burgage tenements in the old market place precluded removal; at Shaftesbury, although the market was so cramped that wealthy corn farmers threatened to carry their grain elsewhere, the site was not altered [20].

The topography and facilities of market towns

The topographical layout of market towns in the sixteenth century was thus of considerable importance. Though no two towns were identical, there were certain distinctive shapes or types of market place. The simplest form, characteristic of small country towns, consisted of a single, long, wide street, expanding in the middle and narrowing at either end, such as may be seen today at Yarm, Thame, or West Malling. Little less common were the triangular shape, often formed at the meeting place of three roads, as at Sevenoaks or Ormskirk; the plain rectangle, as at Grantham and Preston; and the cross-shape, as at Warrington and Maidstone. In larger towns there were many deviations from these basic patterns. In some places, like Canterbury and Northampton, the expansion of the market obliterated the original layout or necessitated the dispersal of trade through various streets devoted to the sale of particular commodities. Quite modest towns, like Banbury and Newark, had their 'horse fair', 'beast market hill', or 'cornhill'; such names are still met with in places as small as Ottery St Mary. At Exeter there was a Butcher Row, Shambles, Fish Market, Corn Market, Cloth Market and Wool and Yarn Market [21]; at Northampton a Horsemarket, Cattle Market, Marehold, Hay Market, Cornhill, Sheep Street, Woodhill and Malthill. At Warrington the market stalls and standings extended along the four arms of the cross-roads in the centre of the town, with the Butter Market to the east, the Horse Market to the north and the Forum or Corn Market in the north-west angle of the cross-roads. At Liverpool the general market was held round the White Cross, extending along the High Street into Castle Street and along Dale Street. In the High Street was the Corn Market, the Lancashire dealers standing on one side and those of Cheshire on the other; nearby were the Shambles; while the fish boards stood next to the Town Hall, and the fruit and vegetable stalls near the High Cross. Until 1567 the Liverpool Cattle Market was also held in this part of the town; but about 1570, owing to the 'greater repair of people than in times past', it was removed first to the Castle fields and then to Chapel Street: for like many other towns Liverpool was rapidly outgrowing its original site [22].

Situated alongside the market place of every country town were its public and official buildings. Practically every town had its market cross. In the smallest places, like West Malling, it was the solitary symbol of market status. With the expansion of markets in the sixteenth century, crosses were often multiplied till in towns like Yeovil and Shaftesbury there were four or five of them: one for the sale of fish, another for cheese, a third for poultry, and others for hemp and butter. The building or rebuilding of these structures was a common act of civic piety in the two centuries preceding 1640. At Shaftesbury the butter cross was built about 1570, by Edmund Bower the mayor, 'for all those who sold butter, cheese, eggs, poultry, or the like to stand or sit dry in during the market' [23]. At Canterbury the old Poultry Cross was built by John Coppin of Whitstable and William Bigg of Canterbury in 1446, and the new Cross by John Somner, brother of the antiquary, 'at the expense of upwards of £400', two centuries later. In the same town there was also a 'Bull Stake' erected for the baiting and chasing of bulls, 'used by an ancient order and custom of the city by the city butchers before their killing, not for pleasure, but to make them proper meat and fit to be eaten' [24].

The principal official building was the market house, variously styled market hall, booth hall, tollbooth, town house, town hall, guildhall, or courthouse. It was generally built in the open market place, often with a row of shops to one end; and it gave rise to a common topographical feature of modern town centres, namely a row of buildings on an island site, with a narrow lane to one side and a wide street on the other. The precise functions of the market house varied from place to place. Some were little more than covered crosses, or open shelters supported on rows of pillars, as at Oakham; many included a hall or court room built above, with a weigh house, toll chamber and gaol or cell below [25].

In all parts of the country many market houses were rebuilt under the Tudors and Stuarts. The market house at Rothwell and the pillared guildhall of Much Wenlock both date from 1577. The guildhall at Sandwich is also Elizabethan. At Liverpool the Common Hall was the gift of John Crosse, a London vicar, who in 1515 bequeathed to his native town his 'new [house] called our Lady house to keep their courts and such business as they shall think most expedient' [26]. At Barking the Town House was rebuilt early in Queen Elizabeth's reign, the structure itself being erected by the Crown, while the inhabitants spent £100 in levelling the site and putting up sixteen shops 'and certain sheds' for the benefit of the market. At Clare, in Suffolk, the timber, tiles and workmanship for the new market house were supplied by Roger Barrow, a local grocer, while the townsmen agreed to raise a fund amongst themselves to repay him [27]. At Newtown, in Montgomeryshire, the town hall was built by Thomas Turner under a lease of the market tolls from the corporation; it comprised 'a courthouse where the bailiffs keep their courts and the judges keep their great assizes' for the county, with 'two or three fair chambers in the lower end thereof', 'two strong rooms to keep prisoners', and an open chamber beneath 'for market folks to sell their grain of corn, meal, malt and such like'. At Shaftesbury three market halls appear to have been built in this period: the Old Guildhall, where the mayor's court was held every Saturday afternoon; the new 'market house or guildhall near adjoining unto St Peter's Church there, wherein the said balances and weights do stand'; and 'a fair building made with timber and covered with lead over the said cornmarket, and a bell to ring when the said market shall begin' [28].

The statutory obligation to provide a 'common beam', with its accompanying weights and measures, was one of the principal reasons for erecting market halls. Goods sold in the open market were usually supposed to be weighed by the common balances, and, as trade increased, the right to levy toll at the beam often became a valuable source of revenue. At Crediton

> cries [were] usually made in the said market to call such as had
> anything which ought to be weighed at the said common beam, to
> bring it away to the beam. And if any were found to weigh any
> commodities away from the common beam . . . such commodities
> were threatened or declared to be forfeited, half to the king, and
> half to the lord of the market.

In the great summer wool market at Doncaster the mayor appointed yearly four sufficient men, with weights and scales, to levy toll of ½d per stone from the wool sellers, allowing large merchants to compound at 6d per pack of 15 or 16 stone, 'in regard they were good customers to the said market' [29].

In practice there were many loopholes in these urban regulations. At Doncaster in Charles I's reign the freemen of Lincoln claimed to be toll-free by virtue of their charter, and many merchants refused to pay the dues demanded, alleging 'deceit and cozenage' on the part of local officials. In other towns private beams were set up. At Crediton one Shilston let out one of his rooms with a beam to a woolman from Chudleigh; another Chudleigh woolman set up a beam in Clement Piddesley's house; and Mistress Katherine Berry had a beam 'openly set up in her hall'. Although not a 'half part' of the wool sold in Crediton market was lawfully weighed; the town was so full of a 'great multitude of weavers' that every market day great quantities of wool and yarn were carried 'away out of the market and weigh[ed] . . . at their own or other private houses' [30]. In the neighbouring wool market of Ashburton two rival beams were set up, and a heated dispute arose between two local claimants to the profits, Thomas Prideaux and William Abarrow. For 'divers market days together' Thomas Prideaux

> did walk up and down the said market . . . with a sword by his side,
> and did threaten the said William Abarrow . . . that his
> father . . . would spend a thousand pounds but that he would have
> and keep the profits . . . and . . . did also unhang the weights set up
> by the said William Abarrow to weigh wool and yarn, and did also
> threaten the market people there coming to sell their wares, that if
> they did not weigh their wool and yarn at our weights they should
> pay for it . . . [and] did also overthrow the stalls and standings of
> others and terrify them much. [31].

In addition to crosses and halls, market towns also possessed shops and shambles. The two terms were not sharply distinguished, but the latter were generally small premises erected for the sale of fish and flesh by the town, and let out to townsmen or foreigners on market days only. Frequently, as at Crediton, the shambles stood in the centre of the market place adjoining the market house; the borough court, as at Tavistock, was sometimes called the 'Shammel-Moot' [32]. In some places shambles still survive, and at Sevenoaks butchers' shops are still gathered near them.

Shops were more permanent structures and shambles, generally burgage tenements, built with pentices before them, with signposts set up in their pavement, and opened for sale to the public each day [33]. Some places, like Westerham, had their row of mercers' and grocers' shops many years before they acquired a market; there were sometimes shops in villages, too, like Leeds in Kent, where no market grant seems to have been sought. In thriving towns, like Blandford and Chichester, competition for shop sites was keen, and many new shops were built in this period. At Shaftesbury in James I's reign 'shops and houses', had recently been erected, it seems, called 'Chapman's Standings'. At Crediton there was a street of new shops, some let out at rents of 40s and 56s a year [34]. Such buildings were sometimes of considerable size. The two shops of Edward Baylie, a butcher at Frome Selwood in Somerset, consisted of '17 felde of building'; the three of Robert Acourt, another butcher, of '25 felds'; that of Anthony Treheren, a smith, was smaller, comprising only '6 felds'. Like other shops in the town, they were of 'timber and stone building, and ... covered with stone tile' [35]. Sometimes shop tenants were expected to undertake their own 'glazing [of windows], making of partitions, setting up of shelves, lining the walls with boards, [and] hanging up of a cupboard' for their 'more convenient occupying of the said rooms and premises ...'. Ranged as they were round the market place, and often rented by the same family for several generations, such buildings provided an element of continuity in the market town which would otherwise have been lacking [36].

The wooden pentices formerly attached to shop fronts have disappeared from the modern country town. Their position is still visible in the pavement of a number of market places, and the cloth 'tilts' or awnings occasionally employed were a direct ancestor of the modern shop blind. In the sixteenth century, when business was still carried on in open premises, the wooden pentice was a necessity of trade. It extended several feet into the street, as far as the 'eavesdropping'; the work of shoemakers or tailors was carried on beneath it, under the public eye, the master sitting in the centre of a trestle table, with his apprentices at either end [37]. The right to erect 'standings' with 'balks' or counters beneath the pentice and to let them out to country folk on market days was sometimes a valuable privilege of burgage tenure. In most towns burgage tenants also claimed the right to erect stalls or sheep pens in front of their shops, as far as the channel in the centre of the street. At Ashburton those who held 'ancient burgages near the places where the said market is kept' claimed this right in virtue of their responsibility for 'reparations of the pavements afore their several houses'. At Shaftesbury freeholders who were responsible for repairing the 'pavements and pitchings right before their houses and lands unto the channel' claimed the right 'to take the profits of the pickage and standings set before their said houses and lands on fair and market days'. At West Malling, where one side of the High Street lay in the Bishop of Rochester's liberty and the other in the manor or lordship of Malling, stalls were erected by shopkeepers on either side of the 'posts of dowls' set up in the centre of the street to mark the manorial boundary [38]. In corporate towns the erection of stalls and pens was usually the responsibility of municipal authorities. At King's Lynn the profit of the market reaped by the corporation must have been considerable, for the butchers alone rented thirty stalls in the Tuesday market from the corporation [39].

No summary can do justice to the infinite variety of market towns. Each had its own customs and peculiarities, familiar to those who frequented it, a source of curiosity and wonder to strangers. One instance of an unusual market was the annual 'great mart' held at Howden in Yorkshire. Each year the old manor house of the Bishop of Durham was let out as warehouses to merchants from London and the West Riding; stalls were erected in the courtyard and against the kitchen walls; the stables were converted into shops; and goods were transported by ferry boats from the river Ouse to the Briggate [40].

Regulation of market towns by local authorities

Everywhere marketing was subject to more or less strict regulation. Each town had its own company of market officers, varying in number from the four or five of Newtown or Ashton-under-Lyne to the forty or fifty of Manchester or King's Lynn. Sometimes they were elected annually by the borough or manorial court; sometimes appointed for a term of years; not infrequently the office descended *de facto* from husband to widow or father to son. Virtually every town had its toll-gatherers, sweepers and bellmen, and many appointed a couple of 'market lookers' for the general inspection of the market. Aleconners and bread-testers enforced regulations and statutes governing the price and quality of bread and beer; leather searchers carried a hammer with a die or seal in its head and stamped skins and hides; 'aulnagers' performed similar functions for various types of cloth; and 'appraisers' were appointed to settle the value of goods in event of dispute. In large market towns there might be half-a-dozen of these officials. In Manchester there were six or seven corn-lookers, four fish-and-flesh-lookers, and ten whitemeat-lookers; in Liverpool there was a host of paid employees, ranging from the stewards of the Common Hall and the keeper of the Common Warehouse to the setters of booths and fleshboards [41].

Under the auspices of these officers the market was closely controlled in the interests of the consumer or the lord of the market. Market days were usually fixed in the original charter, but market hours were settled by the town, and as a rule no one was allowed to sell his corn till the country folk had arrived from distant villages and the toll-gatherer had made his round of the cornsellers, dipping his toll-dish into the mouth of each man's sack. The provision and testing of measures, balances and weights; the control and licensing of badgers, broggers, corn-carriers, maltsters, engrossers, forestallers and other traders; the fixing of prices of bread, malt, meal and corn; the prevention of cozenage and civil disturbance: these and other activities were among the responsibilities of market authorities [42].

Their most onerous task was the levying of tolls and the entering of receipts and expenditure therefrom in toll-books kept in the market hall or tollbooth. The fiscal value and utility of these dues varied greatly. No tolls were payable in the corn markets of Shaftesbury, Huntingdon or St Ives. At Hertford in 1536-37 they amounted to no more than 18s 8d. At Gainsborough no official corn toll was levied, but the bellman took 'some small quantity of corn to his own use . . . and in consideration thereof he kept clean the streets', for which he was also given 'twenty shillings in the year . . . and some old coat' by the lord of the market. At Romford the corn toll amounted to one pint in every four bushels, or 6d a cartload, and the beast toll to 2d a head; the butchers paid 6d for every stall, or 12d if 'twice filled', and other tradesmen 3d, 2d, 1d, 'or what could be gotten of them'. At Newark the tolls appear to have been sufficiently valuable to farm out to five or six different people: the passage toll and 'week toll' to Richard Stacye; the beast-market toll and swine drift to Nicholas Hopton; the horsemarket toll to an inhabitant of Balderton; the corn toll to the man who 'dresseth . . . the market place'; and the toll for 'pickage and stallage' to the Earl of Rutland and Mr Anthony Foster. Generally, dues levied on townsmen were lower than those paid by strangers, perhaps half or less. Quite frequently local people refused to pay toll. An angry scene occurred at Denbigh in 1537, when the Welsh countrymen came in arms on market day and proclaimed at the cross 'that Welshmen were as free as Englishmen and that they should pay no stallage there' [43].

The proceeds from tolls, when not farmed out to private people, were generally devoted to some charitable or civic purpose. At Crediton they were employed in paying the rent of the market, mending the standings of butchers and shoemakers, cleansing the town wells, providing a ladder and fire-buckets, improving the pavements and causeways, enlarging the weighing house, repairing the almshouses and market clock, relieving the sick, and purchasing corn for the poor, 'a shroud for poor Rose', and bread, wine, beer and cheese, spent 'at the passing of this account' [44]. This annual auditing of the toll-gatherers' accounts was often a local ceremony of some importance. At Dover it was heralded by blowing the borough horn through the streets of the town; at Stow-on-the-Wold the town bailiffs came to the courthouse 'attired in their gowns, and round Leominster caps, with other velvet night caps under them, and their sergeants . . . before them with maces and sergeant's staves' [45].

Some glimpses of market regulation may be gleaned from the Courts' Books of the borough of Ipswich. By regulations passed in the reigns of Elizabeth and James I, no one in Ipswich was permitted to have a stall upon the Cornhill 'but only such as shall be free of this town, and every of them shall pay for his standing there 4d for every market day, to be paid to the chamberlains'. None of the 'butchers of this town or country' were to sell 'in any other place but in the butchers' stalls of this town', on pain of forfeiting their licence for one year. No one was to bring any wheeled vehicles into the market except 'carts and tumbrils unshod'.

No one was allowed to open his shop doors or windows upon the Sabbath day, and the carriers of the town who had caused 'great offence [to] Almighty God' and brought 'infamy and slander' on the town by travelling on Sunday were ordered to discontinue their profanity. Elaborate regulations were passed regarding the selling of tallow, hides and cloth, the licensing of foreigners who wished to rent stalls in the market, the charges of carriers and wagoners, and the purchase of corn for the poor [46]. Similar restrictions could be traced in the records of many another town: of Manchester, Leicester, Whitchurch, Beverley, Royston or Northampton, for instance [47]. When we come to study private marketing, however, we shall find that this kind of restriction was not altogether unnecessary.

The community of the market town

The market town was not simply a centre of trade; it was the focus of the rural life around it. Its square and taverns provided the meeting place for yeomen and husbandmen, not only to buy and sell, but to hear the news, listen to sermons, criticise the government, or organise insurrection [48]. Its carpenters, wheelwrights, ploughwrights and other craftsmen existed principally to minister to the needs of its dependent villages. Its society was closely intertwined with that of the countryside and its prejudices and convictions governed those of the farmers who bought and sold in its streets. Its conservatism was upheld and strengthened by the hard core of aldermanic families who by the end of the period had come to dominate the society of many country towns. At Ipswich, Daundys, Sparrows and Bloyses governed the borough from the early sixteenth century till the end of the seventeenth. In Northampton a number of shops remained in the same ownership for seventy or eighty years, and families like the Maynards, Mackerneses, Scrivens and Lyons dominated the town for upwards of a century. At Petworth there was a succession of Libards as millers, Barnards as chandlers, Lucases as locksmiths, Bowyers as shoemakers and Haslens as barber-surgeons. In Leicester three freemen out of four followed in their fathers' footsteps; and even in the smallest towns, like Westerham and West Malling, family businesses sometimes descended from father to son for three or four generations [49]. Many town churches still contain memorials to half-a-dozen local trading dynasties of this kind, whose history would repay detailed investigation. Although the drift of wealth back into the countryside precluded the development of rigid burghal hierarchies like those of continental cities, the web of urban society was remarkably close-knit and enduring.

The wealth of urban tradesmen varied much with the size and situation of the town [50]. In the small market towns of East Anglia, like Diss and Bungay, the tradesman's property was often worth no more than £30 or £40. In the middle-sized towns of Hertfordshire, such as St Albans, many merchants possessed goods worth £80 or £90, and some more than £600. In Northampton, a town of three or four thousand people in this period, the richest mercers and innkeepers left over £1,000. In Newcastle, one of the principal ports of the country, a number of grazing butchers possessed personal property valued at over £2,000, and merchant-venturers more than £3,000. Since most towns still retained their open fields and commons, much of this wealth was invested in agricultural goods. In many places, such as Leicester, leading tradesmen were often graziers or farmers; and in large ports like Ipswich and Newcastle agrarian wealth still accounted for half the property of a number of burgesses. In few towns was there as yet a complete divorce between the trading community and the land, although by the end of the seventeenth century that breach was becoming much clearer in a county town such as Northampton.

In urban communities as much as in the countryside everything was still carefully made by craftsmen. Essentially it was still a hand-made world, and the trading classes often enjoyed a substantial measure of comfort. Thomas Webster, a tanner of St Albans who died in 1612, left domestic goods worth £175 out of a total estate of £600. His house contained no fewer than seventeen rooms. The hall and parlour were furnished with carpets, cushions and chairs. In the kitchen hung a fine array of dripping pans, frying pans, pothooks, spits and bellows; in the offices and outhouses stood the powdering troughs, boulting hutches, churns, hogsheads, stills and other paraphernalia of a large farming-tradesman. His pewterware was valued at £5 and his silver at £2. His wife's store of linen, perhaps spun on the spinning wheel in the parlour, comprised 20 pillowcases, 30 pairs of sheets, 15 table-cloths and 42 napkins; it was worth nearly £20. Both the house and goods of Thomas Webster bear witness to the solid prosperity of an urban tradesman, and to a kind of wealth not easily spent or quickly come by, but the fruit of a lifetime of patient toil. For the society of the Stuart market town was no mushroom growth; it was embedded in traditional ways of life of exceptional strength and obstinacy. Those ways of life have now vanished, but they survived every wind of fortune, with only minor changes, until the time of George Eliot's *Middlemarch*.

The open market

Products and specialities of market towns

There can be little doubt that in the sixteenth century most towns still served a purely local area and specialised in marketing no particular types of commodity. Nevertheless, a tendency for the more important towns to market certain kinds of product had inevitably gone hand in hand with regional specialisation in agriculture. By the end of the period, or a little after, the broad pattern of specialisation becomes clear. About two English towns in five and one Welsh town in three tended to specialise in the marketing of either corn, cattle, horses, sheep, cheese and butter, poultry, fish, wool, yarn, cloth or some other product or group of products. For the country as a whole the available sources do not admit of very precise differentiation; local studies would doubtless reveal more minute specialisation, in some towns, in marketing different types of grain and cattle [51]. Neither was there a sharp distinction between all corn markets and all cattle markets; nor were their specialities mutually exclusive. To some extent specialisation varied with the time of year, and many markets specialised in the sale of more than one kind of product. An important city, such as Exeter, might be equally noted as a trading centre for cattle, corn and wool. The town of Bedford, situated near diverse agrarian regions, was both the chief cattle market and the chief corn market of its area, the former held on the south side of the river on Tuesday, the latter on the north side on Saturday [52]. Only a general outline of the subject, however, can be given here. In this outline six different regions of the country are distinguished, each with its peculiar features: north, south, east, west, Midlands and Wales.

The pattern of specialisation emerges most distinctly in the east of England [53]. In this area seventy-seven out of a total of nearly 200 market towns showed a tendency to specialise in one or more products. Four were largely devoted to the sale of cheese and butter, nine to poultry, ten to fish, six to swine, five to sheep, ten to cattle, thirteen to malt and as many as forty-six to corn. The cattle markets were mainly situated on the Midland fringe of the area in Bedfordshire, or near the fenland pastures of East Anglia; the fowl and fish markets near the fens, or in other wildfowl areas, or on the sea-coast. The principal corn markets were almostly uniformly sited near navigable rivers. Here, as elsewhere, there were many purely local corn markets, but few English towns were likely to develop into major grain entrepôts unless they were situated on the sea-coast or near a navigable stream [54]. And no other region of England was so plenteously served by waterways as the eastern counties. Nottinghamshire and Lincolnshire were watered by the Witham, Trent and Foss Dyke; Norfolk, Cambridge, Bedford, Huntingdon and west Suffolk by the Wensum, Welland, Nene, Cam and Great and Little Ouse; Hertfordshire by the river Lea; and Buckinghamshire, Middlesex and Surrey by the Thames. Of the many great corn markets of the area, Gainsborough was sited on the river Trent, Peterborough on the Nene, Bedford, St Neots and King's Lynn on the Ouse and Oxford, Abingdon, Wallingford, Reading, Kingston and Brentford on the Thames.

The Midland counties provide a marked contrast with the east [55]. Here the predominant speciality was not corn and malt, but livestock. Out of about eighty markets where specialisation is discernible, of a total of over 160 in the area, twenty-five concentrated on cattle, fourteen on sheep, at least seven on horses and seven on swine. A further six towns held markets for leather products, including Northampton for shoes, Burford for saddles and Congleton for 'purses and points'. Among the numerous cattle markets of the Midlands were Kington in Herefordshire; Banbury, Bicester and Thame in Oxfordshire; Shrewsbury, Oswestry, Whitchurch, Ludlow, Bridgnorth, Wem and Newport in Shropshire; Newcastle, Leek, Uttoxeter, Wolverhampton and Tamworth in Staffordshire; and Coventry, Birmingham and Southam in Warwickshire. A number of these towns also held large sheep markets; while others were held at Hereford, Leominster, Loughborough, Market Harborough, Daventry, Kettering and Stow-on-the-Wold. Among the principal horsemarkets of the area were Banbury, Daventry, Hinckley, Northampton and Market Harborough; among the chief cloth markets Shrewsbury and Oswestry [56].

In the west of England the pattern was again different. Here there were about fifty-five specialised markets, or rather more, out of a total of some 170 [57]. Of these, twenty-four were devoted largely to the sale of cattle; five to cheese and butter (including Yeovil, Chipping Sodbury and Wincanton); and three to leather or gloves (including Ilminster and Grampound). The principal specialities of west country markets, however, were wool, yarn and cloth. According to Hooker, virtually every town in Devon was a market for kerseys, wool, or yarn [58]. One such town was Crediton, where there dwelt 'a great multitude of weavers' who every market day dealt 'very much in buying and selling of wool'. Another was Norton St Philip, where for three weeks before SS. Philip and James's day 'the great house or inn called the George' was converted into an emporium for use of Somerset clothmen, and all the 'tables and household stuff' were 'displaced . . . out of the hall, kitchen, two parlours, cellars and chambers' to receive their woollen and linen packs and fardels. Among the many other wool markets of the area were Launceston in Cornwall, Ashburton in Devon and Shaftesbury in Dorset [59].

In both the west of England and the Midlands there was also a goodly number of grain markets: seventeen in the former area and nineteen in the latter. Most of these corn marts were of merely local importance, but a few were remarkably lively centres. The two markets of Bruton and Wincanton in east Somerset supplied corn to nearly seven thousand people in the surrounding clothing villages; most of it, apparently, imported from other districts. The corn market at Derby served a similar function for the miners and quarrymen of Derbyshire, and was furnished with corn principally by way of the river Trent [60]. At Shaftesbury as many as twenty cartloads of corn were brought in for sale, each market day, by farmers from Dorset and Wiltshire, 'besides divers other horseloads'; while it is clear that only the restrictions of the site prevented further expansion [61].

In the north of England over half the 124 market towns and villages of the area showed a tendency towards specialisation, a higher proportion than in any other region [62]. Of the twenty-five corn markets of the area, ten were situated near the drier arable areas of the north-east, many of them close to navigable rivers; a further four were found in the manufacturing dales of the West Riding and distributed corn imported from Hull and York; while the remainder were probably of local importance only, among them being Penrith, Ulverston, Wooler and Keswick [63]. More truly characteristic of the area were its seventeen major cattle markets, with which many north-country cattle fairs must also be reckoned. Equally significant were the nine or more markets devoted to wool or yarn, and the nine to cloth. The rising cloth marts of south Lancashire and the West Riding were by 1640 of considerable importance, and the great wool market at Doncaster was undoubtedly one of the largest in the kingdom, attended by purchasers from all parts of Yorkshire and the Midlands [64].

Of the sixty market towns in Wales only twenty-three are known to have specialised to any marked degree. Most Welsh towns were exception- ally small. In the mid-sixteenth century only Carmarthen had over two thousand inhabitants, and only five other towns more than one thousand, most of them situated either near the border or by the sea-coast [65]. Of the nineteen, fourteen were devoted primarily to the sale of corn. Presteigne was the market town for the Maelienydd district of Radnorshire (the north-east corner of the county); Denbigh, where 'the confluence to the market on Tuesday [was] exceeding great', for the vale of Clwyd. Brecon, Builth and Tenby were other corn markets of some consequence [66]. All these towns were situated in the drier areas near the border or the southern sea-board. Ten Welsh markets also specialised in the disposal of livestock, to which must be added numerous annual fairs; for in Wales, as in the north of England, cattle and sheep were more usually sold by private contract or at fairs than in the weekly markets.

In the south of England only one market town in four tended to specialise [67]. There were a few grain markets in Surrey and Berkshire, such as Dorking and Newbury, and in the rich cornlands of north-east Kent. There was also a handful of important sheep and cattle markets in Hampshire, Sussex, Kent and the Berkshire Downs; together with three or four markets for poultry and wildfowl in Essex, Surrey and Sussex. In an area accessible to the metropolis and supposedly progressive, the comparative absence of specialisation may seem surprising. In part it may be due to a less specialised economy; in part, perhaps (though this is improbable) to a tendency to deal privately rather than in the open market; and in part to certain *lacunae* in the sources. It was also affected by the absence of navigable rivers, the notorious state of the roads, the presence of extensive forests and heathlands and a plethora of exceptionally tiny market towns, such as Smarden, Elham, Ditchling, Tarring, Havant and Kingsclere. The situation in southern England as a whole, however, is a salutary reminder that, even within the orbit of the metropolis, commercial penetration of agriculture was limited to pockets or *caches* of farmland in a countryside still largely given over to peasant husbandry. As Mr Kenyon found at Petworth and Mr Chalklin at Tonbridge, the market towns of the south were surprisingly self-centred and self-sufficient places [68]. It is difficult to avoid the conclusion that, away from the sea-coast, many of them were still largely asleep.

In summary, it appears that out of a total of some 800 market towns in England and Wales, rather more than three hundred tended to specialise in the marketing of some particular product. Of these 800, 133 specialised in the sale of corn, 26 in malt, and 6 or more in fruit; 92 in cattle, 32 in sheep, 13 in horses, and 14 in swine; 30 or more in fish, 21 in wildfowl and poultry and 12 in cheese and butter. There were probably well over 30 wool and yarn markets, and 27 or more cloth markets; 11 markets for leather or leather products, 8 for linen and at least 4 for hemp [69]. Scattered about the country were a number of highly specialised markets, such as Bewdley for caps, Malton for farming implements, Langport for pecked eels, Evesham for stockings and Wymondham in Norfolk for wooden spoons, taps and handles. Of the corn markets, one third were situated in the east; of those for cattle, one third in the Midlands, a quarter in the west and a fifth in the north country. The markets for sheep and horses were also mainly situated in the Midlands; those for swine in East Anglia and the Midlands; for butter and cheese in East Anglia and the west; for poultry in the east and the south; and for wool and cloth in the west, the north and East Anglia.

How far this pattern of specialisation in Caroline England obtained before, say, 1575, it is impossible to say with precision. The information given by Leland, though in general confirmatory, is patchy and incomplete. Short of a series of local monographs, there is no means of arriving at a generalised picture. But it is probable that it was clearly marked by the fourth quarter of the sixteenth century, and that some of its principal features were emerging by the 1530s. Certainly many of the corn markets of East Anglia had appeared on the map at least by Henry VIII's reign, and in all probability many of the cattle markets of the Midlands.

Market areas

The 800 or so market towns of England and Wales in the sixteenth and seventeenth centuries were distributed by no means evenly over the landscape. In Yorkshire there were at least 54 markets, in Devonshire 45, in Somerset 39, in Lincolnshire 37, in Gloucestershire 34 and in Kent 33. In Northumberland, on the other hand, there were only eight markets, and in several of the small Welsh counties no more than three or four. The regions served by market towns thus varied greatly in different parts of the country. The average market area in Wales extended to 100,000 acres, or 156 square miles; in England it averaged 45,000 acres, or 70 square miles, ranging from 20,000 acres for each of the twenty markets in Hertfordshire to the 161,000 acres of the eight markets in Northumberland [70].

On the whole, towns clustered most thickly in the south-western counties, in Hertfordshire and the neighbouring Midland areas, and in Suffolk and Kent. In these shires there was, generally speaking, at least one market town to every 35,000 acres of countryside. Next came Lancashire and the remaining Midland and East Anglian counties; followed by a group of shires containing extensive tracts of moorland, forest, heath or fen — Cambridge, Nottingham, Hampshire, Surrey and the Welsh Marches — where the average market area exceeded 45,000 acres [71]. At the foot of the scale stood the six remaining Pennine counties, with one market, or less, to every 63,000 acres of countryside. The great county of Yorkshire, despite its large number of towns in the aggregate, was more poorly served by markets than any other county except Durham and Northumberland.

Perhaps the ideal distribution of market towns in England would have been at a distance of eight or ten miles apart, varying with the density of population and the kind of husbandry of the area. Such a distance would afford time for the unmounted countryman to walk to market, transact his business, and reach home again by daylight. But even in a county like Kent, where towns were numerous, many folk lived twelve or fifteen miles from their nearest mart; there was not a single market town in the Isle of Thanet, the Stour Levels or the Forest of Blean. Few shires were without extensive tracts of downland, forest, heath or moor, from which towns were usually absent. On winter days many a yeoman must have driven his corn-wains to market long before sunrise, and many a labourer returned home to his cottage by starlight.

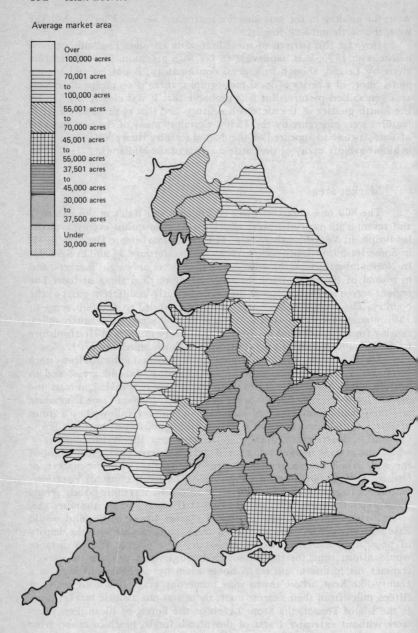

Average market area

Over
100,000 acres

70,001 acres
to
100,000 acres

55,001 acres
to
70,000 acres

45,001 acres
to
55,000 acres

37,501 acres
to
45,000 acres

30,000 acres
to
37,500 acres

Under
30,000 acres

Fig. 8.4   Market areas in England and Wales, *c.* 1500-1680.

Table 8.1   Market areas: distances travelled to market

Region	Percentage of people travelling			
	1-5½ miles	6-9½ miles	10-19½ miles	20 miles and over
North	17	13	20	50
South	31	38	31	0
East	60	25	13	2
West	25	35	25	15
Midlands	36	14	29	21
All England	39	26	20	15

The *average* market areas of English and Welsh towns, however, are no more than a part of the story. How far did people travel to market in fact? An analysis of the distances travelled by several hundred people in all parts of England shows a remarkable variety in different areas of the country, and for different types of product [72]. In England and Wales as a whole the average distance travelled was seven miles, varying from under one mile to over one hundred.

The market area tended to be least extensive for corn markets. Much corn, it is true, was conveyed great distances by sea and river. In the north of England (for the most part an importing area) many thousands of quarters were sold annually at York and Hull to the chapmen of Yorkshire and Lincolnshire, and transported by way of the Aire, Don, Trent and other rivers to the markets of the north Midlands and the woollen towns of the Pennines [73]. But elsewhere few people, always excepting merchants and badgers, travelled so far. In East Anglia not many buyers or sellers of corn went more than ten miles to their market, and most no more than five. At Spilsby in Lincolnshire corn was brought from the surrounding villages of Scremby (three miles to the north-east), Hundleby (one mile to the west), Toynton (two miles to the south) and Orby (six miles to the east); only two out of the twelve villages served by Spilsby lay more than six miles away. Even at High Wycombe, one of the principal corn markets of Buckinghamshire, most cornsellers travelled no more than seven miles to market.

At livestock markets the position was different. Cattle and sheep were more easily transportable than corn; and though most sales were still local, the average cattle-market area extended to a radius of eleven miles, while to the great sheep marts of the Midlands and the north people occasionally travelled forty, fifty and even seventy miles. At Rotherham market, late in Queen Elizabeth's reign, one purchaser came from Carlton in Lincolnshire, forty miles to the south-east, and one seller from Ellerburn in the vale of Pickering, seventy miles to the north-east. At Newcastle-under-Lyme sheep were brought from Macclesfield and from Wales; and in Somerset they were conveyed across the Bristol Channel from Wales and sold at Minehead, Chard and Taunton.

The market areas of wool, yarn and cloth towns were sometimes very large. Their radius generally exceeded twenty miles and not infrequently forty. One of the greatest of these wool markets was

Doncaster, to which buyers in Charles I's reign came from Gainsborough (21 miles away), Lincoln (40 miles), Warsop (25 miles), Pleasley (26 miles), Blankney (50 miles) and many other places in Yorkshire, Lincolnshire, Nottinghamshire, Derbyshire, Leicestershire and Warwickshire [74].

Regarded regionally, market areas were equally diverse. Villagers in the Midlands, the west of England, and especially the north often travelled further afield in their weekly trading activities than in the east and south. In the sample here analysed more than half the north countrymen attended markets upwards of twenty miles from their homes; half the inhabitants of the Midlands and two-fifths of those in the west country travelled more than ten miles. In eastern England, by contrast, nearly two-thirds of the population lived within six miles of their habitual market, and in the south of England the proportion was larger still. In part these differences are explained by the comparative fewness of north-country towns, separated as they often were by extensive moorlands; in part, perhaps, by the unavoidable vagaries of the sample. But only in part: they also reflect regional differences in agrarian specialisation and in economic outlook. The broad market areas of the north arose from the region's concentration on cattle and wool; those of the Midlands from an emphasis on cattle and sheep; the comparatively narrow areas of East Anglia from its numerous corn markets; and the yet narrower ones of the south from its plethora of small towns and a certain lack of commercial push on the part if its inhabitants.

It must not be supposed, however, that market areas were sharply defined or mutually exclusive. Everywhere large towns trespassed on the territory of their neighbours, and nowhere was it unusual for villagers to frequent two or three different markets. When towns began to specialise in selling particular types of product, such trespassing was inevitable. In east Devon the people of Broadhembury regularly marketed in Honiton, Ottery St Mary and Exeter, and an inhabitant of Broadclyst in Exeter, Honiton, Ottery and Cullompton. In Berkshire the townsmen of Hungerford sold their grain in the important corn market of Newbury; in Buckinghamshire those of Amersham and Wendover at High Wycombe; and in Oxfordshire those of Watlington at Reading. At Crediton the wool mart attracted buyers and sellers from the market towns of Chedleigh, Bow and Exeter itself; at Doncaster from towns all over the Midlands and the North. In Lancashire the rising county town of Preston succeeded in stealing a good deal of the trade of Kirkham, Chorley, Walton-le-Dale and Garstang [75]. In almost every county the same process is discernible. For economic *concentration* is one of the salient themes of inland trade in this period: everywhere agricultural traffic tended to be drawn away from the smaller markets, ports and fairs, and centred in the larger provincial centres like Maidstone, Canterbury, Reading, Newcastle or King's Lynn.

From the standpoint of many a commercially minded farmer, there was thus often not one market to be considered in disposing of his produce, but several. There might be nothing in the way of published treatises or trade directories to guide him in his selection; but a keen yeoman, such as Henry Best of Elmswell, in Yorkshire, would be thoroughly versed in the marketing ways of his own county. Best knew well that the north country shipmasters bought their corn at Bridlington and sold it at Newcastle; that a fine Tuesday would bring the Lincolnshire mealmen to the Wednesday market at Beverley (they crossed the Humber the previous night); that in summer time Malton was a better barley market than Beverley; that if you would catch the 'moorfolk' from the Cleveland Hills, you must get there early; and that if the king was at Malton (as he was in 1641) the market was like to be 'very quick'. In all parts of the country and among all classes of people (except the peerage and the poor) the same lively observant interest in agricultural markets was apparent. In Suffolk Sir Nathaniel Barnardiston, the richest man in the county, might be seen every week in the market place of Haverhill or Clare. In Kent, families like the Oxindens and Twysdens were fully aware that Canterbury was a rising hop market, that Maidstone was the best fruit mart and Ashford a flourishing centre of the cattle trade. In Lincolnshire, John Hatcher of Careby was in the habit of selling his wethers at Stamford and his cows and oxen at Newark, while he bought his steers at Spilsby, his fish at Boston, his wine at Bourne and his luxuries in London [76]. In Lancashire the Shuttleworths of Gawthorpe Hall sold their beans and wheat at Preston and Ormskirk, their meal at Padiham, their horses at Wigan, their heifers at Blackburn, their sheep at Haslingden and their geldings in London [77].

Nevertheless, for most people the economic horizon was still bounded by the local market town. The great majority of agrarian debts and credits recorded in farmers' probate inventories relate to purely local transactions. Those of Richard Green of Little Wyreley in Staffordshire did not extend beyond Walsall, six miles to the south, and West Bromwich, five miles beyond; nor those of Richard Coveney of Elmsted in east Kent beyond the neighbouring villages of Monks' Horton, Wootton and Boughton Aluph, or the market towns of Sandwich and Wye [78]. In Tudor and Stuart England a certain temerity was required to venture into unfamiliar territories, and the poorer peasant did not often possess it. If he was wise, he restricted himself to the regulated safety of his local market: the records of the Courts of Chancery and Requests contain numerous cases recording the sad fate attending temerarious village labourers who sought to break away from traditional practices.

Expansion and disputation

The Tudor market town was clearly neither a moribund nor a stagnant place. From about 1570 onwards its trade began to expand rapidly, and the expansion did not go unremarked by contemporaries. Market tolls suddenly became an important source of revenue; the half-forgotten customs of urban freemen began to take on a new significance; burgage rights were stretched or challenged by tradesmen, corporations and manorial lords; and a spate of lawsuits flooded the Tudor courts. Of these disputes, perhaps the most interesting may be found in the records of Special Commissions and Depositions in the Court of Exchequer, of which about one hundred have been examined for the present study. With much variation in detail, nearly all run to a similar pattern. The market at Great Newton, we learn, has greatly expanded in the last twenty years, after having been 'little worth' so long as any one can remember. Not infrequently the tolls have fallen into desuetude and the market charter has been lost or mislaid. Someone has suddenly realized the potential value of the tolls, staked a claim to them and acquired a new grant from the Crown. After a while the corporation challenges his rights, or a sturdy group of townsmen or countryfolk refuse to pay toll and are prosecuted. In their defence these people usually assert that no one has ever paid tolls before; or that at any rate their village is exempt; or that Mr Smith the complainant is 'a great rich man' and a notorious oppressor of the poor. Not infrequently the defendants themselves turn out to be wealthy local tradesmen, or unscrupulous manorial lords, or graziers who have erected half-a-dozen stalls without licence on the king's highway, and are determined to reap their profit [79]. Two or three examples will suffice to illustrate this general theme.

During the early years of Queen Elizabeth's reign the town of St Neots, on the river Ouse, began to emerge as a corn market of some importance, serving the barley farmers of the neighbouring parts of Bedfordshire, Cambridge and Huntingdon. Its capabilities were readily apprehended by Robert Payne, the local squire, 'a gentleman of great wealth' who 'might pleasure and displeasure many inhabiting in the said town . . . and in the country'. He railed in the Cornhill, paved it at considerable expense, caused it 'weekly to be swept and kept clean for the safeguard of the sacks of corn' — and proceeded to levy toll of one quart of corn for every quarter sold, or twopence for each cartload. There was apparently little legal justification for his action, but the benefit could not be gainsaid, and people conceded it for quietness' sake and because they 'would not contend with the said Robert Payne'. But there was a more sinister side to Payne's action. He had leased his rights, such as they were, to one Thomas Newman, whose brother Hugh had obtained a commission as purveyor to the Queen's household. Those who denied toll to Thomas Newman were quietly mulcted, an hour or so later, by his brother Hugh. Unfortunately for Payne and the Newmans, there were a few redoubtable (or possibly perverse) farmers who refused to be coerced. Men like Thomas Archdeacon of Paxton, who had frequented the market for fifty or sixty years, asserted that toll had never been paid in *their* time; and Robert Payne's son and heir Edward was therefore obliged to go to law to establish whatever claim he may have had [80].

At Doncaster in Yorkshire the position was more complicated. In this case the aggrieved parties were the mayor and corporation. By Charles I's reign the Doncaster wool market had become one of the largest in the country, sometimes as many as eighty packs, or about six thousand fleeces, being sold each Saturday during the summer months. The traffic was so considerable that it was impossible for the four men appointed by the corporation to weigh all the wool sold in the market: it became the custom for some buyers to accept the weight of fleeces on the seller's own word. For those weighed at the corporation's beam a toll of ½d per stone was levied on the seller. Or was it in fact a toll — or a mere gratuity? That was the great question. The corporation affirmed that it was a toll, the defendants a voluntary gratuity. Most probably, as in other towns, the dues had originated as small, amicable gratuities when the market was in its infancy, and had become more strictly enforced as the market expanded and the corporation perceived their fiscal potentialities. But in this instance there were two complicating factors. In the first place the official wool-weighers were accused of 'cozenage'; they engaged, on the quiet, in a considerable trade in wool on their own account, and it was alleged that they used their official position to blackmail a number of factors and farmers who habitually sold their wool in the market. In the second place, a number of the wool-sellers who came from the city of Lincoln claimed to be toll-free in all markets and seaports throughout the country. They had recently won their claim to be free in the city of London, and now incited a number of their colleagues to refuse to pay toll in the market at Doncaster too. The corporation, as a consequence, was damnified, and brought the whole question of the Doncaster tolls before the chancellor of the exchequer [81].

The third dispute relates to the market for butter, cheese and sheep at Yeovil, and to the right to the profits of the town beams and the stalls and standings in the market place. Until the closing years of Queen Elizabeth, Yeovil had boasted only one town beam, used principally for the weighing of wool, and lent or leased to one Master Hobbes, the portreeve's bailiff. The informality of the arrangement is shown by the fact that after Hobbes's death his widow was permitted to remove the beam to her own house, and make what profit she could of it, 'in regard of her poor estate'. With the expansion of Yeovil's trade, however, the profits of the market became a valuable piece of property, and everyone was anxious to lay claim to them. A second beam for the weighing of cheese and butter was set up about 1595, and the right to the profits of the old one was disputed. According to one deponent, the wool beam had been set up by Sir John (or was it Sir Ralph?) Horsey, the lord of the market; according to another by Mr Penny of East Coker, the farmer of the parsonage; according to a third, by the portreeve of the borough. Meanwhile, as everyone was busy disputing, the inhabitants of the neighbouring manor of Hendford (*alias* Newland), whose boundary actually traversed the middle of the market place, quietly took it into their heads to assume that their tenements were ancient burgages, and claimed the right to the profit of stalls and pens which they had recently erected in front of their doors. Before long a number of valuable standings had been set up in Hendford manor; and by the middle of James I's reign there were at least two lawsuits in progress — between Jonathan Penny and the inhabitants of Hendford, and between the corporation and Jonathan Penny — over their respective rights to tolls, beams, stalls, pens and burgage rights in general. Sir Ralph Horsey, it seems, more wise than his hot-headed rivals, had made his peace with the corporation in private [82].

Finally, the case of Builth in Breconshire may be cited. By the seventeenth century Builth was becoming an important centre of the Welsh cattle and sheep trade, visited by drovers from the counties of Radnor, Brecon and Carmarthen on their way to fairs and markets across the border. The tolls levied at the bridge over the Wye — 3*d* for every beast and 1*s* for every score of sheep, in addition to a 'drift' or 'passage' toll — were a lucrative source of revenue. They were acquired, either by purchase or grant from the Crown, by Sir Edmond Sawyer, whose right was disputed by the local squire and justice of the peace, John Williams of the Park. Mr Williams was a colourful, if illogical, personality. He maintained, in the first place, that the tolls were due to himself or his tenants; in the second place, that no tolls were due to anyone. He forbade the townsmen to pay any dues to Sir Edmond Sawyer — no doubt a highly popular act — and, accompanied by a group of his followers, strode into the market on 5 July 1631 to enforce his command. Seeing Sir Edmond Sawyer's octogenarian bailiff, William Thomas, exacting toll 'under the market house', he at once demanded by what authority he did so. Thomas rashly replied by putting his hat on his head and defying the squire to his face. Thereupon Mr Williams struck the hat off again with his own hand and did 'throw the same to the ground' while his attendants 'took hold on the said William Thomas and hauled him and pushed him into the Cage, by means whereof the said William Thomas fell to the ground . . .' The Cage, as one inhabitant remarked, was 'a very loathsome place'; through the bars the market folk could 'see the said William Thomas sitting upon the stocks'. When Mr Williams returned later in the day, however, with the town constable, the wretched bailiff pleaded to be left there, where at least his life was safe from the incensed squire and the crowd. But Mr Williams willed the constable 'to haul or pull out the said William Thomas out of the Cage in quarters or in pieces if he would not come forth by fair means'. Next morning, Mr Williams despatched Thomas, by his own *mittimus*, to the county gaol. And shortly afterwards Sir Edmond Sawyer cited Mr Williams before the chancellor of the exchequer [83].

These disputes were not merely parochial feuds. They bear witness to the expansion of the agrarian economy and to certain fundamental changes in English rural life. Their geographical distribution is of considerable interest. Two cases in five relate to the eastern counties, with their many corn markets; nearly one quarter to the south-western counties, with their wool and cloth markets; a further seventh to the Midland counties; and only one quarter to the whole of the south of England, the northern counties and Wales [84]. Barley, malt, wheat, wool, cloth: these were the great culprits. Or in other words, it was in those areas where the influence of 'man's manufacture' was most powerful, by way of the clothing and brewing industries, that the new tensions became most acute.

The widespread attack upon market tolls also bears witness to an impatience of old restraints which was highly characteristic of the period. At Wells in Somerset, where tolls were levied by the bishop, a group of tradesmen went so far as to assert that

> there ought not any toll at all, by the laws or customs of this realm,
> to be taken of any corn or grain sold in any market, but the buyers
> and sellers there ought to be free. And if any such outrageous
> toll . . . be taken in the said market by the owner . . . the king's
> Majesty shall seize the said market into his hand as forfeited. . . .
> And this by the Statute of Westminster the first, the thirtieth
> chapter [85].

Even in the closely regulated community of the market town, the force of individual enterprise was breaking down the barriers of social custom.

Notes

Abbreviations: AO: Archives Office; *CSPD: Calendar of State Papers Domestic; LP: Letters and Papers of Henry VIII;* RO: Record Office (PRO: Public Record Office).

1   H. W. Knocker, 'Sevenoaks: the manor, church, and market', *Archaeologia Cantiana,* xxxvii (1926), 51-68.

2   See H. P. R. Finberg, *Gloucestershire Studies,* 1957, pp. 64 *sqq.*; G. H. Tupling, 'The origin of markets and fairs in medieval Lancashire', *Lancashire and Cheshire Antiquarian Society,* xlix (1933), 75-94.

3   G. H. Tupling, 'An alphabetical list of the markets and fairs of Lancashire recorded before the year 1701', *Lancashire and Cheshire Antiquarian Society,* li (1936), pp. 88-110.

4   See maps, pp. 169, 171, 174, and cf. Finberg, *op cit.,* pp. 86-8; Tupling, 'Origin of markets and fairs', pp. 92-3. The Lancashire figures relate to grants up to 1625. For the figure of 130 for Norfolk I am indebted to Professor W. G. Hoskins. Mrs J. R. Green, in *Town Life in the Fifteenth Century,* 1894, ii, 26, states that almost 5,000 markets and fairs were established by grant between 1200 and 1482; R. B. Westerfield, in *Middlemen in English Business . . .,* 1915, p. 334, gives a figure of over 2,800 between 1199 and 1483. Both figures appear to be exaggerations. The *Royal Commission on Market Rights and Tolls,* 1889, i, 108-31, lists 2,713 grants between 1199 and 1483; but some of these were to places overseas, some were for the translation of the market to a new site, many were regrants to places already possessed of market rights and many were for fairs only.

5   Richard Blome, *Britannia,* 1673, *passim*; Edward Hasted, *History of Kent,* 2nd edn, i, 260; cf. *CSPD 1639-40,* p. 252, regarding Attleborough (Norfolk).

6   Leicester and Grantham, for instance, obtained the right to hold wool markets: *CSPD 1598-1601,* p. 197; *1603-10,* p. 115.

7   PRO E 134, 9 Car. I, E 30; SP 14, 141, f. 352; *CSPD 1598-1601,* p. 155; *1625-26,* p. 367; W. Le Hardy, *County of Buckingham: Calendar to the Sessions Records,* 1933, i, p. 344; *LP,* iv, pp. 81, 898, 902.

8   Tupling, 'Alphabetical list of the markets and fairs', pp. 89, 93, 96, 99, 103, 109.

9   Tupling, 'Origin of markets and fairs', pp. 89, 92.

10   PRO Req. 2, 213, 15.

11   PRO C 2, James I, F 9, 33. Similar disputes occurred in connection with the new market grant at Bovey Tracey in Devon: Req. 2, 45, 93.

12   PRO E 164, 37, f. 386.

13   For towns in Sussex, Bucks. and Rutland, see Julian Cornwall, 'English country towns in the fifteen-twenties', *Economic History Review,* xv, 1 (1962) 54-69.

14   The terms 'shire town' or 'county town' came into use by Henry

VIII's reign (cf. *LP*, viii, 241, referring to Dorchester in 1535), but were unusual before the end of the century.

15   Peter Heylyn, *A Help to English History...* , 1709 (first published in 1641), p. 504; Daniel Defoe, *A Tour through England and Wales*, Everyman edn, 1959, i, 115.

16   W. G. Hoskins, 'English provincial towns in the early sixteenth century', *Transactions of the Royal Historical Society*, 5th ser., vi (1956), 5.

17   Based on C. A. F. Meekings, *Dorset Hearth Tax Assessments*, Dorset Natural History and Archaeological Society, 1951, pp. 108-10.

18   William Burton, *The Description of Leicestershire* [1622], p. 160; Heylyn, *op. cit.*, pp. 375, 389. According to Tupling, however, the Manchester market-place was severely congested: 'Lancashire markets in the sixteenth and seventeenth centuries', *Lancs. and Ches. Antiq. Soc.*, lviii (1947), 15-16. The Soar was not navigable to Leicester in this period.

19   PRO C 2, Eliz., H 22, 34.

20   PRO E 134, 5 James I, H 22.

21   PRO E 134, 42 and 43 Eliz., M 3; E 134, 3 James I, E 20; W. G. Hoskins, *Industry, Trade, and People in Exeter, 1688-1800*, 1935, pp. 23, 25; cf. M. W. Beresford, *History on the Ground*, 1957, chapter vi, for Toddington and Higham Ferrers. The name 'cornhill' arose from the need to choose the driest and cleanest site for the sale of grain; livestock were generally penned in the lower-lying parts of the market.

22   J. C. Cox, ed., *The Records of the Borough of Northampton*, 1898, ii, 186 (most of these Northampton street names still survive); Tupling, 'Lancashire markets in the sixteenth and seventeenth centuries', pp. 12-14; cf. pp. 15-16, 19. For a valuable account of the markets of York, see H. Richardson, *Medieval Fairs and Markets of York*, St Anthony's Hall Publications, no. 20, 1961, pp. 21 *sqq.*

23   PRO E 134, 5 James I, H 22; E 134, 9 James I, M 31.

24   Hasted, *op. cit.*, xi, 115n. The new 'cross' comprised a 'handsome market place, with several rooms over it for public use, part of which was used as a repository for corn, against a time of dearth'. The Crediton market accounts refer to a 'bull collar': Devon RO, 252 B, APF, Bdle 75, no. 13. The custom seems to have been usual.

25   In large towns the legal and municipal functions were usually carried on in a separate building.

26   Tupling, 'Lancashire markets in the sixteenth and seventeenth centuries', p. 4. Crosse's house served till 1675, when a new building was erected at the High Cross.

27   PRO E 178, 843; C 2, Eliz., B 5, 58. The Clare market house was put up in 1592 to shelter market folk 'from the rain, which might and did fall to the great loss and spoil' of their corn.

28   PRO E 134, 12 James I, E 16; E 134, 12 James I, T 2; E 134, 5 James I, H 22; E 134, 18 James I, E 1.

29   PRO E 134, 9 James I, M 31; E 134, 4 Car. I, E 36; E 134, 17 Car. I, M 8.

30   PRO E 134, 4 Car. I, E 36. Private beams were legitimate in shops.

The Crediton weigh-house had been enlarged in 1615, but was evidently still too small.

31 PRO E 178, 5236.
32 PRO E 134, 4 Car. I, E 36; Tavistock deed of 1315 cited in W. G. Hoskins and H. P. R. Finberg, *Devonshire Studies*, 1952, p. 181.
33 'Signposts' are referred to at Brackley, Crediton, etc., Northants. RO, Ellesmere MSS, 2345/77; PRO E 134, 4 Car. I, E 36. A sign-rent was often payable to the lord or corporation, in addition to shop rent.
34 PRO C 2, James I, F 9, 33; Req. 2, 114, 17; Req. 2, 55, 64; E 134, 18 James I, E 1; E 134, 4 Car. I, E 36. Many village 'shops' were workshops rather than trading centres.
35 PRO E 178, 1934. The width of a 'feld' is not stated, but an inn of '21 feld' is described as a 'house of great room'.
36 PRO C 2, James I, P 25, 4. Treheren's shop at Frome was held by a succession of smiths who drew their custom from the market folk, 'for that the same was the nearest smith house' to the market place. A shop at West Malling was held by at least three generations of the Tresse family: PRO E 134, 15 Car. I, E 13.
37 PRO E 134, 4 and 5 Car. I, H 1.
38 PRO E 178, 5236; E 134, 18 James I, E 1; E 134, 12 Car. I, E 26; E 134, 15 Car. I, E 13. For this right the Malling shopkeepers paid a rent called 'street gable'. The erection of market stalls back to back in the middle of the street, as at Malling, may well explain the broad high streets of many country towns. In some towns, as at Rayleigh, stalls descended from father to son and were bought and sold like other forms of real property: Req. 2, 303, 74.
39 PRO E 134, 24 Car. I, M 7. According to E 178, 6104 one-fourth of the profits were claimed by private individuals.
40 Durham, Prior's Kitchen, Ch. Com. 23, 384.
41 The above account is based principally on Tupling, 'Lancashire markets in the sixteenth and seventeenth centuries', pp. 20-5, supplemented by information in Exchequer Special Commissions and Depositions relating to Newtown, Gainsborough, St Ives, St Neots and Reading.
42 For a detailed account of market regulation in one county cf. G. H. Tupling, 'Lancashire markets in the sixteenth and seventeenth centuries', *Lancs. and Ches. Antiq. Soc.*, lviii, 1947, pp. 26-34, lix, pp. 1-33.
43 PRO E 134, 9 James I, M 19; Herts. RO, Hatfield Deposit, Bailiff's Account of Hertford Vill; E 134, 24 Car. I, E 9; E 134, 42 and 43 Eliz., M 3; *LP* xii (i), 543. At King's Lynn, about 1648, tolls were apparently worth at least £130 p.a.
44 Devon RO, 252 B, APF, Bdle 75, no. 13. Cf. PRO Req. 2, 77, 77; E 134, 18 James I, E 1; Devon RO, 257 M/T.5, lease of 30 Jan. 1629; C2, James I, G2, 19, for Dulverton, Shaftesbury, Tiverton and Burton-upon-Trent.
45 *LP* iv, p. 3113; PRO E 134, 7 James I, E 18.
46 Ipswich and East Suffolk RO, Ipswich General Courts' Books, 1582-1608 and 1609-43, *passim*; Historical Manuscripts Com-

mission, *Reports*, ix, 1, pp. 254, 256; cf. E 134, 43 Eliz., H 18.

47   At Royston in 1633 more than 100 traders were fined at the manor court 'for overcharging': Herts. RO, No. 66,344, Royston Manor Court Book. For Northampton cf. J. C. Cox, *op. cit.*, ii, pp. 278, 280-4, 290, 293 *et passim*; for Whitchurch, Salop, RO, Bridgewater Collection, no. 212.

48   Henry VIII's activities were frankly discussed in Fakenham market place in 1534, where 'honest men . . . marvelled much what the king meant by polling and pilling the realm . . . more than he did in times past, and thought he intended to make a great hand by money, and then to avoid the realm and let the people shift as they could': *LP* viii, 46. Public sermons were preached on market days in many places, such as Cranbrook, for 'the amendment of men's manners': Cf. *Thomas Wotton's Letter-book, 1574-1586*, ed. G. Eland, 1960, pp. 24-5.

49   Nathaniel Bacon, *Annalls of Ipswiche*, 1884, *passim*; Northants. RO, Northampton wills and probate inventories; G. H. Kenyon, 'Petworth town and trades, 1610-1760: Part I', *Sussex Archaeological Collections*, xcvi (1958), pp. 64-6; W. G. Hoskins, 'An Elizabethan provincial town: Leicester', in *Studies in Social History: a tribute to G. M. Trevelyan*, ed. J. H. Plumb, 1955, p. 60; cf. D. Charman, 'Wealth and trade in Leicester in the early sixteenth century', *Leics. Archaeological Society*, xxv, 1949, pp. 69 *sqq.*

50   The following paragraph is based on tradesmen's probate inventories for thirty-three towns situated mainly in Hertfordshire, East Anglia and the north.

51   Best's farming book, for instance, shows that Bridlington was noted for oats, Malton for wheat and maslin, Pocklington for barley: Henry Best, *Rural Economy in Yorkshire in 1641 . . .*, Surtees Society, xxxiii (1857), 100-1.

52   Richard Blome, *Britannia*, 1673, p. 44. The following generalised account is based on numerous cases in Exchequer Special Commissions and Depositions, and many references in *State Papers Domestic* and local histories. I have also relied heavily on Leland, and on Richard Blome, though I have checked the latter's information, whenever possible, from other sources, and I believe his facts to represent, broadly speaking, developments apparent by 1640. There is urgent need for local monographs on market specialisation; they would probably reveal many specialities I have not discovered and modify or amplify the conclusions of the following paragraphs.

53   The area so designated here includes Middlesex, Suffolk, Norfolk, Hertfordshire, Buckinghamshire, Cambridgeshire, Bedfordshire, Huntingdonshire, Lincolnshire, most of Nottinghamshire, part of west Essex and a few Thames-side markets in Oxfordshire, Surrey and Berkshire.

54   In Kent, for instance, the chief corn-towns were Faversham, Maidstone and Sandwich; in Sussex corn for the royal household was furnished at Chichester, Arundel, Shoreham and Newhaven: Allegra Woodworth, 'Purveyance for the Royal Household in the reign of

Queen Elizabeth', *American Philosophical Society*, ns, xxxv (1946), 44. Leicestershire, by contrast, could not develop as a corn county, for it was 'far remote from any means of exportation of corn': PRO SP 14, 112, 91. For river navigation see T. S. Willan, *River Navigation in England, 1600-1750*, 1936, especially pp. 125 *sqq*. and 136-8; cf. also R. B. Westerfield, *Middlemen in English Business*, 1915, pp. 150, 169-70; P. Mathias, *Brewing Industry*, 1959, pp. 441-7.

55　'The Midlands' here comprises Warwickshire, Worcestershire, Northamptonshire, Rutland, Leicestershire, Staffordshire, Shropshire, Derbyshire, Cheshire, Herefordshire, Monmouthshire, part of Nottinghamshire, Gloucestershire (north of the Stroud Water) and Oxfordshire (except Oxford and Henley).

56　For Shrewsbury and Oswestry, see T. C. Mendenhall, *The Shrewsbury Drapers and the Welsh Wool Trade . . .*, 1953.

57　'The west' here comprises Dorset, Devon, Cornwall, Somerset, Wiltshire and Gloucestershire south of the Stroud Water.

58　W. J. Blake, 'Hooker's Synopsis Chorographical of Devonshire', *Devonshire Assoc.*, xlvii (1915), p. 346. The transcript has 'voirne', but no doubt 'yarn' is intended. Hooker probably exaggerated, but local searches would doubtless reveal many wool and cloth markets in the West.

59　PRO E 134, 4 Car. I, E 36; E 134, 37-8 Eliz., M 15; E 178, 5236; E 134, 20 James I, E 10; E 134, 5 James I, H 22. For the great Exeter serge market, at a rather later date, cf. W. G. Hoskins, *Industry, Trade, and People in Exeter, 1688-1800*, 1935, pp. 41-3.

60　PRO SP 16, 187, 51; cf. SP 14, 113, 17 and 90.

61　The corn market was constricted by the cattle market, likewise expanding: one large corn farmer from Bridmore (Wilts.), who had sold in Shaftesbury for forty years, threatened to 'bring no more corn into the said market' unless 'such straitening of the corn market place be reformed': PRO E 134, 18 James I, E 1.

62　The region comprises Lancashire, Yorkshire, Durham, Westmorland, Cumberland and Northumberland.

63　Very large quantities of grain were dispensed from Hull and York. The two towns were jealous rivals in this trade: Hull was said to have purchased 30,000 quarters of corn in 1622 (?) from 'strangers' and to have resold it to 'country chapmen . . . not suffering the marchants of York to buy any part thereof': PRO SP 14, 138, 120.

64　PRO E 134, 17 Car. I, M 8; E 134, 18 Car. I, E 9.

65　L. Owen, 'The population of Wales in the sixteenth and seventeenth centuries', *Hon. Soc. Cymmrodorion*, 1959, pp. 107-12. For this reference and other information regarding Wales I am indebted to Mr Frank Emery.

66　*The Itinerary in Wales of John Leland . . . 1536-1539*, ed. Lucy Toulmin Smith, 1906, pp. 10, 41, 97.

67　The region comprises Kent, Sussex, Hampshire, most of Essex, and Berkshire and Surrey excluding Thames-side markets. Judged by its marketing specialities, Essex seems to group more naturally with these counties than those of eastern England, though its marketing economy was somewhat enigmatic.

68   Cf. Kenyon, *op. cit.*, pp. 45, 94; C. W. Chalklin, 'A seventeenth-century market town: Tonbridge', *Arch. Cant.*, lxxvi (1961), p. 160. Mr Chalklin shows the intense poverty of most inland towns in Kent at this time, and suggests similar conditions obtained in Surrey and Hampshire.

69   For further information on wool markets, see P. J. Bowden, *The Wool Trade in Tudor and Stuart England*, 1962, pp. 57 *sqq.*

70   See Table 8.1, and Fig. 8.4.

71   Cambridgeshire had only eight markets (one to 69,000 acres), but with these must be reckoned towns just over the border of neighbouring counties, such as Royston and Newmarket.

72   The following account is based principally on information in Exchequer Special Commissions and Depositions, State Papers Domestic, farming diaries, and private estate account books, printed and manuscript; it relates almost entirely to the period after 1560. For Wales the available sources are too scanty to bear much weight; the situation there probably resembled most closely that of the north. See Table 8.1.

73   PRO SP 14, 138, 120; cf. SP 14, 113, 17.

74   PRO E 134, 17 Car. I, M 8; E 134, 18 Car. I, E 9. See also Bowden, *op. cit.*, pp. 57-72.

75   H. B. Rodgers, 'The market area of Preston in the sixteenth and seventeenth centuries', *Geographical Studies*, iii, 1 (1956), 49-55.

76   Best, *op. cit.*, pp. 100-1; Essex RO, B, 7 . 13, 38 . 1502, Clopton Diary, *passim*; Lincs. AO, Holywell MS, 97, 22, *passim*.

77   John Harland, ed., *The House and Farm Accounts of the Shuttle-worths of Gawthorpe Hall . . .*, Chetham Soc., xxxv, 1856, *passim*. The Shuttleworths also bought cattle at Chorley, Bolton, Bury, Blackburn, Wigan, Newburgh, Colne and Preston.

78   Kent AO, PRC 10, 35.

79   Many of these disputes turned on a question of town boundaries. They were thus common in towns of late creation, like Stow-on-the-Wold, where the urban area had been carved out of other parishes and was small in extent.

80   PRO E 134, 3 James I, E 20.

81   PRO E 134, 17 Car. I, M 8; E 134, 18 Car. I, E 9.

82   PRO E 134, 9 James I, M 31; E 134, 13 James I, E 19. The deponents' evidence is contradictory, but I believe the above account to be substantially correct.

83   PRO E 134, 7 Car. I, M 19; E 134, 7 Car. I, E 19.

84   In the two latter areas, however, market disputes may have been dealt with by the councils of the North and Marches.

85   PRO C 3, 262, 7. Tenants of Duchy manors (cf. E 134, 3 James I, H 19) and inhabitants of London, Lincoln and some other towns invoked genuine claims to be toll-free in English markets. The significant fact is that frequently such rights had fallen into desuetude (though not, of course, in London) till their revival under the impulse of Elizabethan expansion.

9 London as an 'Engine of economic growth'

F. J. Fisher

The concepts of centre and periphery do not easily fit the economy of a country except, perhaps, in a metaphorical sense. For economies progress from a state of self-sufficiency to one of regional specialisation, and regional specialisation creates a pattern that is essentially policentric. Different activities develop around different centres that are linked to each other by a web of communications and trade. One may easily speak of textile centres, of mining centres, of commercial centres. But it is with less confidence that one can speak of a centre to the economy as a whole; and especially when the economy in question is largely agricultural, for agriculture is essentially a dispersed activity that defies centralisation. Yet it can be argued that, in the seventeenth century, London was in an important sense the economic centre of England.

The arguments for seeing it as such are basically two. The first, and minor, may be dealt with briefly. It lies in the fact that, when one looks for emerging areas of specialisation in Tudor and Stuart England, London is prominent under a variety of headings. It was the largest centre of population in the country; at the beginning of the sixteenth century it was probably five times as large as the largest provincial town; at the end of the seventeenth century it was fifteen times as large. Consequently it was the most important single market for consumer goods and, in an age when most consumer goods industries were carried on in close proximity to the consumer, it was the largest centre of such industries. It was the country's largest port, and as a result its chief commercial and financial centre. As the country's largest town, and as the centre of government, it was the obvious location for ambitious professional men. The centralisation of the English political and legal systems meant that only in London were the rewards of government service or legal practice of much substance. Then, as now, it was the most profitable location for doctors, especially as many were content to diagnose and prescribe for an illness by correspondence. As the one town in which commercial publishing and printing were allowed, it naturally attracted the professional writer. And although ecclesiastical posts in London do not seem to have been exceptionally remunerative, ambitious bishops and clergymen were likely to spend considerable time there in search of preferment, if not for more spiritual

F. J. Fisher, 'London as an "Engine of Economic Growth" ', in J. S. Bromley and E. H. Kossmann, eds, *Britain and the Netherlands: iv*, The Hague, Martinus Nijhoff, 1971, pp. 3-16.

reasons. As the largest town — and moreover one in which the Court normally resided — it offered a wider range of urban amenities than any other place in England and thereby attracted the gentleman bored with the intolerable tedium of country life: an attraction that was intensified by the possibility, when in London, of dabbling in politics, obtaining favours from those in power, borrowing money, buying or selling land, arranging marriages for his children and generally meeting men of his own social class from other regions.

In all these respects London both influenced and was influenced by developments in the provinces, and the main difference between the sixteenth and seventeenth centuries was one of degree. London was already the centre of commerical and professional life in the early sixteenth century, but it was only in the 1580s that the development of the theatre, the conversion of large houses into taverns and the complaints of contemporaries began to suggest that London was becoming important as a centre of social intercourse; and its population seems to have grown more substantially after 1600 than before. Consequently, on the principle that, when carried beyond a certain point, differences of degree become differences of kind, it might well be argued that, whereas during the sixteenth century London was highly influential, in the seventeenth century it took on the role of the country's economic centre.

But the major argument for attributing to it that role is more substantial. It can be appreciated only if the nature of the English economy at that time is borne in mind. That economy was, above all else, small. Not only was its total population small — about a tenth of that of modern England — but the great majority of that population lived in small communities and worked on small farms or in small workshops by methods that yielded only a small output per head. The fact that most men lived in small communities meant that a large proportion of them still had some access to land and could produce at least some of their own food-stuffs; and to that extent there persisted a strong subsistence element in the economy. The fact that communities were small, and that most goods were produced in or near the place at which they were consumed, meant that much commercial production was for small local markets. The fact that output per head was low meant that the national income was small, not only in its total volume, but also in the range of goods and services that composed it. Experience suggests that few economies of that nature contain within themselves self-generating tendencies to change. They can remain stable for centuries. For neither subsistence production nor production for small local markets encourages either a growth in investment or the division of labour — the twin engines of economic growth. And the availability of only a narrow range of consumer goods and services is notoriously a great disincentive to effort, and an encouragement to what in the sixteenth and seventeenth centuries was denounced as laziness, but is now more politely described as leisure preference.

In such an economy, substantial change is likely to come about only as a result of one or both of two factors. A growth in population will increase the demand for basic necessities and, by enlarging the markets for them, stimulate both investment and the division of labour. A growth in non-local trade will not only widen markets, and thereby stimulate investment and specialisation, but will provide an additional stimulus to effort by widening the range of goods available. Both of these factors were at work in Tudor and Stuart England, and it was with respect to them that the role of London changed in such a way as to justify the concept of the capital as the centre of the economy.

Anything said about population change in the sixteenth and seventeenth centuries must of necessity be largely speculative, for the scanty data afford hints rather than firm conclusions. Yet two propositions seem reasonably secure. In the sixteenth century the growth of population was fairly general throughout the country, and although the rate of growth was highest in London the greatest volume of growth took place in the provinces. A reasonable guess might be that, whereas the population of England and Wales increased by something like a million, that of London may not have increased by more than one hundred and fifty thousand. Thus the major impetus to increased agricultural and industrial production came from provincial rather than from London demand, especially as London was in some measure fed on imported grain. In the seventeenth century, however, there were signs of a new demographic pattern. In many parts of the provinces the growth of population seems to have slowed down; substantial growth seems to have been confined to three areas. One was Tyneside, where the coal industry was expanding largely in response to London demand. Another was in the West Midlands, where the metal industries were flourishing. But the most pronounced growth occurred in and around London. The reasons for these changes are still obscure. In some areas the age of marriage seems to have risen and the birth rate to have fallen. There is some evidence of a major epidemic in the 1640s. But one factor was undoubtedly the massive migration to London that both increased the population of the capital and depressed that of the provinces. And whatever the reasons for that migration may have been, its result was that, in the seventeenth century, the dynamic effects of population growth on the economy as a whole were increasingly mediated through London.

A comparable change may be discerned in the case of foreign trade, the most obvious form of that non-local trade that provides a stimulus to simple economies. In purely quantitative terms, it appears that London's proportion of total overseas trade may have declined slightly in the seventeenth century. But what is important is a change that occurred in the nature of English trade. Economists draw a useful distinction between trade expansion that is primarily export-led and expansion that is primarily import-led. In the first case trade expands because, as in modern Germany, of the efficiency of the export industries and their ability to undersell competitors abroad. In such circumstances the dynamic factor is obviously to be found in the exporting industry; merchants may add an additional dynamic factor by opening new markets; but on the other hand their role may be the largely passive one of moving a larger quantity of goods along established channels. In the case of sixteenth-century England, it is clear that trade expansion was primarily export-led. Trade was buoyant in the first half of the century when the superiority of the English cloth industry was marked. It became sluggish in the second half of the century, and by the end of the century there were increasing complaints about the difficulties of competing with the reviving textile industries on the Continent. This was the standard explanation of commercial difficulties from the 1590s until the 1630s. It was this competition that made the increase of export taxes by king and Merchant Adventures so burdensome in the early seventeenth century. It was this competition that inspired so much legislation and so many projects designed to prevent the export of English and Irish wool and English fuller's earth to foreign rivals and to improve the quality of English textiles. The rise in exports was, of course, accompanied by a rise in imports. But it was not always easy to find returns that could profitably be sold in England, and in consequence there was an influx of bullion that contributed to the rise in prices. In this process, the role of the London merchants seems to have been largely passive. Their efforts to find new markets were more spectacular than fruitful, and for the most part they performed the passive role of moving increasing quantities of goods into the Netherlands for distribution throughout Europe by foreigners. Thus in overseas trade, as in demographic change, the dynamic factor during the sixteenth century has to be sought in the provinces rather than in London.

But in seventeenth-century England, as in the England of today, trade expansion became increasingly import-led. Trade grew, less because of the competitive efficiency of English industry, than because of the English demand for foreign goods. For to the demand for such traditional imports as linens, expensive silks and wines — a demand that grew with the population — there was added a vigorous market for the fruits, the cheap silks, the cheap spices, the cheap sugar, and such new commodities as tobacco and calicoes that flowed in gradually mounting quantities from Spain, the Mediterranean, Africa, America and the East and West Indies. That appetite for imports was a dominant feature of English trade throughout the seventeenth century and goes far to explain why, in that century, Englishmen were so often concerned with the problem of the balance of payments — for later experience has shown that import-led trade expansion and balance of payments problems often go together.

Moreover, the timing of the first balance-of-payments scare in seventeenth-century England may suggest one reason why English trade was becoming import-led rather than export-led. That scare came at the beginning of the second decade of the century — just before the notorious Cockaigne experiment — and it is tempting to see it as a delayed result of that big switch in agricultural incomes in favour of landlords and larger farmers that had taken place since the 1580s. It is reasonable to suppose the beneficiaries of that redistribution of income had a more than average propensity to consume imports — contemporary comment certainly suggests as much — and the delayed response to that redistribution may well be accounted for by the fact that it was those beneficiaries of income redistribution who largely met the cost of the Irish and Spanish wars through the payment of subsidies and the purchase of royal lands. It is easy to believe that, once the demands of wartime finance were ended, they indulged in an import spree. But if the change in the nature of English trade from export-led to import-led was started by a redistribution of the national income in favour of those with a greater propensity to consume imports, it was perpetuated by the gradual cheapening of such imports as spices and sugar and the introduction of new imports such as tobacco and calicoes — to name only the most obvious.

This change from export-led to import-led commercial expansion had one obvious implication: it meant that the dynamic element in trade expansion had shifted from the manufacturer to the merchant. Export-led growth depended on the competitive efficiency of the manufacturer; import-led growth depended on the enterprise of the merchant who scoured the world in search of desirable commodities to meet the English appetite for foreign wares. And a shift of the dynamic element from manufacturer to merchant meant, in seventeenth-century England, a shift from the provinces to London. And this new role of London was reinforced by two further circumstances. Imports, of course, had to be paid for. But they were paid for only in part by an increased export of English manufactures, despite the versatility of the provincial textile industries in producing new draperies for new markets. In large part, they were paid for by re-exports; and re-exporting was essentially the function of London merchants. Moreover when, as is usually the case, the rising tide of imports led to a movement for import substitution, that movement took an interesting turn. On paper, there were plenty of schemes for establishing in England the production of substitutes for imported manufactured goods. Some of the notorious monopolies granted by the early Stuarts were designed to that end. But most of these schemes remained on paper; most of the monopoly projects failed. The truth of the matter was that, textiles apart, most imports were of commodities that could not be produced in England. In textiles, there was some success in developing a silk industry on the basis of raw silk imported from the Levant — a development that took place mainly in London. But little success was achieved in the case of linen, for a linen industry would have required for its growth a large mass of cheap female labour that was already well employed in the woollen industry. And it was impossible for English workers to compete with the low-wage labour of India in the production of cottons. For the most part, import substitution took a different form. It took the form of substituting English colonies for foreign countries as sources of supply. Above all, it took the form of substituting the services of English ships and merchants for those of foreigners. The great import-substitution measures of the seventeenth century were not protective duties but the Navigation Acts. The competitor to be eliminated was not England's great industrial rival, which was France, but her commerical rival — the Netherlands. To rephrase the matter in modern jargon, it was in the realm of invisible rather than in the realm of visible import that substitution occurred. And it is well known that in the financing of colonies and in the provision of shipping and mercantile services London played a major role. Once more, the dynamic factor is found in London rather than in the provinces.

Moreover, these demographic and commercial changes both promoted and were further stimulated by one of the major developments that took place in pre-industrial England — the creation of a system of communication that linked London to all parts of the provinces. The physical manifestations of that system were a rapidly growing fleet of coastal vessels that plied between London and all provincial ports; a growing fleet of barges on the Thames and its tributaries such as the Lea; a spreading network of carriers, who with their packhorses or carts linked every town in England to the capital with a regular schedule of services; and a rash of shopkeepers in every town and important village linked by these carriers and these vessels to wholesalers in London. This distributive system not only brought produce to be consumed in or exported from London, and not only distributed London's imports throughout the country, but also brought wares from one part of England to be shipped onwards to other parts and provided channels along which news and people moved with ease. It was in the seventeenth century that London became the centre of England in the sense of being at the centre of a regular system of communications; a fact that was confirmed in the later seventeenth century by the establishment of a general post office based on the capital.

Thus, it can be argued that in the course of the sixteenth and seventeenth centuries the role of London in the English economy changed significantly. In the sixteenth century, London was important as being the largest town with the largest mercantile community and offering the widest range of urban amenities — but it was in no real sense the economic centre of the country. In the seventeenth century it became the centre of the economy — not only or even mainly because it became larger and its range of urban amenities became wider — but because the two dynamic factors conducing to change became increasingly channelled through it. The problem is to consider what can usefully be said about the pattern of relationships that consequently emerged between London and the rest of England. At a very high level of generalisation, certain obvious comments suggest themselves. It is clear that the development of London was made possible or at least stimulated by some of the major changes that were occurring in English provincial life. Obviously the congregation of half a million people in a single urban community was made possible only by the increase in agricultural production and productivity that occurred in the England of the time. The migration of labour to the capital owed much to the nature of the English agrarian system. For in that system the effects of population pressure tended to be, not the subdivision of holdings into dwarf allotments that held men on the land, but the creation of a landless class that was usually able and often willing to move. In the sixteenth century they seem to have moved mainly to the remaining areas of woodlands and marsh where land, or at least the use of commons, was still available. But in the seventeenth century, as the forests dwindled and the marshlands were drained, they moved more and more towards London. At a rather higher social level the system of primogeniture, which often cast the younger sons of the gentry on to the world to shape their own fortunes, often sent them running in search of careers in either trade or the professions. The ability of the more prosperous landowners to make frequent visits to London obviously owed something to the rising rents that swelled their incomes after the 1580s. And it may have owed something to the development of the coach which, by making it more difficult for them to leave their wives at home, operated to make their visits both longer and more expensive. Clearly, London's commercial expansion was heavily dependent both on the capacity of provincial industry to supply it with exports and on the capacity of provincial consumers to take off its imports; in both respects the general expansion of the Tudor and Stuart economy made the growth of London possible.

Looking in the other direction, it is easy to accept the verdict of seventeenth-century writers that the London market was a major stimulus to production and regional specialisation in the provinces. What is more speculative is the effect on provincial life of the wider range of goods and services, whether imported or locally produced, that London had to offer. This wider range of goods and services must have raised the standard of living of those who were able to enjoy them, for it is a commonplace that beyond a certain very low level of consumption rising standards mean that a greater variety of goods rather than a greater volume of goods is consumed. What is less certain is the effect of the availability of this wider range of goods and services on productivity in England as a whole. It is tempting to believe that it did something, and possibly something very substantial, to reduce that leisure preference that is so serious an obstacle to economic expansion in simple economies. To test any such proposition empirically is impossible. But certainly Hume, Adam Smith and the classical economists — men who knew from first hand an economy not greatly dissimilar to that of Tudor and Stuart England — attached enormous importance to this effect of commercial growth. And modern growth economists have used very much the same arguments under the title of the demonstration effect of foreign commodities in underdeveloped economies.

In this respect it may be pertinent to ask who it was that consumed imported goods and was thereby open to their pressure to increase productivity. One class clearly was that of the landowners and it was a commonplace of contemporary satirists that some landlords, to meet their expenses in London, demanded greater rents from their tenants; and the need to pay these greater rents may well have led tenants to increase their output where possible. But had the consumption of imports and city-made goods been confined to the upper classes it is doubtful whether much weight could reasonably be attached to them as a spur to production. The significant feature of some of the most rapidly growing imports was that they penetrated a considerable way down the social scale. Tobacco seems to have been consumed by all classes except the very poor. Currants were so widely consumed that the Venetian ambassador was able to report somewhat mysteriously to the Doge and Senate that there was a season in England when it was so dishonourable for a man not to be able to consume currants that he would hang himself in shame if such a tragedy occurred. Cheap silks and cheap sugar were both enjoyed by the middle ranks of the population, and one of the standard objections to cheap Indian calicoes was that they made it impossible for a man to distinguish between his wife and his serving girl, a situation that causes embarrassment in all ages. The penetration of imported goods down the social scale is perhaps best illustrated by a comment made by Defoe in the reign of Queen Anne. One of the many objections to that lady was that she had many relations, with the result that deaths among them repeatedly plunged the English Court into mourning. One consequence was that the London Mercers were left with a stock of coloured ribbons and silks that they could not sell, and with a demand for black ribbons and silk that they found it difficult to supply. Explaining why the repercussions of the death of some minor German aristocrat were so profound, Defoe pointed out that by aristocratic convention every member of the court was bound to wear black on such an occasion, that every lady in or near London wore black in the hope of persuading her neighbours that she was connected with the court, and that every shop girl wore black in the hope of persuading the world that she was a lady. The truth of that explanation is, of course, irrelevant; the point is that Defoe's readers would accept the proposition that the shop girls were consumers of imported goods. And observations that point to a similar conclusion could be multiplied with ease.

Some years ago Professor Nef argued that in the seventeenth century the economic histories of France and England parted company. France, he asserted, remained true to the habits of civilised society by concentrating its resources on the production of articles of grace and beauty. England sank to a lower cultural level by diverting those forces to the production of cheap commodities in mass demand; he poured scorn on an economy that devoted so much labour and capital to the digging of coal. His point might have been made more effectively, although perhaps less dramatically, had he observed that much of England's import trade was aimed at the middle and lower classes. Nor is this fact perhaps very surprising. The calculations of the national income made by Gregory King at the end of the seventeenth century are no doubt unreliable in detail, but the interesting thing about them is that he places only about a quarter of the population on a level of extreme poverty. To the remaining three-quarters of the population, he attributes an income that leaves some margin over the basic needs for subsistence and therefore a margin from which imported and London-made goods might be purchased. And the buoyancy of what may be called the popular market for imported goods owed something to the fact that, in England, not only was taxation normally light but the upper classes were not able to claim exemption from it. Given this considerable penetration of society by imports and London-made goods, it is not difficult to believe that they were having some effect in diminishing men's leisure preference and so stimulating economic growth.

At a rather lower level of generalisation, it is perhaps possible to make half-a-dozen points without sinking into details of local history that would be inappropriate here. Something can reasonably be said of the multitudinous complaints that were made at the time about London's development. On examination these complaints fall into three main groups of which one may be quickly dismissed, since it dealt essentially with problems of urbanisation within London rather than with any relationship between the City and the provinces. The second group of complaints were really variants on the general theme of opportunity cost. The availability of goods and services in London and from London meant a change in men's patterns of expenditure that adversely affected the provinces.

If landlords went to the capital, employment, hospitality and charity in the provinces declined; if workers went to the capital, agricultural rents declined; if London merchants brought in East India calicoes, the provincial textile industry declined. Arguments of that type were abundant and not always ill-founded.

Finally, there was a third group of complaints based on the theme that Londoners used their economic power and political influence unjustly to exploit their provincial fellows. That theme found its most vigorous expression with respect to London's dominating position in England's trade in the late sixteenth and early seventeenth centuries. The reasons for London's dominating position were, of course, largely geographical: lying on a navigable river sixty miles inland and with easy overland access to all parts of the country, it was the obvious place for the collection of exports and the distribution of imports, especially when the main market to be served was that of the Netherlands. A merchant in a provincial port could draw only on the products of his hinterland for his exports and sell his imports only to the inhabitants of that hinterland. A merchant in London could draw exports from all parts of the country and distribute his imports as widely. As was said in the late seventeenth century, by comparison with London an out-port was a prison. Yet there seems to have been some substance in the argument that for a time the merchants of London used their predominance which these advantages gave them, first to obtain excessive privileges from the Crown, and then to use those privileges to exploit the producers and consumers of provincial England. Certainly it is difficult to refute that accusation with respect to the Merchant Adventurers of London during the reigns of Elizabeth and James, for it is clear that they then expanded their fortunes less by finding new markets for English cloth and cheaper supplies of English imports, than by squeezing both provincial and foreign merchants out of the profitable trade with the Netherlands. And it is easy to believe that having excluded foreign merchants so largely from that trade, they used their oligopolist position both to depress the price of English cloth at home and to raise the price of the imported goods that they placed on the English market. To that extent, at least, there was some justification for the argument that London was parasitic on England. But it was a justification strictly limited in time for it did not apply to most of the sixteenth century, when foreign merchants were still active in English trade, and it did not apply to most of the seventeenth century, when the weaknesses of the English cloth industry and the development of trade with other parts of the world had greatly reduced the Merchants Adventurers' capacity for either good or evil.

Another topic that permits of some general remarks is the effect of London's growth on the economic geography of the country. For reasons of transport, London's demand for such bulky commodities as grain, hay and wood fuel, and for such perishable commodities as fruit and vegetables, was met for the most part from the counties adjacent to it; and for the same reason the same area provided it with most of its meat supply. The result was to intensify the agricultural nature of south-eastern England and to push the major industrial areas away from the capital even before that process was completed by the use of steam power. In the sixteenth and early seventeenth centuries there were considerable textile industries in Kent, Surrey, Hampshire and Berkshire and a flourishing iron industry in the Weald. By the end of the seventeenth century those textile industries had virtually disappeared and the Wealden iron industry was languishing. One reason given by contemporaries was that the London demand for food kept food prices high; in consequence wages in the area from which London drew its food were high; and so industry was lost to areas where both food and labour were cheaper. Unfortunately the price and wage data that have survived do not enable us to test that argument, although it is clear that from the 1590s wages in London itself rose increasingly above their level in the more distant parts of the country. And whether or not the wage argument was valid, it is clear that entrepreneurs within sixty or eighty miles of the capital found agriculture more profitable than industry. The textile areas of Kent turned to the fattening of cattle; the textile towns of Reading and Newbury turned to the processing of and trading in grain for the metropolitan market. In the Weald it was found more profitable to root up coppices and convert the land to pasture than to continue it under wood for the supply of the iron industry.

London's demand for food and fuel was not, of course, confined to the neighbouring counties. But elsewhere it was less intense and more selective. Dairy produce came from Cheshire and Suffolk, coal from Newcastle; store cattle for fattening in the south-east came not only from the north and west but in increasing numbers from Scotland and Ireland.

For the most part, London's own industries were able to overcome the handicap of high wages. Many of them — such as building and tailoring — were by their nature best carried on, or necessarily carried on, in close proximity to the consumer. Luxury trades, in which labour formed only a small proportion of costs, were best carried on in the capital that formed their largest market. Some, such as tanning and sugar-refining, remained tied to the capital because of the availability of their raw material. Others, like silk-weaving, were carried on largely by alien immigrants who found the capital more congenial and more hospitable than small country towns. But there can be discerned some movement of industry from London to the provinces, the most notable examples being the movement of the hosiery industry to Nottingham, of the shoemaking industry to Northampton, of the silk-throwing industry to north Essex. And it is possible to discern a significant division between London and the provinces in the matter of industry; Londoners added the finishing touches to many wares, but the initial stages of production were carried on in the provinces where labour was cheaper and water power more abundant. Clothes were made in London not only for Londoners but for the provincial upper classes; but cloth was made in the provinces. London had a large cutlery industry, but it used blades forged in Sheffield or the West Midlands. And as Professor Barker has recently shown, the flourishing London clock and watchmaking industry was based on the assembly of parts in Lancashire.

There is, however, only a limited profit in thus discussing London and the provinces, for a major feature in the English scene was the fact that Londoners and provincials did not crystallise as completely separate groups of people. One of the most obvious characteristics of the English gentry was that they tended to retain their provincial homes and take lodgings or houses in London rather than shift from the countryside permanently to the city. At any time in the seventeenth century many

Londoners were first-generation immigrants to the city; many who were permanently domiciled in the city retained some property or at least family connections in the countryside; and a significant part of the city's population consisted of people visiting it for purposes of education or business or pleasure for a period that, although it might last for some years, was not intended to be permanent. It was this situation that made the influence of London so pervasive.

A final point that may be worth making is that the pattern of relationships that appeared so clearly in the seventeenth century proved not to be permanent. In the course of the eighteenth century population growth became less confined to the city and consequently the increase in the demand for agricultural produce became more diffused, especially with the growth of subsidised exports. Also in the course of that century foreign trade became once more export-led rather than import-led, so that the dynamic factor shifts once more to the manufacturing areas. And the improved network of communications could be used by provincial merchants and by provincial manufacturers to distribute goods other than through the capital. And as one observes this modification in the pattern, one is inevitably reminded of the theory of international trade that depicted international trade as 'an engine of economic growth' by virtue of the fact that, although in the earlier stages of development industrialised countries stimulated mainly primary production in other parts of the world, in the course of time the latter producers by a process of import substitution tended to become industrialised themselves. There is, perhaps, sufficient similarity between that model and what happened in seventeenth-century England to justify the title of this paper.

10 Socio–economic status and occupations in the City of London at the end of the seventeenth century

D. V. Glass

This paper represents a further stage in the analysis of archival materials bearing upon the social demography of London at the end of the seventeenth century [1]. Two sets of data are drawn upon here. The first is derived from the 1695 enumeration of the population of London, an enumeration carried out under the Act of 6 & 7 William & Mary, c. 6, for levying taxes upon burials, births and marriages and annual dues upon bachelors over twenty-five years of age and upon childless widowers. The Act provided for civil vital registration and for population statistics, and also prescribed modifications of the parochial registration system designed to make it both more speedy in its operation and more comprehensive in its coverage. In the present paper it is only the population statistics which are considered, covering not only total numbers but also certain subdivisions of the population, particularly with reference to marital condition and socio-economic status.

The second set of data consists of the 1692 poll tax statistics. In connection with this tax, collected under the Act of 3 William & Mary, c. 6 – and, like the taxes on marriage, births and burials, designed to provide revenue for prosecuting the war against France – a nominal roll was prepared for each administrative area, listing families and their members in considerable detail, though not in quite as much detail as the 1695 enumeration. That enumeration listed and named each individual and indicated all the personal characteristics which were relevant to the system of taxes and annual dues. The 1692 poll tax gave the name of the head of the family and indicated whether there was a wife and children (and the number of such children) but did not generally name these other members of the family. On the other hand, the occupations of 'employed' persons were given (it is men who are in the majority of cases listed, though the occupations of some women are also stated), and it is fairly clear from the lists that the occupations are real, and not simply gild memberships. Both the marriage tax and the poll tax were graduated. It is thus possible to obtain from the basic data a quantitative estimate of the distribution of socio-economic status and, in the case of the poll tax returns, to look at the relationship between occupation and wealth. But before presenting the

D. V. Glass, 'Socio-economic status and occupations in the City of London at the end of the seventeenth century', in A. E. J. Hollaender and W. Kellaway, eds, *Studies in London History*, Hodder and Stoughton, 1969, pp. 373-89.

results, it is necessary to discuss the nature of the 'universe' to which the statistics relate, as well as to consider the limitations of the basic data.

So far as the 1695 enumeration is concerned, the assessments preserved in the Guildhall relate to eighty of the ninety-seven parishes within the Walls (there are also assessments for thirteen parishes without the Walls, but they are not included in the present analysis). The inner parishes represent only the 'core' of London. Jones and Judges estimated the population of that core in 1695 at about 70,000 [2], for London as a whole, including the twenty parishes without the Walls, fifteen parishes in Middlesex and Surrey, and seven parishes in Westminster; Gregory King's estimate (including an allowance for omissions) was a population of about 528,000. Even in the London of 1695, the East End had around 80,000 people, a somewhat larger number than that in the City within the Walls. It was this core which lost resident population throughout the nineteenth century and which may well have shown some overspill after the middle of the seventeenth century — the poorer people moving to the East End, and the wealthier towards the West, to escape — according to Sir William Petty — the 'stink' of the town, given the direction of the prevailing winds. At present, the data for the populous outer ring of late seventeenth-century London are far less firm than those for the core, and this must be allowed for in considering how representative of London as a whole are the statistics for the City within the Walls.

Further, partly because the analysis of the 1695 enumeration is very time-consuming, the documents actually used are not the eighty parish assessments preserved in the Guildhall archives, but a stratified sample of forty parishes. The City was first divided into four approximately equal geographical segments, and within each segment a one-in-two sample of parishes was selected from an alphabetically ordered list. In addition, a sub-sample of one-in-four parishes was taken from each of the four geographical segments, both for the purpose of a more detailed analysis of household structure and also — as will be explained later — for comparison with the 1692 poll tax statistics. The main sample of forty parishes had a recorded population of almost 28,500 persons, while the population in the sub-sample (consisting of twelve parishes) amounted to just under 9,200. The broad social and demographic characteristics of the main sample and of the sub-sample are shown in Tables 10.1 and 10.2. It is clear that, although there are some differences between the structure and composition of the main sample and of the sub-sample, the differences are small. A complete matching could not be expected — both because of the chance error involved in the smaller numbers of the sub-sample, and also because the sampling units (the parishes) are neither homogeneous nor equal in population. But the similarity of the two sets of results is sufficiently close to justify inferences drawn from the sub-sample, which is the basis of the poll tax analysis to be discussed subsequently.

Tables 10.1 and 10.2 present a general indication of the social and demographic structure of the City of London within the Walls. The proportion of the population liable to surtax — the relevant heads of families and their dependants — suggests a sizeable top economic stratum, namely some 17 per cent with incomes of £50 per year or over, or with personal estate worth £600 or more, these constituting the minimum level

Table 10.1   City of London within the Walls, 1695. Some social characteristics of total sample of 40 parishes and of sub-sample of 12 parishes..

	Per cent of population liable to surtax	Persons per house	Children per house*	Servants and apprentices per house†	Total population
1. Total sample of 40 parishes	16·6	6·03	1·38	1·43	28,498‡
2. Sub-sample of 12 parishes §	17·2	5·91	1·31	1·33	9,199

Notes

*   Children include those so designated in the assessments and also
     individuals referred to as sons or daughters.

†   The information on apprentices appears to be incomplete, but it is
     possible that in some parishes there was confusion between apprentices
     and servants. The latter designation is by no means always restricted to
     domestic servants.

‡   Excluding nine persons of unknown sex.

§   The sub-sample consists of the following parishes: St Alban Wood
     Street; St Lawrence Jewry; St Mary Staining; All Hallows London Wall;
     St Helen; All Hallows Bread Street; St Benet Paul's Wharf; St Matthew
     Friday Street; All Hallows Barking; St Botolph Billingsgate; St George
     Botolph Lane; St Mary Abchurch.

Table 10.2   City of London within the Walls, 1695. Demographic structure of
total sample of 40 parishes and of sub-sample of 12 parishes (percentage
distribution by marital condition).

	Males						Females				Ratio: males per 100 females
	Single										
	under 25	25 and over	all	Married	Widowed·	Total	Single	Married	Widowed	Total	
1. Total sample of 40 parishes	54·6	10·2	64·8	33·2	2·1	100·1	65·0	29·0	6·1	100·1	87
2. Sub-sample of 12 parishes	55·8	9·7	65·5	32·7	1·8	100·0	65·7	28·8	5·5	100·0	89
3. London, 1851 Census	50·5	10·1	60·6	36·1	3·3	100·0	58·6	32·6	8·8	100·0	88

at which surtax was payable. Theoretically, this should be an accurate figure in that no one was excluded from the enumeration. Even though some categories of people were exempt from some of the taxes, no category was exempt from all. For example, fellows, students and scholars in universities were exempt from the bachelor tax, but not from the duty on burials or, if they came to marry, from the duty on marriages. Similarly, though persons in receipt of alms were exempt from most of the taxes, the parish had to pay the duty if they or their wives or children died. Accordingly, everyone was 'exposed' to the risk of some tax and everyone should have been listed, and the parish assessments do include the names of individuals who were exempt from some of the taxes. Nevertheless, there is no doubt that there was under-enumeration. Gregory King was aware of this, attempted to measure the amount in two parishes, and made an allowance for it in his estimates. The evidence suggests that his allowance was too small and that perhaps a quarter or more of the total population was omitted — though it should be emphasised that the tests of under-enumeration are difficult and have not yet been fully checked. These omissions do not contradict the earlier, qualitative evaluation by Jones and Judges that the 1695 assessments were carried out very conscientiously and were likely to be the most reliable of all the late seventeenth-century fiscal returns [3]. On the contrary, the experience of working on the parish data confirms the general impression of enumerations conducted with unusual care. But that there were omissions is no less evident and they may well have been selective, consisting disproportionately of the poorer people. In that case, the estimate of 17 per cent of the population in the surtax categories would be excessive and overstate the wealth of the inhabitants of the City of London.

Because the surtax was graduated, it is possible to show the distribution of the population within the surtax categories, and this is not without interest. The data for the sub-sample are summarised in Table 10.3. As might be expected, the largest proportion consists of the population in the lowest surtax category. The population of gentlemen, esquires and higher ranks (omitting the three recognized professions)

Table 10.3 City of London within the Walls, 1695. Sub-sample of 12 parishes. Population liable to surtax under Act of 6 & 7 Wm. & M., c. 6, classified by category.

Category	No.	Per cent
1. Total population liable to surtax	1,579	100·0
2. Persons (and dependants) with £50 p.a. or £600 personal estate	1,181	74·8
3. Doctors of divinity, law or medicine, and ministers from Canon upwards (and dependants)	38	2·4
4. Gentlemen and esquires (and their dependants)	296	8·7
5. Knights, Knights bachelor, Baronets (and their dependants)	34	2·2
6. Others	30	1·9

amounts to some 21 per cent of the surtax population and about 3·6 per cent of the total population.

Disproportionate under-enumeration of the poorer people might also affect the more specifically demographic characteristics shown in Table 10.2. It is not unlikely, for example, that among those poorer people there would be a smaller proportion of apprentices and servants, who were predominantly unmarried. If the selective omissions could be allowed for, the total population might thus show a smaller proportion of single males and females — perhaps nearer to the proportions reported for London as a whole in the 1851 Census. But even taking that into account, the data for 1695 and for 1851 show a strong similarity, namely the large proportion of single males and females. This would be expected with a relatively high age at first marriage — as was the case in England and Wales in 1851 — and particularly in the largest urban centre with substantial employment opportunities for young unmarried men and women and, in 1695, with a heavy emphasis upon apprenticeship opportunities for young men. The quantitative role of apprenticeship in London will be considered later.

Apart from the question of household composition, which will not be discussed here, the 1695 enumerations as a whole do not provide much additional information on the socio-economic structure of London. In a few cases there are data on occupations — especially comprehensive for the parish of St Mary le Bow — but such information was not required by the Act and is not sufficiently general to furnish a picture of the City as a whole. In the case of the 1692 poll tax records, however, occupations are given for the majority of relevant individuals, and the rest of this paper will be mainly concerned with an analysis of those records.

In trying to make use of both the 1695 enumerations and the 1692 poll tax records, it was obviously desirable to relate the analysis to the same geographical areas. But the 1695 enumerations were undertaken on a parish basis, while the 1692 tax records are on a ward basis, the customary basis of fiscal returns for London. However, by using the data for precincts within wards, it was possible to obtain a reasonably close match between the two sets of records. For nine parishes, the match is fully satisfactory; for the remainder, there is some overlapping with other parishes. In total, the poll tax data relate to thirteen parishes (plus some additional fringes) rather than the twelve in the 1695 sub-sample, the thirteenth parish being St John the Baptist. Analysis of the 1695 enumeration for that parish shows that it has a smaller proportion of surtax payers than the average for the sub-sample of twelve parishes, and also has smaller percentages of unmarried males and females. The overall figures for the thirteen parishes would be slightly closer to those for the main sample of forty parishes in Tables 10.1 and 10.2, and the comparison is not unreasonable, though the absolute figures are different [4].

The 1692 poll tax was payable quarterly, the basic rate being 1s per quarter, payable for every man, woman and child, with the following exceptions: almsmen and their children under sixteen; poor housekeepers and their children under sixteen; children (under sixteen) of day labourers and of servants in husbandry; all children (under sixteen) of those who had four or more children and who were worth less than £50 in lands, goods and chattels. There were four main surtax grades, the members of which had to pay the specified surtax in addition to the basic charge. These grades were:

1. 10*s* per quarter: tradesmen, shopkeepers and vintners with estates worth £300 or more.
2. £1 per quarter: gentlemen and above (but not peers); relatively wealthy women (e.g. with estate of £1,000 or more); the clergy (but excluding the lords spiritual); merchants and brokers; and a variety of professions.
3. £2 per quarter: clergymen with more than one benefice worth £120 per year or over.
4. £10 per quarter: lords temporal and spiritual. There were also special charges for persons keeping a coach and for those liable to provide a horse and horseman for the militia.

This surtax coverage is wider than is specified for the taxes on marriages, births and burials and the sub-categories are not comparable. Further, the enumerations appear less complete than those of 1695, in that the number of paupers totally exempt from the tax is extremely small, amounting to only fourteen families in the sample. It would thus seem probable that, in general, families which were exempt were simply not listed in the returns. Accordingly, it would be more realistic to exclude the few recorded pauper families from the analysis and this has been done, so that the subsequent statistics refer only to families, at least one member of which was liable to tax.

The total population listed in the sample amounted to 6,701, very substantially smaller than that reported in the sub-sample of 1695 enumerations. Though it is not possible at present to say how far the difference is explained by under-reporting and how far by lack of exact comparability in the area coverage, it seems very probable that the former factor is mainly responsible. Of the total, the number liable to tax is 4,126 — 2,617 males, 1,501 females, and eight whose sex could not be determined. Taxpayers, of course, include individuals (predominantly women) who were not gainfully employed, but the information provided is not sufficiently precise to measure participation in the labour force. This is especially the case because, even for men, there are many taxpayers with unspecified occupations. For women, apart from servants, in only a small number of cases is a specific occupation stated.

So far as tax liability is concerned, the simplest analysis is that of the distribution of primary taxpayers as such. For the sample area, 83·4 per cent of taxpayers were liable only for the common tax of 1*s* per quarter; 10·1 per cent for the additional 10*s* tax; and 6·5 per cent for the additional tax of £1 quarterly. The higher tax brackets are not represented in the sample [5]. It is also possible to show the distribution of the total reported population by the tax liability of the head of the family and by apparent marital condition. This is both more complicated and less precise, for in a substantial proportion of cases marital condition is not specified and can only be presumed. But the results, which are summarised in Table 10.4, are not without interest. Thus most of the chief taxpayers (those whose tax rate is taken as the basis for classification) are males, and this is especially so for the surtax categories. Again, in the main primary male taxpayers are married, whereas female taxpayers are single. This is brought out more clearly in Table 10.5, in which only the primary

Table 10.4   City of London within the Walls. 1692 poll tax sample. Total population classified by tax liability of the head of the family.

		1s tax only	10s additional tax	£1 additional tax	Total
(A)	Families headed by males:				
	1. married, wife present	2,070	916	502	3,488
	2. presumed widowed	39	45	49	133
	3. presumed single	1,230	113	72	1,415
		3,339	1,074	623	5,036
(B)	Families headed by females:				
	1. presumed widowed	244	20	42	306
	2. presumed single	1,334	1	24	1,359
		1,578	21	66	1,665

Notes

The married couples represent those cases in which both husband and wife are listed. The presumed widowed are those in which children are listed, but no spouse. The presumed single are individuals listed without either spouse or child and may, of course, include an unknown proportion of widows or widowers without dependant children living at home.

Table 10.5   City of London within the Walls. 1692 poll tax sample. Primary taxpayers classified by tax liability.

		1s tax only	10s additional tax	£1 additional tax	Total
(A)	Males:				
	1. married	748	272	134	1,154
	2. presumed widowed	17	16	15	48
	3. presumed single	1,230	113	72	1,415
		1,995	401	221	2,617
(B)	Female:				
	1. presumed widowed	115	7	20	142
	2. presumed single	1,334	1	24	1,359
		1,449	8	44	1,501

taxpayers (unmarried male and female adults, and heads of families) are taken into account. Both tables show a higher proportion of surtax payers among the married and widowed — not unnaturally, since age is a factor both in marital condition and in relative wealth.

As for occupations, there is once again a considerable element of uncertainty. First, substantial numbers are reported as servants or apprentices, and it is not always possible to distinguish the meaning of the two categories. Further, apprentices are simply so reported, without an indication of the occupation in which they were apprenticed. It is not always clear that they were attached to the families next to which they are listed in the records. Finally, there are many cases in which, though a tax liability is noted, no occupation is recorded. A classification of the basic material is given in Table 10.6, and shows that individuals in respect of

Table 10.6   City of London within the Walls. 1692 poll tax sample. Primary taxpayers classified by type of occupational designation.

	Males	Females	Total
1. Specified occupations	772	39	811
2. Non-specific occupations:			
(a) Servants	721	971	1,768*
(b) Apprentices	164	9	176†
3. No occupation stated	841	456	1,306‡
4. Gentry	47	19	66
	2,545	1,494	4,127

Notes

* Including 76 of undetermined sex. Of the total servants, 53 males and 246 females could be fairly clearly categorised as domestic servants and 418 males and 462 females as probably not domestic servants. The categories of the remainder could not be determined.

† Including 2 of undetermined sex and 1 journeyman (so recorded).

‡ Including 8 of undetermined sex.

whom no occupation was stated constitute almost a third of all the primary taxpayers. Although it is possible that a considerable proportion of the women in that category were genuinely not part of the labour force (in the sense that they were not normally gainfully employed) it is difficult to believe that this would be true of the men, for whom the proportion with no stated occupation is also about a third. Part of the problem arises in connection with lodgers. There were 470 lodgers so designated in the sample area; occupation was not stated in respect of 403, of whom 213 were males. But this, too, is only a partial explanation. One point is clear, namely that the vast majority of the individuals whose occupations were not stated came within the lower income groups. Of the 841 males whose occupations were not stated, 751 were liable only to the 1s tax, and this was so for 427 out of the 456 women in the same row in Table 10.6. For individuals with specified occupations. however, this applied to only 324 out of a total of 811, though most of the women with specified occupations (35 out of the total of 39) were in the 1s tax category. (Servants and apprentices are all listed as liable to the 1s tax.) Hence in looking at the distribution and nature of the specified occupations (and, apart from servants and apprentices, these constitute the only fairly clearly described segment of the working population as shown by the 1692 poll tax returns), it must be remembered that in general these constituted the 'wealthier sort' in the City within the Walls. Accepting these limitations, the occupations listed have been allocated to broad categories and are shown in Table 10.7. Given the size of sample, it is only to be expected that the numbers in each occupation would be generally small — what is more interesting is the long list of occupations serving the society. And with small numbers, a scatter across the parishes is inevitable. But there is also some concentration of those occupations, the practitioners of which were all in the surtax categories. The occupations with the largest numbers of members in that group are merchants, haberdashers, mercers and silkmen, with a total of 158 persons listed. Of these, 93, or 59 per cent, were reported in four parishes, namely St Matthew Friday Street;

Table 10.7   City of London within the Walls. 1692 poll tax sample. Occupations specified in the returns, divided into broad categories.

Occupational category		No. of individuals
I Legal, administrative and financial		28
II Clerks		15
III Clergy		13
IV Teachers (including ushers and writing and dancing masters)		6
V Medical and para-medical (including midwives and nurses)		26
VI Military		9
VII Production and distribution:		

1. All paying surtax

coachmaker	1	shopkeeper	1
cakeman	1	skinner	5
diamond cutter	1	smoker	4
distiller	1	soapboiler	2
flaxman	1	steward	1
haberdasher	33	stocking presser	1
hosier	6	throwster	2
merchant	88	vintner	11
needlemaker	1	warehouseman	9
packer	1	whaling master	1
refiner	3	wharfinger	3
saddler	2	winecooper	1
silkman	19	woodmonger	2
			201
			201

2. Majority paying surtax

brewer	3	jeweller	3
button seller	3	leather seller	3
coachman	5	linendraper	5
coatseller	3	mercer	18
colourman	3	oilman	7
draper	13	plumber	3
druggist	3	salter	15
factor	14	stationer	3
goldsmith	13	tobacconist	10
grocer	20	tradesman	57
hatter	3	upholsterer	3
hot-presser	3	warehouse keeper	3
innholder	7		

223   223

Surtax payers   188

3. Less than half paying surtax

baker	6	painter	2
callender	5	pewterer	3
carpenter	5	potter	4
cheesemonger	3	stable-keeper	2
cook	2	sugar-baker	2
glazier	5	tailor	9
hosefactor	2	tallow-chandler	4
ironmonger	13	victualler	29
joiner	16	watchmaker	3
milliner	4	wiredrawer	17

136   136

Surtax payers   42

4. Paying 1s tax only

alehousekeeper	2	journeyman	1
barber	17	labourer	10
blacksmith	6	linen-dresser	1
bookbinder	1	looking-glass maker	1
bookseller	1	mariner	1
boxmaker	4	mason	2
brazier	1	mastmaker	1
bricklayer	2	merchant tailor	1
brushmaker	1	painter's agent	1
buttonmaker	1	painter-stainer	1
cabinetmaker	3	pattenmaker	1
capmaker	1	perfumer	2
chairmaker	1	periwig maker	2
chairman	2	plainman	1

chandler	2	porter	5
clothdrawer	4	poulterer	1
clothmaker	1	razormaker	2
coffeeseller	10	salesman	1
confectioner	1	seamstress	14
cooper	5	shoemaker	3
cosse	1	silkdyer	1
engraver	2	silversmith	7
farrier	1	smith	5
founder	1	sword-cutler	1
fruiterer	1	tinman	1
ginman	1	trunkmaker	2
glover	1	turner	2
hatmaker	1	virginal maker	1
housekeeper	1	waterman	1
innkeeper	1	waxchandler	2
instrument maker	1	weaver	1
		154	154
		Total	811

All Hallows Bread Street; St Lawrence Jewry; and St Helen. According to the 1695 enumerations, these parishes contained only 30 per cent of the total population of the sub-sample of parishes in Tables 10.1 and 10.2, but they were relatively wealthy parishes. The proportions of the population liable to surtax in respect of the taxes on marriages, births and burials were: St Matthew Friday Street, 40 per cent; All Hallows Bread Street, 38 per cent; St Lawrence Jewry, 27 per cent; and St Helen, 17 per cent. The average for the twelve parishes in the sub-sample was just over 17 per cent, so that the four parishes are in the upper band of wealth.

Table 10.8   City of London within the Walls. 1692 poll tax sample. Distribution of occupations reported for women in the sample.

Occupation	No.	Occupation	No.
bookbinder	1	milliner	2
boxmaker	1	nurse	2
coffeewoman	2	perfumer	1
cooper	1	periwig maker	1
draper	1	schoolmistress	1
exchangewoman	1	seamstress	14
goldsmith	1	skinner	1
haberdasher	1	victualler	1
housekeeper	1	wiredrawer	3
ironmonger	1		
joiner	1	Total	39
midwife	1		

The number of women with specified occupations is very small, and the details cannot be regarded as of more than antiquarian interest. Nevertheless, they are given in Table 10.8, simply to show the kind of distribution found in the sample. With four exceptions, all the women were taxed at the 1s level — the exceptions are two wiredrawers, a haberdasher and skinner, all paying an additional tax of 10s — and some two-thirds of the women were in occupations of the kind which might well be regarded as typically 'women's occupations'.

At this stage of the analysis of the 1695 enumeration and 1692 poll tax data, there is little more to add. It is hoped subsequently to consider household structure in some detail — for a sample of parishes — and also to select three or four parishes beyond the City Walls for purposes of comparison. For the moment only one point will be taken up for further discussion here, namely the question of apprentices.

This question has been examined in detail by J. R. Kellett, but his contribution is more concerned with the eighteenth than with the seventeenth century, and his data are largely qualitative [6]. He provides estimates of the annual average numbers of apprentices enrolled in 1700-10 and 1740-50, but these statistics are for sixteen selected companies. It is possible to use a somewhat different approach, making use of the records of freedoms and redemptions available in the Guildhall. And these records have the additional advantage of providing information on the provenance of those applying for admission to the freedom of the City [7]. The records used here are those relating to the years 1690, 1695 and 1700, but some later years have been looked at to see the general trend.

Table 10.9   Admissions to the freedom of the City of London.

Year	By Apprenticeship	Patrimony	Redemption	Total
1690	1,590	137	123	1,850
1695	1,346	137	62	1,545
1700	1,508	213	118	1,939
1725	1,306	279	197	1,782
1750	755	190	190	1,135
1775	672	156	226	1,056
1800	546	182	301	1,029

The crude data are summarised in Table 10.9. Immediately after the Great Fire, for reasons discussed by Kellet, the numbers of admissions increased. In 1668, according to the unpublished statistics of P. E. Jones, the total was 2,133, of which 1,766 were by apprenticeship, 272 by patrimony and 95 by redemption. Thereafter the numbers fell, but for the period between 1690 and 1725, the figures in Table 10.9 do not suggest a wild fluctuation. The picture from 1750 onwards is, of course, quite different [8]. For the period around 1690, however, it would not be too unreasonable to accept the actual 1690 figure of 1,590 as about the number of admissions by apprenticeship. Now the typical period of indenture was seven or eight years; of the admission to freedom in September to December 1690, 480 were of apprentices with a seven years' indenture, ninety-two with eight years and only two with a longer period. If seven years were taken as a not too unrealistic figure, and if apprenticeships began at around fourteen years, wastage by mortality would probably be quite light. Thus with an expectation of life at birth of thirty years, the probability of surviving from age fourteen to age twenty-one would be about 93 per cent. Small changes in the age at indenture would not make much difference, for mortality would be heavily concentrated on the years between birth and age five. Given the other assumptions, mortality can be left out of account, in which case the number of apprentices to be expected in London in 1690 would be around (7 × 1,590) or, say roughly 11,000. How realistic that estimate is depends, of course, upon another possible wastage factor, namely drop-outs during apprenticeship, on which I have no information. But the estimate is certainly on the conservative side [9]. Even so, a figure of around 11,000 is a substantial one both absolutely and in relation to the employed population.

No less important is the fact that the London apprenticeship system brought together young men (and a few women – in 1690, twenty-three women were admitted to the freedom, twelve by apprenticeship, nine by patrimony and two by redemption) from all over the country to the largest urban centre in Western Europe and certainly one of the major intellectual centres of the period. The information on place of last residence, as recorded in the documents, shows that, taking only those admitted by apprenticeship to the freedom in 1690, forty counties in England and seven in Wales were represented, and there were a few from Scotland, Ireland and the Channel Islands. The data are summarised in Table 10.10, in which the various counties are arranged in descending order of the numbers of apprentices emanating from them. Plotted on a map these figures suggest something comparable with the Ravenstein 'law of migration' – namely, that migration was inversely proportionate to distance – save that the size of the population of the county of origin is also obviously of importance.

In a later publication I hope to look more closely at the pattern of apprenticeship migration in the seventeenth and eighteenth centuries, especially with reference to competing alternative opportunities. In the context of the present paper I should like only to add that it might well be relevant to look at the role of the London apprentices in broader terms than their immediate economic contribution. The 1690 data on admissions to the freedom of the City suggest that the apprentices came from a fairly wide social spectrum. Of the 1,850 admitted by apprenticeship, patrimony or redemption, there were, at one end of the scale, twenty-six whose fathers were labourers and 150 with husbandmen as fathers; while at the other end of the scale there were among the fathers two knights, 177 gentlemen or esquires, twenty-one farmers, twenty-eight members of the professions or near-professions and 241 yeomen [10]. Further, minimal literacy was fairly high. Of the individuals admitted by apprenticeship, the proportion signing their indentures was at least 60 per cent and more probably over 80 per cent [11]. And there must have been some subsequent movement out of London, with possible effects on other parts

Table 10.10   City of London, 1690. Admissions to the freedom by apprenticeship. Apprentices allocated to county of last residence, in descending order of numbers in each county.

County	No.	County	No.
London	317	Cumberland	11
Middlesex	149*	Nottinghamshire	11
Surrey	89†	Huntingdonshire	10
Northants.	71	Dorest	9
Berkshire	61	Flint	7
Leicestershire	61	Cheshire	6
Gloucestershire	56	Westmorland	6
Buckinghamshire	54	Durham	5
Oxfordshire	53	Carmarthen	4
Wiltshire	52	Denbigh	3
Yorkshire	46	Devon	3
Essex	43	Merioneth	3
Warwick	42	Northumberland	3
Hertfordshire	33	Caernarvon	2
Hampshire	32	Cornwall	2
Somerset	32	Montgomery	2
Hereford	27	Rutland	2
Derby	26	Brecknock	1
Kent	26	Anglesey	1
Lancashire	26	Pembroke	1
Shropshire	21	Radnor	1
Staffordshire	20	Scotland	2
Worcestershire	20	Ireland	5
Sussex	19	Channel Isles	2
Bedfordshire	17	Illegible	5
Lincolnshire	15	Not known	37
Norfolk	14		
Suffolk	13	Total	1,590
Cambridgeshire	11		

Notes
* Including 78 from the parishes bordering on London and from Westminster.
† Including 35 from Southwark.

of the Kingdom. Exactly how much movement is not known, but a rough idea may be gained by checking the names of individuals admitted to the freedom in 1690 against the 1695 parish enumerations. Of the 1,850 admissions, only 1,007 could be identified, identification being based upon the Christian name and upon a reasonably close approximation of the surname. Loss by death is not likely to have been substantial at the ages concerned, but allowance has to be made for the absence of returns for seventeen of the ninety-seven parishes within the Walls, as well as for under-enumeration. Even so, supposing that, if the basic documents had been more comprehensive and reliable, the figure of 1,007 might have been increased to, say, 1,500, 300 or more outward migrants in five years would be far from negligible in relation to the size of the initial cohort. It may well be, as John Graunt believed, that London owed its population increase to continuing, substantial net inward migration. But a figure of net migration may easily hide much larger numbers of outward and inward migrants. It would be worth investigating whether there were in fact sizeable streams of trained individuals moving away from London and contributing to the development of trade and industry in other parts of the country [12].

Notes

I am indebted to a number of graduates who, at various times, took part in analysing the archival materials drawn upon in my attempts to study some aspects of the historical demography of London — notably Miss G. Charing, Miss A. Davies, Miss D. Filson, Dr T. R. Gourvish, Mr B. J. Betham and Mr D. Lazar. Miss E. South has worked on the materials much more continuously, and has been especially helpful in respect of the 1692 poll tax data and the records of admission to the freedom of the City of London. I wish no less to acknowledge my indebtedness to Mr P. E. Jones, for his unfailing advice on, and help with, these and many other records of the City of London.

1   The materials are discussed more fully in two earlier papers, namely, in the Introduction to *London Inhabitants within the Walls, 1695* (London Record Soc., ii, 1966); and 'Notes on the demography of London at the end of the seventeenth century', *Daedalus* (Spring 1968).

2   P. E. Jones and A. V. Judges, 'London population in the late seventeenth century', *Economic History Review*, vi (Oct. 1935), 58-62.

3   *Ibid.* p. 48.

4   With one exception, the poll tax returns used are for the first quarter of the first year of the tax. The returns are in the Corporation of London Records Office. The matching precincts were drawn from the following wards — Bread Street, Castle Baynard, Candlewick, Cripplegate Within, Bishopsgate Within (2nd quarter), Broad Street, Cordwainer, Cheap, Tower, Aldersgate Within and Billingsgate.

5   Only 19 individuals are listed as liable to the tax on coaches — 3 coachmen; 6 merchants; and 6 members of the gentry represent the main categories.

6   J. R. Kellett, 'The breakdown of gild and corporation control over the handicraft and retail trade in London', *Economic History Review*, 2nd ser. x, no. 3 (1958), 381-94.

7   The statistics for 1690-1800 were compiled from the completed indentures deposited with the chamberlain's court when the appli-

cants were admitted to the freedom of the City. The Registers of Freemen compiled by the chamberlain's court were also drawn upon.

8 The sharp decline in the number of admissions does not necessarily mean that apprenticeship declined but only that freedom of the City became less attractive. The increase in the number of admissions by redemption suggests that the freedom came to be much more significant politically, or in terms of status, than directly valuable in economic terms.

9 The estimate also leaves out those who completed an apprenticeship but did not apply for admission to the freedom.

10 A similarly wide range is shown for the fathers of apprentices in Southampton. See *Calendar of Southampton Apprenticeship Records, 1609-1740*, ed. A. J. Wills and A. L. Merson (1968), p. xxxi, Table E (I am indebted to Professor F. J. Fisher for referring me to this publication). Of course, the numbers of apprentices enrolled in Southampton are small — only 600 in the period 1610 to 1683. Using the much larger numbers for London for a series of years, I hope later to examine the relationship between fathers' occupations and the gilds to which sons were admitted. The Southampton data indicate that the sons of clergymen and gentlemen were very largely apprenticed to mercantile crafts (including, later, surgeon, apothecary and goldsmith). Sons at the other end of the social scale were very largely apprenticed to handicrafts.

11 The percentage depends upon the way in which the calculation is undertaken. Of the 1,590 individuals, 965 had actually signed and 153 had signed with a mark; a total of 1,118. But there were also 472 unsigned indentures (including 138 replacements for original indentures). The ratio 965 to 1,590 is 60 per cent; that of 965 to 1,118 (probably more justifiable) is 86 per cent.

There are no comparable figures for minimum literacy for the general population of the City. The apprenticeship figures relate to individuals at a young age — say, fourteen years. The evidence from the marriage certificates relates to older ages and, of course, to a later period, since it was provided under the Hardwicke Act of 1753. But it is not entirely without interest to cite some of those later figures and for that purpose the marriage entry data for the thirteen parishes used in the poll tax sample were analysed for the period 1755-59. For that period, there were 424 marriage entries, the groom signing in 390 of them, or 92 per cent. (Female minimum literacy was also high, the bride signing in 315 cases, or 74 per cent.) But I have not examined the data further to see how far the marriages were actually those of London residents or to inquire into the economic or social status of the brides and grooms. The figures for double illiteracy (that is, with both bride and groom signing by mark) are certainly remarkably low — only fourteen cases, or 3 per cent.

As to literacy in London, Comenius was greatly impressed, during his visit in 1641, by the numbers of men and youths who, attending church on Sundays, took down the sermons in shorthand.

Comenius wrote of these men, 'Almost all of them acquire this art of rapid writing, as soon as they have learnt at school to read the Scriptures in the vernacular. It takes them about another year to learn the art of shorthand', R. F. Young, *Comenius in England* (1932), 65. John Graunt was one of those who practised shorthand; this was reported of him by John Aubrey, who knew him well.

12   There must, of course, have been considerable cross-movement. Thus the apprentice records for Southampton show that, although Southampton naturally had a much smaller catchment area than London, it received apprentices from other parts of the country, notably the Isle of Wight, Dorset, Wilts. and, in the early seventeenth century, from the Channel Islands. In addition, the Poor Child Register, which gives the location of the masters with whom poor apprentices were enrolled, shows that some were sent to places outside Southampton — a few in Portsmouth, for example, in Shadwell, London, and even one in Newfoundland, *Cal. Southampton Apprenticeship Records*, pp. xxix and lv-lvi.

11 A provincial capital in the late seventeenth century: the case of Norwich

Penelope Corfield [1]

'As to Norwich, it is a great city and full of people', commented Baskerville in 1681; 'the whole Citty lookes like what it is, a rich thriveing industrious place', Celia Fiennes agreed in 1697; and in 1723 Defoe confirmed that Norwich was 'antient, large, rich and populous' [2]. Not all travellers' tales are true. Yet these comments reflected accurately enough the importance of the city of Norwich in the late seventeenth and early eighteenth centuries. At this time, it was the second city in the kingdom (a position sometimes wrongly ascribed to Bristol) and it had experienced considerable expansion in the course of the seventeenth century, at a rate of growth faster than that of most other provincial cities. Between 1600 and 1700 the population had increased from an estimated 12,000 or 13,000 to an authenticated 30,000 [3]. This essay is concerned to chronicle the growth of the city in the latter half of the century and to examine some of the factors which brought this about.

The growth of the city attracts attention for two reasons. In the first place, it was among the comparatively small number of provincial cities that were expanding, in a period which was not one of general urban growth. While there was undoubtedly an increase in the urban population of England and Wales, both in absolute and proportionate terms, much of this increase can be accounted for by the growth of the capital city. London was not only much larger than all other cities, but it was also growing at a faster rate. Indeed, fears were expressed that London would swallow up all England. In the second place, Norwich was among an even smaller number of inland towns that were expanding in this period. By 1700, Norwich was by far the largest inland town in the country, with over twice the population of Birmingham, its nearest rival in this respect [4]. Most of the other leading provincial cities in 1700 were ports. Indeed, the late seventeenth century saw a considerable expansion of overseas trade, to such an extent that the period is sometimes labelled that of 'the Commercial Revolution'. The growth of Norwich suggests that there were other developments in the late seventeenth-century economy which deserve investigation.

Analysis and explanations are alike complicated by the dearth of statistics relating to the demographic and economic history of the city.

Penelope Corfield, 'A provincial capital in the late seventeenth century: The case of Norwich', from P. Clark and P. Slack, eds, *Crisis and Order in English Towns 1500-1700*, Routledge, 1972, pp. 263-310.

There are no reliable figures for the size of the urban population before 1693, when the first local enumeration was taken. In this respect Norwich resembles many other towns. With regard to data relating to the economic life of the city Norwich fares rather worse. As an inland town, the city has left no commercial statistics, since inland trade was not subject to any control or fiscal imposition. Furthermore, the official records of the Weavers' Company, which regulated the city's staple industry, were destroyed in the early eighteenth century when formal supervision was ended [5]. Paradoxically, therefore, some of the conditions that assisted in the expansion of the city in the seventeenth century have made it difficult, at a distance of three centuries, to recover evidence for that growth.

The population of the city of Norwich multiplied in the course of the seventeenth century some two-and-a-half times. It is easier to sketch this in outline than to clothe the skeleton. But it seems probable that the growth of the city was not continuous and cumulative throughout the century, but occurred in two discrete periods, in the first three and last three decades of the century. These periods of growth were separated by a population plateau in the mid-century. This is a pattern similar in outline to the growth of the population in the country as a whole, although in both periods of growth the urban population was increasing at a faster rate than that of the rest of the country.

This essay is concerned with the second of these two periods of growth. But in order to establish the size of the city's population by the mid-century plateau, it is necessary to look briefly at the earlier period. That there was an increase in the city's population can be seen from the returns of the city's Bills of Mortality from 1582 to 1646. These show marked increases in the totals of both baptisms and burials in the early years of the seventeenth century. The most rapid growth occurred in the late 1610s and early 1620s. The average annual number of baptisms showed an increase of over 50 per cent between the first and second decades of the century, rising from an average of 478·6 between 1601 and 1610, to an average of 748·9 between 1611 and 1620. In the following decade the average number of baptisms rose again to 836·2. This then fell to the slightly lower figure of 710·6 between 1631 and 1640 [6]. Other records indicate a movement of population into the city in the early years of the century. In 1622, the Ordinances for regulating the city's trading companies spoke of the vast increase in numbers of 'foreigners' coming into Norwich [7].

The Mortality Bills, however, do not so readily yield the size of the total population. There are two problems here. In the first place, there is no means of testing either the accuracy or the consistency of the Bills. The returns were made weekly to the Mayoral Court, and there may well have been errors and omissions in the collection of the material. And the original parish registers, from which the information was culled, were not themselves above reproach as a complete record of the demographic statistics of the city [8]. The second problem consists in the selection of the appropriate birth rate for the city's population at this time. Since there is no evidence to suggest one figure rather than another, the inflation of the number of baptisms to produce the total population can only be a very arbitrary exercise. It has been noted that the increase in the number of baptisms in the early part of the century was so great that, assuming a standard birth rate of 1 in 33, or 30 per 1,000, the population of the city would have reached almost to the total of 30,000 by 1622 [9]. Such a total is theoretically feasible, and cannot be disproved given the present state of the evidence. But it is unlikely that the population had reached such a high total by this date. Such an assumption implies a very rapid rate of growth in the early part of the century, followed by a steep decline in the following decades. The population rise can be flattened out by the selection of a higher birth rate. This would be consonant with what is known about the effects of high levels of immigration into a community, which tends to increase the proportion of those in the reproductive age-groups in the population as a whole, and hence pushes up the birth rate [10]. A birth rate of 1 in 25, or 40 per 1,000, would produce the smaller total population of some 20,000 inhabitants in the 1620s.

Certainly any population expansion was halted in the late 1620s and the 1630s, as the result both of renewed outbreaks of plague in 1625-26, 1631 and 1637-38, and of emigration from the city for religious reasons in the 1630s [11]. The average yearly baptismal and burial figures for the decade from 1631 to 1640 were lower than those for the previous decades, and showed, for the first time this century, a preponderance of baptisms over burials, which suggests that there was some emigration [12]. But there is no evidence for any protracted population decline in the middle years of the century. Puritan exiles returned in the 1640s, and some foreign co-religionists also settled in the city in the 1650s [13]. The population of Norwich probably fluctuated therefore around the figure of 20,000 in the mid-seventeenth century.

The evidence for the demographic history of the city in the second half of the century is unfortunately even more scanty than for the earlier period. The Bills of Mortality were still collected (though not without administrative difficulties) [14] but there is a complete hiatus in the records between 1646, when entries in the Mayoral Court Books ceased, and 1707, the date of the earliest surviving local paper, which printed monthly totals. Nor has it proved possible to recover the data on baptisms and burials from the original parish registers. Although many of these registers have survived, the amount of information that can be collected is far from complete, as a result of illegibility and gaps in the records [15].

Some indices for the growth of the city's population can, however, be devised from fiscal records. Mutilated but legible returns of the inhabitants paying the hearth tax in 1662 have survived, although they do not cover the whole city. These returns, for parishes which in 1693 contained 79 per cent of the city's population, listed 1,538 taxpayers, paying for 5,864 hearths, at 3·8 hearths per person. This suggests for the whole city a total of 1,947 taxpayers, paying for 7,423 hearths [16]. Allowance then has to be made for those who were exempted from payment. According to a list of 1671, 61·7 per cent of all householders were exempted [17]. This proportion is very high in comparison with those found in some other cities, but it is not unreasonable in view of the fact that Norwich was a manufacturing city, and that there was some uncertainty about the taxable status of industrial hearths [18]. Assuming an exemption rate of 60 per cent in round figures, the total number of householders was 4,868. With an average household size of 4·2 individuals in Norwich [19], the total population comes to 20,446 inhabitants. While it is obvious that this calculation is far from exact, it gives some indications of the order of magnitude of the city's population.

A similar calculation can be made for 1671, on the basis of a list of assessments for the same tax. This list is more detailed, in that it contains the names of all householders, including those eventually exempted from payment, but it too is incomplete. The returns survive for parishes which in 1693 contained 76 per cent of the total population. They suggest for the whole city a total of 4,904 householders, with 11,683 hearths, an average of 2·38 hearths per householder [20]. This produces a total population of 20,597 inhabitants, a total not significantly larger than that calculated for 1662. It has, however, been pointed out that the efficacy of the assessments tended to decline over time, as resistance to the tax increased [21]. It may be, therefore, that the figure for 1671 is too low. The evidence of the Compton Census returns, however, also seems to confirm that the population of the city had not reached much above 20,000 by 1676. This census listed 12,562 adult communicants in the city. Assuming that 40 per cent of the population were too young to take communion, this suggests a total of approximately 21,000 inhabitants. But the returns of the Compton Census for the city of Norwich also present problems. Many of the parish totals of Conformists are given in suspiciously rounded numbers. It is also clear that the number of Nonconformists (totalling less than 5 per cent of the whole population) is too low for this traditional Puritan stronghold, but it is not known whether they were counted as Conformists or simply omitted [22].

These estimates deal in probabilities and not certainties. They do, however, suggest that there was very little population growth in the 1660s, which was a decade of high mortality due to epidemics of plague and smallpox, and that population expansion was not resumed before the 1670s, and possibly not until the end of this decade. The 1670s and 1680s must therefore have seen a return to the sort of growth rate seen at the start of the century, in order to produce the total of 28,881 inhabitants found at the enumeration of the city and county in 1693 [23]. This total may be assumed to be reasonably reliable, subject to the inevitable inaccuracies found in all early censuses. It was confirmed by the figures given independently by Gregory King, whose two estimates of 29,332 and 28,546 made in 1695 and 1696 are very similar to the total found by enumeration [24]. On this basis, it seems likely that the population of Norwich had reached a total of 30,000 by 1700.

It is probable that the growth of the city's population was brought about by immigration in this period as in the earlier part of the century, rather than by a 'natural' increase produced by a preponderance of births over deaths. It is difficult to be precise about this, in the absence of relevant statistics. There is a certain amount of circumstantial evidence relating to mortality in the city. Contemporaries showed the preoccupation with death characteristic of an age of high mortality and low expectation of life: indeed Arderon in the eighteenth century considered that the inhabitants of Norwich took an exceptional interest in funerals which were attended by vast crowds [25]. On the other hand, there is a complete dearth of information relating to births and marriages. But, on the basis of this negative evidence, it has been assumed that there were no major changes in either birth or marriage rates in Norwich in this period.

As far as death rates in the city are concerned there was probably no reduction in the prevailing high level of urban mortality. The most significant changes came in the causes of mortality, with the ending of the cycle of plagues in Norwich, culminating in the epidemic of 1665-66. Mortality in this outbreak was heavy: in the twelve months from October 1665 to October 1666, a total of 2,251 plague deaths were reported out of a total of 3,012 reported deaths from all causes. This figure almost certainly underestimates the number of deaths from plague, since registration was especially defective in periods of crisis [26]. The mortality in this epidemic did not in fact constitute as great a proportion of the total population as did the mortality in some of the earlier outbreaks of plague in the city, such as that of 1603 [27]. But its effects were nonetheless very serious. Fear of the contagion kept people from the markets and disrupted supplies of food. Commercial and industrial activities were suspended, causing widespread unemployment. The wealthy began to leave the city, and, to the consternation of a government correspondent, there was also a threat of social subversion from the poor:

> Our city lookes sadley, most of our chefest shopkeepers in the market ar gon and ther shopes shut up. I doe beleve before 10 days come a 4 part of the city will be gone. The pore does much murmur at it and says they will live in beter howses then now they doe, but I hope to God they will be prevented.

The Town Clerk was as frank: 'Wee are in greater feare of the poore than the plague, all our monie beinge gone . . .' As these accounts suggest, the epidemic strained the administrative and financial resources of the city to the utmost [28], and threatened a complete breakdown of its economic life.

The disappearance of the plague after this outbreak, however, did not produce any permanent reduction in the level of mortality in the city, although it did remove a potent cause of social and economic instability. The successor to the plague as the major urban killer was smallpox, which was endemic in cities at this date, while also breaking out in epidemics of increased intensity from time to time. The incidence of mortality from smallpox was highest among small children and survival conferred immunity in the majority of cases, thus producing the erroneous view that the disease was not contagious [29]. Smallpox was not therefore a 'panic' disease in the same way that the plague had been. Specific outbreaks of smallpox were reported in the city in January 1670, when the Town Clerk noted that 'the smallpox rageth still, and poverty daily invades us like an armed man', and in December 1681, when Sir Thomas Browne observed: 'I hardly remember the smallpox so much in Norwich, as it hath been of late and still continueth' [30]. There may also have been other epidemics, about which no information has survived. Evidence relating to other diseases is scarce. Sir Thomas Browne recorded as a general phenomenon an increase in the incidence of both smallpox and rickets in the late seventeenth century, and a decline in the number of cases of great pox (syphilis). Throughout this period the incidence of mortality was highest among the very young. Sir Thomas Browne observed melodiously: 'Nothing is more common with infants than to die on the day of their nativity, to behold the worldly hours and but the fractions thereof' [31].

There is no evidence to suggest that there was any reduction in levels of mortality through improvements in medical care. The period was not one which was distinguished by major advances in medical practice. An extensive range of medical assistance was available in the city, ranging from doctors, apothecaries and surgeons on the one hand, to optimistic quacks and vendors of patent medicines on the other. But it is hardly necessary to point out that there is no automatic correlation between the number of practitioners and the efficacy of medical care. Without more detailed information than is available (or is ever likely to be available), there is no means of estimating the value of their labours.

Nor does the evidence suggest that there was any radical reduction of mortality through improvements in standards of public health and living conditions. Indeed, it is probable that the growth of the city in itself tended to worsen living conditions in the city centre, and thus to increase levels of mortality. At this date the city's population was concentrated within the medieval city walls, which were still standing. In 1693, 90·5 per cent of all inhabitants lived within the walls. The area thus encircled was, however, the largest of any ancient city centre. As Defoe remarked, the walls seemed to have been laid out with prospects of future expansion in mind. The overall density of population in the city and county of Norwich was 6·68 inhabitants per statute acre in 1693 [32]. But this figure conceals many variations. There were fields and pastures within the walls, which, with the flower gardens of the artisans, gave the city a rural air. This was frequently commented upon by visitors. Fuller, for example, described the city as: 'Either a city in an orchard or an orchard in a city, so equally are houses and trees blended in it, so that the pleasures of the country and the populousness of the city meet here together' [33]. But there were also pockets of densely built-up areas, especially in the low-lying parishes alongside the river in Wymer and Coslany Wards, where the population was crammed into houses in a maze of courtyards and alleyways. There was in this period a certain amount of rebuilding of the city's housing stock, which may have tended to improve living conditions, as the old houses of wood and plasterwork were replaced by brick buildings [34]. But the improvements brought about by this means were probably not of very great significance, and the basic layout of the city was hardly altered at all.

The streets and public places seem to have been reasonably well maintained by the standards of the day. Such at least was the verdict of Celia Fiennes who wrote in 1697 in her characteristically breathless manner: 'The streets are all well pitch'd with small stones and very clean and many very broad streetes' [35]. But cleanliness lies in the eye of the beholder. There is certainly no evidence to suggest that the Corporation was doing any more than keeping pace with the problem, and that without any spectacular efficiency. The accounts of the River and Street

Committee, which was responsible for dredging the river and for the general upkeep of the city, did not show any great increase in expenditure in the late seventeenth century [36]. Expenditure is not, of course, a conclusive index to efficiency. But this certainly does not suggest any great increase in the activity of the Committee. The Corporation issued frequent proclamations against the practice of allowing cattle and swine to roam the streets, and reminders to individual householders of their responsibility for the upkeep of the highway abutting upon their property [37]. No doubt individual officials and householders performed their duties reliably, but the system as a whole depended upon exhortation after the deed rather than preventive measures. There seems, therefore, no reason to doubt that the city of Norwich in this period was both noxious and insalubrious.

Growth was therefore brought about by migration of population into the city. The net rate of immigration must have been in the region of some 400 newcomers per annum in the 1670s and 1680s to produce a net increase of 8,000 inhabitants in these twenty years. Gross totals must have been even higher, to take into account the movement of population out of Norwich. But emigration totals are completely irrecoverable. Poll books from the early eighteenth century list the names of Norwich citizens living outside the city who returned to cast their vote. As might be expected, the largest contingents returned from Yarmouth and London, both cities with which Norwich had close commercial links [38]. But there is no way of estimating what proportion of all emigrants was represented by these figures. On the basis of the estimated immigration figures alone, it seems that the number of 'foreigners' in the city may have constituted as much as one-quarter of the total population in 1700, a proportion which is almost identical with that found in Norwich at the third local enumeration in 1786 when 26 per cent of the population were without a settlement in the city [39].

Most of the migration in the late seventeenth century probably followed the usual pattern of movement of single individuals or small family units. But there was one instance of group immigration. This was the arrival in the city in the 1680s of a number of Huguenot exiles. According to a near-contemporary source, the Huguenots had been invited to Norwich by Onias Philippo, one of the city's leading manufacturers, who was himself a descendant of the Walloons who came as exiles to the city in Elizabethan times. There is some uncertainty about the number of Huguenots that eventually settled in Norwich. Estimates vary from 'very few' to 'many', which may or may not mean the same thing. At a guess, they numbered some 100 to 200 individuals. Certainly the refugees arrived in sufficient numbers to provoke the indigenous population to riot in 1682 in the fear that the newcomers would undercut wages and cause unemployment. Tensions did not immediately die away. A petition of 1690 from the French weavers of Norwich to the Houses of Parliament complained of harassment by informers who were reporting the newcomers for working without fulfilling the formal apprenticeship requirements [40]. After the initial problems, however, the Huguenot community was integrated without further difficulties, as indeed a century earlier the much larger numbers of Dutch and Walloon refugees had been assimilated into the host community.

The arrival of 'strangers' is easier to identify than movement among the indigenous population. Information is either too particular, such as removal orders against single individuals who had fallen foul of the city authorities; or too general, such as complaints from freemen of the city against competition from 'foreigners' [41]. Complaints and removal orders were most frequent in periods of economic depression. Although they attest to the reality of movement of population into the city, they provide no information about its timing or quantity.

It seems likely that the major sources for immigration were the agricultural counties of Norfolk and Suffolk, since movement of population at this time usually took place over short distances. But as one of the major urban centres, Norwich would also exercise something of a 'pull' outside its immediate hinterland, since migration distances tended to correlate with the size of the city. No complete documentation of removal orders in the late seventeenth century has survived. Eighteenth-century figures provide some evidence. The surviving accounts of the removal of 433 paupers and vagrants, and their families, in the period from 1740 to 1762 demonstrate the importance of the city's rural hinterland as recruitment ground: 40 per cent of these migrants came from East Anglia; another 15 per cent came from east coast and east Midland counties, within an approximate hundred-mile radius of the city; 6 per cent came from London and Middlesex; as many as 39 per cent, however, came from the rest of the country, including thirty-three migrants from Scotland and sixteen from Ireland [42]. Beggars and vagrants may have been an exceptionally mobile section of the populace. Analysis of the place of origin of 1,601 apprentices whose indentures were taken out in Norwich in the period from 1710 to 1731 shows a more circumscribed catchment area: 43 per cent of the apprentices were sons of residents of Norwich; 22 per cent came from Norfolk; and 6 per cent came from elsewhere, leaving a further 29 per cent whose place of origin was not recorded [43]. Neither of these sources is exhaustive, but together they confirm the preponderance of short-distance migration, although comparison of the two sources suggests that distance of migration might also vary with the social status of the migrant.

It should be emphasised that the growth of the city was not taking place at the expense of its rural hinterland. The population of Norfolk was probably not growing very fast in the late seventeenth century, and certainly not as fast as the city of Norwich. But in 1700, Norfolk, with a population of over 200,000, still remained among the most densely populated areas in the country [44]. And the growth of Norwich may have stimulated expansion in its immediate vicinity. As Celia Fiennes observed: 'Most of the great towns and cittys have about them little villages as attendants or appendix's.' Certainly when Defoe visited the county, he was impressed with the concentration of population in the central and eastern region of the county:

> This side of Norfolk is very populous, and throng'd with great and
> spacious market-towns, more and larger than in any other part of
> England so far from London, except Devonshire and the West Riding

of Yorkshire; . . . Most of these towns are very populous and large; but that which is most remarkable is, that the whole country round them is so interspers'd with villages and those villages so large, and so full of people, that they are equal to market-towns in other counties: in a word, they render this eastern part of Norfolk exceeding full of inhabitants [45].

Although the city still maintained the physical attributes of an enclosed and walled community in the late seventeenth century, and Norwich citizens evinced an attitude of suspicion, and even hostility, towards newcomers, it is clear that recruitment was taking place on a considerable scale. In this period, as in most periods of growth, there was progressive weakening of the institutional barriers which attempted to restrict and control entry into the city. Poor law policy acted only as an *ex post facto* system of control, which removed the economically unsuccessful, and it was not administered with any great degree of efficiency. Furthermore, the formal regulations governing admissions to the city's trades and industries were falling into desuetude in the later part of the century and the Corporation was finding it increasingly difficult to enforce the obligation to take out the freedom of the city [46]. The relaxation of such regulations, which were protective in nature, both reflected and contributed to urban growth; on the one hand, the urban economy demanded ready supplies of labour, while, on the other, the administrative problems of enforcing restrictive regulations were accentuated as the city grew in size.

Investigation into the development of the urban economy illuminates the basis of the city's growth. But reconstruction of the pattern of employment in Norwich involves further documentary problems. There is no comprehensive information relating to occupations in the city at this time. The admissions to the freedom provide information relating to a section of the population. But the material contained in the freemen lists is open to two damaging criticisms: it is highly selective, and the selection is not completely consistent even on its own terms.

In theory, all adult males engaged in trade and industry were obliged to take out the freedom within six months of taking up work in the city [47]. The freemen probably accounted for about half the adult male work-force in the late seventeenth century. They excluded servants, apprentices, and casual labourers. They also excluded women and children who constituted at this time a sizeable proportion of the work-force. Furthermore, the information contained in the freemen lists relates only to the major occupation of each individual, and excludes part-time and secondary occupations. And, needless to say, the information concerns legal occupations only, and provides no guide to the numbers of those making their living by crime, although it is quite possible that the growth of the city produced an increase in the criminal population (the larger the city, the better the lurking-places and the better the prey, not to mention the better the chances of escaping detection).

It is also evident that by this date many of those who were theoretically qualified for the freedom were evading the expensive honour. This is demonstrated by the frequent proclamations issued on this topic by

Table 11.1   Occupational groups in Norwich, 1660-1749: freemen of the city (percentages)

Occupations	1660-69	1670-79	1680-89	1690-99	1700-09	1710-19	1720-29	1730-39	1740-49	Total
Textiles	41·3	46·8	40·9	37·5	57·6	57·7	64·0	41·7	42·8	49·8
Leather	8·1	9·3	7·0	9·8	8·0	7·4	7·0	8·7	5·9	7·9
Metal	3·1	3·9	2·0	4·2	2·5	4·5	2·3	3·1	4·0	3·2
Building	5·3	6·5	8·3	7·2	5·3	5·9	3·2	6·5	6·4	5·8
Food and drink	10·3	10·4	15·1	16·3	11·1	9·8	7·2	9·1	11·0	10·5
Clothing	18·1	12·8	13·6	11·6	5·7	6·8	4·3	6·9	6·7	8·9
Professions	3·8	3·0	5·1	7·7	5·4	5·8	4·1	6·3	9·1	5·4
Miscellaneous	10·0	7·3	8·0	5·7	4·4	2·1	7·9	17·7	14·1	8·5

Source: See Appendix

the Corporation. In 1677 and in 1701, the Corporation also attempted, unsuccessfully, to obtain legislation 'to bring in freemen' [48]. It is therefore possible that some trades and industries were under-registered, and that some of the newer or smaller trades were completely omitted. This seems to have been the case with the small carpet-manufacturing industry, which admitted no freemen in this period [49]. Despite all these inadequacies, however, the freemen admissions do provide a general guide to the range of occupations in the city, and throw some light on the relative importance of the different trades and industries.

The admissions from 1660 to 1749 were dominated by employment in the textile industry (see Table 11.1 and Appendix, pp. 260-2). By the early eighteenth century worsted weavers and others engaged in the various stages involved in the production of worsted stuffs accounted for over 50 per cent of all admissions. At the same time, the textile industry may have employed almost the same proportion of the total work-force, since the industry was organised on a domestic basis, and the weaver was assisted by his wife and children. Its dominance was confirmed by visual evidence. Defoe commented:

> If a stranger was only to ride thro' or view the city of Norwich for a day, he would . . . think there was a town without inhabitants . . .; but on the contrary, if he was to view the city, either on a Sabbath-day, or on any publick occasion, he would wonder where all the people could dwell, the multitude is so great: But the case is this; the inhabitants being all busie at their manufactures, dwell in their garrets at their looms, and in their combing-shops, so they call them, twisting-mills, and other work-houses; almost all the works they are employ'd in, being done within doors [50].

Norwich therefore manifested a considerable degree of functional specialisation as a textile manufacturing centre. This had not always been a feature of the urban economy. The numbers of those employed in both the production and the distribution of textiles in the mid-sixteenth century was considerably lower: in 1525 they constituted approximately 30 per cent of all freemen; by 1569 the proportion had fallen to 21 per cent [51]. The urban population at this time was static or even declining. The revitalisation of the textile industry in the 1570s inaugurated a new period of urban expansion, and thereafter, during the seventeenth century, the numbers of freemen admitted in the production of textiles alone (excluding distribution) increased steadily, from 23 per cent in 1600-19, to 58 per cent in 1700-19 (see Table 11.2). The growing importance of the industry in the city can also be traced through other sources. The changing occupations of the individuals elected to the mayoralty show the emergence of worsted weavers into the urban ruling class in the second half of the century, joining the mercantile elite that had hitherto dominated the city (see Table 11.3). Of course, 104 mayors do not make an urban elite. But the trend is instructive. By the end of the century, the wealthiest man in the city, according to Dean Prideaux, was Robert Cooke, a weaver and conventicler, who became sheriff in 1674 and mayor in 1693 [52].

While Norwich continued to function as a market centre and local capital, the labour-intensive textile industry provided the major demand for labour in the city and the growth of the city was linked closely with its specialisation as a textile centre. This is not to say, of course, that each individual coming to the city was impelled by a desire to work at the loom. But there is at least some evidence to suggest that some textile workers were being recruited specifically from other textile centres. Weavers from Taunton and Exeter were found in Norwich in 1674. And some specialised workers were also moving into Norwich: Michael Brown, a silk-dyer newly arrived from London, was advertising his special fats for dyeing blues and greens in Norwich in 1725. There may have been an unofficial network of communication between textile centres, by which information relating to employment opportunities was circulated. Such at least was implied by reports of the migration of weavers between different textile centres in the depression of 1719 [53], and this may well have applied in the late seventeenth century.

Table 11.2   Admission to the freedom of the city in textiles, 1600-1739

Period	% of all freemen
1600-19	23
1620-39	31
1640-59	37
1660-79	44
1680-99	39
1700-19	58
1720-39	53

Sources: K. J. Allison, 'The wool supply and the worsted cloth industry in Norfolk in the sixteenth and seventeenth centuries', unpublished Ph.D. thesis, University of Leeds, 1955, for figures to 1660 and P. Millican, *The Freemen of Norwich, 1548-1713*, Norwich, 1934, and *The Freemen of Norwich, 1713-1752*, Norfolk Record Society, xxiii, 1952, for figures to 1739.

The continued vitality and expansion of the Norwich worsted weaving industry over a period of two-and-a-half centuries is a subject in itself. The Norwich worsted stuffs were among the 'New Draperies' that were successfully introduced to England in the late sixteenth century [54].

Unlike the 'New Draperies' introduced elsewhere in East Anglia, the Norwich industry continued to flourish and develop throughout the seventeenth century. In this, it contrasted with the Colchester bays industry, which was in decline by the end of this period.

Unfortunately there is no way of constructing a satisfactory index to the economic fortunes of the Norwich industry in the late seventeenth century. No figures have survived relating to either the volume of production, or the value of the trade, or the numbers employed in the

Table 11.3 Occupations of 104 mayors elected in the period 1600-1699*

Occupation†	1600-19	1620-39	1640-59	1660-79	1680-99‡	Total
Weaver			3	5	7	15
Dyer		1				1
Ironmonger	3	1	2		1	7
Pinman				1	1	2
Butcher	1					1
Baker		1				1
Grocer	5	6	4	5	5	25
Brewer				3		3
Draper	1	2	2	1	1	7
Mercer	2	3	2	1		8
Hosier			3	2		5
Glover		1				1
Skinner		1				1
Merchant	4	1	3	1		9
Goldsmith	1					1
Scrivener	1	2				3
Apothecary	1	1		1		3
Not traced	2	1	3		5	11
Total	21	20	23	20	20	104

Source: B. Cozens-Hardy and E. A. Kent, *The Mayors of Norwich, 1403-1835* (Norwich, 1938).

* In 1602, 1641, 1649 and 1650 the mayor died in office, and a successor was elected. Two individuals became mayor more than once, Sir Thomas Hyrne, ironmonger, in 1604, 1609 and 1616 and John Tolye or Tooley, merchant, in 1638 and 1644. They have been counted anew at each election.

† In cases of multiple occupations, the major occupation only has been counted.

‡ The mayoral year ran from June to June: dates refer to year of inauguration.

industry. Isolated estimates can be produced, but these are of dubious validity [55]. Representatives of the Norwich industry calculated in 1719 that £600,000 worth of stuffs from all sources was consumed annually in the kingdom of Great Britain, but this may have been exaggerated for polemical purposes. In the same year an estimate was made of the numbers employed by the Norwich industry. This combines reality and fantasy. The declared total of 500 master weavers and 8,000 journeymen and apprentices may well have a basis in reality; the additional figure of over 120,000 other workers, including spinsters, combers, dyers, dressers, throwsters and winders, lacks the ring of verisimilitude. The final estimate of over 130,000 workers engaged in the industry is clearly a partisan and unreliable figure [56]. And estimates for individual years, such as these, give no assistance in constructing an index to changes over time. Nor can admissions to the freedom of the city be used as an index to levels of economic activity. By this date, the number of admissions in any one year was regulated by the exigencies of political conflict, rather than by the dictates of economic activity. In the period from 1660 to 1713, the greatest number of admissions occurred in 1678, the year of the Popish Plot scare, and one of intense political conflict within Norwich. In 1704, another year of vigorous electioneering in Norwich, the mayor was said to have admitted 200 freemen of his own political persuasion [57]. To discover what was happening to the Norwich industry in the late seventeenth century, therefore, reference has to be made to literary evidence. This has the involuntary effect of concentrating attention upon the years of crisis within the industry, since bad trade is more conducive to literary output than is prosperity. Nonetheless, the picture that emerges is not one of unrelieved gloom but one of both expansion and change.

It seems clear that by the later part of the century, the Norwich industry was catering mainly for home demand. This was in marked contrast to the industry both in earlier and later times: in the early part of the century, its expansion was based on production for foreign markets; and in the mid-eighteenth century, the industry again successfully moved into overseas markets when faced with competition in the domestic market [58]. The evidence for the importance of the home market in the late seventeenth century is incontrovertible. At the time of the dispute between the Weavers' Company and the alnage officials, the weavers estimated that in 1688 one-quarter of their output had been sold overseas. This estimate, moreover, was produced at a time when it was in the interests of the Norwich industry to claim the maximum importance for their export sales. By contrast, the alnagers reported, at the same time, that no Norwich stuffs were exported [59]. The truth may be presumed to lie somewhere between the two extremes. The Yarmouth Port Books for 1685 show that some Norwich stuffs were exported in this year [60], but it is impossible to put this in proportionate terms without knowing the total volume of production. But the implication of both of these statements was clearly that a large proportion of the Norwich stuffs was produced for the home market at least by the late 1680s.

The shift to domestic markets probably took place in the middle years of the century. Overseas markets, especially those in Spain, were disrupted in the 1640s and 1650s. This occurred at the same time as an expansion in domestic demand, which provided new outlets for the Norwich stuffs at home. Despite complaints from the city of declining trade with Spain in the late 1650s, the preamble of the Act of 1662 for regulating production of Norwich stuffs noted that the industry 'hath of late times very much increased, and a great variety of new stuffs have been invented' [61]. This wording was in part polite formula, but choice of formulae is in itself of some significance. Expansion of domestic demand in the late seventeenth century was commented upon by numerous contemporary writers, including Sir Josiah Child and Adam Martindale [62]. The flattening out of the prolonged secular rise in prices improved the standard of real wages in the years after 1640 and released purchasing power, especially among the 'middling sort of people'. One of the ramifications of the expansion of domestic demand was an increased demand for good quality textiles, a demand which the Norwich industry was well qualified to meet.

The generic title of 'Norwich stuffs' concealed a considerable range and variety of fabrics. Most were light and brightly coloured textiles. They were made of long-staple wool, which had been combed, spun and dyed in the yarn. Some stuffs were 'mixed' fabrics, composed of worsted yarn and other fibres, such as silk, mohair or linen. After weaving, the material was treated by special finishing processes, which gave the stuffs their characteristic fine and glossy finish [63]. Some coarse cloths were still produced in the city. These included dornix, the linear descendant of the old worsteds produced in Norfolk in medieval times, fearnothing, a hard-wearing cloth worn by sailors, and bewper, used as sailcloth [64]. But the Norwich industry concentrated increasingly upon the 'light' end of the worsted range, while the production of coarse worsted migrated from East Anglia to the West Riding of Yorkshire [65]. The coarser and cheaper worsteds produced in Yorkshire at this date complemented rather than rivalled the output of the Norwich industry.

Norwich stuffs catered for those who wanted fabrics of stylish and attractive design, lighter and more decorative than the heavier serges or bays, but cheaper than the costly imported luxury fabrics worn by the very rich. Stuffs were used for women's and children's apparel, for gentlemen's suits and waistcoats, and as linings for more expensive fabrics. They were also used for furnishings, as curtains, room-hangings, quilts and coverings. Professor Wilson has specified the ideal market for the Norwich bombasine as that of 'the not-too-affluent squire's lady or the tradesman's wife' [66]. This may be termed the semi-fashionable market, since it was neither a luxury market nor a mass market. The hallmark of the Norwich stuffs was their wide range of both styles and prices. Celia Fiennes noted: 'Their pieces are 27 yards in length and their price is from 30 shillings to 3 pound as they are in fineness.' Variations in patterns and styles were used as a means of promoting sales. A chronicler of the city noted in 1711 that the Norwich weavers were famous for their inventiveness, adding happily: 'Gain always sharpens wit and invention, which has never appeared more than in the improvement of this stuff trade.' And Fuller, writing in the 1650s (where he is clearly referring to the home market), described some of the sales techniques used to titillate demand when the market was sluggish. He wrote of the Norwich stuffs:

> Expect not that I should reckon up their several names, because daily increasing, and many of them are *binominous,* as which, when they began to tire in sale, are quickened with a new name. [And he explained] A pretty pleasing name, complying with the buyers' fancy, much befriendeth a stuff in the sale thereof [67].

Some of the range of Norwich stuffs at this time can be seen from contemporary inventories of the stocks of Norwich weavers, which included damasks, russells, satins, tamines, cheyneys, callimancoes, crapes, camblets, jollyboys, druggets and faringdons [68].

Throughout the seventeenth century, there was a constant flow of innovation in finish and design, though there were no major technical changes. Techniques of dyeing were improved in the course of the century as the range of dye-stuffs increased; and according to a nineteenth-century historian, the French immigrants contributed new expertise [69]. The Huguenots were also responsible for the introduction of the Norwich crape, the one new fabric developed in this period. This was made of worsted, or of mixed worsted and silk, and was a very light and fine material. It was retailed at under twenty-five shillings the piece. When first introduced, the crape had an immediate fashionable success. Defoe recalled in 1704: 'The first effort of the French refugees was our thin black crape, a manufacture purely their own, and I refer to the memory of persons conversant in trade, how universally it pleased our people.' Its cheapness had however some disadvantages from the point of view of the woman of fashion. Use of crape spread down the social scale to servant-girls and the fabric then became 'a little obsolete' among upper-class women. This whole cycle, as Defoe makes clear, had taken place within twenty years of its introduction [70]. Norwich crape remained one of the more important varieties of the industry's output in the eighteenth century, although it never regained its first popularity. It subsequently captured two useful markets which were not so subject to the vagaries of fashion. These were the markets for mourning wear and for clerical vestments [71]. The history of the reception of the crape illustrates well the nature of the markets for which the Norwich industry catered and the capriciousness of demand.

The Norwich industry therefore depended for its success upon sedulous cultivation of its markets. In particular, the Norwich weavers paid great attention to the importance of rapid communications with the capital city which was the chief mart for Norwich stuffs. Weavers needed topical information about changing tastes and styles, and merchants needed quick distribution to catch the fashion while it was still in vogue. The bulk of the Norwich stuffs were carried to London by road, which was more expensive but faster and more reliable than transit by river and sea [72]. One of the major reasons behind the weavers' opposition to the alnagers in the late 1680s and 1690s was that the alnagers' practice of stopping waggons on the road to search for unsealed stuffs caused delays and uncertainties in the transport of goods. The alnagers also, the weavers alleged, entered merchants' warehouses and cut or confiscated stuffs [73]. The disruption of trade was more serious than the fiscal imposition on the industry. The conflict was finally settled in 1699, when the weavers agreed to pay an annual composition to the alnagers, who in return abandoned their claim to supervision.

Norwich stuffs were import substitutes, and also relied on protection in the home market from foreign rivals. The markets for which the Norwich industry catered were prone to succumb to the lure of prestigious imported textiles. The industry therefore benefited greatly from the ban imposed on French imported goods from 1679 to 1685. This ban was lifted briefly from 1685 to 1688, but thereafter replaced in the form of heavy import duties, which priced the French textiles out of the range of the markets supplied by Norwich stuffs [74]. The Norwich industry did not play much part in obtaining the ban on their French rivals. It did, however, play a leading part in the prolonged war waged by the English textile interests in the late seventeenth and early eighteenth centuries against imported East India calicoes. The calicoes were light, bright, gaily patterned printed textiles similar in appearance to the Norwich stuffs and with the advantage of being much cheaper. They began to enjoy a fashionable success in the 1690s, to such an extent that a spokesman for the Norwich industry admitted in 1696 that Norwich stuffs were being made 'in imitation of the India goods'. The English textile interests were temporarily successful in 1699 when an Act was passed against the importation of East India calicoes, wrought silks and Bengalls [75]. But the issue was rekindled within two decades, because, through a loophole in the Act, calicoes were being brought into the country in an unfinished state for printing and finishing in England. The fashion revived with alacrity. The Norwich weavers, in conjunction with the silk weavers of London, again took the lead in a campaign for further legislation, which was successful in 1722 [76]. The contest showed that the domestic industries could successfully press for, and obtain, legislation to defend their interests. But the incident again demonstrated the volatility of the consuming public, which constituted an inherent instability in the markets for Norwich stuffs.

Within this framework of protection, the Norwich industry was gradually shedding all internal restrictions and supervision. This was in itself a symptom of expansion. As noted, the Norwich weavers had campaigned successfully in the 1690s against the attempt made by the alnagers to seal Norwich stuffs. In the same period the supervision nominally exercised by the Weavers' Company was increasingly being evaded. This was admitted by the Company itself in 1689 when a number of merchants and dealers in Norwich stuffs petitioned Parliament for the office of search to be made effective. The Company's response was to suggest that the number of officials elected annually to search and seal should be increased. But nothing came of this proposal and in 1705 the practice of sealing was ended. This marked the effective demise of the real powers of the Company, although it continued for a time to act as the official spokesman of the industry. By the 1730s it had been replaced by a Committee of Trade [77]. The Weavers' Company had also fought and lost in the 1690s a battle with the woolcombers over their claim to supervise the standard of yarn. This power had been granted to the weavers in 1650 by their Act of Incorporation. In 1693 the woolcombers of Norfolk and Suffolk mounted a campaign against the methods of search used by the weavers. Ironically, their complaints echoed those made by the Norwich weavers themselves against the alnagers, that the searching disrupted trade for no good purpose and that the weavers' power to issue arbitrary fines was unconstitutional. Parliament upheld the woolcombers in a judgment in 1694 [78]. By the end of the century, the whole unwieldy apparatus of control had been jettisoned.

With the growing importance of domestic markets in the late seventeenth century came changes in the location of the industry. While the industry had always been closely associated with the city of Norwich, as the name of the stuffs implied, there had also been a considerable number of weavers resident throughout the county of Norfolk, especially in the area to the north and east of Norwich (the ancient centre of the worsted industry in Norfolk from medieval times). The revival of the worsted weaving industry in the late sixteenth century did not at first produce any great locational changes. The Incorporation of the Weavers in 1650 provided for equal numbers of Wardens and Assistants from the county of Norfolk and from the city of Norwich [79]. But in the late seventeenth century there was a growing concentration of the weaving processes in the city of Norwich and its immediate vicinity, though spinning remained a rural occupation. Locational changes are difficult to pinpoint. The evidence of the places of residence of 581 weavers, as shown in wills proved in the Consistory Court at Norwich in the period from 1611 to 1750, confirms the tendency of the industry to concentrate in the city (see Table 11.4). This evidence is not in itself conclusive, but its findings are suggestive. Clearly what Tsuru has labelled the 'external economies' afforded by an urban location [80] were important for an industry which was highly dependent on good communications and rapid access to markets. The advantages of concentration outweighed the potential disadvantages of the fact that wage levels tended to be higher in the town than in the countryside. There is, however, virtually no evidence relating to labour costs at this time. A speaker in the House of Commons stated in 1680 that an English weaver could expect to earn 1s a day, or 6s a week, but there is no means of checking this statement. The success of the Norwich industry at this time argues in itself that labour costs were not prohibitively high. The absence of any labour disputes over piecework rates also suggests that the industry did not make any attempts to cut costs by cutting wages [81].

Table 11.4   Location of weavers* in Norwich diocese, 1611-1750

Period	Norwich	Norfolk	Suffolk	Total
1611-30	20	35	6	61
1631-50	22	56	9	87
1651-70	13	26	2	41
1671-90	22	13	4	39
1691-1710	63	26	4	93
1711-30	100	65	4	169
1731-50	56	31	4	91
	296	252	33	581

Source: M. A. Farrow and T. F. Barton, eds, *Index of Wills proved in the Consistory Court of Norwich, 1604-1686* (Norfolk Record Society, xxviii, 1958) and *Index of Wills proved in the Consistory Court of Norwich, 1687-1750* (Norfolk Record Society, xxxiv, 1965).
* Includes all those listed as 'weavers' and 'worsted weavers', but excludes linen-weavers, ribbon-weavers and coarse cloth weavers.

The continued existence of the worsted weaving industry in Norwich was in fact a tribute to the force of tradition or the momentum of inertia. For at first sight Norwich does not seem to be especially suited to the production of worsteds. The industry drew all its raw materials from outside the county of Norfolk. Worsteds did not use the short staple wool of the Norfolk sheep but drew on wool from Lincolnshire, Leicestershire and Northamptonshire, which was then transported into Norfolk and Suffolk for spinning. Furthermore, by the late seventeenth century the demand for yarn in the city was beginning to outrun the capacity of the local spinners to provide for it, and yarn was being combed and spun outside the county for the Norwich industry [82]. But both wool and yarn were relatively cheap and easy to transport. The industry also required supplies of coal for the combing, dyeing and finishing processes. The city of Norwich was always sensitive about the cost of fuel, and in 1696, for example, petitioned Parliament that high coal prices were aggravating discontent among the poor. Similarly, the question of Yarmouth harbour dues on coal was a perennial source of conflict between the two cities [83]. But raw material did not in fact constitute a large proportion of production costs, since labour accounted for five-sixths of the total, according to an estimate made by the weavers' representatives in 1719 [84]. A plentiful supply of labour was, therefore, an essential requirement of the industry. In the absence of any technological changes in methods of production there was no particular reason for the industry to move, but on the contrary, there was ample reason why the industry should remain in a locality which had the accumulated expertise of a long tradition of weaving. Once the city had reached and passed a certain critical point, and the old regulations and restrictions on the recruitment of labour had been broken down, growth was self-sustaining, prior to the advent of mechanisation.

The Norwich industry had, therefore, adapted successfully to meet changing markets and experienced considerable prosperity and expansion in the late seventeenth century. There were years of depression. For example the plague and its aftermath caused considerable disruption in 1666-67. There were complaints of unemployment and the rising cost of poor relief and it was at this time that the Corporation began investigating the possibility of setting up a workhouse in the city (a project that did not achieve fruition until 1712). There was also a recession in the industry in the years from 1674 to 1676. By contrast the 1680s saw a prolonged boom. This probably explains a comment made by one of the witnesses before the House of Lords in 1692-93 who remarked that 'Norwich stuffs were not heard of till within twelve years'. The industry was still vulnerable to competition as the struggle against the East India calicoes made clear. As a result of competition in the home market, coupled with the disruption produced by the recoinage, the industry was reported as being in a depressed state in 1696. And again in December 1699 Dean Prideaux noted that trade was slack, observing lugubriously that Norwich 'now sinks apace' [85]. This comment makes clear that contemporary observers were well aware of the close connection between the wellbeing of the city and that of the worsted weaving industry. But despite these intermittent depressions, the industry was in a fundamentally sound position at the end of the century.

The growth of the textile industry did not prevent the city from continuing to perform other functions. Norwich was a centre of commercial and social life. The city was a natural focal point within the county: it was the county town and cathedral city; it was situated in the heart of the most densely populated area of the county; it was a point of convergence for several roads within the county, which came to cross the Wensum/Yare river complex (avoiding the flat marshy area to the east of the city); and it was well served with communications to London, both overland and via Yarmouth, the city's port, which was itself one of the largest towns in the country [86]. The growth of the industry, by increasing the size of the city, also augmented its importance *vis-à-vis* its hinterland and hence enhanced its role as a centre of distribution and consumption.

Urban growth in itself entailed an increase in the so-called 'maintenance industries' in the city. The term is used to include the occupations of all those who were engaged in supplying essential requirements for the city's population, such as food and drink, clothing and housing. The freemen's admissions show that, as might be expected, those engaged in the provision of food and drink, and of clothing, constituted the major occupational groups after the textile workers (see Table 11.1 and Appendix). The numbers admitted in the clothing trades show a puzzling decline, both in absolute and proportionate terms, in the late seventeenth century: they fell from 18 per cent of all admissions between 1660 and 1669 to 5·7 per cent between 1700 and 1709. There is no obvious explanation for this. It may be simply that those occupied in these industries were ceasing to take out the freedom of the city. This is substantiated by complaints made in 1675 and 1681 by the freemen drapers and tailors against competition from non-freemen [87]. Or it may also be that these occupations were being increasingly taken over by women, who were ineligible for the freedom. There is evidence for the employment of women in dressmaking and millinery. Among the apprenticeship indentures of the early eighteenth century were those of 113 women, of whom 90 were apprenticed in the clothing trades [88]. But this is a problem to which there is no satisfactory answer. The freemen figures are in any case rather an erratic guide. One industry which was clearly flourishing at this time, although this is not shown in the freemen figures, was beer-brewing. Considerable wealth was made in the brewing of Norwich 'Nog', a heavy, dark brew made from local barley. The power of the brewing industry was discovered by the mayor in 1681 when he mounted a campaign against the growing number of alehouses in the city: 'this town swarms with them ... most of them, 'tis said, bawdy houses too.' He was reported to the central government by Excise officials, as politically suspect [89]. He survived, but the campaign was dropped.

Norwich was an important commercial centre, supplying goods for a wide rural hinterland as well as for its own growing population. At this time people travelled long distances for luxury goods and even for comparatively small and inexpensive purchases [90]. Much of the city's commercial life was centred in the large open market in the heart of the city, celebrated for its size, good order and for the quantity and quality of goods on sale. Baskerville's description conveys a graphic impression:

> A little way off from this Castle ... is the chief market place of this
> city, and this being the only place where all things are brought to be
> sold for the food of this great city, they not as in London allowing
> markets in several places, make it vastly full of provisions, especially
> on Saturdays, where I saw the greatest shambles for butchers' meat I
> had ever yet seen, and the like also for poultry and dairy-meats,
> which dairy people also bring many quarters of veal with their butter
> and cheese, and I believe also in their seasons pork and hog-meats.
> ... They setting their goods in ranges as near as may be one above
> another, only allowing room for single persons to pass between.

He added that the Friday market was an important market for fish. The
market regulations stipulated that all meat slaughtered in the early part of
the week was to be sold off by Thursday evening, an unusual provision
devised to assist the Yarmouth fishing industry. Indeed his informant told
him that it was so successful that at times there were no fish to be had in
Yarmouth. There were three markets weekly, of which that on Saturday
was by far the largest and most important [91].

The open market was a very flexible and inexpensive form of
establishing retail outlets. It was flexible since the number of stalls could
be varied to accommodate changes in the volume of trade. Ample room
was provided for country tradesmen. Celia Fiennes noted that special stalls
were reserved for country butchers opposite their city counterparts. And
many country producers traded directly with the consumer without the
intervention of middlemen. Farmers' wives and daughters sat with hampers
or 'peds' of dairy produce in the 'ped market'. The market was also
inexpensive, from the point of view of the salesman. Setting up a stall
required no capital outlay, apart from the cost of renting a stall from the
Corporation (and payments were often in arrears). In addition the market
was free from tolls, with the minor exception of a small herbage toll [92].

In this period there was also a growing tendency towards the setting
up of permanent retail outlets for round-the-week trading. A growing
number of shops were being established in Norwich, especially in the area
in and around the market-place. One of the main shopping areas was the
ancient Cockey Lane, which was renamed in the course of the eighteenth
century as 'London Street' in tribute to its quasi-metropolitan splendour
[93]. It is impossible to quantify the amount of retail trade carried on, or
even to estimate the number of retail outlets there were in existence.
Retail trade was not a specialised occupation; the freeman figures,
therefore, cannot be used to distinguish the craft producers from the
retailers. And there was a considerable amount of casual trading carried on
by pedlars and streetsellers, whose numbers cannot even be guessed at.
William Arderon, writing in the mid-eighteenth century, listed forty-two
different sorts of shops in the city and fifty-seven different street cries
[94]. Retail trade in Norwich is much better documented in the
eighteenth century when advertisements appeared in the local press.
Earlier, shopkeepers relied upon brightly coloured signs, or commissioned
the city Bellman to broadcast information about goods for sale [95]. The
growing importance of regular retail trade was paralleled by the gradual

decline of the thrice yearly fairs, which were ceasing to be of great commercial significance, although retaining their popularity as social occasions [96].

Norwich was also an important centre of wholesale trade. Two roles can be distinguished here. The city was one of the main distribution points for the export of the agricultural surpluses of the county of Norfolk. In particular Norwich specialised as a market for livestock, especially cattle, and for grain. These markets were attended by London dealers or their agents. Grain was then shipped via Yarmouth, while livestock were walked to town. The cattle which were sold in the Norwich market included the celebrated 'Scottish runts', which wintered in the marshland to the east of the city where they were fattened up and sent in 'great quantities' weekly to the capital [97]. Secondly, Norwich acted as a nodal point for the distribution throughout Norfolk of heavy goods and groceries which were imported into the city by the river and sea route. It is noticeable that the city did not operate as a very important market for its own industry, nor for the raw materials used in the textile production. Woolcombers ordered their supplies of wool in bulk, often at the annual Stourbridge Fair, while Norwich weavers consigned their goods directly to London merchants and dealers. An attempt was made in 1700 to establish a formal Exchange in the city to facilitate commercial transactions, but this experiment was concluded within three years after a petition to the City Assembly that the Exchange was detrimental to the staple industry [98].

The economic importance of consumption has also been recognised as a factor of significance in the growth of towns. The sixteenth and seventeenth centuries saw the growing urbanisation of the social life of the landed gentry. This was particularly encouraged from the early seventeenth century onwards with the invention and popularisation of the coach, which meant that a country gentleman could transport his wife and daughters to town [99]. The towns were able to supply luxury goods, professional services and entertainments that were not available in the countryside. London was of course the mecca in this respect. Its dominance in the social world in the late seventeenth century was as great as it had ever been. In the eyes of London society the world outside the city presented a picture of uniform monotony: provincial England was termed generically 'Hampshire' [100]. But such views were exaggerated. Provincial capitals offered a considerable range of services, which, though not on a par with those of London, were sufficient to attract custom to the city. Norwich came into this category: although not newly fashionable like some of the spa towns, it was a recognised centre of social life in the county. Nor was its development as a textile centre any handicap to this function. The staple industry was unobtrusive to eyes, ears and noses. This was a negative factor of some importance, for a city that was too dirty or smelly could lose its role as a social centre. Bristol's Hotwells failed to achieve any great social success, partly as a result of the smoky, oppressive atmosphere of the town, as well as through the rivalry of nearby Bath [101].

The city of Norwich had something of its own winter season, a copy in miniature of that of London, with theatres, shows and assemblies. This catered for the middle-rank gentry, the country clergy and prosperous farmers. On the other hand, it failed to attract the county aristocracy, who tended to gravitate to London. As far as can be ascertained from imperfect records, the leading members of Norfolk society did not keep up town houses in Norwich although they might own property in the city. If they kept a town house it was usually in London. It was in this period that the Howard family ceased to keep up their Palace in Norwich, concentrating their attention instead on their property in the Strand. This decision was taken as much out of disenchantment with Norwich as from the lure of London. The Norwich Palace was on an unattractive site, in a densely built-up and industrial area of the city. Baskerville thought it 'seated in a dung-hole place', and Evelyn concurred that it was 'an old wretched building' despite the fact that the Duke was said in 1681 to have recently spent £30,000 on repairs and rebuilding [102]. In the 1690s the property was in a very dilapidated condition, visited but infrequently. The departure of the family was compounded by a quarrel in 1708 between the Duke of Norfolk and the Corporation, which was jealous of ducal pretensions: the issue was whether the Duke had the right to have himself played into the city with full ceremonial and a procession. The Corporation subsequently leased the Palace and used part of the premises, suitably enough, as the City Workhouse [103]. The departure of their resident nobility must have occasioned the city some loss of custom. Edward Browne's diary gives an account of the great prodigality with which Christmas was celebrated by Henry Howard in 1663. He entertained 'so lavishly the like hath scarce been seen. They had dancing every night, and gave entertainments to all that would come.' But provincial society did not relish ducal glamour at all costs. When a later Duke of Norfolk visited the city in 1696 his reputation was so bad, that, although he prepared a great ball, no ladies attended for fear of being compromised [104].

Besides its miniature winter season, the city had a second string to its bow. When the gentry redispersed to their country estates in the summer months they came into the local capital for specific functions which offered entertainment to relieve the monotony of rural life. Such a function, for example, was the annual inauguration of the Lord Mayor of Norwich, which was attended with much ceremonial every June. Celia Fiennes described the scene:

> All the streete in which this Mayor elect's house is, is very exact in beautifying themselves, and hanging up flaggs the collours of their Companyes, and dress up pageants and there are plays and all sorts of shows that day, in little what is done at the Lord Mayor of London show; then they have a great feast with fine flaggs and scenes hung out, musick and dancing [105].

Another important event in the annual calendar was the Summer Assize week, which was the occasion of many balls, theatres and shows. Mary Chamberlayne wrote to her half-brother William Windham in August 1688: 'As to the Assizes, there happened very little remarkable besides the good company at them, for it was agreed by all, there never was more: nor so pittyful a High Sheriff to entertain them.' Among the 'good company' she noted the Lestranges, the Astleys, the Hobarts, the Earles and the

Potts, all leading Norfolk gentry families [106]. Other functions which brought county society into the city were meetings of the Norfolk Lieutenancy Committee, the quarter sessions, the inauguration of a new Bishop (who was attended to his palace with a retinue of city notables and country gentlemen) and other special occasions, such as the visit of Charles II to the city in 1671 [107]. These occasions brought a great deal of business into Norwich and caused at times acute shortage of accommodation. When the Hobart family leased out Chapelfield House in the 1680s, they prudently made arrangements for two annual visits to the city: a clause in the lease allowed them the use of two rooms free of charge twice a year, each stay to last a maximum of five days and nights [108]. County elections, which were held in Norwich, also brought in large numbers of people. In May 1679 Sir Thomas Browne observed country voters sleeping 'like flocks of sheep' around the cross in the market-place, and he wrote in February 1681, with the prospects of a contested election in mind: 'The people delight in it, and say it will be better for the towne, as causing more concourse of persons, and more money to be spent in the towne' [109].

The Corporation itself made some modest attempts to improve amenities. For example, it was decided in 1710 to present a piece of plate as a prize for an annual horse race to be held near the city. Norwich never rivalled Newmarket, but there was a considerable amount of horse-racing carried on in the vicinity, accompanied by much betting and gambling. Attempts were also made, on private initiative, to give Norwich some of the amenities of a spa. Aylsham spa water, brought fresh every morning to the Black Boy in St Clement's, was advertised in 1710 [110]. Other entertainments, both official and unofficial, included prize-fighting, all-in-wrestling (accompanied by kicking with specially sharpened boots), races, cockfighting, throwing at cocks, bear-baiting, nine-pins and 'camping', described as 'a wild and primitive form of football' [111]. The Corporation made strenuous but unsuccessful attempts to control the amount and variety of popular entertainments in the city, fearing that the industrial population would be distracted from its employment. It was empowered to license plays and shows: for example, permission was given in 1665 for Richard Browne to show an eagle, a vulture and two camels for a fortnight; in 1678 for Isaac Cookson to show 'a girl without bones'; and in 1677 for a group of rope-dancers to perform at the Red Lion in St Stephen's [112]. In addition to entertainment, the city also offered to both town and country society a chance to see and be seen. Hence the growing vogue for promenades along the 'Gentlemen's Walk' in the market-place or in the Chapel Fields, where the walk, 'prettily adorned with young trees' and 'loved by beaux and belles', was described in the mid-eighteenth century as the 'Mall of Norwich' [113].

There was also in this period a growth in the number of professional men in the city (see Appendix). Norwich offered a gamut of services, ranging from sin to repentance. Sin was catered for by the city prostitutes who flourished despite attempts made by the Corporation to close down bawdy houses, although it seems that in this respect Norwich was considered as inferior to Lynn. [114]. Repentance in all its guises was catered for by doctors, lawyers and ministers of religion. Professional men catered for an extensive rural as well as urban clientele. The letters of Sir Thomas Browne show that he was consulted professionally by country gentry families [115]. Other professional services available in the city at the end of the century were those of surveyors, architects, teachers, printers, publishers and musicians [116]. The city also functioned as an informal money-market. Numerous loans, mortgages and pecuniary trans-actions were conducted in the city. The correspondence of gentry families show that city moneylenders (often widows with cash to invest) were important sources of capital. Some of the carriers and waggoners also acted as unofficial bankers and moneylenders [117]. The numerous inns and alehouses in the city exemplified its commercial and social import-ance. They provided refreshment, accommodation and entertainment. In 1685 the city had 550 beds and stabling room for 930 horses, although in this respect it was outshone by some of the ports and staging-posts. Norwich ranked as eighth among English towns in terms of beds available and fourth for stabling [118].

It is notable that the churches of Norwich played a very muted role in the city's economic development. Here there was a contrast between the dominant visual impression created by Norwich as a city of churches, and economic reality. The Church of England no doubt attracted some business to the city for the conduct of diocesan administration and for litigation in the Church Courts. But the evidence suggests that neither was of very great significance: there was no very large ecclesiastical bureauc-racy and the volume and importance of business in the Church Courts was declining. The many small parish churches in the city were small and poorly endowed, and the standard of ministers was low. They were characterised as 'drones' by the acerbic Prideaux. An attempt was made in 1677 to provide for Anglican ministers in the city through a local rate, but this was firmly resisted by the Corporation [119]. Probably the most important economic influence of the Church of England was the custom generated by the household of the Bishop whose social life and standards of entertainment approximated to those of a country gentleman. The impact of the Church on town life in England contrasts with that of the Catholic Church on the Continent. In Beauvais, the 'ville sonnante', and in eighteenth-century Bayeux, for example, the Catholic Church dominated the urban economy, as employer, consumer and purveyor of poor relief [120].

The poverty and dejection of the Church of England in Norwich was both product and cause of the strength of Dissent in the city. The Dissenting churches, however, were decentralised in their administration and modest in their building requirements and they did not, therefore, have such direct impact upon the urban economy. In more indirect ways they may have contributed to the growth of trade and industry by the inculcation of a commercial morality. Such at least was the intention of Dr Collinges, one of the leading Presbyterian ministers in the city in the late seventeenth century. In 1675 he produced the *Weaver's Pocket-book, or Weaving Spiritualised*, which was designed to be read by the weaver at the loom, and which demonstrated considerably familiarity with the processes of worsted production. He urged an ethic of hard work (as a sign of salvation, rather than as a means of redemption); he inveighed against the practice of weaving short lengths, which was as bad as deceiving God, for 'Does not the falseness of our hearts prompt us, to come off as cheap with God as we can?' and he counselled obedience to the officials of the Weavers' Company, provided that they were vigilant, active and disinterested in the execution of their office [121]. The effect of writings such as these must obviously remain incalculable. But they provide yet another illustration of the importance of the city as a textile centre, which overlaid its traditional function as a market town and cathedral city.

In its specialisation of function in the seventeenth century, the city of Norwich differs from the formal model of the pre-industrial city, which tends to be heterogeneous in function [122]. The case of Norwich shows that, within the context of a pre-industrial economy, a considerable amount of specialisation could occur. The expansion of the city and its growing importance as a textile centre were concomitant developments. The textile industry was the leading sector of the urban economy, productive of the greatest demand for labour in the city. 'We want hands to work', announced Thomas Lombe, describing the industry in its heyday [123]. The urban environment also fostered the growth of the industry. The city's economic regulations were revised to accommodate changed economic circumstances, as the restrictions on the recruitment of labour were broken down and supervision of the industry was waived. Contrary to the opinion of some eighteenth-century writers, overly-impressed with the growth of new towns, an old incorporated city could provide a sympathetic environment for industrial expansion. Consequently the expansion of domestic demand in the late seventeenth century which stimulated the growth of domestic textile industries also promoted the growth of Norwich.

The expansion of the city was, however, a cumulative process and did not entail the abandonment of its traditional functions. Indeed these were enhanced as the city grew in size and the volume of business attracted to the city increased. Although the textile industry was the main agent of growth, the other aspects of the urban economy flourished in its wake and may have helped the city to weather the intermittent depressions in the staple industry. Like late seventeenth-century Exeter, which in some ways it closely resembled, Norwich was 'full of gentry and good company, and yet full of trade and manufactures also' [124].

This meant that in both the long and short term, the crucial determinant of the well-being of the city was the worsted weaving industry. In the long term, this can be seen when the erosion of the textile industry in the early nineteenth century produced a fundamental alteration in the status and relative importance of Norwich [125]. The city then fell back upon its traditional function as a market town and commercial centre. In the short term, too, its fortunes fluctuated with those of the industry. A depression in the textile industry upset the whole urban economy, producing a heavy demand for poor relief at the very time when the city was least able to afford it. Problems were intensified when depressions in trade coincided with epidemics which threw greater numbers out of work. Thus to contemporaries the basis of the urban economy seemed very shaky and insecure, although in retrospect the period seems one of successful growth and adaptation.

But despite anxieties about the staple industry, contemporaries were sanguine about the specifically urban problems produced by growth, such as the increased problems of sanitation and housing, supplies of food and water, and maintenance of public order. All these issues confronted the civic authorities at this time but provoked very little public debate. As often happens, people were more concerned with the problems caused by lack of growth than with those consequent upon expansion. And indeed, the growth of Norwich in the late seventeenth century did not cause a breakdown in the administrative and political structure it had inherited from the past: even its physical expansion was almost entirely contained within the old city walls, which remained standing as visible symbols of continuity and urban self-sufficiency. All commentators therefore agreed in lauding unreservedly the city's size and importance. In the eighteenth century its inhabitants were regaled with the story of Johnny Numps, the country bumpkin come to town, who was dazzled by the sophistication and glamour of the big city [126]: the tale would have applied with even more force in the late seventeenth century, when Norwich led the provincial world.

Appendix   Admissions to the freedom of the city, 1660-1749

Occupations	1660-69	1670-79	1680-89	1690-99	1700-09	1710-19	1720-29	1730-39	1740-49	Total
TEXTILES										
Worsted weavers	335	363	212	218	613	564	699	372	242	3,618
Other weavers[a]	17	13	6	3	1	4	29		1	74
Woolcombers	13	18	3	5	10	38	115	55	26	283
Dyers	2	9	6	4	10	12	12	11	3	69
Finishers[b]	3	6	13	10	30	32	25	19	16	154
Total	370	409	240	240	664	650	880	457	288	4,198
LEATHER										
Leather workers	16	4	1	4	7	5	8	10	1	56
Shoemakers	57	77	40	59	84	79	88	84	39	607
Total	73	81	41	63	91	84	96	94	40	663
METAL										
Metal-workers[c]	28	33	12	27	27	49	31	31	22	260
Clockmakers		1			2	2		3	5	13
Total	28	34	12	27	29	51	31	34	27	273
BUILDING										
Carpenters	25	33	34	27	36	33	26	53	31	298
Masons	22	21	15	18	25	30	15	13	8	167
Others	1	3		1		4	3	5	4	21
Total	48	57	49	46	61	67	44	71	43	486

Continued on next page

Appendix   Admissions to the freedom of the city, 1660-1749

Occupations	1660-69	1670-79	1680-89	1690-99	1700-09	1710-19	1720-29	1730-39	1740-49	Total
FOOD AND DRINK										
Butchers	19	18	18	16	28	28	21	15	13	176
Bakers	24	29	37	36	48	38	43	36	27	318
Fishmongers	2	1	7	3	1	1	3	2		20
Grocers	31	22	15	34	30	22	16	22	25	217
Brewers[d]	17	21	12	15	21	21	16	25	9	157
Total	93	91	89	104	128	110	99	100	74	888
CLOTHING[e]										
Drapers	8	6	1	6	6	11	8	11	8	65
Mercers	10	4	7	7	6	6	5	4	6	55
Merchants	12	1	3	1		2	1	2	3	25
Tailors	91	80	63	52	43	44	38	42	16	469
Milliners	1	3	1	1		4				10
Hosiers	23	4	4	2	3	2	1	4		43
Glovers	8	9	1	4	7	5	6	3	8	51
Hatters	10	6		1	1	3		10	4	35
Total	163	113	80	74	66	77	59	76	45	753
PROFESSIONS[f]										
Goldsmiths	3	2		2	1	1	1	1	1	12
Scriveners	9	8	7	3	4	5	8	2	2	48
Apothecaries	4	3		7	8	6	7	7	6	49
Surgeons[g]	18	13	23	37	49	46	39	46	45	316
Attorneys						6	1	13	7	27
Total	34	26	30	49	62	65	56	69	61	452

Continued on next page

Appendix   Admissions to the freedom of the city, 1660-1749

Occupations	1660-69	1670-79	1680-89	1690-99	1700-09	1710-19	1720-29	1730-39	1740-49	Total
MISCELLANEOUS AND NOT STATED	90	64	47	37	52	24	110	195	95	714
Total	899	875	588	640	1,153	1,128	1,375	1,096	673	8,427

Source: P. Millican, *The Freemen of Norwich, 1548-1713*, Norwich, 1934, and *The Freemen of Norwich, 1713-1752*, Norfolk Record Society, xxiii, 1952.

Notes

Years are given old-style.

a   Other weavers include weavers of cloth, dornix, fearnothing, lace, linen, ribbon and silk.

b   Finishers include calenderers, hotpressers, sheermen and twisterers.

c   Metal-workers include blacksmiths, braziers, cutlers, founders, ironworkers, locksmiths and whitesmiths.

d   Brewers include coopers, maltsters, victuallers and wine-coopers.

e   Producers, wholesale dealers and retailers of cloths and clothing are all classified together, since the data do not permit further breakdown.

f   Professions include all those working in law, medicine, finance and allied occupations.

g   Surgeons include barber-surgeons and barbers, since their functions are not clearly differentiated in the data.

Notes

Abbreviations *CSPD: Calendar of State Papers, Domestic*; HMC: Historic Manuscripts Commission; MCB: Mayoral Court Book; NCRL: Norwich, Colman and Rye Libraries of Local History; NNRO: Norfolk and Norwich Record Office; PRO: Public Record Office; *Trans. Roy. Hist. Soc.: Transactions of the Royal Historical Society*; *VCH: Victoria County History*.

1   I would like to thank Professor F. J. Fisher for his help in reading early drafts of this chapter.
2   For useful brief accounts of the city, see HMC *Portland MSS*, II, 268-70, C. Morris, ed., *The Journeys of Celia Fiennes* (1949), pp. 146-150, and D. Defoe, *A Tour Through the Whole Island of Great Britain* (Everyman edn, 1959), i, 62-5.
3   For estimates of the city's population, see K. J. Allison, 'The wool supply and the worsted cloth industry in Norfolk in the sixteenth and seventeenth centuries' (unpublished Ph.D. thesis, University of Leeds, 1955), pp. 604-5, 732-3, and W. Hudson and J. C. Tingey, *The Records of the City of Norwich* (1906-10), vol. ii, p. cxxviii. (Unless stated to the contrary, all figures relate to both the city and county of Norwich, and also include the precincts of the cathedral, which came under separate jurisdiction.) Norwich was the second city for most of the seventeenth century. J. E. Thorold Rogers, *History of Agriculture and Prices*, Oxford, 1887, v, 120, ranks Norwich as second city in 1641. It was not overtaken by Bristol until the 1720s or 1730s. The population of Bristol in 1700 was about 20,000, according to W. E. Minchinton, 'Bristol: the metropolis of the West in the eighteenth century', *Trans. Roy. Hist. Soc.*, 5th ser., iv (1954), 75.
4   C. Gill and A. Briggs, *History of Birmingham,* Oxford, 1952, i, 48, estimate its population at between 10,000 and 15,000 in 1700. The lower of these two figures is probably the more accurate. W. Hutton, *The History of Birmingham*, Birmingham, 6th edn, 1835, p. 77, estimated a population of about 15,000 in 1700. This was based on a list of 2,504 houses in the city, multiplied by an average household size of six. This multiplier is almost certainly too high. P. Laslett, 'Size and structure of the household in England over three centuries', *Population Studies*, xxiii, no. 2 (1969), 207, 211, suggests an average of 4·75.
5   F. Blomefield, *An Essay towards a Topographical History of the County of Norfolk*, 1806, iii, 432.
6   Allison, *op. cit.*, p. 607, gives annual figures collated from weekly returns in the Mayoral Court Books.
7   Bodleian Library [Oxford] MS. G. A. Norfolk, 4°.14: 'Ordinances for crafts ... 19th August 1622'. 'Foreigners' referred to all coming from outside the city.
8   Discussion of the flaws and idiosyncrasies of parish registers is the stock-in-trade of historical demography. For a survey of the problems, see R. Mols, *Introduction à la Démographie Historique des*

Villes d'Europe du XIVe au XVIIIe siècle, Louvain, 1954-6, i, 259-90, and D. E. C. Eversley, 'Exploitation of Anglican parish registers by aggregative analysis', in E. A. Wrigley, ed., *An Introduction to English Historical Demography*, 1966, pp. 45-53. Ideally figures for baptisms and burials should be inflated to allow for under-registration, but selection of an inflation rate is fraught with problems.

9   Allison, *op. cit.*, pp. 604-5, has multiplied by 33 the baptismal figures for every tenth year, producing a population of 13,000 in 1602, 18,000 in 1612, 32,000 in 1622, 21,000 in 1632 and 27,000 in 1642. This exaggerates fluctuations from year to year. Applying the same birth rate to the decennial averages, a lower total population of 27,500 is produced for the decade from 1621 to 1630.

10   See D. E. C. Eversley, 'Population, economy and society', in D. V. Glass and D. E. C. Eversley, eds., *Population in History* (1965), p. 53, and M. W. Flinn, *British Population Growth, 1700-1850* (1970), p. 29.

11   Blomefield, *op. cit.*, iii, 372-3, 376-7, 379-80; and Allison, *op. cit.*, p. 607. See also N. C. P. Tyack, 'Migration from East Anglia to New England before 1660' (unpublished Ph.D. thesis, University of London, 1951), *passim*.

12   Allison, *op. cit.*, p. 607. The yearly average for the decade from 1631 to 1640 (my calculation) was 710·6 baptisms, compared with 615 burials.

13   A. Jessopp, *Diocesan History of Norwich* (1884), pp. 203-4, and M. James, *Social Problems and Policy during the Puritan Revolution* (re-issue, 1966), p. 186. The Corporation was not backward in publicising its grievances, but made no mention in this period of any loss of population. For petitions to the central government in 1649 and 1659, see James, *op. cit.*, pp. 50, 76.

14   NNRO Case 16, Shelf b, MCB, no. xxiv, 30/6/1669, 23/9/1676.

15   NNRO has a number of registers and microfilms. These can be supplemented by miscellaneous Archdeacon's Transcripts (NNRO, Case 31, Shelves d-e), Bishop's Transcripts (NNRO Norwich Diocesan Archives), and register transcripts in the libraries of the Norfolk and Norwich Archaeological Society and the Society of Genealogists. But there are many lacunae in the material. A pilot study for six selected years produced complete statistics for only nineteen of the thirty-four intramural parishes, which contained 57 per cent of the total population at the enumeration of 1693. The figures exclude the records of the French and Dutch churches in Norwich, and probably under-register the city's Nonconformists. The figures cannot, therefore, be used as a basis from which to extrapolate totals for the whole city.

16   PRO E179/154/701 Schedule of taxable hearths, 1662. The estimated total of hearths corresponds closely with the total of 7,302 given in W. G. Hoskins, *Local History in England* (1959), p. 177.

17 PRO E/179/338 lists certificates of 3,028 people exempted from payment of the Hearth Tax for the whole city from January to April 1671. The rate of exemption can be calculated by comparison with the estimated total of those assessed in July 1671. The lists are not strictly comparable since they date from different months of the year. But comparison of names shows a considerable degree of compatibility.

18 *Calendar of Treasury Books 1672-5*, p. 627. Lord Treasurer Danby confirmed to the Mayor of Norwich in 1674 that weavers' and dyers' furnaces were exempt, provided that their chimneys had already been paid for. This suggests that exemption was not *ipso facto* a sign of poverty. Exemption rates elsewhere were 41 per cent in Newcastle in 1671, R. Howell, *Newcastle-upon-Tyne and the Puritan Revolution* (Oxford, 1967), pp. 9-10; just under 40 per cent in Exeter in 1671-72, W. G. Hoskins, *Industry, Trade and People in Exeter, 1688-1800* (Manchester, 1935), pp. 115-16; 20·4 per cent in York in 1672, *VCH Yorkshire: The City of York* (1961), p. 164; and 27·4 per cent in Leicester in 1670, *VCH Leicestershire*, iv (1958), p. 156.

19 D. V. Glass, 'Two papers on Gregory King', in Glass and Eversley, *op. cit.*, p. 177, suggests an average household size of 4·226 for the city of Norwich in 1696. This is confirmed by a partial census for the parish of St Peter Mancroft in 1693/4, which gives a household size of 4·14 for the 255 households of those paying the Poll Tax: NNRO Case 13, Shelf a, 'A certificate of the names'. The household figure is inclusive, so that there is no need to add an additional total for servants and apprentices, as some do: see Howell, *op. cit.*, pp. 8-9.

20 NNRO Case 12, Shelf a, 'Norwich City' Assessment Books, nos 1, 3 and 4, dated July 1671 (no. 2 is missing). A covering letter makes it clear that these are hearth tax assessments: NNRO Case 7, Shelf k, Papers re Hearth Tax, 1666-96. The average number of hearths per householder in Norwich was very similar to those found elsewhere: in Newcastle, 2·06, Howell, *op. cit.*, p. 9; in Exeter, 2·59, Hoskins, *op. cit.*, p. 115; in York, 3·2, *VCH Yorkshire: The City of York*, p. 163; and in Leicester, 2·4, *VCH Leicestershire*, iv, 159.

21 C. A. F. Meekings, *Dorset Hearth Tax Assessments* (Dorchester, 1951), pp. viii, xi-xii, and L. M. Marshall, 'The levying of the hearth tax, 1662-1688', *English Historical Review*, li (1936), 628-46.

22 William Salt Library, Stafford: Compton Census Returns for the Diocese of Norwich. Twenty-three of the thirty-four parishes give totals of Conformists in multiples of ten. The age of communion is conventionally taken to be sixteen: see Glass and Eversley, *op. cit.*, p. 212, for the age structure of English society in the late seventeenth century.

23 The origins of the 1693 enumeration are obscure and extensive search has failed to recover any contemporary references to its making. It was first published in 1752, with the civic enumeration of this date. Printed copies in *Gentleman's Magazine*, xxii (1752), 437; *Norwich Mercury*, August 22-9, 1752, and Bodl. MS. Gough Maps,

24: 'A Parochial List', s.s. fol. One MS. copy in NNRO Visitation Book, VSM/3.

24   Glass and Eversley, *op. cit.*, pp. 177, 199.

25   British Museum Additional MS 27, 966: Arderon Letters and Tracts, 1745-60 (subsequently Arderon), fols 241-3.

26   Blomefield, *op. cit.*, iii, 410-11; *CSPD 1666-7*, pp. 188, 393-4; *CSPD 1667-8*, p. 124. See also J. Graunt, *Natural and Political Observations on the Bills of Mortality* (ed. C. H. Hull, Cambridge, 1899), p. 365, for a note on under-registration of deaths. The Norwich graveyards were reported as being seriously overcrowded by 1671: E. S. De Beer, ed., *The Diary of John Evelyn* (1959), p. 563. See also J. T. Krause, 'The changing adequacy of English registration, 1690-1837', in Glass and Eversley, *op. cit.*, p. 384.

27   Blomefield, *op. cit.*, iii, 360, reports 3,076 plague deaths in 1603. Allison, *op. cit.*, p. 607, gives a lower figure of 2,682.

28   *CSPD 1665-6*, p. 523. In September 1665, Sir Thomas Browne and his family left the city on the arrival of the plague: S. Wilkin, ed., *Sir Thomas Browne's Works* (1836), i, 111. See also for reactions to the plague, R. H. Hill, ed., *The Correspondence of Thomas Corie* (Norfolk Record Society, xxvii, 1956), p. 20; *CSPD 1665-6*, pp. 223, 472, 497, 498, 523, 530, 551; *CSPD 1666-7*, pp. 53, 101, 119, 141, 161-2, 179, 191; and NNRO Case 16, Shelf b, MCB no. xxiv, 20/6/1666, 9/7/1666, 14/7/1666, 20/7/1666, 15/8/1666, 30/8/1666, 26/10/1666, and 3/11/1666.

29   M. C. Buer, *Health, Wealth and Population in the Early Days of the Industrial Revolution* (re-issue, 1968), p. 181.

30   Hill, *op. cit.*, p. 30; Wilkin, *op. cit.*, i, 321.

31   T. Browne, 'A letter to a friend' in Wilkin, *op. cit.*, iv, 41, 44. For figures relating to child mortality in mid-eighteenth-century Norwich, see Arderon, fol. 245. See also for discussion of infant mortality in towns, M. D. George, *London Life in the Eighteenth Century* (1925), pp. 25-6, 406, 408, and J. D. Chambers, 'Population change in a provincial town: Nottingham 1700-1800' in L. S. Pressnell, ed., *Studies in the Industrial Revolution Presented to T. S. Ashton* (1960), pp. 114-15.

32   Defoe, *op. cit.*, i, 63. The 1851 Census Report gives the area of the city and county of Norwich as 4,325 statute acres.

33   T. Fuller, *The Worthies of England* (ed. J. Freeman, 1952), p. 419. See also De Beer, *op. cit.*, p. 562, for Evelyn's comments on 'the flower gardens, which all the inhabitants excell in'. And see T. Cleer's New Map of the City, 1696, reproduced in W. J. C. Moens, ed., *The Walloon Church of Norwich: its Registers and History* (Huguenot Society of London Publications, i, 1887), frontispiece.

34   Morris, *op. cit.*, p. 149: Celia Fiennes noted that some rich factors owned houses of brick, but thought that otherwise there were very few. By 1718, however, much of the housing stock was built in brick: *A Compleat History of the Famous City of Norwich* (Norwich, 1728), p. 2. At the same time thatched roofs were being replaced by tiles: see NNRO Case 16, Shelf b, MCB no. xxiv, 16/3/1672.

35 Morris, *op. cit.*, p. 147.

36 NNRO Case 19, Shelf b, River and Street Committee Accounts, 1643-1717. Average annual expenditure was £70 15s 2d from 1650 to 1659 and £60 16s 2d from 1690 to 1699.

37 NNRO Case 16, Shelf b, MCB no. xxiii, 18/8/1655, MCB no. xxiv, 14/7/1666, 26/1/1667, MCB no. xxv, 14/12/1687, MCB no. xxvi, 25/8/1703, 17/10/1705. Also see NNRO Case 5, Shelves e-k, Scavengers' presentments, and Hudson and Tingey, *op. cit.*, ii, 388-90, for examples of fines for negligence imposed by the Sheriffs' Tourn of 1676.

38 NCRL, *An Alphabetical Draft of the Poll ... October 1710* (Norwich, *c.*1710) lists 150 country voters, of whom 13 came from Yarmouth. *An Alphabetical Draft of the Poll ... February 1714* (Norwich, 1716) lists 492 country voters, of whom 30 came from Yarmouth and 67 from London.

39 *Norwich Mercury*, 8 and 15 July 1786.

40 For the arrival of the strangers, see Blomefield, *op. cit.*, iii, 418, *CSPD 1683 July-September*, p. 363, and *CSPD 1700-2*, pp. 553-4. For estimates of their numbers: Moens, *op. cit.*, p. 108, says 'very few'; J. James, *History of the Worsted Manufacture in England* (1857), p. 166, says 'many'. R. L. Poole, *A History of the Huguenots of the Dispersion* (1880), p. 90, makes it clear that a colony settled in Norwich, but gives no estimate of their numbers. See also NNRO Case 31, Shelf g, 'Actes du Consestoire de l'Eglise Wallonne de Norwich', which show very little increase of business in the 1680s.

41 For removal orders, see NNRO Case 16, Shelf b, MCB no. xxiv, 11/2/1665, 18/2/1665, and 13/10/1676. For agitation against 'foreign' traders, see *ibid.*, 2/10/1667, 12/1/1676, MCB no. xxv, 13/8/1681, 20/6/1685, and NNRO Case 10, Shelf d, Petition to prohibit non-freemen from trading (n.d. 1690?) with 165 signatures.

42 NNRO Case 15, Shelf c: Orders for Passing Vagrants, 1742-62. For comparison with some sixteenth-century figures, see J. F. Pound, 'An Elizabethan census of the poor', *University of Birmingham Historical Journal*, viii (1962), 139.

43 PRO IR/1/41-9, July 1710-September 1731 (hiatus June 1725-October 1728).

44 N. Riches, *The Agricultural Revolution in Norfolk* (2nd edn, 1967), p. 159, puts the population of Norfolk in 1700 as 210,200, quoting *Annals of Agriculture*, xlii, 267; P. Deane and W. A. Cole, *British Economic Growth, 1688-1959* (1962), p. 103, give a population of 242,511 in 1700, using Rickman's estimates. For population densities, see J. N. L. Baker, 'England in the seventeenth century' in H. C. Darby, *The Historical Geography of England before 1800* (Cambridge, 1951), p. 524.

45 Morris, *op. cit.*, p. 146; Defoe, *op. cit.*, i, 62.

46 It is always difficult to prove that regulations which were partially administered did not exert much influence. For comments on the efficacy of the Act of Settlement, see P. Styles, 'The evolution of the Law of Settlement', *Univ. Birmingham Hist. J.*, ix (1963-4),

33-63. For Company regulations, see NNRO Case 16, Shelf b: Trade Bye-laws, 1543-1714. By the early eighteenth century, at least, the Companies had ceased to exercise formal supervision of the standard of goods produced or on sale: see NNRO Case 16, Shelf b, MCB no. xxvi, 21/6/1703, MCB no. xxix, 19/1/1732. The names of their annually elected officers ceased to be registered in the Mayoral Court Books by the 1720s, with one or two rare exceptions: see MCB nos. xxviii-xxix, *passim*. For the concomitant decline of the apprenticeship system, see P. Millican and W. Rising, *Index of the Indentures of Norwich Apprentices* (Norfolk Record Society, xxix, 1959), pp. xi-xiii. For the freemen, see P. Millican, *The Register of the Freemen of Norwich, 1548-1713* (Norwich, 1934), pp. xi-xx.

47   *Ibid.*, pp. xiv-xv. Admissions to the freedom averaged seventy-five per annum from 1660 to 1699, suggesting a total of approximately 2,500 freemen at any one time.

48   For proclamations on this subject, see NNRO Case 16, Shelf b, MCB no. xxiv, 2/10/1667, MCB no. xxv, 20/6/1685, and Case 16, Shelf c, Assembly Book, 1665-82, 3/5/1675. For attempted legislation, see *ibid.*, 16/3/1677, and Assembly Book no. vii, 24/2/1701. The Corporation was partially successful in 1723, when it obtained an act to qualify textile workers: see Assembly Book no. viii, 7/1/1723 and *Commons' Journals*, xx, 114.

49   Carpets were made from the 'niles' or refuse of the wool used in the worsted manufacture. For a reference to the industry in Norwich, see *Calendar of Treasury Papers, 1731-4*, p. 57.

50   Defoe, *op. cit.*, i, 63.

51   J. F. Pound, 'The Social and Trade Structure of Norwich, 1525-75', *Past and Present* no. 34 (1966), 55-63. See also A. R. Bridbury, *Economic Growth: England in the Later Middle Ages* (1962), p. 49, for figures from fifteen-century Norwich.

52   See B. H. Allen, 'The administrative and social structure of the Norwich merchant class, 1485-1660' (unpublished Ph.D. thesis, Harvard University, 1951), *passim*. See also E. M. Thompson, ed., *Letters of Humphrey Prideaux, sometime Dean of Norwich ... 1674-1722* (Camden Society, new series, xv, 1875), p. 167.

53   NNRO Case 16, Shelf b, MCB no. xxiv, 13/10/1676, and *Norwich Gazette*, vol. xix, no. 287, 1725. See also for movement of labour among textile centres in the eighteenth century, PRO CO/388/21, fols 137-40, and E. Hobsbawm *Labouring Men* (1964), p. 36.

54   See D. C. Coleman, 'An Innovation and its Diffusion: the New Draperies', *Economic History Review*, 2nd ser., xxii (1969), 417-29.

55   *Magna Britannia et Hibernia, Antiqua et Nova* (1721-30), iii, 320, quotes an estimate of 1711 that the annual value of the industry was £100,000, but this seems a suspiciously round figure.

56   PRO CO/388/21, part ii, fols 196,286. Defoe, *op. cit.*, i, 62, quotes a figure of 120,000 employed in the industry, which is clearly derived from these estimates. J. H. Clapham, 'The transference of the worsted industry from Norwich to the West Riding', *Economic Journal*, xx (1910), 196, took Defoe to task for this statement, but Defoe had in fact toned down the estimates given to him.

57 Millican, *op. cit., passim* (my calculation). See also HMC *Portland MSS*, iv, 27. For the same reasons the freemen admissions cannot be taken to be an adequate index to the growth of the city's population.

58 For markets in the early part of the seventeenth century, see C. Wilson, *England's Apprenticeship, 1603-1783* (1965), p. 55, and Allison, *op. cit.*, pp. 542-608. For eighteenth-century markets, see J. K. Edwards, 'The economic development of Norwich, 1750-1850, with special reference to the worsted industry' (unpublished Ph.D. thesis, University of Leeds, 1963), chap. i, *passim*.

59 BM Lansdowne MS. 846, fol. 284 and J. James, *op. cit.*, pp. 172-4.

60 PRO E190/503/18 Yarmouth Port Book, Overseas, Dec. 1684-Dec. 1685: 125,053 lb of worsted stuffs were exported in this year. I am grateful to Anthony Michell of Corpus Christi College, Cambridge, for this information.

61 M. James, *op. cit.*, p. 76. See also J. James, *op. cit.*, pp. 157-9, for legislation of 13 and 14 Charles II, c. 5 (1662).

62 *Ibid.*, p. 170, quoting Sir Josiah Child: 'Formerly gentlewomen esteemed themselves well clothed in a serge gown, which a chambermaid would now be ashamed to be seen in.' See also Wilson, *op cit.*, pp. 185-6, and C. Hill, *Reformation to Industrial Revolution* (1967), p. 137.

63 There are no contemporary descriptions of the processes involved in the production of worsteds. But there was general agreement on their final effect. See Morris, *op. cit.*, p. 149 and HMC *House of Lords MSS 1692-3*, p. 37: it was reported that Norwich stuffs were so light that seals dropped off them. But some white and unfinished stuffs were still produced at this time: see Morris, *op. cit.*, p. 149 and *Commons' Journals*, xii, 74.

64 Millican, *op. cit.*, pp. 55-8 and P. Millican, *The Freemen of Norwich, 1714-52* (Norfolk Record Society, xxiii, 1952), pp. 30-1. For Norwich bewpers, see *CSPD 1664-5*, p. 137.

65 H. Heaton, *The Yorkshire Woollen and Worsted Industries* (2nd edn, Oxford, 1965), pp. 263-9.

66 PRO CO/388/21, part ii, fol. 196; HMC *House of Lords MSS 1696*, pp. 240-3; Wilson, *op. cit.*, pp. 76-7.

67 Morris, *op. cit.*, p. 149; *Magna Britannia, op. cit.*, iii, 320; Fuller, *op. cit.*, pp. 419-20.

68 NNRO Case 33, Shelf e, Norwich Archdeaconry Inventories, Bundle iii, no. 200 (1674), Bundle iv, no. 69 (1692).

69 J. James, *op. cit.*, p. 166.

70 *Ibid.*, pp. 166-7, quoting D. Defoe, *Review*, 30 December 1704.

71 *Ibid.*, pp. 200-1. See also D. C. Coleman, *Courtaulds. An Economic and Social History* (Oxford, 1969), i, 25.

72 BM Various Tracts 816. m. 14 'Reasons humbly offered . . . why the waggoners ought not to be obliged to carry any certain weight' (n.d.).

73 After the civil war, the alnagers made an unsuccessful attempt to impose the alnage on Norwich stuffs: see PRO PC/2/55 fol. 206, Petition against the alnage (1661). The issue revived again under James II. For petitions against the alnage, see *Commons' Journals*, x,

203, 361, and also HMC *House of Lords MSS 1692-3*, pp. 34-42.

74   J. James, *op. cit.*, pp. 169-72. The Corporation had also petitioned Parliament against the proposal to license the import of Flemish textiles: NNRO Case 16, Shelf b, MCB no. xxiv, 29/5/1674.

75   See J. James, *op. cit.*, pp. 167-8, 178-81, *Commons' Journals*, xi, 437, ff., and HMC *House of Lords MSS 1696*, pp. 240-3. Legislation was passed in 1699 by the Act of 11 and 12 William III, c. 10, 'for more effectively employing the poor'.

76   See J. James, *op. cit.*, pp. 216-19, and N. Rothstein, 'The calico campaign of 1719-21', *East London Papers*, vii (1964), 3-21. Also *Commons' Journals*, xix, 168 ff., and PRO CO/388/21-2.

77   *Commons' Journals*, x, 129 ff. The Norwich Committee of Trade was advertising a competition for cotton weaving in 1736: *Gentleman's Magazine*, vi (1736), 169.

78   The Woolcombers had been incorporated and empowered to maintain standards of combed wool in 1686, see NNRO Case 17, Shelf d. This seems to have been the prelude to the contest with the weavers: see *CSPD 1700-2*, pp. 579-80, 'Case of the Woolcombers', 1693; *CSPD 1663-4*, p. 189, 'Reply of the Norfolk and Norwich weavers' (wrongly dated ?1663); and BM Tracts 814. m. 14 (124), 'A Brief Reply to the Weavers' Answer . . .' (wrongly dated ?1718). For the outcome of the debate, see *Commons' Journals*, xi, 95, and E. Lipson, *Economic History of England*, vol. ii: *The Age of Mercantilism* (1931), pp. 48-9.

79   Allison, *op. cit.*, pp. 379-80; Blomefield, *op. cit.*, iii, 399.

80   S. Tsuru, *Essays on Economic Development* (Tokyo, 1968), pp. 76-92.

81   Labour disputes were frequently symptoms of a declining industry. For comments on weavers' earnings, see J. James, *op. cit.*, pp. 168, 191-3. For labour disputes in Exeter, see Hoskins, *op. cit.*, pp. 58-61, and cf. K. H. Burley, 'A Note on a Labour Dispute in Colchester', *Bulletin of the Institute of Historical Research*, xxix (1956), 220-30.

82   Allison, *op. cit.*, pp. 553-4 and Defoe, *op. cit.*, i, 61.

83   For disputes with Yarmouth, see Blomefield, *op. cit.*, iii, 412, and *Commons' Journals*, xv, 99 ff.

84   PRO CO/388/21, part ii, fol. 286.

85   See NNRO Case 16, Shelf b, MCB no. xxiv, 10/10/1667, 12/1/1676, 30/8/1676; HMC *House of Lords MSS 1692-3*, p. 37; Thompson, *op. cit.*, pp. 175-6, 181, 193; and M-H. Li, 'The great recoinage in England, 1696-9' (unpublished Ph.D. thesis, University of London, 1940), pp. 206-57.

86   See W. G. East, 'England in the eighteenth century', in Darby, *op. cit.*, p. 498 and R. H. Mason, *History of Norfolk* (1884), p. 433. See also Pound, *op. cit.*, pp. 49-69, for comparison with sixteenth-century Norwich.

87   NNRO Case 16, Shelf b, MCB no. xxv, 13/8/1681 and R. H. Hill, *op. cit.*, pp. 37-8.

88   PRO IR/1/41-9, *passim*.

89   See Thompson, *op. cit.*, p. 120; *CSPD 1680-1*, pp. 631-2; and

Wilkin, *op. cit.*, i, 323. Arderon, fols 232-3, lists 176 alehouses and taverns in the mid-eighteenth century.

90 D. Davis, *A History of Shopping* (1966), p. 144.

91 HMC *Portland MSS*, ii, 269.

92 Morris, *op. cit.*, pp. 147-8; P. Browne, *The History of Norwich* (Norwich, 1814), p. 174. For regulations governing the hours of sale in the market, see NNRO Case 16, Shelf b, MCB no. xxv, 8/8/1685.

93 J. Kirkpatrick, *The Streets and Lanes of the City of Norwich* (Norwich, 1889), p. 45.

94 Arderon, fols 228-9, 235. See also Davis, *op. cit.*, p. 45.

95 NNRO Case 16, Shelf b, MCB no. xxiv, 31/1/1667.

96 Celia Fiennes (Morris, *op. cit.*, p. 148) noted the 'vaste concourse' of people at the fairs. See also Browne, *op. cit.*, pp. 244-5, and Hudson and Tingey, *op. cit.*, ii, cxxxv-cxli.

97 Defoe, *op. cit.*, i, 64-5, considered that approximately 40,000 cattle passed this way yearly. See also Riches, *op. cit.*, pp. 30-1.

98 Blomefield, *op. cit.*, iii, 399, 427, 431.

99 J. Crofts, *Packhorse, Waggon and Post* (1967), pp. 109 ff.

100 See F. J. Fisher, 'The development of London as a centre of conspicuous consumption', *Trans. Roy. Hist. Soc.*, 4th ser., xxx (1948), 37-50. See also G. Etheredge, *The Man of Mode, or Sir Fopling Flutter. A Comedy* (1676), p. 88.

101 See V. Waite, *The Bristol Hotwell* (Local History Pamphlet, no. 1, Bristol, 1960), pp. 3-15.

102 See HMC *Portland MSS*, ii, 270, and De Beer, *op. cit.*, pp. 562-3.

103 See L. G. Bolingbroke, 'St John Maddermarket, Norwich', *Norfolk Archaeology*, xx (1921), 221, and E. A. Kent, 'The houses of the Duke of Norfolk in Norwich', *Norfolk Archaeology*, xxiv (1932), 81-7.

104 'Journal of Edward Browne', in Wilkin, *op. cit.*, i, 44, and Thompson, *op. cit.*, p. 184.

105 Morris, *op. cit.*, p. 149. R. Beatniffe, *Norfolk Tour* (5th edn, Norwich, 1795), pp. 89-90, describes the Guild Day Feast provided by the St George's Company.

106 R. W. Ketton-Cremer, 'Assize week in Norwich, 1688', *Norfolk Archaeology*, xxiv (1932), 15.

107 See B. Cozens-Hardy, ed., *Norfolk Lieutenancy Journal, 1676-1701* (Norfolk Record Society, xxx, 1961), *passim*. The Commission met three or four times a year, and more frequently in times of emergency. For the visit of the King in 1671, see R. H. Hill, *op. cit.*, pp. 32-6.

108 B. Cozens-Hardy, 'The Norwich Chapel-Field House Estate since 1545', *Norfolk Archaeology*, xxvii (1941), 377-8.

109 Wilkin, *op. cit.*, i, 241, 306.

110 *Norwich Gazette*, 5 August 1710.

111 See R. W. Ketton-Cremer, 'Camping, a forgotten Norfolk game', *Norfolk Archaeology*, xxiv (1932), 88-92; Arderon, fols 241-3; and Wilkin, *op. cit.*, i, 49, 322.

112 Blomefield, *op. cit.*, iii, 409. The Corporation's powers were superseded by those of the Royal Fishing Company from 1665 to

1670: *CSPD 1664-5*, pp. 139, 438; *CSPD 1668-9*, p. 627; and *CSPD 1670*, pp. 39, 71. For shows licensed by the Corporation, see NNRO Case 16, Shelf b, MCB no. xxiv, 5/3/1665, and MCB no. xxv, 1/12/1677, 5/10/1678.

113   W. Honeycomb (pseud.), *The History of Pudica, a Lady of Norfolk* (1754), pp. 21-2;

114   NNRO Case 16, Shelf b, MCB no. xxiv, 1/2/1668, and *CSPD 1681, July-September*, pp. 631-2. For reference to the Lynn prostitutes, see V. H. H. Green, *The Universities* (1969), p. 298.

115   For city doctors, see Wilkin, *op. cit.*, i, 371-3, and R. W. Ketton-Cremer, *Felbrigg, the Story of a House* (1962), pp. 44-6. For doctors employed by the Corporation, see NNRO Case 16, Shelf b, MCB no. xxiv, 24/4/1667, and MCB no. xxv, 14/12/1678.

116   For professional services available in the city, see *Norwich Gazette, passim*. For teachers in the city, see also H. W. Saunders, *History of Norwich Grammar School* (Norwich, 1932), chap. vii, *passim*. For the first printer in the city, see Blomefield, *op. cit.*, iii, 427. For the City Waits, see NNRO Case 16, Shelf b, MCB no. xxv, 2/10/1678, 18/8/1683 and 17/11/1683.

117   W. Rye, ed., *Calendar of Correspondence and Documents relating to the Family of Oliver Le Neve, 1675-1743* (Norwich, 1895), pp. 30-1, 39-40, 104-5, 162. For carriers as money lenders, see C 5/558/58 Southgate v. Crome, 1683.

118   PRO WO/30/48. Bristol led the list both for beds and for stabling.

119   For comments on the poor standard of ministers, see Thompson, *op. cit.*, pp. 148-9, 151, 160-1. For the proposed rate to finance ministers, see Blomefield, *op. cit.*, iii, 317, and C. Hill, *Economic Problems of the Church* (Oxford, 1956), p. 288.

120   See P. Goubert, *Beauvais et le Beauvaisis de 1600 à 1730* (Paris, 1960), pp. 233-41, and O. H. Hufton, *Bayeux in the Late Eighteenth Century* (Oxford, 1967), pp. 20-40, 89-91, 100-2.

121   NCRL J. Collinges, *The Weaver's Pocket-book, or Weaving Spiritualised* (1675), *passim*.

122   See G. Sjoberg, *The Pre-Industrial City: past and present* (Chicago, 1960), pp. 87-91; and for a critique of Sjoberg, O. C. Cox, 'The pre-industrial city reconsidered' in P. Meadows and E. H. Mizruchi, *Urbanism, Urbanisation and Change: comparative perspectives* (Reading, Mass., 1969), pp. 19-28.

123   HMC *House of Lords MSS 1696*, pp. 240-3.

124   See Hoskins, *op. cit.*, *passim* and Defoe, *op. cit.*, i, 222.

125   For discussion of the decline of the Norwich textile industry, see Clapham, *op. cit.*, pp. 195-210; M. F. Lloyd Pritchard, 'The Decline of Norwich', *Ec.H.R.*, 2nd ser., iii (1951), 371-7; D. C. Coleman, 'Growth and Decay during the Industrial Revolution: the Case of East Anglia', *Scandinavian Ec.H.R.*, x (1962), 115-27; and J. K. Edwards, 'The decline of the Norwich textiles industry', *Yorkshire Bulletin of Economic and Social Research*, xxvi (1964), 31-41.

126   Bodl. Gough Norfolk. 59: 'The Cabinet of Curiosities' (n.d.).

12 The evolution of Leeds

W. G. Rimmer

The regional predominance of Leeds in the West Riding could be explained simply as the outcome of nineteenth-century developments. Industrialisation proceeded at a much faster pace in the Aire valley than elsewhere in the clothing districts. In 1801 there had been two people in the neighbouring Calder valley to the south for every one in the Aire valley [1]. But by 1901, both valleys had populations of about the same size. Not only had the Aire valley caught up with the Calder during the nineteenth century in respect of its total population, but in the process it became more urbanised. Leeds had 428,000 inhabitants in 1901; ten miles farther up the valley, Bradford, a worsted centre, had 280,000 — a population equal to that of the four largest towns in the Calder valley added together.

Yet even in 1801 Leeds, with over 30,000 inhabitants, had four times as many people as any other town in the clothing district. By any measure — population, wealth, markets, as a social centre, or as the hub of the region's transport network — Leeds was at that time already acknowledged as the capital town of the clothing region. John Marshall, the millionaire flax-spinner, went even further, claiming that 'Leeds ... may justly be considered the capital of the North-eastern part of England' [2]. When, during the eighteenth century, the English textile industry began to concentrate in the West Riding, Leeds had become one of Britain's boom towns and its population increased fivefold.

Before the introduction of steam-driven machinery, woollen cloth was made entirely by cottagers in the rural villages of the region. Every week they collected wool from a nearby market-centre and then returned to sell their cloth. Since the Calder valley had a much larger population than the Aire valley we might reasonably expect to find the principal urban centre of the clothing district located in the Calder valley, and until the seventeenth century this was in fact the case. For a long time, Wakefield, lying at the mouth of the Calder valley, had been the main town in the Riding. The rise of Leeds to regional predominance in the seventeenth and eighteenth centuries thus coincided with the decline of Wakefield. And since this displacement took place *before* the 'Industrial Revolution' which began to shape urban growth in the region only at the close of the eighteenth century, and since the development of neither

W. G. Rimmer, 'The evolution of Leeds to 1700', *Thoresby Society Transactions*, **50**, 1967, pp. 91-2, 107-29.

town owed much to its ecclesiastical, military or governmental functions, this change in the relative positions of Leeds and Wakefield has to be explained primarily in terms of the changing mercantile activities of these neighbouring towns . . . .

[*Sections I-III on the medieval clothing industry omitted.*]

IV

In the fourteenth century, the Pennine valleys were less developed than the Vale of York. Only 7 per cent of the fairs granted in Yorkshire during the peak period of such grants between 1220 and 1350 were in the Aire and Calder valleys [3]. In 1394-96, 87 per cent of the Yorkshire cloth stamped by the Aulnager for sale was made on the plain. Because they were faked, these returns are unreliable and have to be treated as 'works of art rather than transcripts of fact' [4]. So the only available details relating to cloth production cannot be utilised to show the progress of the industry. However, they may perhaps be taken as a *rough* guide to the regional distribution of the industry at two points in time. They then show that only 13 per cent of the Yorkshire cloth stamped in 1394-96 was made in the villages of the West Riding, a figure *excluding* kerseys which escaped duty at this time. Two generations later, in 1468, 54 per cent of the stamped Yorkshire cloth was made in the valleys, and in 1473-75 57 per cent — two-thirds of which came from the Aire and Calder valleys and one-third from the Ripon district.

From this evidence, it appears that whatever happened to the level of total output, country clothmakers in the West Riding began making a larger proportion of total output than those in the towns of the Vale. In this sense — and only in this sense — the industry was shifting from town to countryside in the fifteenth century. A familiar explanation of this change is the decline of the urban industry owing to war, civic faction, and the 'extreme exclusiveness, excessive regulation and heavy taxation' of the gilds [5]. On the rural side, two factors probably played a part. In the first place, rural skills must have improved steadily to the point where valley products could compete with those of the town on the basis of quality. Rural specialisation has already been discussed, as much as the evidence allows. That it was a response to specific local conditions is illustrated by the preamble to the Halifax Act of 1555:

> . . . the parish of Halifax . . . being planted in the great waste and the moors where the fertility of the ground is not apt to bring forth any corn nor good grass, but in rare places and by exceeding industry . . . the inhabitants altogether do live by clothmaking, and the great part of them neither getteth corn nor . . . keep a horse to carry wool, nor yet to buy much wool at once, but hath ever used only to repair to the town of Halifax . . . there to buy upon the wool driver some a stone and to carry the same to their houses, some three, four, five and six miles off, upon their heads and backs and so to make . . . into yarn or cloth. By means of which industry the barren ground in

these parts be now much inhabited and above five hundred
households there newly increased within these forty years past [6].

Secondly, the decline in exports of wool after the mid-fourteenth century
would benefit rural clothiers by decentralising internal wool sales.
Precisely how the abbeys reacted to restrictions on wool exports is not
known. They could have reduced the supply from their own flocks,
stopped buying from lay farmers, or rented their granges. Whatever their
response, provided the total supply of wool remained fairly constant, the
quantity available for home production would be much more than it had
formerly been. Furthermore, much less wool was probably sold by the
abbeys. Unfortunately there has not yet been a study of the internal wool
trade in England before the sixteenth century [7]. In the fourteenth
century the abbeys perhaps started selling wool to English middlemen who
would seek to supply more native producers. Both town and countryside
were likely to be well supplied with wool. But the latter would gain
relatively in so far as it was in the interests of woolstaplers to ignore the
limitations on cloth production characteristic of the towns. Much later in
1552, when an Act permitted only cloth manufacturers to buy wool,
Halifax clothiers secured exemption from it by stressing their need for
dealers. Wool drivers were important not merely because Halifax clothiers
operated on a hand-to-mouth basis, but also because they wanted fine
wool from Lincolnshire, a journey which no clothier could contemplate.
The traffic in wools that developed in the sixteenth century indicates a
fairly advanced specialisation both of dealer and district.

How did the expansion or rural clothmaking affect the development
of the Aire and Calder valleys? Initially the Calder valley industry grew
considerably. It had four times as many fullers reckoned by their surnames
as the Aire valley in 1379. Further, from a comparison of the lay subsidy
and poll tax returns for Aggbrigg Wapentake, it is clear that in the
fourteenth century the lower part of the Calder valley developed faster
than the upper region. Walker asserts that 'at the beginning of the fifteenth
century [Wakefield] was the most important centre for the manufacture
of cloth in the West Riding' [8]. And there is ample evidence of the
town's subsequent growth: the extension of the parish church, the
construction of large mansions such as Haselden Hall, the royal grant in
1509 of free trade throughout the kingdom. But the lower part of the
Calder valley was not the only rural district to benefit from the growth of
clothmaking at this time. It has been suggested by Heaton that the upper
reaches of this valley and the lower part of the Aire valley developed even
more rapidly in the late fifteenth century. Both Halifax and Leeds emerge
from obscurity about this time. Leeds began to come to life in the
fourteenth century when Kirkstall's Cistercians contributed to the
economic life of the town. The higher quality wool hitherto collected for
exports was perhaps sold locally. This would stimulate rural clothmaking
in the lower Aire valley, especially in the parish of Leeds. There the parish
church was rebuilt in the early fourteenth century and at the time of the
1379 poll tax, Leeds ranked second as the most populous and highest
assessed town in the Aire and Calder valleys. This quiet, unobtrusive
development continued throughout the fifteenth century. The abbey

found it worth while to accumulate property in the nearby town; a stone bridge was built across the Aire, and the parish church was again enlarged. Henceforth Leeds grew as the central township in a clothmaking parish, a parish which had seven fulling mills in 1547 [9].

V

When Leland passed through these valleys in the 1530s, Wakefield was undoubtedly the principal town of the clothing district. A century later it was slipping into second place behind Leeds.

The Aire valley developed rapidly in the later sixteenth century. Between the accession of Elizabeth I and the death of James I, the number of annual baptisms in upper Airedale parishes increased several times, and the population of Leeds doubled. There were schemes to promote clothmaking as far west as Skipton; and in 1638 a witness claimed that 'in the town of Shipley, and places adjoyning there are now about an hundred clothiers for one that was in these Townes' a generation before [10]. These changes made Leeds an important mercantile centre. For two hundred years Leeds had been raising itself above the other villages around. The dissolution of Kirkstall Abbey in 1540 accelerated its growth. For the brisk trade in real estate which followed the dissolution brought many newcomers to the valley. Simultaneously Leeds secured its first toll-free trading privileges. A grammar school was built in 1552 and a Moot Hall in 1561. Leeds was thus a growing town by the mid-sixteenth century. But only after an outburst of expansion between 1580 and 1630 did Leeds surpass Wakefield in size and prosperity. In the hearth tax returns made at the Restoration, Leeds had three times as many houses as Wakefield; and Wakefield ranked as the second largest town of the district, though not much larger than Halifax at the western end of the Calder valley. And this ranking is the same as that in the first Census of 1801. Although seventeenth-century Wakefield was still 'a large market for kerseys and wool', and although 'its prestige and importance increased during the [seventeenth] century ... its industrial and economic expansion was not so rapid as that of some of its neighbours' [11].

Why did Leeds become the principal trading town of the clothing district? How is the relative decline of Wakefield to be explained?

Urban growth in the clothing district was nourished by several roots. First, as regards the cloth trade, rural clothiers wanted markets where they could buy wool. This became particularly important by the end of the sixteenth century. Not only did West Riding weavers use the whole local supply of wool, but they took all the coarse wool produced in the four northern counties, and some high-grade fibres from the Midlands and Lincolnshire. Secondly, unless the clothier worked on a commission basis or as an employee for a merchant-manufacturer, he wanted a market in which to sell his cloth. Finally, the cloth had to be finished — cropped and perhaps dyed. These processes were best undertaken centrally, close by the cloth market so that they could be directed by the merchants who knew what different customers wanted. Clothmaking was thus a joint venture, involving clothier, merchant and finisher. In 1588, fifteen persons took a week to make one short broadcloth of the kind made around Leeds and Wakefield. This suggests one important cause of urban growth. In 1579 when the output of the district was '30 packes of brode cloths ever weecke, and ev'y packe is 4 whole clothes', over 700 town workers were needed to grade wool and finish cloth [12]. And as output increased more would be needed. There is a second cause of town growth. Over the centuries many travellers commented on the inability of the clothing district to meet its own food requirements. 'The whole country from Leeds westward into Lancashire, does not produce grain or feed cattle sufficient to supply one-fifth of the inhabitants' [13]. These things had to be imported into the region, and sold to townsfolk and clothiers. This, too, resulted in markets and shops, again promoting urban growth.

Any conveniently situated town or group of towns could discharge these functions. Markets for distributing wool grew up at Halifax and Leeds as well as at Wakefield. Likewise all such towns had regular cloth markets. On the other hand, only certain cloths needed dyeing; and with the development of intraregional specialisation in different types of cloth, the market towns dealing in cloths requiring more finishing and dyeing grew faster. Furthermore, towns near the plain were better placed to buy cattle and grain for the region. In theory, and indeed in practice, there was considerable diversification in the discharge of these urban functions as the trade of the district increased. Wakefield's quasi-monopoly of these activities, acquired at a time when the valleys were much less developed, and when settlement was concentrated in the lower Calder valley, could not be expected to persist for ever. Other centres would arise to perform some of these functions in those parishes where the cloth industry expanded. To some extent therefore the relative decline of Wakefield simply reflects the subsequent expansion of clothmaking in other parts of the valleys. This in turn was governed by the availability of land and the advance of settlement. However, the decline of Wakefield has usually been attributed entirely to the misguided mercantile policy of its inhabitants. Therefore it is necessary to consider the validity of this view as it is expressed in some recent writings.

J. W. Walker maintained that Wakefield's relative decline begins early in the fifteenth century.

> As time went on the other towns of the West Riding . . . forged ahead, the cause of [Wakefield's] decline being due to a rigid protection by the merchants, who tried to keep the trade in their own hands, and, as we have seen in the case of provisions, imposed onerous tolls or duties on outside merchants. These prohibition rules had the effect of driving away both population and prosperity. The tyranny of the merchants drove commerce and industry to rural districts and to smaller 'free trade' towns, where the natural expansion was not hampered by ancient privileges; thus came about the decay of once powerful boroughs in the fifteenth and sixteenth centuries, and there can be no doubt that the gild merchant and his trade restrictions was one of the most potent factors which led to this revolution [14].

This argument rests on weak foundations. In the first place, to date the decline of the town, Walker draws heavily on the Aulnagers' returns as analysed by Heaton. But such evidence would not now be regarded as reliable for this purpose. Furthermore, whereas Heaton cited supplementary evidence to confirm the decline of the ancient cloth towns, Walker is content to argue the case of Wakefield by analogy. He assumes that Wakefield can be put in the same category as York and Beverley, and then infers that the decline of Wakefield can be attributed to the same causes. Such a method is very questionable.

The point about the rural industry centred on Wakefield was its different development. The town did not trail behind York and Beverley on the same path; it took a different course. Whereas the production and marketing of cloth took place mainly *within* York, the spinners and weavers of the Calder lived in rural hamlets and homesteads. Indeed, the argument that steep tolls repelled traders from Wakefield, thereby sending them to nearby small free-trade towns, is bereft of meaning *unless* most of the cloth sold at Wakefield was made in outlying villages. When Leland visited the Riding in 1538, he considered Wakefield to be twice as large as Leeds or Bradford [15]. Although this does not rule out the possibility that Leeds, Bradford and perhaps Halifax had higher growth rates in the fifteenth century simply because they were starting from scratch, it does not provide a compelling reason for dating Wakefield's relative decline from the early fifteenth century. There was no effective challenge to the town's regional hegemony before the reign of Elizabeth I.

Experience shows that any town, or a group of towns, can decline temporarily in size and prosperity and then grow again. This may have been so in the case of Wakefield, York and Beverley in the fifteenth century. But the point at issue in this instance, the loss of regional supremacy, is more specific. As long as Wakefield remained the sole market and finishing centre for the cloth of the Aire and Calder valleys, its size and prosperity would simply reflect the condition of trade in the surrounding rural district. If prosperity ebbed out of the valleys for a time, Wakefield would cease to grow. A revival of trade would show itself in further expansion of the town. But the emergence of rival market centres channelling the flow of goods into and out of the region would bring this sequence to an end. The establishment of other regular markets might sever roots which had hitherto ensured the revival of the town. That something like this happened is confirmed by Wakefield's later experience. When important rival markets appeared, the town shed its former role and became a sedate administrative centre and a wholesale market. Little processing took place in the town which remained outside the main stream of industrialisation in the nineteenth century.

The testing-time and transition came in the late sixteenth and early seventeenth centuries when rival market towns matured and elbowed Wakefield from its paramount position in the valleys. Whilst confirming this timing, Waters in *Wakefield in the Seventeenth Century* still clings to the view that the relative decline of the town at this period was due to trading barriers. His argument has three parts. First, Wakefield grew on the basis of administration and trade. The main reason for its local commercial pre-eminence was the special privileges granted to its inhabitants which placed them in a more favoured position than others in the valleys. But the people of Wakefield failed to enlarge their area of free action to the extent of freeing themselves entirely from seigneurial control and assuming such powers themselves [16]. Secondly, by virtue of his powers, the Lord of the Manor could hinder trade by imposing 'irritating restrictions' and 'market tolls'. 'A very comprehensive system of tolls existed in Wakefield ... on cloth, wool, corn and cattle. ... These tolls, particularly those on cloth and wool, were bitterly resented by the rest of Yorkshire ...' because they were levied 'on all "foreigners" who sold goods in the town' [17]. Thirdly, these taxes on trade drove commerce and therefore the finishing of cloth away from the town. 'Progressive and enterprising industrialists and merchants must have chafed under them [i.e. these restrictions], and looked elsewhere for openings, so that Wakefield did not advance at the rate it should have done in view of its many natural advantages' [18].

This view, like that of Walker, attributes the decline of Wakefield to commercial impositions. But it deserves further scrutiny because it is based on additional evidence. It should be understood that Waters was concerned only incidentally with the problem of Wakefield's decline. Consequently he fails to elaborate his argument. The substance of his case is that Wakefield did not have men of sufficient enterprise to acquire the lord's manorial powers and bring new trade into the town. 'It is probable that the failure of Wakefield to emulate Leeds at this time was due to a lack of similar outstanding men' [19]. Why was this so?

Other towns under manorial administration until the nineteenth century, Manchester for instance, grew very rapidly and produced businessmen of outstanding ability. Of course, Manchester and Wakefield differed in a fundamental respect. No nearby town challenged Manchester's regional position. Lancashire traders had no alternative but to trade in Manchester. But in the case of Wakefield, business shifted to Leeds. Consequently it is necessary to weigh the relative disadvantages of trading in Leeds and Wakefield. The heart of Waters's case is that Wakefield had no outstanding men because the Lord of the Manor suffocated enterprise by imposing onerous tolls; so enterprising men migrated elsewhere. This reasoning raises a question: how onerous were these taxes on trade? Waters appears to lump all taxes together as uniformly harmful in their effects. But this was simply not so. The purpose and incidence of a tax has a bearing on its consequences. The duties levied on strangers at Wakefield, it has been suggested, originated in the opposition of the townsfolk to seigneurial taxes. When the Lord of the Manor tried to impose tolls on their dealings, they agreed instead to assist him to tax strangers living outside the parish who came there to trade. If this is what transpired, the inhabitants of Wakefield were clearly short-sighted. Wool sold at Wakefield had to bear a toll of $4d$ a stone, compared with $\frac{1}{2}d$ at Doncaster: and each pack of cloth had to pay $6d$. But these duties only amounted to a tax of between 2 per cent and 5 per cent on wool and 1 per cent on cloth, perhaps a little more in periods of falling prices such as 1610-25. Tariffs at this level are imposed simply to raise revenue. It is difficult to see how they prohibited trade, especially when consideration is given to the high cost of transporting wool and cloth to an alternative market [20].

In fact, a comparison between the tolls imposed at Leeds and Wakefield reveals only slight differences. The principal tolls at Wakefield 'were farmed out for £50 per annum in 1700': the toll at Leeds was leased in 1676 for ten years at 'the yearely Rent of Eighty pounds' [21]. In both cases, the purpose was to raise revenue, not to stifle trade. Furthermore, Leeds Corporation Minutes, the 1628 Survey of the Manor, and the Aulnage case involving Metcalfe, show that Leeds merchants, who suffered no manorial impositions whatsoever, were as forceful as the bailiff or inhabitants of Wakefield in collecting tolls and rallying against strangers, especially in bad times.

Multiplying such examples leads nowhere. Xenophobia and taxes are meaningful only in the context of their immediate background, and not over long periods of time. Unless sufficient data exist for the construction of time series, this line of enquiry is unlikely to produce fruitful results. However, enough has been said to cast doubt on Waters's argument that Wakefield suffered from the effects of excessive tolls. Indeed, the challenge of Leeds Corporation and other towns to Wakefield's right to levy tolls might be regarded as an indication of just how important this market was in the seventeenth century [22]. Of course, it was also an assertion by traders in the other towns involved of their legal privileges; for although the toll itself was small, the penalties for evasion amounted to the full value of the commodity in question, and this was worth fighting about.

Those who maintain that Wakefield committed economic suicide attribute an unusually high degree of stupidity to the people about whom they write. And there is no evidence that this was the case. Driving trade away would injure the interests of both the Lord of the Manor and the inhabitants. Such behaviour was unlikely to characterise that branch of the Saville family which occupied the office of Chief Steward in the Manor from the late fifteenth century. With roots in the wool and cloth trade of both Lincolnshire and Yorkshire, the Savilles stood to gain from increasing commerce at Wakefield [23]. Furthermore, the town itself had considerable advantages. It was very well situated in the most developed part of the valleys. It was until the 1770s the only town in the district lying on the main route south to London. This was particularly important in the sixteenth century when so much cloth was sent south for sale in Blackwell Hall or at St Bartholomew's Fair. Wakefield, like Kendal, another cloth market on this north-south trading axis, 'served as a . . . collecting centre for . . . manufactured goods from the villages between Wakefield and the Pennines. . . . These goods were sent chiefly to the market at Blackwell Hall, London. One of the chief benefactors of the town, George Saville, was a Blackwell Hall man' [24]. Much of this cloth would be shipped abroad by London merchants, so much so that Wakefield's protest against the payment of ship-money rings true. 'There was not one person inhabiting in Wakefield, or in the precincts thereof . . . that venteth any cloth in the port of Hull' [25]. Of course, in so far as much of the cloth despatched through Wakefield ultimately went overseas, the prosperity of the town was governed by the level of cloth exports. In national terms, reckoning the products of several manufacturing districts, broadcloth exports reached a peak in the first half of the sixteenth century, fell a third in the third quarter, then stabilised during the remainder of the Queen's lifetime [26]. During this period, one producing district might have gained at the expense of another; or commodities like kerseys or new draperies might find more eager buyers overseas. But, at least as a starting point, the slower growth of Wakefield in the later sixteenth century — assuming that it was slower — could have been due to stagnant overseas demand.

In this estimate of the situation, being overtaken by a nearby market town would depend upon the rival discovering a buoyant market, involving perhaps a change in both the cloth produced and also in the ultimate direction of the trade. Without new trade or fabrics, the old pattern of business would persist. Personnel, location, resources, all favoured the hegemony of Wakefield if the position remained unaltered. To displace Wakefield, the challenger would have to embark on a different trade and overtake the established business houses of Wakefield before they realised that an opportunity had been lost.

VI

The growth of Leeds coincides with the revival of Hull as a port [27]. Numerous instances of friction between Leeds and Hull merchants over the conduct of trade occur in early seventeenth-century records. They indicate an increase in the amount of West Riding cloth being shipped through the port. Coarse northern woollens comprised nine-tenths of the value of Hull's exports in the early seventeenth century; and in 1638, three-quarters of the West Riding's kerseys were exported through Hull and other east coast ports. All this suggests a change in the direction of some West Riding trade. Instead of moving along the north-south axis which had hitherto dominated the region's trade, some cloth went in a west-east direction. This shift coincides with three other changes. In the first place, the development of new markets: opportunities presented by the rise of the United Provinces led after 1604 to a post-war boom and an upward trend lasting twenty years in broadcloth exports, the first sustained increase for half a century. Secondly, authorised dealers throughout the trade began to fight a running battle against the activities of outsiders. 'The majority of them [i.e. Hull's merchants] traded as interlopers' despatching goods 'wherever they could find a market' [28]. Consequently, chartered trading companies adversely affected by this traffic in cloth across the North Sea endeavoured to place the commerce of Hull under their control. This produced a confused and fluid situation in the port. To complicate matters, conflict between the Regulated Companies and organised groups of Hull traders were matched by disputes between shippers and inland merchants. Who these Humber merchants were and where they came from requires investigation: many came from York, but only one — a Merchant Adventurer who shipped 10 per cent of the cloth leaving Hull in 1609 — came from Leeds. Leeds merchants generally had to transfer their cloth to a Hull house for shipment. The result was that their prime concern was to prevent any shippers forming a quasi-monopoly and controlling the markets to which goods could be sent. Thus the interests of the Hull trader and the Leeds merchant frequently diverged. Thirdly, the growth of Leeds coincides with the production locally of more dyed cloth. The coarse cloth sent south from Wakefield was mostly white. But much of the cloth sent from Leeds to the United Provinces and the Baltic was coloured. In asking for a charter of incorporation in 1626, Leeds merchants objected chiefly to the deceptive dyeing of cloth by clothiers. They had an interest to safeguard. 'The cloths ... made in the ... town and parish [of Leeds] have been sold and exported before other cloths of the country there, from their fit, good, and true workmanship' [29]. In the same vein, Sir John Saville, who was closely associated with Leeds, protested in the Commons against the Cockayne Scheme which granted to the Eastland Company a monopoly of dyeing prior to exporting cloth to the Baltic. Thus the rapid development of Leeds and the expansion of clothmaking in the Aire valley was associated with a change in the direction and organisation of the trade in Northern Dozens.

Leeds grew substantially in the half century after 1580. The number of annual baptisms recorded in the Parish Register doubled. At its incorporation in 1626 the town had a population of between five and six thousand. The physical size and appearance of the town are described in surveys of 1612 and 1628. Besides the earliest district to be settled around the parish church, the town

> ... hath a large and broad streete — (paved with stone) — leadinge directlie north and continuallie ascendinge. The houses on both sides thereof are verie thicke and close compacted together, beinge ancient meane and lowe built; and generallie all of Tymber; ... only some fewe of the richer sort of the Inhabitants have theire houses more large and capacious, yett all lowe and straightened on their backsides. In the middle of the streete (towards the upper end wheare the Markett place standeth) is built the Court or Moote House [30].

Then, at the top of this main street, New Town was being developed as a residential district for the wealthier burgesses. The grammar school was transferred there in 1624 and, seven years later, St John's Church was built. Around this small urban-core lay enclosed fields, the out-township villages, and the larger farms and estates of the parish, all of which had a population of some 4,000 in the 1620s. In cottages everywhere, spindle and loom made cloth for sale in Briggate; and the merchants of Leeds had it finished in their workshops, one 'dayly setting on worke about forty poor people in theire Trade' [31].

The architects of the town's growth, its merchants, were for the most part newcomers to Leeds. On the evidence of surnames, none of them had descended from prominent Leeds families of the thirteenth and fourteenth centuries. Nor is it the case that from amongst the ordinary clothiers of the sixteenth century, such as Pawson, 'we find the beginnings of the great families which directed social and municipal life in their locality for the next two centuries' [32]. Those who came to the fore in local affairs in the early seventeenth century were merchants and merchant-manufacturers. They prospered, built conspicuous houses such as Wade Hall, North Hall, and the Red Hall, acquired the right to organise many aspects of local life, supported St John's, and organised charities. To take one measure: twenty-four of the twenty-nine families in the 1626 Corporation were either first or second generation newcomers to the district. Their ancestry deserves a thorough investigation. Several descended from yeoman families which had come to the valley in the mid-sixteenth century and settled on what had formerly been Abbey estates. Two of these families — the Wades and Sykes — came from as far apart as Coventry and Carlisle. Their offspring, attracted by the opportunities for trade in Leeds, went there at the end of the sixteenth century, and presumably inherited sufficient resources to set up in business. Others were amongst those freelance wool dealers whose activities were censured and regulated from the mid-sixteenth century. Whatever their background, those associated with the Corporation of 1626 were mainly newcomers. Only three aldermen, all local gentry, present an obvious link with old local families. Even amongst the gentry, newcomers to the valley like the Ingrams and Lowthers soon outnumbered such ancient families as the Calverleys, Leghes and Nevilles. Indeed between *c.* 1550 and *c.* 1750 every local landed estate passed into 'immigrant' hands. However, few gentry meddled in the affairs of Leeds, certainly not before the eighteenth century. So the prosperity of Leeds was brought about mainly by a group of upstart traders, 'young adventurers . . . lately sprung up at Leeds . . . who at little or no charges buy and engross as they please' [33].

This mercantile group sought not merely wealth but also social advancement in the embryonic urban society of Leeds. Both goals could be attained by directing the affairs of the town. To do this, the newcomers endeavoured to acquire the legal right to control local affairs. In this respect, a municipal situation developed in Leeds very different from that at Wakefield. Many privileges were sought after simply to advance new commercial interests. Between 1596 and 1626, Leeds merchants received four charters exempting the town's traders from tolls at Ripon and Boroughbridge, both of which were wool markets, and throughout the Duchy of Lancaster estates. These privileges placed them on an equal footing with Wakefield traders and must have been very welcome to newcomers who operated outside the pale of the regular trading companies. When, in February 1617, Wakefield secured nomination as one of the twenty-three staple towns chosen to put into practice a monopolistic scheme designed to revive the waning fortunes of the Company of Staplers, Leeds merchants promptly protested. As a result, Leeds and two other towns were added to the list of authorised markets in the next year. This removed a threat to the town's trade that would have followed from the restriction of wool sales to Wakefield. It proved a superfluous victory, however. A Bill introduced in 1621 to repeal the laws against middlemen, reached the Statute Book in 1624. And this was simply one facet of a general reaction against privilege, especially the statutory privilege of the metropolitan merchant. Strident local traders in expanding regional economies asserted their right to buy, sell, and organise trade in their districts so as to suit their own interests. In this wave of unrest, Leeds merchants featured more than those of Wakefield who had long been accustomed to old, regulated patterns of trade [34].

The crowning achievement of the Leeds mercantile group, secured after half a century of urban expansion, was a Royal Charter of Incorporation granted in 1626. In this perspective, the Charter appears simply as one of a long series of actions initiated by the town's traders to increase their control over local affairs. At a time when they supported a Commons so intent on sweeping away privileges distributed by the Crown, the same men raised enough money to buy the right to control the economic life of the parish. Under the Charter, Leeds became a free borough governed by a self-perpetuating Corporation. In their corporate capacity, the town's leading businessmen could regulate the borough's markets, make provision for its roads, dispense justice in minor cases, and decide whether to accept the work codes drawn up by the gilds which the borough's craftsmen were instructed to form. Endowed with these powers, they lost no time consolidating their own position. Outsiders were immediately excluded from the town's markets: 'If strangers may have as much libertye and privilidge to buy Rough Cloth as they that are free . . . yt ys need lesse . . . for anie man that hath money to bind himselfe apprentice to the said Trade' [35]. Following this resolution, clashes with outsiders, especially those from York, grew apace. At the same time, when the out-township clothiers protested that the Charter had been secured without their knowledge, the Corporation informed the Privy Council that the plaintiffs were 'men of mean quality' who had displayed 'greate disorder and contempt of government at the first', and 'opposed . . . our orders' [36]. Clearly, the merchants of Leeds wanted to monopolise the local wool and cloth trade. In addition they tried to enforce apprenticeship rules and lay down standards of work. In this way they could perhaps control the quality of work which may have declined as marginal workers were employed to raise output. Alternatively, as Bowden suggests, the well-being of a coarse-cloth centre like Leeds depended not on cutting costs after the depression of the early 1620s because they were fixed, but on improving quality. In either case the acquisition of a charter was in part the outcome of the need to safeguard production standards. Subsequent efforts might also be viewed in the same light. In 1639, the town's merchants wanted a member of Parliament 'to have voice upon any occasions arising touching abuses or other matters of Cloathing. . . . None can be soe apt or able to judge of as those who live amongst theis places of Cloathing, and have . . . experience of their deceipts' [37]. Subsequently, they sought to extend their jurisdiction over rural clothiers outside the parish boundary so that reforms forced upon clothiers in the Parish of Leeds could be applied 'in all parts of ye said Ryding' [38]. When Leeds had a member at Westminster for a short time after 1653, this scheme was pushed with all possible haste. But not until 1662 was a Bill passed setting up a Corporation 'for the better regulating' of broadcloth manufacture in the West Riding [39]. If all these powers were sought to ensure quality-control over a dispersed rural industry, they might also be explained as a desire to extend the town's market monopoly. For until the construction of the Aire and Calder Navigation and the development of an

Atlantic trade at the end of the seventeenth century, the regional supremacy of Leeds was not assured beyond doubt.

Another aspect of the way in which Leeds merchants enlarged their control over local affairs was by the acquisition of the manor's administrative functions. The opening shot in this campaign was fired in 1600 when leading townsmen accused the royal bailiff of misappropriating the revenue of a charitable trust. This evoked a Duchy decree by way of disciplinary action. The outcome was a Royal Commission of Enquiry in 1619 which vested future control of such charities in a 'Pious Uses Committee' consisting of thirteen prominent citizens. Their nominee, together with the bailiff, would jointly collect and share all revenues that had to be divided between the manor and charities. Three years later, John Harrison led the movement to raise £700 in order to purchase the lease of the bailiwick from Sir Arthur Ingram. Then in 1628 Richard Sykes took the initiative in acquiring the Manor of Leeds. This had been mortgaged along with other royal estates to a group of London merchants in 1619, and Charles I now allowed its sale in order to help towards repaying his father's debts. This acquisition was very important. Eighty per cent of the property in Leeds township was subject to manorial dues; and the manor court had as much jurisdiction over the behaviour of the townsfolk as the newly empowered borough court. By purchasing the manor, these powers were transferred to the town's merchants. At first, both the lease of the manor and its reversion were owned privately by individual merchants. But the holdings of these two parts were merged, and between 1655 and 1709, the rights of the manor, though not its revenues and ownership, were conveyed to the Corporation. The administrative functions of the manor — the common oven and tolls — thus passed to the Corporation in the seventeenth century. In future no outside individual would have any voice (as a right) in the affairs of the town. Furthermore, by immediately enfranchising copyhold land in return for a substantial fine — £620 was raised in 1630, and £120 in 1631 — the 'merchants of the manor' converted a large part of Leeds township into freehold property. Only the soke, the monopoly of milling, remained in private hands until 1839. But this right brought only financial gain, not administrative power. For a generation, the town's merchants thus gathered the strands of local power into their hands, not to destroy these vestiges of an old order, but to exploit them for their own purposes. And those merchants who had acquired these powers as individuals invariably transferred the exercise of them to the corporate body. For instance, in 1638, Harrison vested the patronage of St John's in the Corporation and the vicar of Leeds [40].

Among the specific factors accounting for the growth of Leeds are a new channel for trade, upstart traders, and their control over local administration. But the town's regional supremacy was not assured until the end of the seventeenth century. The forces underlying the expansion of Leeds waned in the second quarter of the seventeenth century. Foreigners protected by tariffs produced their own cheap cloth, and the coarser wool used in England lowered the value of her products. Consequently, broadcloth exports declined. The West of England broadcloth producers were very seriously affected by shrinking European demand, and cheap broadcloth manufacturers could no longer count on a buoyant market. The prosperity of the early seventeenth century gradually ebbed out of the Aire valley. Plague, civil war, and the uncertainty of foreign markets added to the tribulations of the local inhabitants. The physical growth and new building which characterised Leeds during the first quarter of the century came to an end. Very little expansion occurred during the next sixty years. The number of annual baptisms for the built-up core of Leeds which had risen to 200 a year by the 1620s, did not surpass this level until the eighteenth century. The fall-off in population growth was of course a national phenomenon. But its incidence was not uniform. Some textile towns, Norwich and Exeter for instance, prospered and continued to increase in numbers. Unfortunately, the clothiers of the Aire valley did not produce worsteds or serges, light woollen cloths which could be sold in the warmer climes of southern Europe. The West Riding's prosperity was for long under a cloud and, like others similarly placed, its businessmen looked to the government in the later seventeenth century for measures that would bring general relief [41]. Meanwhile, locally, merchants and clothiers tried to keep the remaining trade for themselves. In the 1620s, the Steward of Wakefield reserved the reduced amount of work available there for those living in the town and parish, thereby forcing outsiders to sell their cloth elsewhere. In 1662, when 'all or most of the trades within this Borough [of Leeds] are much decreased and the poore thereof much increased occasioned by the . . . setting on worke Forreners and strangers', the Corporation decreed that work be restricted to gild members and apprentices who were natives of the town [42]. Protective policies, dictated by the stagnant trading situation, lasted until the 1690s. Then the tide turned. The reopening of old markets and the development of new ones brought a flood of prosperity, resulting in a great expansion of Leeds and the Aire valley during the eighteenth century.

VII

During the seventeenth century, Wakefield's merchants might have found a good deal of satisfaction in the trading predicament of Leeds had they not been in much the same position themselves. After the mid-sixteenth century, Leeds merchants had drawn upon an increasing proportion of the region's resources, thereby preventing Wakefield from growing as rapidly as it might otherwise have done. The London trade in which the town was involved did not yield the same opportunities as the more irregular markets seized by Leeds. In the 1620s, however, when broadcloth exports declined, Leeds and Wakefield traders were hit alike. And this long-drawn-out recession deprived Wakefield of any real chance to catch up with Leeds. That she failed to do so was not for lack of effort. Wakefield, not Leeds, secured the privilege of being a staple town in 1616. 'During the reign of James I, the men of the clothing towns formed a project to make the river Calder navigable, from the sea to Wakefield' [43]. Two Bills, one in 1621 and the other in 1626, were laid before Parliament to make the

Aire and Calder navigable. But York and other northern towns successfully opposed their enactment. Nor would Thomas Saville, the manorial steward, promote the project again when asked to do so in 1627. Permission for a navigation was not secured until 1699. This gave both Leeds and Wakefield a decisive advantage over other towns in the clothing district; but by that time, the supremacy of Leeds was ensured. For during the seventeenth century the promise of a revival at Wakefield, still an important though surely not 'the greatest markett ... of Clothiers, Drapers and other traffickers for cloath in these parts', came to naught [44]. Part of the town's trade was in kersey cloths made in the Calder valley. These fabrics escaped Continental tariffs in the 1620s. But in the 1660s Colbert taxed them, virtually excluding kerseys from the French market. Then towards the end of the century, Wakefield began making bays, and later worsteds, which as 'new draperies' had brought prosperity to Norwich. In particular, the town specialised in tammies, 'a thin worsted fabric, a glazed variety of which was used for window-blinds and curtains ... both at home and abroad' [45]. In 1710, Wakefield opened a cloth hall, 'with design to engross the woollen trade' of the West Riding at the expense of Leeds. But this venture did not bring the town to the fore again. Wakefield remained a cloth market and finishing centre throughout the eighteenth century; 'a town exceedingly populous, upon account of the great number of hands it employs in the woollen manufacture' [46]. But it failed to draw abreast of Leeds or even to keep pace with the growth of the town in the Aire valley.

Wakefield's inability to regain her former position in the valleys was due to several factors. First, despite efforts to recapture the cloth trade, the town could never regain its role as the unrivalled market of the district. Clothiers further west in the Calder and those in the Aire valley repaired to markets at Halifax and Leeds. And after the 1740s, successive westward extensions of the Calder Navigation and the construction of turnpikes encouraged the development of marketing at Huddersfield and Halifax. Secondly, Wakefield could not hope to gain her former position by making 'new draperies'. Norwich and other East Anglian centres were much better worsted producers. This trade did not take deep root in the West Riding until late in the eighteenth century. Thus the proportion of those concerned with trading and finishing cloth in Wakefield declined as the eighteenth century progressed. Only three merchant dynasties survived into the nineteenth century, and none hastened to introduce mill-production in the town. 'The aristocracy of Wakefield, who had already made their fortunes ... refused to permit mills or factories to be established there. ... This sent the manufacturers to Leeds or Bradford' [47].

The relative decline of Wakefield had occurred much earlier than the Rev. E. C. Camidge supposed. It cannot be attributed to the fact that early nineteenth-century manufacturers 'removed from the town, and left poor Wakefield without its aristocracy, and without the manufacturing wealth and importance which otherwise would have remained here' [48]. The town's economy had been gradually changing throughout the eighteenth century, assuming a new pattern which lasted until the 1870s. Shortly after the mid-eighteenth century, the cloth hall was closed. The Tammy

Hall, opened in 1778, languished within a generation. Instead of dealing in cloth, Wakefield became a raw material market and an administrative centre. The West Riding Registry of Deeds was located there in 1704, and the annual hirings of the Aggbrigg and Morley Wapentakes took place in the town. Since then Wakefield has been the seat of local government for the unincorporated parts of the West Riding. It was, in addition, a major raw materials market. Regular cattle, corn and leather markets were started in the seventeenth century which replaced the local fairs hitherto held in the district. With the opening of the navigation, the town became a funnel through which passed much of the raw material and food produced in eastern England for consumption in the expanding industrial areas of south Lancashire and the West Riding, especially the populous Calder valley. The most conspicuous buildings erected in the town during the eighteenth century were grain warehouses and a Corn Exchange. Whilst Leeds merchants invested in an expanding cloth trade, the accumulated resources of Wakefield went into buying wool, cattle and corn. In 1800 the town had fifty woolstaplers; in 1837, it had more corn merchants and insurance offices than Leeds, almost as many maltsters, and at least twice as many attorneys and banks per head of the population. The presence of so many factors and professional men, together with the absence of much in the way of industrial processing, made Wakefield 'an opulent and handsome town' [49]. Its imperceptible growth, the substantial houses and squares of its north-western suburbs, its quietness and the lack of a growing proletariat, gave Wakefield a 'genteel' atmosphere.

The first challenge to Wakefield's new market role came at the end of the eighteenth century. The Leeds and Liverpool canal, opened as far as Skipton in the 1770s, enabled grain to be shipped west along the Aire valley. Then in the 1820s, Leeds and Manchester, both at the hub of new smoky factory districts, began to reorganise their produce markets to meet the needs of growing populations. Between 1823 and 1828 nearly £90,000 was spent on five new market halls in Leeds. To the detriment of Wakefield's trade, factors started extensive dealings in corn, cattle and hides. The next blow fell in the mid-century when Wakefield lost her function as a wool market. Less than a score of woolstaplers remained in the town at the time of the Great Exhibition. Half the wool used in British mills came from abroad. Most of it was carried to London for auctioning and then moved by rail or water to a factory warehouse in the industrial districts. Besides, with the shift to factory production and a new pattern of local specialities in fabrics, each district of the clothing area had its own special raw material requirements. On both counts, Wakefield's woollen markets became less important.

Finally, in the 1870s grain was imported from North America to meet the needs of the northern industrial regions. These imports were unloaded at Liverpool and then distributed throughout the north. By reversing the earlier flow of grain from east to west across the north, the remaining exchange function of Wakefield was radically undermined. It is not surprising that the average yearly increase in population for the forty years before World War I was half what it had been in the previous seventy years [50].

Notes

1   *The Census of Great Britain*, 1801, 1901.

2   *Leeds Mercury*, 14 January 1826. *See also* W. Cobbett, *Rural Rides* (Everyman edn, 1924), ii, 216, 'for the *capital* it is in fact, though not in name'.

3   K. L. McCutcheon, 'Yorkshire Fairs and Markets', *Thoresby Society Publications*, xxxix (1940), 161-71.

4   E. M. Carus-Wilson, *Medieval Merchant Venturers* (1954), 291; H. Heaton, *The Yorkshire Woollen and Worsted Industries* (1920), 69-76.

5   Heaton, *op. cit.*, 52; *see also* 50-3; Carus-Wilson, *op. cit.*, 207-9.

6   E. Lipson, *Economic History of England* (1937), i, 504. *See also* J. Watson, *The History of the Parish of Halifax* (1775), 1-9.

7   For a later period, see P. J. Bowden, 'The internal wool trade in England during the sixteenth and seventeenth centuries', University of Leeds, Ph.D. thesis, 1955. *See also* D. Knowles, *The Religious Orders in England* (1948), i, 64-9; and Bowden, *op. cit.*, 91-3.

8   J. W. Walker, *Wakefield, its History and People* (1939), ii, 388. *See also* J. W. Walker, *Wakefield Town Life in the Fifteenth and Sixteenth Centuries* (1924), 1-10.

9   Heaton, *op. cit.*, 76-9; W. T. Lancaster, 'Possessions of Kirkstall Abbey in Leeds', and 'Adel', *Thoresby Society Publications*, iv (1895), 37-41, 271; J. Stansfield, 'Rent roll of Kirkstall Abbey', *Thoresby Society Publications*, ii (1889), 4, 13; P. H. Booth, *History of Gildersome and the Booth Family* (1920), 31.

10   Heaton, *op. cit.*, 197. *See also* 220; and M. Slack, 'Economic aspects of the Upper Wharfe and Airedale', University of Leeds M.A. thesis (1954), 25, 112.

11   S. H. Waters, *Wakefield in the Seventeenth Century* (1933), 119; *Thoresby Society Publications*, ii (1891), 180-204; iv (1895), 17-36; *The Hearth Tax, Lady Day, 1666* (for Leeds south of the River Aire), PRO [Public Record Office], E. 179/210/394 A, copy in the Leeds Reference Library.

12   Heaton, *op. cit.*, 79; *see also* 118, 108-9.

13   J. Aikin, *A description of the country from thirty to forty miles around Manchester* (1795), 574. *See also* J. Watson, *The History of the Parish of Halifax* (1775), 8.

14   Walker, *Wakefield*, ii, 388-9

15   Waters, *op. cit.*, p. xiv.

16   *Ibid.*, 7-8.

17   *Ibid.*, 134-5, 125.

18   *Ibid.*, 137.

19   *Ibid.*, 125.

20   For the rates cited in this paragraph, see Heaton, *op. cit.*, 145, 197, 205; Waters, *op. cit.*, 135; Bowden, *op. cit.*, 152; McCutcheon, *op. cit.*, 108; E. Charlesworth, 'A local example of factors influencing industrial location', *Geographical Journal* (1938), 347-50. Miss Charlesworth also ascribes the decline of Wakefield's textile industry to onerous tolls due to gild organisation, and shows that as a result

the district to the north-west of Wakefield continued to produce textiles but for the Leeds market, whereas the district to the south-east became agricultural.

21   'The Court Books of the Leeds Corporation', *Thoresby Society Publications*, xxxiv (1936), 54; Waters, *op. cit.*, 135; Heaton, *op. cit.*, 198-203.

22   'The Court Books of the Leeds Corporation', 52, 67; Waters, *op. cit.*, 136; Heaton, *op. cit.*, 365.

23   Walker, *Wakefield*, ii, 580-3, 647-8; Waters, *op. cit.*, 9.

24   Waters, *op. cit.*, 121; *see also* 122; Walker, *Wakefield*, ii, 390, 395-6; Heaton, *op. cit.*, 146 ff.; McCutcheon, *op. cit.*, 134-6.

25   *CSPD Charles I*, (1858), April 1627; Waters, *op. cit.*, 51-2. *See also* E. Simpson, 'The wool industry in Wakefield during the seventeenth and eighteenth centuries', University of Leeds, B.A. thesis, 1938.

26   Bowden, *op. cit.*, 80.

27   W. J. Davies, 'A description of the trade and shipping of Hull during the seventeenth century', University College of South Wales, M.A. thesis (1937), *passim*; Heaton, *op. cit.*, 150-1; Bowden, *op. cit.*, 80; A. Fries, *Alderman Cockayne's Project* (1927), 120-3. In this discussion, a West Riding 'dozen' is taken to be a short broadcloth.

28   Davies, *op. cit.*, 89; Heaton, *op. cit.*, 153-70; *Victoria County History, City of York* (1961), 129-31, 168-9.

29   J. Wardell, *The Municipal History of the Borough of Leeds* (1846), xxxi and App. vii; Heaton, *op. cit.*, 163-7, 187; Davies, *op. cit.*, 143; B. Hall, 'The trade of the north-east coast', University of London, Ph.D. thesis, 138.

30   Nicholas Raynton, 'Survey of Leeds in 1628', Corporation of London MSS., R(oyal) C(ontract) E(states), No. 60. *See also* Leeds Parish Registers, *Thoresby Society Publications*, i (1891) and iii (1895).

31   Heaton, *op. cit.*, 99. *See also* M. A. Hornsey, 'John Harrison and his times', *Thoresby Society Publications*, xxxiii (1935), 103-47.

32   Heaton, *op. cit.*, 99; *see also* 97-9.

33   Heaton, *op. cit.*, 78. *See also* Hall, *op. cit.*, 193, 151; Bowden, *op. cit.*, 67 and App. A; Wardell, *op. cit.*, pp. clix, clxiv; Leeds Parish Registers, *Thoresby Society Publications*, i (1891), iii (1895). R. Thoresby, *Ducatus Leodiensis*, 2nd edn by T. D. Whitaker (1816).

34   This paragraph is based on Wardell, *op. cit.*, 16-24; Bowden, *op. cit.*, 125-61, 208, 232; Heaton, *op. cit.*, 166-8; *CSPD, James I, 1611-18*, p. 467 (May 1617).

35   'Answer to petition in Council, 22 August 1632', Temple Newsam Collection, Leeds City Archives, TN. LA. 3/2. *See also* Wardell, *op. cit.*, App. vii and App. xxxi; and Heaton, *op. cit.*, 220 ff.

36   Heaton, *op. cit.*, 225-6.

37   *Ibid.*, 226. See the two petitions from Leeds to the King in 1639, *CSPD, Charles I, 1639-40* (1877), 251-2; Bowden, *op. cit.*, 255-61.

38   Heaton, *op. cit.*, 229.

39   Statute 14 Charles II, *c.* 32.

40   I wish to acknowledge the generous assistance of Mr R. Dell,

formerly the Leeds City Archivist, for providing information on which this paragraph is based. The records of Leeds Manor were recently discovered in the office of Messrs Dibb, Lupton of Butts Court, Leeds. *See also* Wardell, *op. cit.*, 16-24.

41 Heaton, *op. cit.*, 192 ff.; Bowden, *op. cit.*, 255, 100; Leeds Parish Registers, *Thoresby Society Publications*, iii (1895); vii (1897); x (1901).

42 'The Court Books of the Leeds Corporation', ii. *See also* Heaton, *op. cit.*, 254.

43 Walker, *Wakefield*, ii, 452. *See also* Bowden, *op. cit.*, 204 ff.; Waters, *op. cit.*, 86; Walker, *Wakefield*, ii, 452-4.

44 Waters, *op. cit.*, 51-2.

45 Heaton, *op. cit.*, 271, 365. *See also* Waters, *op. cit.*, 126.

46 Historical Manuscripts Commission, Portland MSS, vi, 140. *See also* Walker, *Wakefield*, i, 262.

47 E. C. Camidge, *A History of Wakefield* (1866), 8.

48 *Ibid.*, 8.

49 J. Houseman, *Topographical Description . . . of the West Riding of Yorkshire* (1800), 183; E. Day, *Works* (1805), 35. *See also* Heaton, *op. cit.*, 271-3; Charlesworth, *op. cit.*, 348-50. There is an interesting eulogy in verse by T. Brown, 'A poetical description of Wakefield' (3rd edn, 1841). In verse xii, Wakefield is described as a 'pleasant and pretty' town with 'markets unrivall'd for cattle and corn' (verse x), and in verse lix the Corn Exchange Building is called 'the DON of the town'.

50 For an account of Wakefield in the eighteenth century, see Walker, *Wakefield*, ii, ch. 26, 27. A discussion on the woollen industry can be found in E. M. Sigsworth, *Black Dyke Mills* (1958), and in an unpublished D.Phil. thesis, University of Oxford, by R. M. Hartwell, 'The Yorkshire woollen industry in the early nineteenth century'.

13 Places of origin of a group of immigrants into Sheffield 1624 – 1799

E. J. Buckatzsch

From 1624 to 1814 the cutlery trades in Hallamshire were regulated by the Cutlers' Company [1]. Among the surviving records of the Company are lists of indentures of apprenticeship signed during the period of the Company's rule. The lists for a few years are missing, but in general are probably fairly complete. Admission to the Freedom of the Company was not confined to men who had served formal apprenticeship. The privilege could be claimed by sons of Freemen who had been taught their trade by their fathers. Thus the list of indentured apprentices does not, even in principle, represent a complete list of all new entrants into the cutlery trades. We have no direct evidence of the number of unapprenticed sons of Freemen who started to learn their trade in any given year. Most, if not all, of the numerous grants of freedom to men not known to have served apprenticeships were presumably made to members of this group, but we do not know when they actually first entered the industry and there were in any case many men who entered the industry without ever claiming freedom of the Company. The lists of indentures and freedoms are thus of somewhat limited value as a basis for estimates of the growth of the labour force of the industry, particularly in the second half of the eighteenth century.

In spite of this, the list of indentures contains a great deal of interesting information, some of which is summarised in this note. The list, together with that of grants of the Freedom of the Company, is published by Leader in vol. ii of his History of the Company [2]. The two lists are there arranged alphabetically, and have had to be rearranged chronologically for the present investigation. They contain about 24,000 entries, of which about 4,700 are of grants of the Freedom of the Company to men not known to have been formally apprenticed.

The indentures give the name of the apprentice, the name and trade of the master and the date of signature. In addition, in nearly every case they give the name, occupation and place of residence of the father of the apprentice. From this information we may make certain deductions as to the geographical origins of the apprentices bound to masters in various periods.

These deductions are interesting because they bear on a question on which we have very little numerical information, namely, labour migration

E. J. Buckatzsch, 'Places of origin of a group of immigrants into Sheffield 1624-1799', *Economic History Review*, 2nd series, 2 (1949-50), 303-6.

in periods before the nineteenth century. It is clear that the apprenticeship data do not represent the total amount of immigration into the Sheffield district during the period reviewed. They relate to only one component of this immigration, since many people no doubt entered the district to carry on other trades. The cutlery trades, however, employed a very large proportion, perhaps between 30 and 50 per cent, of the male population of working age [3] in Sheffield, the township which contained the greater part of the population of Hallamshire. On general grounds one would expect that the growth of Sheffield, which seems to have become rapid about 1700, would involve some immigration from the immediate neighbourhood but not from any considerable distance. In this investigation of the origins of the apprentices no apprentice has been treated as an immigrant if his father lived less than five miles from either Sheffield or one of the neighbouring villages in which the cutlery trades were carried on. This convention was adopted so as to avoid any tendency to exaggerate the scale of immigration. Another arbitrary convention was adopted in estimating the distance travelled by the immigrants. By this convention distances were measured along straight lines from the centre of Sheffield (the parish church). These methods are arbitrary and crude but probably have little effect on the results obtained.

Since the number of immigrants recorded in single years is generally small the numbers have been calculated for seven periods of 25 years each. The results are shown in Table 12.1. The number of immigrants increased from about 160 in the period 1650-74 to about 1,400 in the period 1775-99. As a percentage of the total number of apprentices bound in each period, the number of immigrants varied in the seven periods between about 15 and about 25 per cent. This percentage does not show a clearly marked trend though it was higher (25 per cent) in the second half of the eighteenth century than it was in the first half (i.e. about 15 per cent). In the fourth quarter of the seventeenth century it had been about 25 per cent; in the third quarter about 20 per cent. The proportion of the *total* labour requirements of the industry (as distinct from that part of them met by indentured apprenticeships) which was met by immigrant apprentices was rather smaller than the percentages stated above. This follows from the fact that the varying but unknown number of sons of Freemen who contributed to the supply of new entrants consisted *ex hypothesi* of natives. In addition, a certain number of new entrants may have evaded the apprenticeship rule. If these evasions were less numerous among immigrants, as we may perhaps suppose they were, than among residents, the number of immigrants as a percentage of the total intake of labour into the trades would be still further reduced. The effect of these adjustments might be to reduce the proportion of immigrants in the total intake of labour in the second half of the eighteenth century to about 20 per cent and that in the first half of the century to about 12 per cent.

With such sketchy figures before us it is perhaps futile to attach much importance to the differences between them. We might be tempted to explain the fall in the immigrant proportion in the first half of the eighteenth century as compared with the higher proportion observed in the fourth quarter of the seventeenth by supposing that the resident population was too small in the earlier period to supply the labour needed

Table 12.1 Immigration of cutlery workers into Sheffield and Hallamshire in 25-year periods, 1625-1799, according to distance travelled. Number of immigrants

Period	Distance (miles)						All distances
	5-10	11-15	16-20	21-30	31-40	>40	
1625-49	140	27	23	40	46	19	295
1650-74	94	25	8	16	9	10	162
1675-99	191	83	18	25	5	7	329
1700-24	166	93	27	40	9	13	348
1725-49	209	127	26	83	8	32	485
1750-74	348	243	116	223	58	76	1,064
1775-99	694	218	131	226	41	111	1,421

by the industry. During the seventeenth century the annual number of recorded baptisms in Sheffield parish church fell slightly short of the number of burials. From 1700 onwards, however, the balance was reversed and an increasing apparent excess of births over deaths was recorded. About the same time a rising trend in the annual number of marriages was established, a fact which tends to support the suggestion that a rising trend in the population began at this time. Such a trend might explain the apparently increased ability of the town to supply the labour needed by the cutlery trades in the first half of the eighteenth century.

The immigrants recorded in each period have been classified according to the distance from Sheffield of their places of origin. The results are shown in Table 12.1 and as percentages of the total number of immigrants in Table 12.2. It will be seen that the number of immigrants declines rapidly as the distance travelled increases. Throughout the whole period about two-thirds of all immigrants came from places less than twenty-one miles from Sheffield, and less than one-tenth (generally many less) came from places more than forty-one miles away. The effective distance over which the Hallamshire cutlery trades exerted an attraction as a source of employment was therefore very limited [4].

It is interesting to observe that the figures in Table 12.2 do not show a systematic shift from short-distance to long-distance migration in the course of the eighteenth century. It is true that the proportion (7-8 per cent) of immigrants coming from places more than forty miles away was rather larger in the period 1750-99 than it was in the period 1675-1724, but it was not much higher than the percentage recorded in the period 1625-74. There are few indications here that Sheffield was much affected by the general increase in the geographical mobility of labour observed by contemporary writers towards the end of the eighteenth century. Our results appear to be in general agreement with those obtained for an earlier period, and for a different type of population, by Cox in his study of the origins of the freemen of York [5].

The indentures provide some information as to the status of the apprentices. Orphans, foundlings and bastards make up about 15 per cent

Table 12.2   Percentage distribution of total number of immigrants according to distance travelled, in 25-year periods

| Period | Distance (miles) | | | | | | All distances |
	5-10	11-15	16-20	21-30	31-40	>40	
1625-49	47·5	9·2	7·8	13·5	15·6	6·4	100·0
1650-74	58·0	15·4	5·0	10·0	5·6	6·0	100·0
1675-99	58·0	25·2	5·5	7·6	1·5	3·0	100·0
1700-24	47·7	26·7	7·8	11·5	2·6	3·7.	100·0
1725-49	43·2	26·2	5·4	17·2	1·7	6·3	100·0
1750-74	32·4	23·6	10·8	20·8	5·4	7·1	100·0
1775-99	48·7	15·3	9·2	15·9	2·9	8·0	100·0

of all indentured apprentices. Somewhat unexpectedly the percentage is about the same among immigrant apprentices. Towards the end of the eighteenth century the number of 'poor children', some of them coming from London parishes, increases. So does the number of sons of soldiers. About this time too, a number of apprentices was supplied by the Ackworth Foundling Hospital. It is, however, not the case that socially unattached lads of this type made up a larger proportion of the immigrant proportion included in the whole apprentice population than of the native proportion.

It was supposed at the beginning of the inquiry that the immigration data would give information about changes in the employment opportunities offered by the surrounding countryside. In a very general sense it no doubt does so but not on a microscopic scale. Lads presumably left their native villages in the hope of bettering themselves, but it is not easy to correlate changes in the annual number who did so with fluctuations in the economic fortunes of those villages. This is mainly because the number involved in the case of any given village is very small and because the data relating to the economic development of these villages are not available.

It is not proposed to enumerate the places of origin of the immigrants. The figures in Tables 12.1 and 12.2, showing the large proportion of immigrants coming from places less than twenty-one miles from Sheffield, virtually imply that a large number came from the Peak District and from places in South Yorkshire. Table 12.3 shows the numbers of immigrants from places in Derbyshire and South Yorkshire.

The occupations of the fathers of the immigrants were very mixed. Sons of yeomen, farmers and labourers made up about 45 per cent of the total number of immigrants. No attempt has been made to detect fluctuations in this percentage from time to time, or to classify the non-agricultural occupations.

Summary   The places of origin of lads apprenticed to the cutlery trades in Hallamshire between 1624 and 1799 have been studied. Lads coming from places more than five miles from the centre of the cutlery district have been defined as immigrants, and their number ascertained in seven twenty-five year periods. The numbers have been related to the total

Table 12.3   Number of immigrants coming from Derbyshire and South Yorkshire

Period	(1) Derbyshire	(2) South Yorkshire	(3) All immigrants	(4) (1) and (2) together as % of (3)
1624-49	64	105	295	57
1650-74	49	74	162	76
1675-99	150	127	329	84
1700-24	138	150	348	82
1725-49	218	146	485	75
1750-74	445	228	1,064	63
1775-99	473	516	1,421	69

numbers of apprentices bound in corresponding periods and found to make up between 15 and 25 per cent of the latter number in different periods. It is found that throughout the period about two-thirds of all immigrants came from places less than twenty-one miles from Sheffield and less than one-tenth from places more than forty miles away. It is also found that there was no systematic shift from the shorter to the longer distances during the eighteenth century. Nearly half of the immigrants were sons of men engaged in agriculture. The results of the investigation are offered as throwing some light on the range over which Sheffield and its predominant industry exercised an attraction as a source of employment, and as illustrating some aspects of the industrial growth of the town.

Notes

1   G. I. H. Lloyd, *The Cutlery Trades* (1913).

2   J. D. Leader, *History of the Cutlers' Company in Hallamshire* (1905).

3   Judging from a study of occupations recorded in some of the Parish Registers. See E. J. Buckatzsch, in *Economic History Review* (1949), i, 145.

4   The *maximum* distances recorded are of the order of 200 miles. London (150 miles) supplied a few immigrants, Ireland less than half a dozen in the whole period.

5   J. R. Cox, *Population Studies* (1948), i, 4, p. 396.

14 Bristol – metropolis of the west in the eighteenth century*

W. E. Minchinton

Although anticipated by earlier writers, the clearest formulation of the idea of a metropolis as the focus of economic activity is to be found in Professor N. S. B. Gras's *The Evolution of the English Corn Market*. There he writes:

> The metropolitan market may be described as a large district having one centre in which is focused a considerable trade. Trade between outlying parts of course may take place, but it is that between the metropolitan town and the rest of the area that dominates all. This is chiefly the exchange of the raw products of the country for the manufactured or imported goods of the town. The prices of all goods sent to the metropolitan centre are 'made' there, or, in other words, prices diminish as the distance from the centre is increased [1].

And the idea may be extended to include a consideration of the role of the centre in investment and banking and as the hub of social and cultural activity. That is, the function of a metropolis may be considered not merely as that of market centre but as the focus for all the activities of its area.

Within Great Britain, London has the pre-eminent and obvious claim to consideration, and Mr F. J. Fisher, in a series of articles 'of more than municipal significance', has outlined the importance of London in the sixteenth and seventeenth centuries as an export market, as a food market and as a centre of conspicuous consumption [2]. But, important though London has been, there are other towns in Great Britain which can claim to have exercised, to a greater or lesser extent, a quasi-metropolitan function, to have served as the focus of the economic and social life of their area. Of none is this more true than of Bristol, which has long been an important provincial centre. It is the purpose of this essay to examine the extent to which, in the eighteenth century, Bristol acted as a metropolis of the west [3].

None will question the importance of the part played by Bristol in foreign trade in the eighteenth century. Indeed, in studies of this period concerned with Bristol, a preoccupation with overseas commerce, and in particular with the African trade, has tended to exclude consideration of

* Part of the research on which this paper is based was aided by a grant from the Research Fund of the University of London.

W. E. Minchinton, 'Bristol — Metropolis of the west in the eighteenth century', *Transactions of the Royal Historical Society*, 5th series, iv (1954), 69-85.

all else. It was from foreign trade that Bristol derived its wealth and influence, and if to be free from the domination of any other city was a sign of metropolitan status, in the field of overseas commerce the claims of Bristol were amply substantiated. As Defoe wrote:

> The merchants of this city not only have the greatest trade, but they trade with a more entire independency upon London than any other town in Britain. An 'tis evident in this particular, (viz.) That whatsoever exportations they make to any part of the world, they are able to bring the full returns back to their own port and can dispose of it there [4].

Further, as London grew at the expense of the outports in the sixteenth century, so Bristol engrossed some of the trade of the English Bristol Channel ports in the eighteenth century. Bideford, Barnstaple and Minehead, in particular, lost ground to Bristol and by the end of the eighteenth century drew their supplies of foreign goods coastwise from Bristol instead of direct from overseas [5]. Its commanding position in foreign trade was one source of its importance in the economy of the west.

The second was its geographical position. The upper reaches of the rivers, the Avon and Frome, at whose confluence it stands, were of little consequence as arteries of communication with its hinterland, although the Avon became navigable to Bath in 1726 [6]. But seaward the Avon placed Bristol at the focal point of two major systems of water communication, at the orifice of two funnels, which served through the centuries to direct the produce of the west to Bristol. The first was the Bristol Channel which linked Bristol with the ports of Somerset, Devon, Cornwall and South Wales and with more distant ports: the second was the river and canal network of the Severn and Wye, still in course of improvement, which served the marches of Wales and the west Midlands. The Severn was navigable above Shrewsbury, the Stratford Avon to within sight of Warwick, the Stour served the Staffordshire iron and coal industries and brought water communication close to Birmingham, the Salwarp served the Droitwich salt works, and the Wye was navigable to Hereford and the Lugg to Leominster [7]. The limits of Bristol's hinterland were, in great measure, defined by this system of sea and river and canal communication, most of her domestic trade being waterborne since, as Adam Smith wrote: 'By means of water carriage a more extensive market is opened to every sort of industry than what land carriage alone can afford it' [8].

Throughout the eighteenth century, the Bristol Avon was thronged with coastal craft, with market boats and with the river barges or trows. No continuous set of figures is available to indicate the volume of trade, but calculations for the random years for which port books still exist give some information about the number of coastal and river craft sailing from Bristol in the eighteenth century. In 1698-99 449 ships left Bristol, in 1733-34 477, in 1752 453 and in 1788-89 575 [9]. Figures for repeated voyages in and out of Bristol coastwise between 1752 and 1782, though fluctuating from year to year, are somewhat more than double these figures. They rose from an average of 900 per year in the 1750s to over 1,700 per year in the 1770s [10].

Most of the coastal and river craft were owned by the outports, the master and merchant often being the same person [11]. Between 1772 and 1786, years for which details are available, never more than 35 coasting vessels were owned by Bristol citizens [12]. It is impossible to state how many vessels altogether were engaged in the trade. For the river barges, however, an estimate exists, for it was stated in 1789 that '103 trows from 50 to 130 tons carry goods upon the Severn, to and from Bristol' [13].

Supplementing the waterborne commerce was that carried by road. Although the improvements of the eighteenth century increased the ease of road communication, there was a considerable volume of road traffic before these changes took place [14]. Bristol stood at the meeting point of five main roads. Neither the clay lands of the vale of Berkeley to the north [15], nor the flats of Somerset to the south [16] had roads which were passable in all weathers, but the three roads to the east, to Tetbury and Oxford, to Chippenham and London and to Bath and Warminster, were in better condition. By these roads Bristol merchants, Defoe reported,

> maintain carriers just as the London tradesmen do, to all the
> principal countries and towns from Southampton in the south, even
> to the banks of the Trent north; and tho' they have no navigable
> river that way, yet they drive a very great trade through all these
> counties [17].

Though dearer than water transport, road carriage was both safer and more regular. By 1750 there were ninety-four carriers plying to and from the city to Leeds, Nottingham and other distant towns [18] and an even more extensive service was in existence by the end of the century [19]. Standing at the centre of this web of land and water communications, Bristol was the commercial capital of the west [20].

First of all, Bristol was the main market for the agricultural produce of this area. Despite the growth of the London food market, this was a trade which London did not completely dominate. In his analysis of the metropolitan market in the sixteenth century, Professor Gras stated that the area around Bristol must be excluded from the metropolitan area [21]. Here prices were 'made' not by the London but by the Bristol market. And Bristol continued to exercise this metropolitan effect on prices in the eighteenth century. The single exception to Arthur Young's generalisation, that as the distance from London increased so the price of agricultural produce fell, was the neighbourhood of Bristol, 'which variations', he stated, 'I attribute to the Bristol market boats constantly buying up all sorts of provisions' [22].

Like London in the sixteenth century, Bristol's demand for agricultural produce was selective rather than indiscriminate. Each district was called on to supply those victuals which it was best fitted to produce [23]. Of the grain crops, wheat came chiefly from the Midlands, barley from west Wales and Gloucestershire, and oats from Cardigan and Carmarthen [24]. Consignments were also from time to time brought from more distant parts, as in 1731-32 when wheat was obtained from Hull and Yarmouth [25], and in 1760 from London and some south coast ports [26]. Foreign supplies were called on, as in 1767 when grain was brought from Dantzig [27], chiefly because of the failure of the harvest, but during the last decades of the century there were regular imports from North America [28]. Peas and beans came from Gloucestershire and from Bridgwater, for use as provender in the inns and for the sustenance of the Negroes on the middle voyage [29], while from Devonshire by sea and from Herefordshire down the Severn and Wye came cider and perry [30].

Of the dairy products, butter was supplied by Cardigan, Pembroke and Glamorgan, 'in very great quantities, salted and barrel'd up, just as Suffolk does the city of London' [31]. The dairy farms of Somerset, Gloucestershire and Wiltshire were the chief source of milk, eggs and poultry, while cheese came from Cheshire both coastwise by sea and down the Severn from Shrewsbury. From the environs of Bristol itself, from the vale of Evesham and from the vale of Glamorgan, especially near Llandaff, were brought regular supplies of vegetables. By the end of the eighteenth century, the stimulus of the urban demand of Bristol and Bath had led to a steady expansion of the cultivation of potatoes in south Gloucestershire [32].

The main source of meat was South Wales. Cattle came on the hoof and were ferried across the Bristol Channel from Sully near Cardiff to Uphill in Somerset or across the Passage from Beachley to Aust. Warner, walking through south Wales in 1791, has recounted how his

> progress was frequently retarded by numerous droves of black cattle from Pembrokeshire and Carmarthenshire travelling towards the Passage to be transported across the Avon (*recte* Severn) and driven to the market of Bristol and the other large towns of Somerset, Gloucester and Wiltshire [33].

To remedy the effects of the long journey, the cattle were fattened on the rich pastures of north Somerset and south Gloucestershire before they were brought to market. In Cardigan pigs were reared for the Bristol drovers and calves in both south Wales and Wiltshire were sold for veal rather than kept as stock so pressing was the demand of the Bristol market. Supplies of fish were less satisfactory and more than once in the century the common council of Bristol offered bounties to any who would supply the city with 'good fresh saleable fish' [34].

During the eighteenth century, Bristol provided a growing market for such victuals. Already, about the beginning of the century, it had outstripped Norwich to become the second largest town in Great Britain, with a population, according to a recent estimate, of 20,000 in 1700 [35]. Though it grew less rapidly than Manchester, Liverpool and Birmingham, all of which were larger than Bristol in 1801, its population more than doubled in the century. According to the census, there were 41,000 inhabitants of the city and 64,000 inhabitants of the whole urban area in that year [36]. Thus, in agriculture, this growing market provided a stimulus for the adaption of cultivation to market needs and the specialisation of production upon particular commodities.

The second category of goods for which Bristol was a market was industrial raw materials. For some of them Bristol was a distribution point. Naval timber, imported from the Baltic or brought down the Severn from the Forest of Dean, was sent coastwise, mainly to London [37]. Teazles from Bridgwater were sent to supply the textile industries of the Cotswolds and Yorkshire [38]. Cornish tin was delivered to tinplate works, like Caerleon and Melingriffith in south Wales or Bringewood in the Midlands [39], while diminshing amounts of lead from the Mendips were dispatched, chiefly to London [40]. Supplies of wool were brought from Milford or Cardiff and transferred to barges or trows for conveyance to Gloucester for use in the Cotswold industry [41], and towards the end of the century these domestic supplies were supplemented by imports of Spanish wool [42]. Early in the century, as Celia Fiennes reported, coal from the mines at Kingswood Chase was sent from Bristol to Taunton [43], but this trade came to an end before 1800 and Bristol became a coal-importing port, obtaining most of its supplies from Newport.

There were two main reasons for this entrepôt trade in raw materials. First, the vessels engaging in the Bristol Channel trade were not normally suitable for conveying cargoes up the Severn nor the barges for service in the channel, and Bristol was a convenient place for transhipment to be carried out. Second, many of the consignments were quite small, so that cargoes were completed with other goods, most of which were dispatched to Bristol. Where the trade was large enough, as was the case with the cross-channel coal trade from south Wales to north Devon and Somerset, it was carried on directly without resort to Bristol.

Other cargoes of raw materials were brought to Bristol to supply the needs of the local industries. Even at the end of the eighteenth century, Bristol was 'not more a commercial than a manufacturing town' [44]. Some local coal was available, water-power was obtained from the Frome, across which a considerable number of weirs had been constructed, and there was a large local market, with easy access to other markets by sea or land. From Cornwall came tin and from Anglesey copper for the local brass and copper works [45]. The local soap works obtained wood ashes and kelp from the Somerset ports, and kelp and clay from Stourbridge were used by the glass industry. This latter industry was the most important of Bristol's manufactures. Window glass and bottles were the chief products, though the reputation of the city now rests on the enamelled and coloured glassware made at this time. As a local directory noted:

> The great demand for glass bottles for the Bristol water, for the
> exportation of beer, cider and perry; for wine, and for the use of
> Town and Country keep the various bottle glasshouses here
> constantly at work. The call for window glass at home, at Bath and
> in the Towns about Bristol: in the Western Counties, Wales and from
> North to South wherever Bristol trade extends, and the great
> quantities sent to America, employ several houses for this article [46].

Early in the century, in 1703, a Bristol glassmaker came to an agreement with a group of Stourbridge glassmakers 'which practically amounted to the cartellisation of the broad (window) glass industry' [47], a shortlived attempt at monopoly, but indicative of the importance of Bristol both as a manufacturing and as a marketing centre. Sugar refining, dependent on imported raw materials, was the other major Bristol industry. By the end of the century there were twenty sugar refineries in Bristol [48]. Ancillary to these were the distilleries, while Bristol also had a number of breweries which used grain 'the growth of the adjoining counties' [49]. Tobacco was the other industry dependent on imports. Then there was the building industry, which obtained tiles from Cornwall and freestone by barge down the Avon from Bath [50] as well as bricks, drain pipes and chimney pots from the local pottery industry. Finally, Bristol had a wide range of finishing trades, woollen, leather, lace and tinware, which had expanded at the expense of similar trades in the nearby towns. Gloucester, it was stated in 1780, 'formerly had many manufactures but Bristol hath since supplanted it: and there is nothing remaining of that kind worthy of observation' [51]. In industry, as in trade, the growth of a metropolis is often at the expense of its near neighbours.

Some of these manufactures were consumed in Bristol, some were exported, but all made their contribution to Bristol's domestic trade. The cargoes of manufactured goods sent coastwise, which alone of the consignments of domestic commerce are available for analysis, were so various as almost to defy description. Ironmongery, glass, haberdashery, mercery, apothecaries' ware, furniture and household goods and earthenware were the chief categories, but this catalogue does little to convey the immense range of articles which were sent out from Bristol. Among the articles sent to Barnstaple in 1810, for example, there was a malt mill, a chaffing machine and a harpsichord [52]. Not all these goods were the product of Bristol industries, for Gras's formulation of the role of a metropolis in trade as 'the exchange of the raw products of the country for the manufactured or imported products of the town' is too rigid a description of eighteenth-century commerce. Many of the manufactures were the product of Bristol's hinterland for which it acted as distribution centre. Particularly was this so for the western cloth trade, in which the influence of London was negligible [53]. Some of these manufactures were brought to Bristol for export. Guns and metal ornaments came from Birmingham, Indian textiles from London, Manchester cotton goods from Lancashire and woollen fabrics from Somerset for the Africa trade, to name but one of the branches in which Bristol engaged. Others were distributed by barge or coastal craft, by packhorse or wagon through Bristol's hinterland.

Among the articles in which Bristol dealt were goods imported from foreign countries and from Ireland. No cargo outwards coastwise from Bristol was complete without some of these goods: timber from the Baltic, linen from Germany, oil, fruit and wine from the Mediterranean, dyewoods, sugar, rum and cotton from the West Indies, rice and logwood from the Carolinas, tobacco from Virginia, timber and skins from New England and fish from Newfoundland. From Ireland came mainly leather, tallow, linen yarn and dairy produce. Some of these imported goods no doubt figured in the groceries which were present in so many of the cargoes from Bristol in the coastal and river trade. 'Not only all south Wales is supplied from Bristol with every article of foreign commerce', stated a contemporary, 'but likewise the cities and towns of the Severn' [54]. And one might add, the south-west of England as well. All these commodities, raw materials, agricultural produce, manufactured goods and imports contributed to Bristol's position as the chief market of the west. 'If we consider domestic Trade, or inland Navigation,' Campbell stated in 1774, 'Bristol is without rival' [55].

The machinery of distribution differed with the product. For agricultural produce and fish, the weekly markets were the main outlet. These were held in the streets and on the quays, but so great became the congestion in the eighteenth century that a considerable building programme was embarked upon to provide the city with suitable accommodation for the sale of these goods. The sale of vegetables was removed in 1716 and that of hay in 1731 to markets on either side of the city, that in Broadmead catering for the produce of Gloucestershire and that in Temple Street for the produce of Somerset. The fish market was removed to the quay in 1717 and a new corn market was built in 1726 [56]. On the Back a covered market was erected 'for the sale of poultry, fruit and other provisions from Wales' [57]. In addition to these markets, it was reported in the late eighteenth century, 'all sorts of fish, vegetables and fruit, fresh butter and numerous other articles are cryed about the streets, which are resounding from morning to night with the harsh music of those ambulatory, mercantile orators' [58]. These were supplied by the weekly market boats which came from Chepstow and Gloucester, the collecting points for the Wye and Severn valleys, and from the nearer ports of Wales.

For many manufactured goods, for cattle and grain, the Bristol fairs dominated the trading year. By the eighteenth century the eight fairs of the Middle Ages had been reduced to two, the St Paul's or winter fair and the St James's fair. Until 1731 the first began on 25 January and the second on 25 July, but as a result of the protests of traders the dates were changed to 1 March and 1 September. While manufactures were disposed of at each fair, the summer fair was the great cattle fair. But, as Dr John has told us, they were more than just places of trade: 'for most of the people of south Wales the economic life revolved around two pivots, the local fairs and markets and the great September fair at Bristol' [59]. There they were called on to discharge their 'shop debts' not only to Bristol traders but to the itinerant salesmen as well [60]. The fair provided an opportunity for a general settlement of obligations. As Henry Escricke, a Bolton middleman, wrote in the summer of 1739: 'I hope to send you some good bills as soon as the Bristol fair is over. I am got in with 3 or 4 travellers that keeps the fair, and they pay but once in twelve months' [61]. Nor should it be forgotten that it served as a social occasion as well as a business function, the normal business of the city being 'set aside until after the fair'.

With the expansion of business and the improvement of communications, regular and organised channels of trade developed and the fairs declined. Agricultural products were purchased by Bristol dealers who went through the western counties, the Midlands and south Wales. The liquor trades led the way: corn factors bought in bulk for the Bristol brewers, and cider was purchased in large quantities by Bristol dealers who had places in the country where they 'worked their liquors'. They bought by sample or sometimes without seeing the crop at all [62]. Thus the merchant secured the large supplies he required and the farmer was able to dispose of his crop in a single transaction. Some complained that the prices paid by the dealers were lower than could be obtained in Bristol, but it was pointed out that 'the dealer must take care in buying to provide for storehouse rent, porterage, freight, insurance by sea, commissions on the sales at the port he sends it to and lastly for his own trouble and capital employed'. Though there were complaints that dealers made little difference in price between a good and a bad sample, there were only a few who took their goods to the market in Bristol and an increasing number who sold direct to the factors. Butchers, too, no longer waited for the fairs or markets in Bristol but went to the local markets and carried away the carcases whole [63].

In a similar manner the importance of the Bristol fair for woollen products declined. Bristol merchants dealt direct with the manufacturer, visited the local markets, or bought by sample. John Pinney, for example, sent his clerk to Bridgwater fair each year and purchased cloth direct from manufacturers at Kilve and Wiveliscombe [64]. Samuel Munckley, another Bristol merchant, had regular dealings with cloth manufacturers in Somerset [65], while some makers, like Samuel Brown of Chard, brought their samples to Bristol and collected orders direct from their customers. As in agriculture, sale by sample replaced the annual visit to Bristol fair [66].

The development of a regular system of marketing had gone farthest in the trade in iron for which Bristol was the great distributing centre. Foreign pig and bar iron, imported through Bristol [67] or brought coastwise from London, was transported to the forges and smithies of the Black Country [68] or south Wales. Bar iron from the Midlands, Cumberland or Lancashire was sent to iron works in South Wales and Welsh iron to iron works in the Midlands [69]. The greater part of the trade was in the hands of Bristol iron merchants, of whom Nehemiah Champion [70] and Graffin Prankard [71] were probably the most important, but some establishments elsewhere like the Bringewood [72] and Caerleon Works [73] had agents in Bristol. Through the intervention of Bristol merchants, local forge masters were faced with competition from works in other parts of the country or from imported iron, and there prices were keenest [74]. The Severn was the principal highway of the iron industry [75], and while London came a good second to Bristol as a market for wire, Bristol was easily the most important centre for the trade in merchant iron [76]. In some measure, Bristol prices were accepted as the ruling prices in the iron trade. In 1780, for example, when the tinplate makers met in London to discuss prices, they drew up two lists, the Bristol list and the London list [77]. Again, when in 1748 the smaller wood-owners in the Furness area were faced with a combination of iron makers, they agreed to deliver charcoal to a new furnace at a price to be regulated under a sliding scale by the price of pig iron in the Bristol market. This agreement lasted for thirty years [78]. Thus, in the iron trade, Bristol exercised a quasi-metropolitan influence on price.

From trade it was but a short step to capital investment. The second function of Bristol in the life of its hinterland was as a source of capital. Although Bristol was suitably situated for the finishing trades, it was becoming in the eighteenth century a high-cost location for heavy industry, particularly in terms of labour and fuel. Thus, from the early eighteenth century, Bristol capital was invested in enterprises in its hinterland, not in the already developed, mature textile industries but in the growing mining and metal industries. It found its major outlet in south Wales. In the early years of the century the Welsh copper industry was 'almost entirely in the hands of English financiers, many of whom were Bristol merchants' [79]. The earliest was Dr John Lane, who established the first copper works in the Swansea area in 1717 [80]. The White Rock Copper Company, a partnership of Bristol merchants, was formed in 1737 to operate in Swansea, and other concerns followed as the cost advantage of that area for copper smelting became apparent. Thereafter the industry declined in Bristol, though the finishing processes continued to be carried on there. In this industry mining and merchant interests were closely allied, and this governed, as Dr John has pointed out, the sources from which capital was obtained for its development [81].

Coal and iron were the other industries in which Bristol capital was to be found. The expansion of the sea-coal industry in the later eighteenth century, which till then had been financed mainly by local landowners, was carried out with capital drawn from Gloucester, Birmingham and Cornwall, as well as from Bristol [82]. Already by this time Bristol interests had invested in the iron industry. There were Bristol partners in the enterprises formed in the first decade of the century to exploit the iron and coal deposits on the earl of Plymouth's land in the Dowlais area [83], in the Myrthy Furnace (1759), where the four Bristol partners supplied half of the capital of £4,000 [84], in the Dowlais Company (1763) and in the Sirhowy iron works (1799) [85], while two new works set up at Abercarn and Cardiff were founded by Welsh ironmasters, who were financed from Bristol [86]. But the most important single Bristol interest was that of the Harfords, who had shares in the Redbrook, Machen, Bassaleg, Lydbrook, Monmouth and New Weir forges, in Ebbw Vale, in partnership with Jeremiah Homfray, and in the Melingriffith iron and tinplate works [87]. Richard Reynolds, too, had wide connections in the iron industry in south Wales.

While copper, iron and coal were the chief ventures in which Bristol capitalists engaged in south Wales, other enterprises received their support, including the Chepstow glasshouse established in 1764 [88], the printing press operated by Samuel and Felix Farley, the Bristol master printers, at Pontypool for a brief period from 1740 [89], and lead mines in Cardiganshire [90]. The importance of this investment lay less in its volume, which was not substantial, than in its timing. It performed a 'pump-priming' function, if the term may be excused, stimulating further development by native capital. Like other merchant interests which invested in south Wales at this time, Bristol merchants were well placed to carry out such a task because of their knowledge of market conditions and their control of the machinery of distribution.

Outside south Wales, Bristol investment was slight and scattered. Dr Lane and Thomas Coster were concerned in tin-mining in Cornwall [91]. Bristol capital was to be found in glasshouses at Nailsea and Chelwood [92] and in copper works at Warmley, Saltford and Keynsham [93].

Thomas Goldney was a partner of Abraham Darby in Bristol and later in Coalbrookdale, of which works Richard Reynolds, another Bristol Quaker, became manager [94]. There were Bristol partners in the Cilgwyn and Cefn du Slate Company in north Wales [95]. Finally, although the finance of canals and turnpike trusts was largely in the hands of local landowners, Bristol capital was to be found in a number of the projects carried out round Bristol. There were Bristol shareholders in the Bristol and Bath, the Stroudwater and later the Kennet and Avon Canal [96]. Caleb Dickinson, Bristol merchant and landowner, had shares in several turnpike trusts, the Toghill, the Bristol, the Somerton, and the Ilchester and Shepton Mallet [97]. Such a concentration of investment in the hinterland of Bristol was indicative of the nature of the capital market, which was still largely personal and specific. The growth of a more impersonal capital market led to a diffusion of capital among projects more widely scattered and the loosening of the bond forged by capital investment between Bristol and its hinterland.

As a source of short-term as well as of long-term capital, Bristol was of some importance. Goldsmiths carried on the business of banking there until 1750 when the first Bristol bank, the Bristol Old Bank, was founded. Within fifty years there were seven banks in existence in the city [98]. They discounted bills, made advances over a wide area, and from 1812 began to set up branches in the west of England and south Wales. Some of the banks set up in south Wales which had small resources had a Bristol bank as correspondent 'on which it, or its customers, could draw, and from which notes and coin could be obtained by discounting bills' [99].

As a centre of marine and fire insurance, Bristol was second only to London, individual underwriters carrying on business as in the capital. The first provincial fire office, the Bristol Crown, was established there in 1718. By 1787 a second company, the Bristol Fire Office, founded twenty years earlier, had 'agents in all the towns of the North and West' and was underselling London offices [100]. Less information is available about ship insurance, but both Isaac Hobhouse and Samuel Munckley, for example, acted as agents, insuring ships from other provincial ports [101]. In these various ways, Bristol acted as a financial centre of the west.

In this Bristol might be found 'all the throng and bustle of the metropolis . . . so exactly the confusion of London that it requires a very slight exertion of the fancy to imagine oneself absolutely in the Strand' [102]. But there was another Bristol which is oft-times overlooked. Those who were critical of the dirt and squalor of the city — and there were many [103] — extolled the beauty of Hotwells, the spa on the bank of the Avon at the foot of St Vincent's Rock. 'The season for drinking is from April to September, during which time the place is greatly frequented', reported a visitor [104], and the volumes of the Historical Manuscripts Commission provide an aristocratic commentary on this statement [105]. Hotwells flourished as a spa for the greater part of the eighteenth century, but was increasingly overshadowed by Bath, entirely consecrated to such social pleasures. The fairs and the spa made Bristol, in some slight way, a centre of conspicuous consumption.

In other ways, also, Bristol influenced the life of its hinterland. Newspapers had been established there early in the eighteenth century

[106] and they circulated over a wide area [107]. Bristol was not slow to follow the new urban style of architecture for which Bath set the mode, and the Georgian terraces of Clifton, though generally less admired, do not suffer by comparison with their more publicised rival [108]. While Bath led the fashion it was Bristol which brought the new style to the attention of those engaged in business and commerce. From Bristol the new architecture spread throughout the west of England [109].

In many ways the life of the west was linked with Bristol. It was to Bristol that towns or interests appealed for support for the remedy of grievances, the carrying out of important projects or the finance of matters beyond local resources. To the construction of both the Flatholm and the Mumbles lighthouses, Bristol merchants made contribution. The Society of Merchant Venturers sent money to the relief of those who suffered from fires in two north Devon towns and to found libraries in the market towns of south Wales [110]. The role of metropolis was no purely economic affair.

But it would be absurd to overestimate the importance of Bristol in the life of its hinterland. There were other towns like Exeter, Hereford, Gloucester and Bath which had their smaller spheres of influence in the west. Such was the nature of Bristol's hinterland, too, that a substantial volume of commerce was carried on between ports in the Severn valley and in the Bristol Channel without the intervention of Bristol. Chiefly was this so in the coal trade from the Staffordshire coalfield and the south Wales ports. There the volume was sufficient to carry the overhead charges. In other directions, too, other parts of the hinterland made their contribution. Capital for south Wales came from Cornwall and the Midlands, as well as from Bristol. Its newspapers were challenged by the *Gloucester Journal*, which had a wide circulation, and much legal work for south Wales was done in Gloucester and Hereford [111]. And overall there was the influence of London. At many points the effect of the London market was apparent. Much smaller in size, the pull of the Bristol market cannot be compared with that of London, yet within its area, the lines of attraction towards the London markets were deflected by the rival magnetism of Bristol's demand. London, too, was important as a source of capital and as the main centre of banking and insurance. But all of this said in qualification does not detract from the premise of this essay, that Bristol dominated the trade of its area, that it influenced prices, that its initiative in investment and banking was of no little importance to the west and that in other directions, too, it performed metropolitan functions.

Towards the end of the eighteenth century the position of Bristol began to decline, a decline which continued into the nineteenth century. For this there were a number of reasons. First, its importance as a metropolis of the west had been founded on a network of predominantly water communications. The construction of canals in the north Midlands in the later eighteenth century shifted the outlet of trade away from Bristol, and goods which formerly came south for export now went to Liverpool. The linking of the Stroudwater and the Thames provided a canal route to London which did not pass through Bristol [112]. The improvement of the roads increased the influence of London and reduced local variations in prices. As Henry Cruger wrote as early as in October 1765: 'The conveyance of Goods from that Port to this, and from this to that, are so easy the difference of the Market seldom continues long or material, the Prices of the London market generally regulates this' [113].

Further, Bristol's importance had been founded on foreign trade, and here it lost ground. Its American trade did not recover after the revolution and in the West Indies trade it was surpassed by Liverpool, while no new staples were found to replace the old. There were delays in modernising the harbour. Local industries, some of them dependent on foreign trade, declined, and the textile trades of Devon and the Cotswolds stagnated while the industrialisation of south Wales proceeded. Bristol ceased to be an important centre for the textile trade and lost the Welsh trade to the growing ports of Cardiff, Newport and Swansea. The growing volume of trade increased the amount of direct marketing and reduced the importance of Bristol as an entrepôt.

Already by 1829, as a banker's circular commented, Bristol had ceased to be 'the metropolis of the west'; by 1850 it was no longer the 'Welsh metropolis'. In successive directions regional isolation was broken down and the coming of the railway made the influence of London all pervasive. For a period Bristol was able to exercise a quasi-metropolitan function over its hinterland in the west. But it was a transitional phase in economic development, when trade was comparatively small in volume, communications as yet imperfect, industry not fully developed and capital investment personal and specific. The improvement of communications and the growth of institutions and methods of organisation appropriate to the expanding industrialism were responsible for the decline in Bristol's position. If the sixteenth century saw 'the rise of the metropolitan market' of which London was centre, then the nineteenth saw the process completed. In the new order Bristol was no longer 'the metropolis of the west'.

Notes

Abbreviations: *Econ H R: Economic History Review;* HMC: Historical Manuscripts Commission; PRO: Public Records Office.

1   N. S. B. Gras, *The Evolution of the English Corn Market*, p. 95.
2   'London's export trade in the early seventeenth century' in *Econ H R*, 2nd ser., iii (1950), 151-61; 'The development of the London food market, 1540-1640' in *ibid.*, v (1935), 46-64; and 'The development of London as a centre of conspicuous consumption in the sixteenth and seventeenth centuries' in *Transactions of the Royal Historical Society*, 4th ser., xxx (1949), 37-50.
3   For the position of Bristol in the fifteenth century see E. Carus-Wilson, 'The overseas trade of Bristol', in E. Power and M. M. Postan, *English Trade in the Fifteenth Century*, pp. 183-246.
4   D. Defoe, *A Tour through England and Wales* (Everyman edn), ii, 36.

5   See port books; also F. Hancock, *Minehead* (1903), pp. 316-17; C. Vancouver, *A General View of the Agriculture of the County of Devon*, pp. 395-6; *Supplement to Collinson's History of Somerset*, pp. 112-13.

6   The Frome was obstructed by weirs. For the Avon see T. S. Willan, 'Bath and the navigation of the Avon', in *Proceedings* of the Bath and District Branch, Somerset Archaeol. and Nat. Hist. Soc., 1936.

7   For details see T. S. Willan, *River Navigation in England, 1600-1750, English Coasting Trade, 1600-1750*, and 'The navigation and trade of the Severn valley, 1600-1750' in *Econ H R*, viii (1937), 68-79; G. Farr, 'Severn navigation and the trow' in *Mariner's Mirror*, xxxii (1946), 66-95; and A. S. Davies, 'The river trade of Montgomeryshire and its borders' in *Montgomeryshire Collections*, xliii (1934), 37-46.

8   *Wealth of Nations* (Everyman edn), i, 16.

9   These figures were obtained from the port books (PRO, E/190). July 1698-June 1699 from 1157/1, 2: 1733-34 from 1211/2, 3: 1752 from 1217/2, 3: and 1788-89 from 1239/2, 3. No 'coastwise In' books exist for Bristol in the eighteenth century.

10   British Museum, Add. MS 11255.

11   For a discussion of the organisation of the coastal trade, see T. S. Willan, *English Coasting Trade*, pp. 34-54.

12   PRO Customs 17/1-22.

13   W. Barrett, *The History and Antiquities of the City of Bristol* (1789), p. 189.

14   See J. L. Baker, 'England in the seventeenth century' in *An Historical Geography of England before 1800*, ed. H. C. Darby, p. 429.

15   Early in the eighteenth century it was stated that wheeled vehicles could use the road only four months in the year (*Journals House of Commons*, xxi, 437-8).

16   As the proverb had it, 'Somerset bad for the rider, good for the abider'. See also Defoe, *A Tour . . .* , i, 270.

17   *Ibid.*, ii, 36.

18   J. Latimer, *Annals of Bristol in the Eighteenth Century*, p. 288.

19   *Matthew's New History of Bristol or Complete Guide and Bristol Directory for the Year 1793-4*, pp. 94-8.

20   See Defoe, *A Tour . . .*, ii, 306. 'Bristol drove a great inland trade with all the western counties and thus it drew to itself the bulk of the water-borne commerce of Wales.'

21   Gras, *English Corn Market*, p. 124.

22   A. Young, *A Six Weeks' Tour through the Southern Counties of England and Wales* (1769), pp. 310, 316-17. But see also Gras, *op. cit.*, p. 122. Figures from Houghton's *Collections* indicate that London had cut into the Severn trade between 1691 and 1702.

23   F. J. Fisher, *Econ H R* v (1935), 56.

24   Both the evidence of the port books (PRO, E/190) and the series of *General Views* drawn up for the Board of Agriculture from 1794 have been used for these and subsequent statements about the

source of agricultural produce. W. Marshall's *Rural Economy of Gloucestershire* has also been used.

25   Willan, *Coasting Trade*, pp. 81, 82, 148.

26   General Committee Books, i (1757-99), City Archives, Council House, Bristol.

27   *Ibid.*

28   *Bristol Presentments*, 1770-1806, Reference Library, Bristol. In 1791, for example, 10,828 bushels of wheat and 5,040 bushels of barley were imported.

29   Marshall, *op. cit.*, i, 153.

30   G. Turner, *General View of the Agriculture of the County of Gloucester*, p. 53.

31   Defoe, *Tour*, ii, 55.

32   PRO, HO 67/3, 11. See also W. E. Minchinton, 'Agriculture in Gloucestershire during the Napoleonic wars' in *Transactions of the Bristol and Gloucestershire Archaeological Society*, lxviii (1949), 169.

33   R. Warner, *A Walk through Wales in 1797*, p. 31.

34   Common Council Proceedings, January 1704 and May 1770. Council House, Bristol.

35   D. V. Glass, 'Gregory King's estimate of the population of England and Wales, 1695', in *Population Studies*, iii (1951), 347.

36   For comparison, the population of London in 1801 was 900,000, of Manchester-Salford 84,000, of Liverpool 78,000 and of Birmingham 74,000.

37   Port books (PRO, E/190).

38   J. Billingsley, *General View of the Agriculture of the County of Somerset* (1795), p. 110.

39   Chappell MSS, National Library of Wales: Caerleon MSS, Newport Public Library: Knight MSS, Kidderminster Public Library.

40   See J. Gough, *Mines of Mendip*, p. 169.

41   See port books. For Cardiff see also PRO, T 64/281 for the years 1739/43 and *An Account of Wool sent Coastwise from Cardiff* for the years 1763/70. Cardiff Public Library.

42   See *Bristol Presentments*, Reference Library, Bristol.

43   *The Journeys of Celia Fiennes*, ed. C. Morris, p. 243.

44   F. M. Eden, *The State of the Poor*, ii, 183. See also HMC, *Charlemont MSS*, p. 40: 'Bristol, a large commercial city remarkable for affording and manufacturing the best woollen nightcaps in the world.'

45   See R. Jenkins, 'The copper works at Redbrook and at Bristol', *Trans. Bristol and Glos. Archaeol. Soc.* lxiii (1942), 145-67.

46   *Matthew's Directory*, p. 40. A writer in the *Builders' Dictionary* (1703) complained that though Bristol window glass was the best it was seldom seen in London owing to the difficulty of getting it there safely.

47   W. H. B. Court, *The Rise of the Midland Industries, 1660-1838*, p. 124.

48   *Matthew's Directory*, p. 40.

49   Barrett, *History of Bristol*, p. 185.
50   *Matthew's Directory*, p. 33.
51   R. J. Sulivan, *Observations made during a Tour (1780)*, p. 118.
52   Account book of John Milton, Quay Master at Barnstaple. County Record Office, Taunton.
53   Willan, *Coasting Trade*, pp. 95-6.
54   G. Walpoole, *The New British Traveller* (1784), p. 362.
55   J. Campbell, *Political Survey of Britain* (1774), p. 147.
56   Details about the markets from Common Council Proceedings, Council House, Bristol.
57   *Matthew's Directory*, p. 44.
58   *Ibid.*, p. 44.
59   A. H. John, *Industrial Development of South Wales*, p. 10.
60   *Ibid.*, p. 14.
61   A. P. Wadsworth and J. de L. Mann, *The Cotton Trade and Industrial Lancashire, 1600-1780*, p. 269.
62   W. Marshall, *Rural Economy of Gloucestershire*, ii, 348.
63   These statements are drawn from the various *General Views* of agriculture for counties in the Bristol hinterland. For a discussion of the general position of the middleman see R. B. Westerfield, *Middlemen in English Business.*
64   C. M. MacInnes, in *The Trade Winds*, ed. C. N. Parkinson, p. 64.
65   Munckley Correspondence in Ashton Court MSS, Council House, Bristol.
66   Account Book of Samuel Brown of Chard, 1773-78, County Record Office, Taunton.
67   See Dickinson Papers, County Record Office, Taunton.
68   The Midland trade in iron has been mapped by B. L. C. Johnson, 'The charcoal iron industry in the early eighteenth century', *Geographical Journal*, cxvii (1951), 167 ff.
69   See A. H. John, 'Iron and coal on a Glamorgan estate, 1700-40', *Econ H R* xiii (1943), 98-9.
70   A. Raistrick, *Quakers in Science and Industry*, p. 100.
71   Dickinson Papers, County Record Office, Taunton.
72   Knight MSS, Kidderminster Public Library.
73   Caerleon MSS, Newport Public Library.
74   A. H. John, *Econ H R* xiii (1943), 99.
75   See T. S. Ashton, *Iron and Steel in the Industrial Revolution*, p. 242.
76   B. L. C. Johnson, 'The Foley partnerships: the iron industry at the end of the charcoal era', *Econ H R*, 2nd ser., iv (1952), 333, n. 2.
77   Reprinted in E. H. Brooke, *Appendix to Chronology of the Tinplate Works of Great Britain, 1665-1949*, pp. 234-6.
78   Ashton, *op. cit.*, pp. 167-8.
79   A. H. John, *Econ H R*, xiii (1943), 94.
80   R. O. Roberts, 'Dr John Lane and the foundation of the non-ferrous metal industries in the Swansea valley', *Gower*, iv (1951), 19-24.
81   A. H. John, *Industrial Development of South Wales*, p. 28.
82   *Ibid.*, p. 28.
83   Plymouth MSS 755, 1404, 1426, 1435, 1437. National Library of Wales.

84   J. Lloyd, *History of the Old South Wales Iron Works*, pp. 23-4.

85   *Ibid.*, p. 148.

86   John, *Industrial Development*, pp. 8, 32.

87   A. Raistrick, *Quakers in Science and Industry*, pp. 128, 148-9; E. L. Chappell, *Historic Melingriffith*, pp. 30-44.

88   F. Buckley, 'The early glasshouses of Bristol', *Journal of the Society of Glass Technology*, ix (1925), 47.

89   I. Jones, *History of Printing and Printers in Wales*, p. 38.

90   F. Green, *Calendar of the Crosswood Deeds*, p. 143.

91   J. Latimer, *Annals of Bristol in the Eighteenth Century*, p. 66.

92   Buckley, *J. Soc. Glass Tech.*, ix (1925), 48.

93   Latimer, *op. cit.*, p. 67.

94   Raistrick, *op. cit.*, pp. 124-140; *Dynasty of Iron Founders*, pp. 47-98.

95   A. H. Dodd, *Industrial Revolution in North Wales*, p. 311.

96   T. S. Willan, *River Navigation in England*, pp. 47-8; Latimer, *Bristol in the Eighteenth Century*, p. 499.

97   Dickinson Papers, County Record Office, Taunton.

98   C. Cave, *A History of Banking in Bristol*, pp. 9-19.

99   T. S. Ashton, *Industrial Revolution*, p. 103. For illustrations see John, *Industrial Development*, p. 49; T. M. Hodges, 'Early Banking in Cardiff', *Econ H R*, xviii (1948), 84-90; F. Green, 'Early banks in west Wales', *West Wales Historical Records*, vi (1916).

100   H. E. Raynes, *History of British Insurance*, pp. 94, 154, 208; J. H. Clapham, *Economic History of Modern Britain*, i, 286.

101   Munckley Correspondence in Ashton Court MSS, Council House, Bristol, and Hobhouse Correspondence in Jefferies Collection, Reference Library, Bristol.

102   E. D. Clarke, *A Tour through the South of England* (1791), p. 148.

103   Among these may be noted Defoe, *Tour*; Samuel Gade, *Journal* (MSS, University of Bristol Library); R. J. Sulivan, *Journal of a Tour* (1778?), pp. 48-9.

104   Clarke, *op. cit.*, p. 148.

105   See, for example, HMC, *Bath MSS*, i, 293; *Charlemont MSS*, p. 400; *Hastings MSS*, ii, 19; *Somerset MSS*, p. 268; *Verulam MSS*, p. 250. Also *Pembroke Papers, 1780-1791*, ed. Lord Herbert, p. 72; *Journeys of Celia Fiennes*, ed. C. Morris, p. 239.

106   Latimer, *Bristol in the Eighteenth Century*, pp. 48-52.

107   John, *Industrial Development*, p. 15.

108   W. Ison, *The Georgian Architecture of Bristol.*

109   See A. E. Richardson and C. L. Gill, *Regional Architecture of Bristol, passim*, for examples of Bristol's influence.

110   These statements are based on documents in the records of the Society of Merchant Venturers of the City of Bristol, to whom I am indebted (and in particular to Miss G. E. Whitaker) for permission to consult the Society's records. See J. Latimer, *A History of the Society of Merchant Venturers of the City of Bristol*, p. 220.

111   John, *Industrial Development*, p. 15.

112   Melingriffith iron works marketed its products this way. See

Melingriffith MSS, in the possession of Mr S. Gazard, to whom I am indebted for permission to see them.

113 *Commerce of Rhode Island*, i, 129. I owe this reference to Dr W. Savadge.

Index

Belgium, urban studies in, 2, 18-19, 29
(n.8)
Benefactions, by merchant classes, 165
Bennassar, B., 14-15
Berengo, M., 14
Berkhamsted, 100
Berkshire, market towns, 174, 179, 190,
194, 202 (n.53), 203-4 (n.67)
Berlin, 7, 80
Best, Henry, 194-5
Betham, B. J., 217, 219, 227, 230
Beverley, Yorks, 184-5, 195, 278
Bewdley, 190
Bicester, 188
Bideford, 94, 298
Bietenholz, P. G., 13
Billesdon, 173, 178
Birmingham
fragmentary available information
on, 25
industrial revolution in, 90
intellectual activity in, 28
markets, 188
size, importance, 91-2, 263 (n.4),
310 (n.36)
source of capital, 305
Birth rates *see* Population
Blackaller family, of Exeter, 149, 151
Blackburn, 177, 195, 204 (n.77)
Blackwell Hall Market, 280
Blake, J. B., 17
Blandford, 183
Bloch, Marc, 9
Blome, Richard, 202 (n.51)
Blundell, Peter, of Tiverton, 165
Bodin, 8
Bodley family, of Exeter, 150, 155, 157
Bologna, 13
Bolton, Lancs., 204 (n.77)
Bonfires, civic, 112, 117
Bordeaux, 9, 10, 12
Boroughbridge, 283
Boroughs, relative size, importance,
23-4; *see also* County towns,
Towns
Boston, Lincs., 92, 195
Boston, U.S.A., 16-17, 18, 55
Boughton Alyph, 195
Bourgeoisie, emergence of, 72; *see also*
Merchant classes, Middle classes
Bourne, 195
Bovey Tracey, 199 (n.11)
Bow, Devon, 178
Bowden, P. J., 284, 290, 37
Brabant, 2, 55
Bradford, Yorks, 100, 273, 278

Bradford on Avon, 94
Bradninch, Devon, 178
Bramante, 63
Braudel, F., 2, 7, 13
Brecon, 190
Breconshire, market towns, 173
Bremen, 7, 66
Brentford, Middlesex, 180, 188
Brewing industry, 252, 302
Brewood, Staffs., 173
Bridenbaugh, C., 16
Bridgnorth, 188
Bridgwater, 300, 301
Bridlington, 202 (n.51)
Briggs, A., 263 (n.4)
Brighton, 103 (n.2)
Bristol
beds, stabling, 257 (n.118)
diversity of trade, 297-8, 299-304, 308
impact of London's trade, 309 (n.22)
local industries, 301-4, 305-6, 308
merchant classes, 95, 96, 97,
149-150, 154, 166 (n.9)
navigable waterways, 298-9
occupational opportunities in, 98
periods of growth, 300
reasons for decline, 22, 307-8
role as market town, 168
size, population, importance, 20, 24,
91, 92, 93, 103 (nn.6, 9), 129-30,
179, 263 (n.3)
'social' capital, 138, 254
source of capital, 305-6
status of craft guilds, 112
Bristol Channel, 298, 307
Bristol Old Bank, 306
Britain, British Isles, urban studies in,
19-29, 35 (n.84)
Brown, T., 291 (n.49)
Browne, Sir Thomas, 237, 238, 266
(n.28)
Bruges, 2, 3, 4, 7, 56, 57
Brulez, W., 3
Brussels, 2, 4
Bruton, 189
Buckatzsch, E. J., 25
Buckinghamshire
markets, 175, 176, 177, 193, 194,
199 (n.13), 202 (n.53)
navigable waterways, 188
studies on, 129
Building industry
in Bristol, 302
phases in British towns, 28
styles, in Norwich, 133-45, 238, 260,
266 (n.34)